Women's Rights in the Middle East and North Africa

Middle East and North Africa

CITIZENSHIP AND JUSTICE

Women's Rights in the Middle East and North Africa

CITIZENSHIP AND JUSTICE

EDITED BY

Sameena Nazir and Leigh Tomppert

FREEDOM HOUSE
NEW YORK ♦ WASHINGTON, D.C. ♦ ALMATY ♦ AMMAN
BELGRADE ♦ BISHKEK ♦ BUCHAREST ♦ BUDAPEST ♦ DUSHANBE
KYIV ♦ MEXICO CITY ♦ LAGOS ♦ TASHKENT ♦ TUNIS ♦ WARSAW

ROWMAN & LITTLEFIELD PUBLISHERS, INC.
LANHAM ♦ BOULDER ♦ NEW YORK ♦ TORONTO ♦ OXFORD

ROWMAN & LITTLEFIELD PUBLISHERS, INC.

Published in the United States of America
by Rowman & Littlefield Publishers, Inc.
A wholly owned subsidary of The Rowman & Littlefield Publishing Group, Inc.
4501 Forbes Boulevard, Suite 200, Lanham, Maryland 20706
www.rowmanlittlefield.com

PO Box 317
Oxford
OX2 9RU, UK

British Library Cataloguing in Publication Information Available
Library of Congress Cataloging-in-Publication Data

Women's rights in the Middle East and North Africa : citizenship and justice / edited by
Sameena Nazir and Leigh Tomppert.
   p. cm.
 Includes bibliographical references and index.
 ISBN 0-7425-4991-7 (hardcover : alk. paper)—ISBN 0-7425-4992-5 (pbk. : alk. paper)
 1. Women's rights—Middle East. 2. Women's rights—Africa, North. I. Nazir,
Sameena. II. Tomppert, Leigh.
 HQ1236.5.M65W66 2004
 305.42'0956—dc22   2005016341

Printed in the United States of America

♾™ The paper used in this publication meets the minimum requirements of American
National Standard for Information Sciences—Permanence of Paper for Printed Library
Materials, ANSI/NISO Z39.48-1992.

Table of Contents

Acknowledgments

Women's Rights in the Middle East and North Africa: Citizenship and Justice is the product of the collective contributions of Freedom House staff and consultants.

The survey project was directed by Sameena Nazir. Country reports were edited by Sameena Nazir and Leigh Tomppert. Adrian Karatnycky, Arch Puddington, Christopher Walker, and Jennifer Windsor provided oversight for the project. The following Freedom House staff and interns also contributed to the various stages of the project: Frances Abouzeid, Lisa Davis, Jeremy Gaspar, Renee Manuel, Mohsen Marzouk, Mikaela McDermott, Sarah Repucci, Jane Stockman, Leonard Sussman, Sanja Tatic, Alex Taurel, and Andrea Trujillo.

Nancy van Itallie copyedited the volume. Anne Green of Greenways Graphic Design was responsible for the design and layout of the book. Translation services were provided by The MID Foundation, California.

Funding for this project was provided by the Middle East Partnership Initiative (MEPI) of the U.S. Department of State.

Contributors

REGIONAL ADVISORS COMMITTEE

Rafiah Salman Al-Talei, *Journalist and editor, United for Press and Publications & United Media Services, Muscat, Oman*

Lisa Anderson, *Dean of School for International and Public Affairs, Columbia University*

Mournira Charrad, *Professor of Sociology, The University of Texas at Austin*

Heba F. El-Shazli, *Regional Program Director, Middle East, American Center for International Labor Solidarity, Washington, D.C.*

Dr. Munira Fakhro, *Associate Professor of Social Development, University of Bahrain*

Leila Hessini, *Senior Policy Advisor with Ipas, North Carolina*

Isis Nusair, *Professor of Women's Studies, St. Mary's College, Indiana*

Mona Yacoubian, *Adjunct fellow, Center for Strategic and International Studies (CSIS), Washington D.C.*

METHODOLOGY COMMITTEE

Leila Ahmed, *Professor of Women's Studies in Religion, Harvard Divinity School*

Karima Bennoune, *Assistant Professor of Law, Rutgers School of Law-Newark*

Dr. Riffat Hassan, *Professor of Religion, Department of Humanities, University of Louisville*

Adrian Karatnycky, *Senior Scholar and Counselor, Freedom House*

Brian Katulis, *Consultant, Freedom House*

Mikaela McDermott, *Senior Program Officer, Freedom House*

Tom Melia, *Consultant, Middle East Projects, Freedom House*

Sameena Nazir, *Director, Survey of Women's Rights in the Middle East and North Africa, Senior Research Coordinator, Freedom House*

Arch Puddington, *Director of Research, Freedom House*

Peter Rosenblum, *Lieff, Cabraser, Heimann & Bernstein Associate and Clinical Professor in Human Rights, Columbia University*

Leigh Tomppert, *Research and Editorial Assistant, Survey of Women's Rights in the Middle East and North Africa, Freedom House*

Jay Verkuilen, *Institute of Government and Public Affairs, University of Illinois at Urbana-Champaign*

Christopher Walker, *Director of Studies, Freedom House*

Jennifer Windsor, *Executive Director, Freedom House*

CONTRIBUTING AUTHORS

Reem Abu Hassan, *Lawyer; Vice President, Jordanian Society for Protecting Victims of Family Abuse, Amman, Jordan*

Haya Al-Mughni, *Sociologist; Consultant to the United Nations*

Shatha Al-Muttawa, *Researcher on UAE; University of Chicago*

Sabika Al-Najjar, *Secretary-General, Bahrain Human Rights Society, Bahrain*

Suheir Azzouni, *Gender Consultant and Human Rights Educator, France*

Amal Basha, *Chairperson, Sisters' Arabic Forum for Human Rights, Yemen*

Catherine D. Bellafronto, *Specialist in business development in the Middle East and North Africa; Georgetown University*

Caroline Sakina Brac de la Perrière, *Coordinator, New Ways International Alliance for Social Innovation, Algeria and France*

Jill Crystal, *Professor of Political Science, Auburn University*

Mary-Jane Deeb, *Head of the Near East Section, Library of Congress; Adjunct Professor, School of International Service, American University, Washington D.C.*

Eleanor Abdella Doumato, *Visiting Fellow, Watson Institute for International Studies, Brown University*

Valentine Moghadam, *Chief of Section, Gender Equality and Development Section, Division of Human Rights and Fight Against Discrimination, United Nations Educational, Scientific and Cultural Organization (UNESCO), France*

Rabea Naciri, *President, Association Démocratique du Femmes du Maroc (ADFM/Rabat), Morocco*

Alison Pargeter, *Research Fellow, International Policy Institute, Kings College, London*

Amal Rassam, *Consultant on Development, Gender, and Civil Society; Specialist on Iraq*

Amira el Azhary Sonbol, *Professor of Islamic Law, History, and Society, Georgetown University*

Zeina Zaatari, *Scholar in Anthropology, University of California-Davis; Program Officer, Middle East and North Africa Region, Global Fund for Women, San Francisco*

FOCUS GROUPS

Brian Katulis, *Director*

Challenging Inequality

OBSTACLES AND OPPORTUNITIES TOWARDS WOMEN'S
RIGHTS IN THE MIDDLE EAST AND NORTH AFRICA

By Sameena Nazir

As the societies of the Arab Middle East and North Africa (MENA) confront the process of democratic change, no issue offers a more formidable challenge than the unequal status of women. This survey presents detailed reports on the state of women's rights in 16 countries and one territory—Palestine—of the MENA region, including countries from North Africa, the Levant, the Gulf, and the Arabian Peninsula. Although the survey provides evidence of progress toward gender equality in a number of countries, its principal findings reflect a pervasive, gender-based gap in rights and freedoms. A substantial deficit in women's rights exists in every country reviewed in this study and is reflected in practically every institution of society: the law, the criminal justice system, the economy, education, health care, and the media.

The Middle East is not, of course, the only region of the world where women are, in effect, relegated to the status of second-class citizens. In Asia, Africa, Latin America, Europe, and North America, women continue to face gender-based obstacles to full realization of their rights as equal participants in society. Indeed, the modern revolution in the status of women in the United States and Europe that began roughly 40 years ago remains incomplete even today. In the United States, the right of women to compete on equal footing with men in the workplace was enshrined in law in 1964, while sexual harassment in the workplace was made a matter of national concern only in the

Sameena Nazir, a senior research coordinator at Freedom House, served as director of the Women's Rights in the Middle East and North Africa project during 2003-2005.

1980s. While women are active participants in U.S. political life, even today their representation in the Congress remains relatively low.

It is, however, in the MENA countries where the gap between the rights of men and those of women is the most visible and significant and where resistance to women's equality has been most challenging. Some of the reforms adopted in recent years, such as the new family code passed into law in Morocco in 2004, have the potential to trigger wide-ranging gains for women's rights. But as this survey repeatedly demonstrates, the passage of laws that putatively guarantee equal rights for women and men means little if those guarantees are not enforced. Most countries examined in this survey have guarantees of equal rights written into the constitution or national legislation, but in no case are these guarantees effectively enforced by state authorities.

The need for change in women's status will grow increasingly urgent as the demands for broad-based democratic reform are felt throughout the Middle East. Democratic change in Arab nations is long overdue. According to *Freedom in the World*, the global assessment of political rights and civil liberties issued annually by Freedom House, none of the countries or territories included in this survey has earned a rating of "Free," and none qualifies as a democracy. But there are growing and encouraging signs of democratic ferment that could have a significant impact on the region's political future. However, a meaningful breakthrough for freedom will require major progress toward women's equality.

The comprehensive reports presented in this survey detail how women in MENA countries face systematic discrimination in both laws and social customs. As a consequence, women do not enjoy equal rights as citizens, nor do they have a full, independent legal identity. In most countries under survey, women do not have legal recourse in cases of domestic violence. Although women's rights organizations have repeatedly raised the issue, not one country in the region has a law that clearly makes domestic violence a criminal offense. Arab women are significantly underrepresented in senior or executive positions in politics, government, the judiciary, and the private sector. The participation of women in political life in MENA countries is the lowest in the world. Women are not allowed to vote in Saudi Arabia. In some countries, women are barred from certain professions, and many women face social pressures to remain at home and eschew a career. Although some countries under review have enacted laws prohibiting gender discrimination, few offer women the practical mechanisms to bring complaints of bias.

In addition to the obstacles to change that women confront in their societies, their status is affected by national, regional, and global political developments. The emergence of extremist Islamic forces stands as a threat to gains women have achieved as well as to future possibilities of reform. Even where radical forces are not influential, the politicization of Islam seriously complicates the challenge of advocating for equal rights. The years of civil strife involving Israelis and Palestinians have had a ripple effect on women's rights, as has the war in Iraq and the earlier civil conflicts in Algeria and Lebanon. The absence of democratic institutions and processes, an independent judiciary, and a lack of good governance in many countries in the region also presents some major roadblocks to women's access to justice. In addition, a large number of migrant and refugee women living in the Middle East region, particularly in the Gulf, face gender-specific obstacles such as discrimination in employment and domestic violence. Migrant women in the MENA region are often more vulnerable to abuse by private employers due to barriers of language, lack of education about their rights, and lack of protections under domestic labor policies. Trafficking of women is also an emerging problem in the region.

This survey has been undertaken to provide an independent, thorough, and comparative analysis of the state of women's rights in the MENA region. Over the past three decades, Freedom House has established a reputation for rigorous and accurate assessment of the state of freedom around the world. *Freedom in the World*, which was launched in 1973, is an authoritative index of global political rights and civil liberties that is widely cited by policymakers and scholars. Freedom House also publishes annual surveys of global press freedom, the state of democratization in East Central Europe and Eurasia, and governance and transparency, and has published surveys of economic freedom and religious liberties worldwide.

Methodology and Approach

This survey is the product of a 20-month-long research effort that involved a team of 40 analysts and advisers, a series of consultations with women's rights leaders in the Middle East, and focus groups on women's issues conducted in three Middle Eastern countries. Consultations with women's advocates were conducted in Bahrain, Egypt, Jordan, Lebanon, Morocco, Oman, Palestinian Authority, Syria, and the UAE. Freedom House staff also consulted with women's rights advocates from Saudi Arabia and Yemen. Focus groups were conducted in Morocco, Kuwait, and Egypt. At the core of the survey is a series of narrative reports that describe the challenges, deficiencies, and progress on women's rights in 16 Arab MENA countries and one territory: **Algeria, Bahrain, Egypt, Iraq, Jordan, Kuwait, Lebanon, Libya, Morocco, Oman, Palestine (Palestinian Authority and Israeli-Occupied Territories), Qatar, Saudi Arabia, Syria, Tunisia, the United Arab Emirates, and Yemen.** The survey methodology and the full list of questions are attached as an appendix at the end of this survey.

The reports were prepared by scholars and women's rights specialists with country or regional expertise who have written widely on political, human rights, and women's rights themes. A number of the analysts live in the countries under evaluation; others are international scholars with expertise in their report country who travel frequently to the region. The methodology was formulated by a committee of specialists on Islam and on human rights, legal, social, political, and women's rights issues in the Middle East and a team of Freedom House staff analysts. The country reports and country ratings were assessed by a team of academic advisers who specialize in social science statistics, Middle East political developments, and women's rights issues.

The survey is comparative from a global perspective; each country or territory receives a numerical rating for each of five broad categories of women's rights. The ratings will be helpful in assessing where in a particular country attention should be focused in order to advance women's equality. The five categories are:

   I. Nondiscrimination and Access to Justice
  II. Autonomy, Security, and Freedom of the Person
 III. Economic Rights and Equal Opportunity
  IV. Political Rights and Civic Voice
   V. Social and Cultural Rights

In rating country performance, Freedom House employed a universal standard of comparability based in part on the Universal Declaration of Human Rights. The survey measures both the de jure and the de facto status of women's rights in all areas under evaluation. Although the major focus of the study is government policy, it also looks at the role of non-state actors in impeding women's rights or in advancing them. The survey reviews the conditions of women in all social groups, residents of urban and rural areas, and both citizens and noncitizens. While the survey is restricted to Arab MENA countries, a country's rating is based on a global standard. Thus readers can ascertain a country's performance both in the region and globally. Ratings are expressed on a five-point scale (1–5), with 1 signifying the weakest performance and 5 reflecting the strongest performance. The survey covers developments up through the end of the year 2003; developments in years prior to 2003 are frequently cited to assist in placing the state of women's rights in its proper context. Significant developments in the year 2004 were cited in rare cases, such as the adoption of a new family code in Morocco.

Findings

The survey identified a complex series of obstacles that prevent women from enjoying the full range of social, political, civil, and legal rights. The survey authors placed special emphasis on the following issues:

Inferior Status Due to Legal Discrimination

The constitutions of most Middle Eastern countries include a clause that guarantees the equality of all citizens. Constitutions that declare, "All citizens are equal and there shall be no discrimination among citizens on the basis of sex," have been adopted in Algeria, Bahrain, Iraq, Libya, Oman, Palestinian Authority, Qatar, Syria, and Tunisia. While Egypt, Jordan, Lebanon, Kuwait, Morocco, the UAE, and Yemen do not include a gender-based nondiscrimination clause in their constitutions, they do declare that "all citizens are equal under the law." Only in Saudi Arabia does the constitution not include a clause or statement committing the government to a policy of nondiscrimination.

Yet even though 16 of the 17 countries and territories examined here enshrine the concept of equal rights in their constitutions or in the body of national legislation, women throughout the region face legal forms of discrimination that are systematic and pervade every aspect of life. In no country in the region are women given equal status in the citizenship laws. In the majority of countries, by law, women are susceptible to harsher penalties than are men charged with the same crime, especially in cases of so-called moral crimes. The legal codes provide no serious protection for women against violence within the family and treat a woman's testimony as worth less than a man's in cases in which rape or domestic violence is brought before the legal authorities. In many countries, the family codes extend to the husband the status of head of household. This confers on the husband the responsibility of providing financially for his family but also gives him social and in some cases legal authority over his wife and the right to demand obedience from her. Several MENA countries still retain the concept of the House of Obedience, under which a wife can be sentenced to a form of house arrest for refusing to "obey" her husband. Police and court officials in many countries often use this law to refuse women means to file complaints of abuse against their husbands. Women are also subject to unequal treatment in the labor laws of most countries in the region, can legally be denied employment in certain occupations, and are discriminated against in labor benefits and pension laws.

Discrimination in Nationality and Citizenship Laws

Women do not enjoy the same citizenship and nationality rights as do men in MENA countries. This particular form of inequality can have a serious effect on the choice of marriage partner. Under the citizenship laws of MENA countries, a man can marry a woman from outside the country with the knowledge that his spouse can take on the citizenship and nationality rights he enjoys. By contrast, a woman who marries a foreigner cannot pass on her citizenship and nationality to her male spouse. Furthermore, with the exception of Tunisia and Egypt, a woman who marries a foreigner cannot pass on her citizenship and nationality rights to her children. Such children must acquire special residency permits, renewable annually, in order to attend public school, qualify for university scholarships, and find employment. In the UAE, the law requires a woman to surrender her UAE citizenship if she marries a man who is not a citizen of a Gulf state.

These restrictions affect millions of women in the region, as it is common practice in many countries for marriages to take place within tribes or extended families that are scattered across the region. Also contributing to transnational marriages are armed conflicts and poverty, which trigger mass movements across borders for security or employment. Limits on citizenship rights are a particular problem for Palestinian women, especially in countries with a large Palestinian diaspora such as Jordan, Lebanon, Syria, and Egypt.

In recent years, modest progress has taken place toward reform of the citizenship/nationality laws in MENA countries. Jordan, Bahrain, and Morocco have adopted measures to allow children from a citizen mother and a non-citizen father to receive more services and benefits if the family decides to reside in the mother's country. But this problem persists and remains a high priority for Arab women's rights advocates.

Domestic Violence

All country reports highlight domestic violence as a serious problem in the Middle East. Contributing factors include lack of legislation criminalizing domestic violence, lack of government accountability and protections for women's rights inside the home, and social stigmas associated with women victims instead of social disapproval of the perpetrators of domestic violence.

Domestic violence can range from wife-beating and marital rape to the brutal battering of female family members by male family members. Gender-based violence such as practices that force women and girls to have virginity tests or undergo female genital mutilation (FGM), as well as the severe physical violence or murder inflicted on women by male family members in the name of family honor also present problems in the region. While domestic violence is widespread, no country in the region has adopted a law that clearly outlaws all its forms and ensures that those guilty of domestic abuse be punished. The authors of the country reports in this study were unanimous in recommending that MENA governments enact strict laws to protect women from all forms of violence, especially domestic violence, and provide punishment for those who commit rape or acts of violence, including violence in the home.

Violence against women within the family is a serious and complex global problem. While no part of the world is immune from the stain of spousal abuse, the Middle East is unique in the array of laws, practices, and customs that pose major obstacles to the protection of women or the punishment of abusers. The problem is intensified by a legal structure that places the burden of proof entirely on the female victim in cases of gender-based violence, something that discourages women from reporting acts of violence or de-manding legal redress.

In many countries, laws exist that actually condone domestic violence. Particularly troubling here is the practice, widespread in the region, of legally encouraging men who rape women to marry their victims. Women are often coerced by social pressure to marry their rapists in order to avoid the social stigma associated with being raped. The countries under review are also notable for the absence of support networks or shelters for victims of abuse. Likewise, few government-supported services exist to provide counseling or legal or financial assistance to help victims reintegrate into society with dignity. All country report writers have recommended public education campaigns on domestic violence and urged governments to allocate funds for victim services and the training of police and court officials.

Lack of Information; Absence of Voice

A major problem for women in the region is a lack of information about wom-en's rights, women's leadership, and women's global achievements. They also lack knowledge of and access to the work of women's advocacy organizations. Overwhelmingly, women in the region are unaware of their rights under the constitution or the laws of their countries. This is due in part to educational weaknesses: Students, especially girls, are simply not taught about their rights as citizens. Governments do not feel obliged to inform their female populations of the available laws and policies that women could use to empower themselves. The media also largely fails to cover the injustices women suffer and problems specific to women. In addition to a lack of information, cultural attitudes, predominant throughout the region, treat women's demands and protests as being in violation of women's traditional, subservient role.

Women's advocacy organizations exist in most countries in the region. In some countries, such as Morocco, women's organizations are free to ad-vocate for any cause, while in other countries, groups must exercise caution when challenging the political status quo. Some women's groups are directly or indirectly tied to the government or political leadership; others are com-pletely independent. Independent women's groups advocating for women's legal equality are not permitted to openly operate in the UAE or Saudi Ara-bia. Women's organizations have made significant headway in certain areas despite the impediments of law and custom. But some countries use licensing and registration requirements to discourage the proliferation of independent advocacy organizations and often prevent nongovernmental organizations from receiving financial assistance from independent sources or from outside the country. Even in the more liberal environments, women's rights advocates do not have easy access to government officials, transparent processes, data on women's issues, national budgets, or state media.

Women's Inferior Status in Family Laws

Throughout the region, legal matters pertaining to family relationships are adjudicated under the Shari'a systems based on Islamic laws. Despite the diversity of legal systems and the diverging interpretations of Shari'a employed in the MENA region, in most countries, all legal matters related to marriage, divorce, custody, and women's legal status are dealt with under what is commonly referred to as the family code or Personal Status Law.

In almost all MENA countries women face gender-based discrimination in the family codes. Among the countries with the most liberal family codes are Tunisia, which has had a relatively liberal family code for many years, and Morocco, which enacted a family code that substantially expanded women's rights in 2004. Egypt has also made recent changes in the family code to give women expanded divorce rights. However, while progressive steps have been taken, women are still treated unequally even under the more liberal family codes.

Reform of the family code has been a high-priority objective of women's rights advocates, as well as liberal-minded lawyers, judges, and Islamic scholars. The Morocco reform has had an important regional impact, as it has strengthened the argument of those who say that equal status within marriage is compatible with Shari'a law. The reforms adopted in Morocco and Egypt are also seen as small but important victories for civil society movements in their ongoing struggle against patriarchal and extremist Islamic forces, for whom the subservient position of women in marriage has been a key political issue.

Outside of Morocco and Tunisia, the existing family laws of MENA countries relegate women to an inferior position within marriage and within the family. Family laws in these countries declare that the husband is the head of the family, require the wife to obey her husband, and give the husband power over his wife's right to work and travel, among other rights. The reports in this study cite specific articles that enshrine a condition of legal inequality for women. The reports further explain how courts have interpreted these laws to deny legal protection to women whose husbands have forbidden them to accept certain jobs. The reports also detail how, in many countries, the law allows a husband to divorce his wife at any time without stated reason and without going to court but requires a wife to meet specific conditions in order to initiate a divorce in a court of law.

Under the family code of most MENA countries, women are not permitted to interpret the religious texts that are the basis for Shari'a or to serve as family court judges. In this way, women are effectively excluded from those aspects of the legal system that have the most intimate and powerful impact on their lives. The patriarchal attitudes, prejudices, and traditionalist leanings of male judges, lawyers, and court officials often contribute to a denial of due process for women, particularly through these functionaries' selective interpretations of what is "Islamic."

Even in Algeria, a relatively secular country with a tradition of more expansive rights for women, the concept of women's unequal status can be found in a number of laws. Although the constitution allows freedom of movement of all citizens, Article 39 of Algeria's family code stipulates, "The duty of the wife is to obey her husband." Consequently, policemen and court officials in Algeria, and in many other countries in the region, consider it an acceptable practice for a husband to forbid his wife to travel without his permission. In Saudi Arabia, women are legally forbidden to travel alone in public transportation or on airplanes. In many cases, a woman is required to seek the authorization of her father, brother, or husband in order to leave the home, and upon failing to do so can expect to face physical violence at the hands of family members or be confined to the home. Most often, governments consider such cases to be strictly family matters. In the absence of proper mechanisms, women often rely on either their educational or social status, or on open-minded government officials, to help ease restrictions on their freedoms. Women can go to the courts to file a complaint against such restrictions in some countries, but in most cases it is unusual for a woman to seek official redress due to the expected social pressure for her to obey her husband.

Many women suffer from a lack of awareness of their legal rights under the country's family law. For example, under Muslim family law, the marriage contract generally contains a section that allows each spouse to stipulate in writing his or her specific rights in the marriage. This feature gives women the theoretical ability to achieve equal rights within the marriage. In practice, however, this feature of the marriage contract is seldom utilized, either due to illiteracy or lack of familiarity with the available legal options or due to patriarchal social traditions under which it is the prerogative of the bride's male guardians to finalize the conditions of the marriage contract. Governments in most countries do not engage in public education campaigns on women's rights in the marriage.

Inheritance laws, which are also included in the family code, are another source of inequality for women. Sisters get half of the share of their brothers, and women generally get a smaller share of family inheritance than do their male relatives. But in most countries, women do not even get their half share of the inheritance because of their lack of access to the legal system. This is a particular problem in countries with large rural populations, such as Egypt, Syria, Libya, and Yemen. In these societies, women's access to inheritance, housing, and property is also affected by their educational level, family support systems, economic status, and access to legal information and legal mechanisms. The governments do not take aggressive steps to enforce women's inheritance and property rights and often allow abuses to go unpunished.

Lack of Complaint Mechanisms

With the exception of Egypt, the governments in the countries under review do not provide mechanisms for women to file complaints against gender discrimination. Women who are discriminated against in the legal system, denied job promotions or benefits, or are excluded from participation in institutions such as the judiciary, do not have access to channels through which they can make confidential complaints or seek redress under the constitution. The absence of special commissions or legal entities to enforce legal protections against gender discrimination reflects a lack of interest in women's rights on the part of government officials. It also reinforces women's inferior status in society and allows violations of women's rights to take place with impunity.

Education

Education has been a prime area of progress for women in the region and is an important avenue for their overall advancement toward equality. Over the past 10 years, women in all MENA countries except Yemen have made gains in access to education, literacy, university enrollment, and the variety of subjects open to study. In several countries, women have a university enrollment rate higher than that of men. There has also been an increase in the availability of vocational training schools and business colleges for female students.

Although women are generally still encouraged to study in such traditionally female disciplines as education and medicine, in many countries women's numbers have increased in the fields of science and engineering. Particular progress has been visible in the Gulf states, where women are now joining new professions in substantial numbers and are increasingly going abroad on government scholarships. There has, however, been something of a backlash in a few MENA countries against women's involvement in non-traditional study areas. In Kuwait, women who want to study in certain traditionally male fields, such as engineering, must achieve a higher grade-point average for admission than men. In Oman, women students often must postpone university study for one year, a limitation not applied to men.

Country Ratings

Although all but two of the countries reviewed in this report, Oman and Saudi Arabia, have ratified the United Nations Convention on the Elimination of All Forms of Discrimination Against Women (CEDAW), a major international agreement on women's equality, none of the countries evaluated can claim to meet internationally recognized standards for women's rights. According to the survey's 1-to-5 rating scale, a score of 3 in any category reflects an imperfect adherence to universally accepted rights standards. In this study, countries seldom receive a score of 3.0 in any of the five broad categories, and some countries receive ratings in the range of the lowest possible score, 1.0. A rating of 3.0 represents conditions in which a woman's ability to exercise her rights is sometimes restricted by the government or by non-state actors, in which some laws that provide adequate protection for women are in place but are poorly implemented, and in which women suffer discrimination in some areas of political, economic, or social life.

Two countries consistently earn the highest scores for the region: Tunisia and Morocco. However, Tunisia scores low in the Political Rights and Civic Voice category due to the country's overall political repression. In all other categories, Tunisia scores highest in the region. The country with the lowest scores in all categories is Saudi Arabia. Its scores ranged from 1.0 for Political Rights and Civic Voice to 1.6 for Social and Cultural Rights.

Among countries with higher ratings, all three—Tunisia, Morocco, and Algeria—are in North Africa. Other countries with comparatively high performances are Egypt, Lebanon, and Jordan. Several of the countries that, according to the survey, score comparatively well on rights issues, such as Algeria and Tunisia, have more secular traditions by the standards of the region and have had periods of socialist government. Yet a secular background is no guarantee of women's freedoms, as evidenced by the relatively low scores the survey found for Syria and Libya. In most categories, the lowest ratings were earned by Saudi Arabia and its fellow monarchical states of the Persian Gulf: Bahrain, Oman, Kuwait, Qatar, and UAE. Yemen, although the poorest country in the Arabian Gulf Peninsula, performed better in the political rights section due to Yemeni women's ability to participate fully in all levels of the electoral process and women's NGOs' scope to work freely. While the Gulf states score particularly poorly on issues pertaining to women's legal rights and women's freedom to advocate for their rights and participate in civic and political life, these countries had somewhat better records on providing educational opportunities and access to health care for women. Nevertheless, despite the availability of higher quality schools and health services in the richer Gulf areas, women still lack the freedom to exercise their rights to healthcare and education independently. In some Gulf countries such as Saudi Arabia, a woman will not be treated in a hospital without a male's permission.

The category of Nondiscrimination and Access to Justice assessed women's equality under the constitution, protection from gender-based discrimination, citizenship rights, equality in the penal code and criminal laws, and women's legal identity. Four countries—Algeria, Egypt, Morocco, and Tunisia—registered scores between 3.0 and 3.6. A second group of countries scored between 2.5 and 2.9: Iraq, Lebanon, and Syria, along with Palestine. The countries with the lowest scores, those below 2.0, were Kuwait, Saudi Arabia, and the UAE.

The category of Autonomy, Security, and Freedom of the Person examined family laws and equality within marriage, freedom of religion, freedom of movement, and freedom from torture and gender-based violence. Only Morocco and Tunisia scored higher than 3.0. Those in the range of 2.5 to 2.9 were Egypt, Iraq, Lebanon, and Palestine. Only Saudi Arabia registered a score below 2.0.

The category of Economic Rights and Equal Opportunity reviewed women's land, property, and inheritance rights, rights to education and employment, and labor protections. Only Morocco and Tunisia received scores above the 3.0 threshold. Countries that scored between 2.5 and 2.9 were Egypt, Iraq, Lebanon, Jordan, Syria, Algeria, Bahrain, Kuwait, Oman, Qatar, and the UAE, along with Palestine. Only Saudi Arabia received a score below 2.0.

The category of Political Rights and Civic Voice examined women's rights to peaceful assembly and freedom of expression, participation in the judiciary and high-level decision making posts, roles in political processes, and visibility in civic rights issues. Algeria and Morocco were the only countries to register a score of 3.0 or better. Scores between 2.5 and 2.9 were accorded to Yemen, Egypt, Jordan, Lebanon, Tunisia, and Palestine. Countries scoring at the low end of the scale, under 2.0, were Kuwait, Oman, Qatar, Saudi Arabia, the UAE, and Libya. Kuwait, UAE, and Saudi Arabia received the lowest scores in this section due to the denial of suffrage rights for women citizens.

The category of Social and Cultural Rights assessed women's health and reproductive rights issues, protection from harmful traditional practices, housing rights and participation in community life, and women's influence in the media. Scores of 3.0 or better were registered by Morocco and Tunisia. Countries receiving scores between 2.5 and 2.9 were Bahrain, Oman, Kuwait, Jordan, Lebanon, and Algeria, along with Palestine. Saudi Arabia and Libya scored below 2.0.

An overall chart of regional comparative ratings for each of the five sections is presented in this survey. Ratings for each country are also presented on the first page of each report along with key country statistics.

Recommendations

The core purpose of this survey is to facilitate local and global efforts to expand the rights of women in the Middle East and North Africa. Each of the five main categories of each country report includes a series of recommendations for reform addressed to the country's government. Although some of the recommendations deal with problems that are specific to the particular society, many deal with issues that affect all, or most, of the countries under survey. These recommendations have been jointly made by the report authors and Freedom House. Among the major recommendations of the survey are:

1. Women should enjoy equal status under the law in all aspects of life. As this survey demonstrates, women face legal discrimination in practically

all countries in the region. Of particular concern are laws on citizenship/nationality, women's legal standing in the judicial system, and discrimination against women within the criminal justice system. Gender discrimination in the name of Islam should not be allowed by the governments. There is thus an urgent need for governments to review and revise national laws and implementation mechanisms so that discriminatory provisions can be removed and women's equal status can be ensured. Governments should also institute public education campaigns to promote women's equal rights as citizens.

2. Family laws should be revised to ensure equal rights within marriage and the family. To ensure nondiscriminatory implementation of family laws, governments should institute significant reforms within the family court system and provide women's rights training to court officials. Islamic Shari'a interpretations that result in a denial of women's equal rights should be revised to ensure women are not discriminated against. Women scholars should be encouraged to work as court experts, and governments should prioritize the appointments of women as lawyers and judges in the family courts.

3. Domestic violence should be considered a serious crime in all instances. This applies to all forms of violence, including torture, rape, marital rape, spouse battering, and violence against women in the name of honor. Court and law enforcement agencies should consider the prevention of domestic violence a major priority. The state should take leadership in and also facilitate NGOs' role in creating awareness of the impact of domestic violence on women and society. Governments should also provide counseling and support services for victims. The international community can help in this process by providing technical assistance and resources to MENA governments.

4. Legal and traditional barriers to women's participation in politics, government, and the private sector should be removed. Governments should take concrete steps to promote women's leadership in politics and business, including various forms of affirmative action and complaint mechanisms for victims of bias. The governments of Kuwait, Saudi Arabia, and the UAE should allow all citizens the right to vote.

5. Governments should increase spending for education, ensure that women in all parts of the country have access to education, and eliminate laws and practices that discriminate against women in education. Education has been an important instrument in promoting the advancement of women in recent years. The reforms that made progress possible should be expanded, and particular attention should be paid to the lack of education in rural

sections of some countries in the region. The international community should increase its assistance to countries that request help.

6. Governments should take aggressive steps to eliminate legal and social obstacles to women's economic equality. In particular, labor laws should ensure that women are not denied equal access to jobs or employment benefits at any level. Governments should facilitate the social needs of women workers, such as transportation and daycare facilities, in order to decrease the social pressures that discourage women from working. Labor laws that mandate equal opportunity should be enforced.

7. Governments should institute reforms in the status of migrant workers. They should take steps to ensure that women migrant domestic workers are not the victims of exploitation or discrimination. Given the large number of female migrant workers in some countries in the region, it is imperative that these workers have access to social services, find protection against violence and abuse, and enjoy the protection of national labor laws. The governments should establish and advertise hotlines for women and allow women's rights groups to work openly as advocates for the rights of migrant women workers.

8. Governments should review all legislation and work to eliminate social traditions that require a woman to seek a male's permission in order to receive medical treatment for her general or reproductive health. The government should work in cooperation with women's NGOs to increase women's access to information on women's health and reproductive health options, with particular focus on diseases affecting women such as breast cancer.

The overarching purpose of this survey is to facilitate and support national and international efforts to empower women in the Middle East and North Africa. It is our hope that the findings of this survey will prove useful to those working for women's equality in the region, whether inside or outside the government, to help to identify priority areas for reform, institute best practices for women's equality, and catalyze further actions.

The Impact of Public Attitudes

by Brian Katulis

The debate over women's rights is among the most divisive issues in the Middle East and North Africa. Critics of a 2003 campaign to enhance women's status in Moroccan family law charged that reforms represented nothing less than an effort to "change Islam." In Kuwait, those opposed to women's suffrage have questioned the morality of women playing an active role in politics. In Iraq and Afghanistan, deliberations over women's legal rights have been as contentious as negotiations over how to structure the future governments in both countries. These debates are not just legal or philosophical struggles among elites—they are emotionally charged political battles that touch upon core values and notions of morality and social order.

To understand the complex environment in which these debates take place, Freedom House conducted public opinion research aimed at gauging social attitudes on women. The rationale behind organizing this public opinion research was straightforward: Public attitudes play a vital role in shaping the opportunities and challenges involved in advancing women's rights. Listening to what a sampling of the general public—both women and men—says helps further the cause of women's advocates in the region by providing insights into how the broader society views changes in the status of women.

Working in close cooperation with established opinion research organizations in Egypt, Kuwait, and Morocco, Freedom House organized focus groups that included a broad cross section of individuals. In Morocco, research was conducted in January 2004, on the eve of the Moroccan government's passage of a family status code. Egypt, the most populous and arguably most

---

Brian Katulis is an opinion research consultant who has worked on democratic development projects throughout the Middle East. In 2004, he served as the director of the focus groups in Egypt, Kuwait, and Morocco.

15

influential country in the region, was selected for the second set of focus groups in May and June 2004. Finally, research was conducted in Kuwait in July 2004, just as debates over a new draft law to give women full political rights began to simmer.

Focus groups are structured group interviews that are open ended enough to capture a deeper expression of the motivations, feelings, and values that shape public attitudes. This type of qualitative research is an invaluable tool for understanding the many shades of gray of public attitudes on sensitive issues like women's rights.

What has emerged is a nuanced story of public perceptions on recent gains and opportunities for women, as well as enduring impediments. The inequalities enshrined in many of the countries' laws are only a part of the challenge. Lack of knowledge and information, societal biases held by both men and women against women, and certain interpretations and understandings of religious doctrine are among the challenges that women's rights advocates face.

Recent Gains and New Opportunities for Advancing Women's Rights

Women's rights advocates in the region are operating in a complex environment in which many men and women alike acknowledge recent gains for women but worry about the social and moral implications of future reforms and changes in women's status.

In Egypt, Kuwait, and Morocco, a consensus exists that women have realized important advances in recent years. When asked to compare the general situation for women today with that of ten years ago, the overwhelming majority of women and men interviewed said that women had made progress. Efforts to increase the quality of women's education and women's increasing presence in the workplace were cited as two of the most important catalysts contributing to positive changes. "Women are more educated and aware. They have raised their level of consciousness. Think about the past, when they stayed at home. They were illiterate and ruled by their husbands; now they rule themselves," said one woman in Rabat, Morocco.

Importance of Education
When asked to choose the two most important rights for women from a list encompassing political, economic, social, and family rights, the right to education was the leading response among most participants, for three main reasons. First, people directly connected education to the chance for a better life, particularly in Morocco and Egypt. Second, many women and men saw education as the first step toward gaining a sense of basic worth and as the

ticket to full membership in society. Many women in particular saw education as the gateway to greater gender equality, with many saying that educated women know their civil and political rights better and are more capable of defending themselves. Women without formal education, including several rural Berber women in Morocco and illiterate women in Egypt, were so lacking in confidence that they would not engage in basic questions on human rights and democracy. Some even denigrated themselves as "zeros" and "cows" for being unable to read and write.

Third, an important rationale for the strong support for women's education is grounded in a view of women's role as the center of the family. Women are seen as future mothers who will shoulder most of the responsibility for raising children; as such, they are viewed, particularly in Morocco and Egypt, as a linchpin for fighting illiteracy. As one woman in Fez, Morocco, said, "Girls are the mothers of the future. If they are not educated, they will not raise their children properly."

Increased Workforce Participation

In all three countries, men and women interviewed noted that women today play a more prominent role in the workplace. In Egypt and Morocco, economic change and necessity were described as leading factors driving this trend. Egyptians and Moroccans interviewed, particularly in urban areas, said that families require two incomes with the rising cost of living. Given this reality, some men are inclined to accept women as co-breadwinners, rather than resent it. But even in wealthy Kuwait, where the economy is booming as a result of high oil prices, women are joining the workforce in increasing numbers in order to make use of the education and skills they acquired in school.

Some participants expressed concerns that an increased number of working women might destroy the basic fabric of society by leading women to neglect what most see as their primary roles of taking care of the home and children. In addition, a few men worried that women are taking too many positions. As one man in Cairo, Egypt, said, "This unemployment [among men] is caused by the increase of women in the workplace." Despite these hesitations, public attitudes toward working women are dynamic and evolving.

One of the main benefits women receive from a job is a degree of financial freedom from families and husbands, something they lacked in the past. Some women saw this as vital insurance against unforeseen problems such as the breakup of their marriage. Moreover, several respondents noted that working women receive greater respect and have a greater voice within their families because they are contributing financial support. As one young woman in Rabat said, "Working gives greater value to women, especially in the family."

In sum, the research findings suggest that work and education may be the most powerful vehicles for positive change for women in the region.

Media Revolution Creates New Opportunities for Changing Societal Attitudes on Women's Rights

Like the rest of the region, Egypt, Kuwait, and Morocco are experiencing a complicated transformation in the media, with a larger share of the general public gaining access to a wider variety of programs. New transnational media outlets like *Al-Jazeera* and *Al-Arabiya* are altering the overall media architecture in the region, introducing new types of programs and creating opportunities for changing public attitudes about women. They also give women—even those who are uneducated—more access to information. Though not a principal object of this research, information on media programs, particularly those on television, gathered by the focus groups indicates that they are impacting how women see themselves and how society as a whole views them.

Egyptian women talked about the influence of television public awareness campaigns addressing health and social issues such as pre-marital check-ups, contraception, family planning, and children's vaccinations. Moroccan women spoke of the news they received from television and radio on the debate over a new family law. Kuwaitis, many of whom have access to hundreds of satellite television channels, noted the impact of seeing women play important roles in business and political life in other countries.

In all three countries, both women and men spoke of the appeal of interactive and participatory programs involving debates and call-in formats that enable the audience to ask questions. Respondents noted that women are often part of these debates and programs, giving them a voice in dialogues broadcast in the media. Young women in particular commented that the women they see on television in leadership positions and as journalists serve as role models, creating new aspirations and expanding the realm of what they think is possible in their lives.

The implications of this regional media transformation are unknown. Some analysts argue that a greater diversity of media outlets has a "democratizing" impact that will serve to promote freedom for women and men alike, while others argue that the new media also give voice to retrograde elements that seek to prevent advances for women. The focus group research shows signs of a complicated transformation in the media that may be offering new role models for women and providing information relevant to improving their lives.

Addressing Four Key Challenges to Advancing Women's Rights

Despite this broadly shared perception of progress, advocates for women's rights in the region face a daunting struggle to change negative stereotypes of women.

Changes to Laws Are a Good Start, but Not Enough

One main finding from the narrative country reports and consultations with women's rights advocates that are part of this survey is that women's unequal status is enshrined in many parts of the law, particularly family law and aspects of the penal code that deal with violence and crimes against women. This institutionalized discrimination is also reflected in the decision by some countries in the region to reject or accept only with reservations the universal standards set out in the United Nations Convention on the Elimination of All Forms of Discrimination Against Women (CEDAW).

Women's rights activists in the region have marshaled their efforts to chip away at this institutionalized discrimination over the past decades. They have achieved some progress through lobbying campaigns to convince their governments to change the laws and fully adopt CEDAW. These efforts require further support, as many powerful legal and institutional barriers remain in place.

The research points to another challenge for women's rights advocates— changing societal perceptions and practices. This challenge is perhaps more formidable than efforts to reform the legal structure, although in many ways they are closely tied. Efforts to reform laws stand a better chance when backed by broad sectors of society, even in dysfunctional political systems that aggregate power among narrow elites, as is the case in many parts of the Middle East and North Africa. Furthermore, legal reforms may have a spillover effect on attitudes that impede women's progress.

Legal changes may be insufficient if not accompanied by efforts to change societal perceptions. To achieve equal status for women, women's rights advocates must work to change attitudes and practices that continue to keep women in an inferior position.

Challenge 1: *Combating Negative Stereotypes and Attitudes toward Women*

Negative stereotypes about women—held by both men and women—are a major challenge. Many people of both sexes perceive a connection between women's rights and responsibilities. In this perspective, women and men have separate and distinct roles, with women seen as responsible primarily for the home and family life. In many instances, women's increased access to education and greater presence in the workforce are leading people to re-conceptualize these gender-defined roles and responsibilities, but certain stereotypes continue to impede women's full equality.

Bias against Women as Leaders

In addition, broad societal biases exist against women holding certain leadership positions in government and society. These biases largely are held by men, but there are women too who would put a ceiling on how high women leaders can advance. A principal argument against women serving as political leaders is that they are too emotional and sensitive—a perspective broadly held by men and a few women as well. As one young Kuwaiti woman said, "Women are emotional by nature. . . . It is better for a woman to stay away from politics."

Furthermore, a common belief is that women should not be permitted to serve as judges, with many respondents relying on a particular interpretation of Islam as a basis for the exclusion of women. As one man in Fez said, "I think that women cannot be judges because the Prophet said that women have weaker minds, and so they shouldn't be judges."

This bias casts women in a weak light, in contrast to men, who are perceived as steely, unemotional, and unyielding. It feeds into a broader culture that places a premium on rule by control from above, rather than consensus and democratic debate in which all members of society are engaged as equals.

Positive examples of women in positions of authority have some influence on societal biases and serve to counteract stereotypes. In the research, respondents who could point to concrete examples of women serving capably as leaders found it easier to accept women's involvement in political life. For example, in Egypt and Morocco, where women are represented in the national assemblies and as ministers in government, respondents broadly accepted the notion that women can serve as capably as men in these positions. But with respect to positions in which women have never served—such as mayors and prime ministers—both women and men were somewhat more divided over whether a woman would be capable.

The example of pioneering women who assume new leadership positions is a potent argument against traditional biases. The achievements of these women stand as a tangible refutation of the proposition that women assuming political leadership would lead to societal decline.

Permissive Attitudes about Violence against Women

Another major challenge involves the issue of violence against women. Though qualitative research such as these focus groups does not measure the extent of violence against women, it does suggest that social attitudes that sometimes justify violence, often by invoking religion, are part of the problem. As one young woman in Morocco said, "Some women deserve to be beaten up." A young man in Kuwait said, "According to the Prophet's sayings, if you must beat a woman, do not use your hands—use a type of stick." Counteracting these permissive attitudes about women poses a major challenge. While transformation of the legal environment is essential, so too is reshaping social attitudes toward violence in the home.

Challenge 2: Implementing Laws and Reforms

The adoption of laws is a critical part of the struggle to expand rights. However, women and men in Egypt, Kuwait, and Morocco expressed deep skepticism about their governments' ability to implement new laws and reforms. Several participants connected the challenge of implementing new laws with the broader struggle for political reform in their countries, and many people expressed concerns that their governments do not follow through with sufficient implementing legislation and regulations to bring the reforms fully to fruition. As one woman in Rabat told us, the laws "are just written in books, but the power remains in the hands of men. We have the rights according to law, but they are not enforced." This sentiment was broadly echoed in Egypt, where people were deeply cynical about the government's capacity to improve their lives.

Women and men spoke of institutionalized biases that affect practices, pointing to the limitations of a strategy that relies solely on reforming the letter of the law. Without follow-through work including training for judges, active efforts to promote women as leaders, and new institutions and practices to guard against gender discrimination, any legal advances run the risk of remaining incomplete.

Furthermore, many participants found it hard to disconnect the struggle for women's rights from the broader struggle of rights for all. The lack of respect for basic political, civil, social, and economic rights in these countries harms both men and women. In these areas, women's concerns are men's concerns too. Some women had a difficult time talking specifically about their particular rights concerns as women, separate and distinct from the concerns of men.

Challenge 3: *Raising Public Awareness of Rights*

The research suggests that for legal advances to have maximum impact, concerted efforts to make the broader public more aware of their rights are required. In particular, respondents with lower levels of education and those living in rural areas were generally less aware of their rights. Many women interviewed in Morocco, for instance, knew only vaguely of the new rights that they had acquired in the revisions to the family code, and some could provide no more than the name of the new law. In Egypt, a large number of women interviewed did not understand basic procedures for registering to vote.

Challenge 4: *Navigating the Backlash against Change*

A fourth challenge that women's rights advocates will likely continue to face is vocal opposition to advances for women, often framed by the emotionally charged terms of religion, tradition, and culture. A small number of respondents, mostly men but some women as well, disapproved of recent legal advances and attempts to expand women's rights.

Some strongly criticized the concept of women's freedom; a few expressed concerns that women have too much freedom. From this perspective, freedom has negative connotations of licentiousness and a degradation of moral values. Some Kuwaiti women disagree with Western notions of women's freedom; one said it is "freedom without purpose." A number of men said women have more rights than men and that there has been too much focus on women's freedom in recent years.

In addition, some critics sought to present women's rights advocates as tools of the West and as people who are advocating for something not grounded in their own values systems. Among certain segments of the population—mostly men but also a few women—women's rights is a hot-button issue that elicited strong and emotional opposition sometimes presented as a clash of religion, values, and culture. One man in Alexandria, Egypt, blamed the West, saying "Women now have more rights than men, because the West keeps talking about women's rights continuously." What some women's rights advocates see as universal standards were viewed by some opponents as standards inimical to their society's basic values.

Women's rights advocates should not allow this opposition to deter them in their struggle to eliminate institutionalized discrimination and to obtain full equality, but nor should they put on blinders and ignore it. In order to ensure that their efforts have maximum impact, women's advocates must take on the difficult challenge of reducing and reversing the negative backlash against progress.

Developing Strategies to Engage the Broader Society

The research suggests some possible avenues for women's rights advocates to advance efforts to change societal perceptions. These include framing the debate in terms that more broadly resonate in MENA countries and working with influential personalities and institutions.

One overall finding is that Islam greatly influences how the general public confronts questions related to change in their lives and society, particularly reforms for women. Even as Egypt, Kuwait, and Morocco undergo numerous changes associated with globalization and political and economic reform, the values systems of the general public remain informed by the rich traditions of Islam.

Nearly every question in this research related to women's rights was met with answers that made reference to religion or the notion of tradition. Most arguments in which religion was invoked were against advances for women. Several individuals' understanding and interpretation of Islam's core principles led them to conclude that, in the words of one woman in Morocco, "Women will never be equal to men. It says this in the Quran. Not because God preferred men to women—it is just that women are more patient, shy, and emotional. Men are more forceful than women."

But many points of view in favor of advancing women's rights were also presented in religious terms. One Kuwaiti woman said, "In our religion, there is justice. Islam makes women equal [to men], but [equality] is not implemented properly." Among many supporters of change, a core issue is the proper interpretation and implementation of Islam's principles.

The research finds that except for the most extreme militants, people in the Middle East are open to a debate over how to advance women's rights in a way that does not contradict core values. The public's views on how to apply the principles of Islam in a changing society are open to dialogue, accommodation, and change, given new realities. This is not surprising, as other major religious traditions have undergone and continue to experience such dialogues.

Since Islam is an important part of the discussions, those engaged in the struggle for women's equality or who are working to promote broader reform should possess a deep understanding of the traditions of the Muslim faith. In order to have a constructive impact, organizations and individuals should seek to understand just how deeply religion serves as a source of values for the general public.

Tables & Graphs

Final Ratings Chart

	Nondis-crimination and Access to Justice	Autonomy, Security, and Freedom of the Person	Economic Rights and Equal Opportunity	Political Rights and Civic Voice	Social and Cultural Rights
ALGERIA	3.0	2.4	2.8	3.0	2.9
BAHRAIN	2.2	2.3	2.9	2.1	2.8
EGYPT	3.0	2.8	2.8	2.7	2.4
IRAQ	2.7	2.6	2.8	2.2	2.1
JORDAN	2.4	2.4	2.8	2.8	2.5
KUWAIT	1.9	2.2	2.9	1.4	2.8
LEBANON	2.8	2.9	2.8	2.9	2.9
LIBYA	2.3	2.1	2.3	1.2	1.8
MOROCCO	3.2	3.2	3.1	3.0	3.0
OMAN	2.0	2.1	2.7	1.2	2.1
PALESTINE	2.6	2.7	2.8	2.6	2.9
QATAR	2.0	2.1	2.8	1.7	2.5
SAUDI ARABIA	1.2	1.1	1.4	1.0	1.6
SYRIA	2.7	2.2	2.8	2.2	2.3
TUNISIA	3.6	3.4	3.1	2.8	3.3
UAE	1.7	2.1	2.8	1.2	2.3
YEMEN	2.4	2.3	2.3	2.6	2.1

Ratings and Results

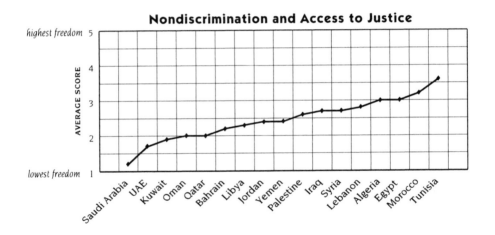

Nondiscrimination and Access to Justice

highest freedom 5

AVERAGE SCORE

4

3

2

lowest freedom 1

Saudi Arabia, UAE, Kuwait, Oman, Qatar, Bahrain, Libya, Jordan, Yemen, Palestine, Iraq, Syria, Lebanon, Algeria, Egypt, Morocco, Tunisia

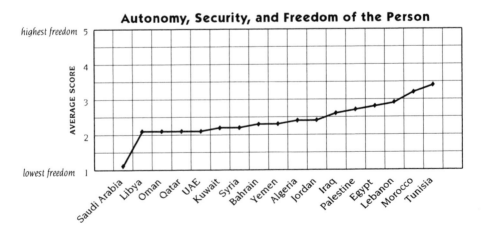

Autonomy, Security, and Freedom of the Person

highest freedom 5

AVERAGE SCORE

4

3

2

lowest freedom 1

Saudi Arabia, Libya, Oman, Qatar, UAE, Kuwait, Syria, Bahrain, Yemen, Algeria, Jordan, Iraq, Palestine, Egypt, Lebanon, Morocco, Tunisia

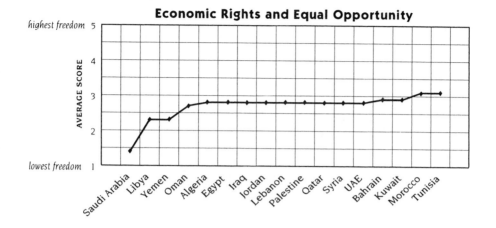

Economic Rights and Equal Opportunity

AVERAGE SCORE

highest freedom 5

lowest freedom 1

Saudi Arabia, Libya, Yemen, Oman, Algeria, Egypt, Iraq, Jordan, Lebanon, Palestine, Qatar, Syria, UAE, Bahrain, Kuwait, Morocco, Tunisia

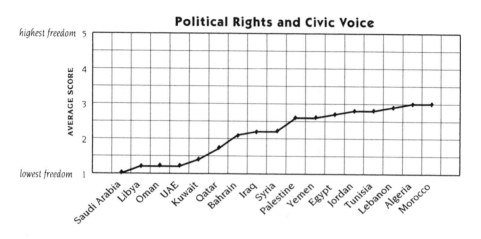

Political Rights and Civic Voice

AVERAGE SCORE

highest freedom 5

lowest freedom 1

Saudi Arabia, Libya, Oman, UAE, Kuwait, Qatar, Bahrain, Iraq, Syria, Palestine, Yemen, Egypt, Jordan, Tunisia, Lebanon, Algeria, Morocco

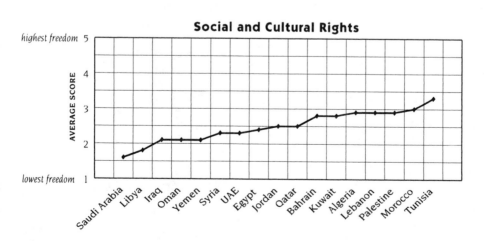

Social and Cultural Rights

AVERAGE SCORE

highest freedom 5

lowest freedom 1

Saudi Arabia, Libya, Iraq, Oman, Yemen, Syria, UAE, Egypt, Jordan, Qatar, Bahrain, Kuwait, Algeria, Lebanon, Palestine, Morocco, Tunisia

Introduction to Country Reports

Women's Rights in the Middle East and North Africa: Citizenship and Justice contains reports on 16 countries and one territory. Each report begins with a section presenting basic political, economic, and social data, as well as key statistics relevant to the status of women. In addition, numerical ratings are provided for the five thematic categories reviewed in the survey including: nondiscrimination and access to justice; autonomy, security, and freedom of the person; economic rights and equal opportunity; political rights and civic voice; and social and cultural rights.

The population, fertility rate, and percent urban/rural figures were obtained from the Population Reference Bureau, 2003. Data on the Gross Domestic Product (GDP), ranking on the United Nations Human Development Index, literacy, and percentage of women economically active were obtained from the *UN Human Development Report 2004*. The date of women's suffrage information was gathered from the Inter-Parliamentary Union and the Carnegie Endowment for International Peace. Note: the literacy rates for Iraq were taken from the UN Economic and Social Commission for Western Asia (ESCWA); the GDP of Palestine (Palestinian Authority and Israeli-Occupied Territories) was obtained from the Palestinian Investment Promotion Agency, 2002; and the literacy rates of Palestine (Palestinian Authority and Israeli-Occupied Territories) came from the Palestinian Central Bureau of Statistics, 2003. The polity and economy designations for all country reports were obtained from Freedom House's *Freedom in the World 2003*.

Each of the five categories assessed in the country reports has been ascribed a numerical rating between 1 and 5. A rating of 1 represents the lowest level and 5 the highest level of freedom women have to exercise their rights within these categories. For a full description of the methods used to determine the survey's ratings, please see the chapters on "Survey Methodology" and "Ratings and Scoring System."

Following the introductory data and categorical ratings, each report includes an executive summary that places the status of women and their rights into a broader country context. The executive summary—jointly prepared by report authors and Freedom House staff—provides information on the country's historical background, the current political, social, and economic environment, and the overall status of human rights for both men and women. The five following sections of the report assess the status of all women in the country and their abilities to exercise their rights in the five thematic categories. Recommendations are made at the end of each section highlighting the areas of most immediate and pressing concern. The recommendations are addressed to the national governments and in some cases to the international community.

The introductory report data, survey ratings, and executive summary reflect the joint efforts of Freedom House staff, consultants, and the report authors.

Country Reports

Algeria

by Caroline Sakina Brac de la Perrière

Population: 31,700,000
GDP Per Capita (PPP): $5,760
Economy: Statist
Ranking on UN HDI: 108 out of 177
Polity: Dominant party (military-influenced)
Literacy: Male 78.0% / Female 59.6%
Percent Women Economically Active: 30.9%
Date of Women's Suffrage: 1962
Women's Fertility Rate: 2.8
Percent Urban/Rural: Urban 49% / Rural 51%

Country Ratings for Algeria
Nondiscrimination and Access to Justice: 3.0
Autonomy, Security, and Freedom of the Person: 2.4
Economic Rights and Equal Opportunity: 2.8
Political Rights and Civic Voice: 3.0
Social and Cultural Rights: 2.9
(Scale of 1 to 5: 1 represents the lowest and 5 the highest level of freedom women have to exercise their rights)

Introduction

Algeria has been a military-backed republic since it achieved independence from France in 1962. Since 1989, the country has taken some steps towards democratic reform, though the process has been difficult and faltering. President Abdelaziz Bouteflika, elected in flawed elections in 1999 and re-elected in 2004, is the nominal head of state. In practice, however, power is shared by various forces, elected and unelected.

Algeria was a virtual one-party regime until the ruling National Liberation Front (FLN) permitted the formation of independent political parties in 1989. This opening allowed the Islamic Salvation Front (FIS), a fundamentalist party, to position itself to win the national elections in 1992. In response, the army cancelled the elections and banned the FIS, triggering the start of a bloody civil war between armed groups of Islamist extremists and the government that has claimed more than 100,000 lives.

Although radical groups have been responsible for the majority of the civil war massacres and assassinations, international human rights organizations have accused Algerian security forces of being responsible for thousands of "disappearances." Thousands of Algerian women who refuse to follow FIS calls for the Islamization of Algerian society have also faced violence, displacement, and exile. Many Islamist fighters surrendered following the government's introduction of the "Civil Harmony" law in 1999 that granted leniency to rebels who renounced violence. However, some armed groups have maintained their resistance, continuing to cause at least 100 deaths each month. Algeria currently clings to a tenuous peace and remains under a declared state of emergency.

Algeria is the second largest country in Africa; 91 percent of the population lives along the Mediterranean coast on 12 percent of the country's total land mass; 49 percent of the population is urban.[1] The country's population of 31,700,000 is young, with over 64 percent of inhabitants under 30 years of age. The Algerian constitution declares Islam to be the state religion, and over 99 per cent of Algerians are Sunni Muslim.

Algeria depends heavily on its oil and natural gas reserves. Since the 1980s, the country has attempted to move from a socialist to a market economy, although free market reforms have proceeded haltingly. Current GDP per capita is $5,760. The country continues to face a number of challenges including an unemployment rate of 30 percent, an overall illiteracy rate of 30 percent, a shortage of housing, and ethnic conflict. Those living under the poverty line account for 23 percent of the population.

Rights of assembly and association have been sharply curtailed since the state of emergency was declared in 1992. While the government has denied registration to certain political parties and organizations due to security considerations, an estimated 50,000 nongovernmental organizations (NGOs) of all kinds are active in Algeria.

Algeria's private press is vibrant, though authorities impose restrictions and strict defamation laws on journalists and media outlets. A lack of respect for due process is reflected in the prevalence of torture and lack of investigations into human rights abuses. Recently, however, the issue of human rights has entered the public debate, and the government has shown itself amenable to improving the overall human rights situation and resolving questions about the issue of disappearances.

While the constitution guarantees equality between genders, the 1984 family code, a set of laws based largely on Islamic law interpretations, treats women as minors under the legal guardianship of their husbands and fathers. The restriction of women's personal freedoms under the law has served to reinforce women's inferior status within society. A large number of women's NGOs work to promote women's rights in Algeria; however, the movement's strength declined in the 1990s due to death threats from fundamentalist groups.

Nondiscrimination and Access to Justice

Algeria's constitution was adopted in 1976 and has since been amended several times, with the latest revisions signed into legislation in December 1996. The country's legal system is mostly founded on French legislation, while nationality, citizenship, and the family code are based on the country's interpretation of *Shari'a* (Islamic law). The government has made significant efforts to bring legislation in line with international conventions on human rights and women's rights in the public sphere, but as far as the application of texts is concerned, these efforts are largely inadequate. Many citizens continue to be victims of arbitrary decisions by authorities.

Algerian women are subject to the family code, a retrograde and patriarchal interpretation of Islamic law passed in 1984 by the Popular National Assembly, under the pressure of religious and conservative representatives. On the whole, laws under the family code serve to reinforce the domination of men over women, contradicting Article 29 of the Algerian constitution, which declares, "All citizens are equal before the law. No discrimination shall prevail because of birth, race, sex, opinion or any other personal or social condition or circumstance."[2] However, the relationship between Article 29 and Article 2 of the constitution, which declares Islam as the state religion, is often a point of contention in debates between different constituencies and groups—some using Article 2 as a pretext to implement and maintain discriminatory practices against women.

Most national legislation ensures women some form of protection from discrimination; and women are treated equally in legislation governing employment, education, health, and the judicial system. However, women are treated unequally in Algeria's nationality code[3] as well as in the family code, in which they are treated as legal minors. According to the nationality code, unlike Algerian men, Algerian women are permitted to confer citizenship on their children only if the father is unknown or stateless or if the child is born to an Algerian mother and a foreign father who was born in Algeria.

The family code discriminates against women in matters of marriage, divorce, inheritance, and child custody and guardianship. According to family law, a wife has a legal obligation to obey her husband. A husband can freely divorce his wife without justification, but a wife must meet very specific conditions in order to initiate a divorce. Moreover, women do not have guardianship over their children under the family code, and they inherit only half of what men inherit. Women's rights groups and human rights lawyers have proposed several amendments to the existing family law, some of which are being debated at the government level and among progressive politicians.

According to the penal code, a woman is considered equal to a man before the courts whether she is the plaintiff or the defendant. While a woman's testimony is considered equal to that of a man, a 1984 Ministry of Justice directive on the requirements for notarized deeds deems the value of two women witnesses equal to that of only one male witness; Algerian notaries actively apply this directive in practice.

Women are judged—by both male and female judges—with more or less severity based on the degree to which their behavior conforms to the traditional role expected of Algerian women. The prejudices and conservative attitudes of judges and lawyers, therefore, can lead to discrimination in practice that does not exist in the legal texts. Most Algerian women's access to justice is further restricted by their lack of financial resources (men continue to maintain strong control over finances in most families), lack of confidence in the public sphere, and lack of knowledge of their legal rights. To date, the government has not taken any specific action to improve this situation for women.

Men and women are treated equally under the penal code except in cases of adultery and the abduction or rape of minors. Article 339 of the penal code punishes those who commit adultery with one to two years' imprisonment, with no discrimination between genders. However, unmarried men who commit adultery with a married woman will not be punished if they were unaware that the woman was married. An unmarried woman, on the other hand, who commits adultery with a married man, will receive the punishment of one to two years' imprisonment whether or not she was aware that the man was married. As for the abduction or rape of minors, the penal code allows for the guilty party to escape all forms of punishment if he marries his victim.

Protections against arbitrary arrest and detention are afforded both men and women under the constitution of 1996, the 2001 amended Algerian penal code, and the National Consultative Commission for the Promotion and Protection of Human Rights, established in 2001. Nevertheless, such laws and protections are not often fully implemented. In reality, most citizens do not feel fully protected from arbitrary arrest and detentions. Most of the cases of arbitrary detentions reported by human rights organizations tend to involve men, but some organizations are beginning to examine the challenges that women face in this area.[4]

Algeria ratified the UN Convention on the Elimination of All Forms of Discrimination Against Women (CEDAW) in 1997, with reservations on Articles 2, 9 (2), 15 (4), 16 and 29 (1). Most of these reservations are based on the Algerian family code and are supported by arguments based on Islam and the status of woman in the family. Algeria has undertaken some efforts to comply with CEDAW, including creating a Ministry of Women's Affairs in 2003 and proposing amendments to the family code. However, the impact of these initiatives is limited by a lack of political will to change societal attitudes that enforce the continuation of gender discrimination in both the public and private spheres. Algeria has also failed to ratify the Optional Protocol to CEDAW.

Top political leaders rarely demonstrate strong support for advancing women's rights. Only after winning the presidential elections in April 2004 did President Bouteflika make a speech in favor of women's rights. In theory, Algerian women's rights defenders and women's NGOs have the freedom to advocate for the advancement of women's human rights and status. However, in practice, they receive no assistance from the state, and their work is often hindered by lack of resources, administrative obstacles, social resistance to change, and the state of emergency laws that limit demonstrations and free association.

RECOMMENDATIONS

1. The government should amend the laws in order to bring all legislation in conformity with the principles of non-discrimination established in the constitution.
2. The government should initiate a country-wide effort to educate the public on legal provisions that protect women's rights.
3. The government should remove all reservations to CEDAW and take steps to implement it locally by bringing national laws in conformity with CEDAW.

Autonomy, Security and Freedom of the Person

Current legal protections for women's security and freedom of the person are overly general and insufficient. Two major obstacles work to limit women's autonomy and individual freedoms; the first is the authority the family code confers on male family members; and the second is the Islamist extremist element in Algerian society. Nevertheless, women's rights defenders have had some success in stirring up debate over the need for reforms in the family code and the need for increased protections against violence.

The Algerian constitution declares Islam the state religion but also prohibits discrimination based on religious belief. The government generally respects this right in practice. Small communities of Christians and Jews are free to practice their religions without government interference. Muslim extremists, however, still manage to influence and intimidate Algerians and act to restrict their abilities to express their beliefs and opinions freely.

The constitution allows for the freedom of movement of all citizens.[5] However, Article 39 of the family code stipulates, "The duty of the wife is to obey her husband," therefore providing the husband with full authority over his wife in law and in practice. Most Algerian policemen and court officials consider it standard social practice for a husband to forbid his wife to travel without his permission. Women's freedom of movement is further restricted by social traditions that support the belief that a woman's social role is to "remain at home."[6] In some cases, a woman is required to seek the authorization of her father, brother, or husband in order to leave the home, and upon failing to do so, can expect to face physical violence at the hands of family members or be confined to the home. The state does not intervene in such family matters. On rare occasions, a woman may find an open-minded government official to help alleviate restrictions on her freedom of movement, or she may go to the court to file a complaint; but, it is very uncommon for a woman to seek official assistance in these situations due to the social pressure placed on women to obey their fathers and husbands and the stigma attached to women who seek legal action against male family members.

The Algerian family code discriminates against women in several ways. Most of the articles in the family code concerning marriage, divorce, child custody, and inheritance ensure men's domination of women. Algerian women's rights groups have been advocating for changes to the family code for decades, and as a result, a draft reform introducing the concept of equality between spouses in certain articles is to be presented by the government to the National Assembly in 2005. However, many women's rights advocates believe that the new draft remains non-egalitarian, and they continue to advocate for additional reforms to the code.

The current family code forbids an Algerian woman, no matter what her age, from marrying without the consent of a male guardian. If she does not have a male guardian, the court will appoint one for her. However, a woman's male guardian is not allowed to force her to marry someone against her will. According to the family code, the minimum age for marriage for men is 21 and for women 18. In practice, however, early marriage of girls is common in rural areas of Algeria where village girls are married by their families in religious ceremonies.

Women are legally permitted to insert certain stipulations into their marriage contract, as long as the stipulations do not contradict the provisions of the family code. Nevertheless, a woman still cannot refuse the "duty to obey her husband."[7] Unlike Muslim Algerian men, Muslim Algerian women are not permitted to marry non-Muslims. Non-Muslim women married to Algerian men must comply with the family code, except in cases involving inheritance, in which case a non-Muslim woman may not inherit from her husband.

The draft family code under consideration introduces measures that would eliminate the requirement for a woman to obtain permission from a male guardian to marry, increase the minimum marriage age for women from 18 to 19, and allow women to stipulate in their marriage contract the right to work. The revised family code would also provide women with additional (but not equal) grounds to initiate divorce proceedings, limit the conditions under which polygamy would be allowed, and give divorced women and women with husbands who are out of the country or ill the opportunity to obtain guardianship of their children.

While the proposed reforms to the family code would improve the status of women in Algeria, women would still not be afforded equal rights with men. The suggested changes to the family code do not nullify the requirement for a woman to obey her husband and do not treat women equally in matters of inheritance.

According to the Algerian government,[8] slavery in Algeria does not exist. However, cases of slavery-like practices have been reported, including the abduction of women and girls by armed groups for the purposes of sexual and domestic services.[9] Little data is available on the trafficking of women for the sex industry, and information is scarce on the possible continued existence of some traditional slavery in southern Algeria. Some researchers and journalists have pointed to the emergence of a new form of slavery involving domestic workers from neighboring countries.

Article 34 of the constitution declares, "[A]ll forms of physical or moral violence or of breaches of dignity are forbidden," and in 1989, Algeria ratified the Convention against Torture and Other Cruel, Inhuman or Degrading Treatment or Punishment. In practice, however, torture continues to be used against opponents of the political regime.[10] While recent human rights reports do not address the torture of women by agents of the state, many cases of the cruel treatment of women by armed groups of religious extremists have been recorded over the past decade.

During the decade of internal conflict and violence, a large number of women[11] fell victim to abduction, rape, and murder by fundamentalist armed groups. While such attacks have decreased significantly since 1999, they continue to take place at the hands of non-state actors. One prominent example occurred in 2001, when several hundred citizens, spurred on by an imam at a local mosque, beat and tortured about 50 women in Hassi Messaoud.[12] Algeria's president, along with the Ministry of Solidarity and other institutions, rallied and supported these women after the press called attention to the case, but police and security forces were slow to intervene and investigate the attacks. Some 40 men were arrested, but those who were actually sentenced (up to three years' imprisonment) were not convicted of rape. Apparently the women victims were not able to provide the required medical evidence to support their claims of rape and violent sexual assault.[13] Women's rights groups in Algeria have been active in demanding justice for the victims, and a coalition of advocates is preparing legal cases to demand reparations.

Algerian women have little or no protection against violence in the family and in the public sphere, and there is very little awareness of this issue at the institutional or societal level. In 2003, under pressure from women's associations and health practitioners, the Ministry of Health ordered a national inquiry into violence against women, with the assistance of the judiciary, the police, and pathologists.[14] The initial study found that only 11 percent of attacks on women are committed by strangers.[15] Algerian women's rights groups, however, estimate that the Ministry of Health survey is likely to understate the nature and extent of the problem, considering that few women register their complaints of violence and rape.

Although women can invoke articles on assault and battery in the penal code in order to initiate legal action against abusive husbands, the grounds for divorce under the family code[16] do not include marital violence. Currently, there are no laws in Algeria that declare domestic violence a criminal offense. According to Article 336 of the penal code, punishment for rape is 5 to 10 years in prison; the punishment is 10 to 20 years if the victim is a minor. Algerian women's groups have observed that as most reported cases of rape have involved mass rapes of women by armed groups, Algerian institutions have become more prepared to help women victims of this type of crime. However, state authorities have not paid the same attention to documenting or addressing the problem of rape and sexual violence within the family. Marital rape is not considered a crime.

Algerian women's rights groups working to combat violence against women have achieved tangible results in recent years. Some civil society groups are working to increase protections for women victims of violence—establishing shelters for women and holding awareness-raising programs on women's rights. Women's rights defenders have also worked with female judges to lobby the government to criminalize sexual harassment in the penal code. Some sources have reported that the government has recently adopted a new provision concerning sexual harassment and included it in the penal code; however, the Algerian public has not been informed about these new changes at this time.

The Algerian women's NGO campaign to reform the family code received strong media coverage during the last year, as well as support from international women's networks. The advances of women under Morocco's new family code in 2004 further encouraged women's rights activists in Algeria. Nevertheless, the role of the government in raising societal awareness around women's issues remains very limited, such as discreetly providing information on national radio.

RECOMMENDATIONS

1. The government should eliminate Article 39 of the Family Code, which requires a wife to obey her husband.
2. The government should revise the existing Family Code in order to ensure women's equality and non-discrimination under the law.

3. The government should enact a law that criminalizes domestic violence.
4. The government, in cooperation with civil society organizations, should initiate long-term national public awareness campaigns on the problem of violence against women and the protection mechanisms available to women victims.

Economic Rights and Equal Opportunity

The Algerian constitution guarantees women the right to own land and property freely, and Article 38 of the family code states, "The wife has the right to freely dispose of her goods." However, Article 39 of the family code, which requires a wife to obey her husband, serves to restrict the right of women to dispose of their incomes and assets independently.

Algerian legal provisions related to inheritance generally suggest that women should inherit a portion equivalent to half of the portion left to a man with the same degree of kinship.[17] However, many Algerian families do not accept or follow such laws in practice. Various studies carried out by women's associations demonstrate that parents and families adopt different strategies to circumvent the current laws in order to distribute inheritance equally between girls and boys; some families resort to donations or fictitious sales in order to provide positive compensation for girls. These practices reveal that Algerian society is beginning to adopt more egalitarian values, even if the laws remain unchanged.[18]

Women have access to all levels of the education system. Article 53 of the constitution and Order 76-31 declare basic education obligatory from the age of 6 to 16; however, the implementation of this legal provision is inadequate, lacking supervision and sufficient financial support. The illiteracy rate of Algerian women aged 15 and above is 40.4 percent, which is almost twice the rate of men at 22 percent. However, women's illiteracy rate falls to 14.4 percent in the age group of 15 to 24 year olds, although this rate is higher in rural areas and sections of southern Algeria.[19]

According to official statistics, 92 percent of girls aged 6 to 14 years attended school in 2003.[20] Girls represent 49 percent of those enrolled in primary school and 53 percent of the population at the university level. Half of all teachers are women. Women are still underrepresented, however, at upper level decision-making positions in education; no woman holds the position of director of education in the *wilayas* (provinces), and less than 10 percent of head teachers are women.[21]

Algerian women are free to negotiate business contracts and financial contracts, as well as work at all levels of employment on an equal status with men. The past few years have witnessed a spectacular increase in the number of female employees and independent women workers; women now represent more than 27 percent of the labor force.[22] In the public sector, women are present in important economic decision-making posts in organizations such as the Bank of Algeria, the Council of Currency and Credit, and the commercial sector of Sonatrach, the largest state-owned company.[23] Nevertheless, while more than 20 percent of women workers fill mid-level executive and manager positions, senior posts remain largely occupied by men.

Algerian women have no legal restrictions on their right to choose a profession. However, a woman's right to work can be revoked by her husband with the family code's "duty of obedience" clause if he does not agree with her choice of career or her decision to work outside the home. Most women who enter the workforce tend to pursue so-called feminine professions in the health and education sectors, which are considered more socially acceptable. Many women make their career choices based on the amount of free time their job will leave them for family life, as child care and family help are difficult to find and domestic chores are a burden that falls mostly on women. In fact, most work performed by women is in the informal sector, ranging from work carried out in the home to illegal work. Little reliable data exists on the extent of this form of employment among women.[24]

Act 90-11 of the employment code (April 1990) states that men and women must receive equal pay for work requiring an equal level of qualifications and performance. Women are further protected from gender discrimination within the labor field by Article 17 of the employment code, which stipulates, "Any provision in a convention or collective agreement or in an employment contract which establishes any kind of discrimination between workers ... based on gender ... is null and void." Articles 142 and 143 lay down sanctions in cases of discrimination. These measures are applied in the public sector, and labor inspectors monitor the private sector for compliance.

The labor law provides gender-specific rights for women, such as maternity leave (Article 55), exemption from night work (Article 29), and special retirement provisions (Article 6). Both state employers and private companies are required to provide such benefits, including two hours a day for breast-feeding and three months of paid maternity leave with benefits. While child-care services are offered only in the largest state companies, public and private child-care centers are increasing in number.

In 2002, the National Committee of Working Women, a section of Algeria's largest labor union, established a center to assist victims of sexual harassment in the workplace. Furthermore, women employees of the National Institute for Public Health and women unionists have been actively campaigning for a law to protect women from sexual harassment in the workplace for some time.

RECOMMENDATIONS

1. The government should address the problem of illiteracy, institute checks on the absenteeism of girls from school, work with women's NGOs to

change the negative images and stereotypes of women in school textbooks, and train teachers to promote values of gender equality.

2. The government should provide financial support and facilitate the efforts of women who want to launch businesses.

3. The government should collaborate with social researchers and labor statisticians to improve survey methods and data collection on female work in the home and in rural areas in order to better understand and evaluate the status of all working women.

4. The government should work to ensure that women are represented in senior level positions in the public and private sectors and labor unions.

Political Rights and Civic Voice

The right of Algerians to change their government is heavily restricted. Although the president and the lower house of parliament (National People's Assembly) are elected by popular vote, and two-thirds of the upper house (Council of Nations) is chosen by elected municipal and provincial councils, these institutions are heavily influenced by members of the old ruling class, consisting of military officers and veterans of the FLN. Algerian legislation recognizes the equal political rights of women, and women are active in civil society and generally take part in politics. However, women remain underrepresented in senior political and government positions.

Articles 41 and 43 of the constitution guarantee freedom of expression, association, and assembly. However, amendments to the penal code in 2001 increased penalties for defamation of any "authority of public order." Freedom of assembly and association are subject to authorization from the Ministry of the Interior for reasons of security and for the purposes of legalization. Requests for permission to hold meetings or establish new organizations often receive no response from the government, therefore obliging groups, such as women's rights defenders, to suspend their plans or to carry on their activities without authorization. Most human rights demonstrations are tolerated, but human rights organizations that focus on investigating the fate of an estimated 4,000 Algerians who have disappeared since 1993 are severely restricted and denied legal registration. Female relatives of the disappeared are prominent activists in this movement.

Algerian women are well represented in the judiciary, particularly at high levels: 34 percent of magistrates are women. In the Council of State, one of the highest institutions of judicial power, 15 of the 38 magistrates are women, and the Council of State's president is a woman.[25]

Algerian women gained suffrage rights in 1962. These rights are guaranteed under Article 50 of the constitution and Order 97-07 (March 1997) relating to the electoral system, which ensures women's right to vote and run for elected office. Eligibility requirements for voting and running for office are the same for men and women.[26] Women have been both appointed and elected to local and legislative positions. In 2004, a woman stood for election to the presidency but was unsuccessful.

Through an informal arrangement, opposition parties reserved 20 percent of their electoral lists for female candidates in the 2002 Algerian legislative elections.[27] Women gained 24 out of 389 seats in the National People's Assembly after the 2002 elections (6.3 percent); and women now hold 28 of the 144 seats in the upper house of parliament (19.4 percent) as a result of the December 2003 elections.

Women are not as well represented in the higher grades of the civil service, filling only 4 percent of available positions. In addition, Algeria has only four female ambassadors, one minister, and three secretaries of state.[28] However, several women have been appointed to executive posts such as *wali* (governor), prefect (the administrative head of a region), or deputy prefect (the administrative head for a subdivision of a region).

In 1999, the government legalized political parties, allowing a few new parties to emerge, including some based on religious politics; however, the FIS remains banned. Article 42 of the constitution guarantees and recognizes the right to create political parties but stipulates, "This right cannot be invoked to attack fundamental freedoms, or values and fundamental components of national identity.... Out of respect for the provisions of the present Constitution, political parties cannot be founded on a religious, linguistic, racial, gender, corporatist, or regional basis."

In theory, there are no restrictions on the participation of Algerian women in politics, but women who attempt to gain positions of higher power within political parties may often face resistance from male members. Just two parties have women serving as president (The Party of Workers and the Party of the Youth Movement) out of Algeria's estimated 40 political parties. To address women's low representation in politics, female members of political parties have presented a manifesto to the government recommending a quota system that would set aside 35 percent of the slots for women in local, prefectoral, and national elections.[29]

Despite wide-ranging access to audiovisual sources of information (90 percent of Algerian households have a television or radio), women still do not gain enough information to be autonomous in their civil or political lives. According to a national study, only 9 percent of women between the ages of 15 and 49 read the newspaper every day.[30] Most women still do not actively participate in political life (93 percent).[31] Some factors that may interfere with women's participation in politics include control exercised by male family members, and an absence of information and communications specifically targeted toward women.

RECOMMENDATIONS

1. The government should allow all political parties that are committed to democracy to participate in the political process, and should facilitate free and competitive elections in the country.
2. The government, in consultation with Algerian civil society groups, should work to prepare effective and clear policies and programs to encourage women's participation in political life, including a proposed measure to set a quota of 35 percent of seats for women in political parties, political elections, and senior government positions.
3. The government should provide leadership training and opportunities for women in the public sector.
4. The government should work with the media and NGOs to educate the general public about women's political rights.

Social and Cultural Rights

In theory, Algerian women are provided the same social and cultural rights as men, but in reality, women do not have equal access to or ability to exercise these rights. Restrictions on women's social and cultural rights are partly due to women's inferior legal status under the Algerian family code, which places women under the guardianship of men, and partly due to the social influence of the country's religious extremist movements. In addition, societal expectations that restrict women's activities to the domestic sphere further limit their abilities to make independent decisions about their health and reproductive rights, or influence community life and social development at the local level.

The state has made considerable efforts to provide family planning for Algerians. Women's fertility rate in 2003 was reported at 2.8 children, as compared to 7 children per woman in the early 1970s; the rate of population growth has dropped to 1.53 percent. The social security system reimburses the purchase of contraceptives, which are distributed throughout the country. An estimated 80 percent of Algerian married women have used contraception at least once in their lives, and 52 percent use modern methods.[32] In 2002, close to 90 percent of births took place in a public-health facility.

Abortion is forbidden and criminalized in Algeria. Article 309 of the penal code stipulates, "Any woman who has intentionally had an abortion carried out or who has attempted to do so shall be punished with 6 months to one year of imprisonment." A *fatwa*, a ruling on Islamic law, issued by the High Islamic Council in 1998, however, allows abortion in cases in which pregnancy resulted from rape by terrorists or armed groups.

Article 54 of the constitution guarantees Algerians the right to health care. However, as a share of gross domestic product, health care expenditure has dropped in recent years to just 3.1 percent.[33] Moreover, disparities exist between certain regions of the country and certain social groups concerning equal access to health services. Poverty and lack of financial resources constitute the major obstacles. An additional factor is the influence of religious extremist teachings that preach that women's social behavior is an assertion of a group's religious and political identity. Algerian civil society groups have observed that this line of thought has a strong impact on women's autonomy and their access to social and cultural rights, particularly in rural communities. For example, a number of Algerian males continue to prohibit women from making independent decisions about their health, restrict women from leaving the home, and forbid their female family members from being examined by a male doctor.

Many Algerian women endure considerable social pressures to use the veil as part of their dress code. For some women, the veil is a precondition to their freedom of movement. This practice has increased, over the past 15 years in particular, due to the influence of religious extremist groups in Algeria. Certain regions of the country are more conservative than others, and women are more often seen covering themselves from head to toe in poorer and more conservative regions of the south. The Algerian government has not taken any public position on the veil issue. Many women employed in state institutions such as public schools wear the *hijab*—a veil that covers only the head and hair; but it is very rare to see a woman employed in government offices veiled from head to toe.

Some Algerian women and girls are subjected to the harmful traditional practice of virginity tests, in which a woman's family asks a doctor to perform an examination to verify whether or not a woman's hymen is intact before she is married. In some cases, if a woman's hymen is not found intact, doctors will perform an operation to reconstruct it.

Women have equal rights with men to own property, but women's right to housing is not equally recognized in practice or in the legal texts. Article 52 of the family code provides that if there is only one family home, it should go to the husband in the case of divorce because he is considered the head of the family. Since 1984, thousands of divorced women—many of whom are victims of Articles 48 and 52 of the family code, which permit a man to divorce his wife verbally and evict his wife and children from the home—have found themselves homeless, without any resources to provide for their children. While a husband is legally obligated to provide for his children after a divorce, government enforcement mechanisms are weak, and many men fail to fulfill this obligation. In situations in which the court system works to address this problem, the financial compensation rarely meets basic living costs.

Moreover, in cases in which housing is allocated by municipal authorities, women are systematically penalized under the pretext that they can be taken in by their families. Few women take legal action in housing discrimination cases. Women's organizations argue that as traditional patriarchal protection has now disappeared with the rise of poverty and increasing housing problems, it is time for the state to introduce new initiatives to protect women's housing rights, particularly those of divorced, widowed, and single women.

The last decade has witnessed a gradual feminization of poverty in Algeria. Since 1992, thousands of women have lost male family members to murder or abduction by armed Islamic extremist groups or the state's security forces.[34] Many of these women have found themselves as heads of household, even though they may have little knowledge of the public sphere or any education or outside work experience.[35] Families of those abducted who request a declaration of absence from the authorities must wait four years before obtaining a declaration of death. During this period, women heads of household are not able to gain access to pensions or any savings or property held in the name of the abducted family member.[36] There are no special programs for widows other than the help of their families, but poor women can sometimes benefit from social care provided by the state.

An additional group of women currently suffering from poverty and social marginalization is made up of the hundreds of female survivors of abductions and rapes carried out by various fundamentalist armed groups from 1992 to 1999. Many families have rejected these women and refused to accept them back into their homes—a woman who has been sexually assaulted is often considered a dishonor to the family—and a majority of these women now live on the streets. The government has provided some assistance to these women, but state personnel are not fully trained or prepared to handle such cases. Women survivors of rape at the hands of armed groups are excluded from economic state benefits, which are available to victims of other armed group abuses who have suffered physical injury or material loss.[37] It took several years after the first cases of mass rapes for psychologists and physicians to provide effective assistance to the victims of these crimes, but the state's ability to provide psychological or economic support remains limited, and the needs of these destitute women remain critical.

Government agencies concerned with development and social welfare programs do not fully recognize the societal gender biases and cultural obstacles that prevent women from enjoying the same opportunities as men. Consequently, state agencies have not been able to establish government action plans to enable women to benefit fully from development programs or gain access to resources at all levels.

More than 50 percent of the state-owned and private print media employees in Algeria are women.[38] While some women journalists write culture and society columns, others contribute political articles, editorials, and economic surveys. Women also constitute close to 50 percent of the journalists employed in national radio stations, and two-thirds of the writers and reporters in television news.[39] Female journalists usually show strong solidarity with women's rights defenders and their agendas, but the influence of women in the media remains limited at the higher level decision-making posts. However, the recent removal from television of a sexist advertisement indicates that the protests formulated by women's rights activists concerning the image of women in the media are beginning to have some impact on content decisions.[40]

Although Algerian women's rights groups have contributed to important recent advances in women's status, women's NGOs are not fully able to operate or advocate for their rights. While women's rights activists are legally permitted to carry out public activities without being subjected to government restrictions, these groups still face a number of obstacles in their work. NGOs working to advance women's rights face especially strong resistance from extremist religious groups and conservative elements of the government. Additional challenges for women's NGOs include the socially and legally ingrained stereotypes and discrimination of women in Algerian society and a prejudice against work surrounding women's equality and rights issues, as well as significant security problems and threats received for engaging in such work in Algeria.[41] Finally, many Algerian NGOs working to advance women's rights lack sufficient financial backing and are in desperate need of national and international funding and support.

RECOMMENDATIONS

1. Government agencies should encourage women to assume leadership positions in development programs.
2. The government should introduce public information campaigns to inform the public about women's rights and services available for women.
3. The government should create policies to address women's housing needs and unemployment, with a special focus on the needs of rural women, widows, and victims of violence.

AUTHOR: Caroline Sakina Brac de la Perrière lives and works in Algeria and France. She is a social and human science researcher and has written extensively on women's rights and the women's movement in North Africa, with a specific focus on Algeria. She is one of the founders of the network New Ways International Alliance for Social Innovation and a member of Collectif 95 Maghreb Egalité and "20 ans barakat." She holds a PhD in History and an MA in Psychology.

Notes

[1] "2003 World Population Data Sheet" (Washington, D.C.: Population Reference Bureau, 2003).

[2] *Constitution of the Democratic and Popular Republic of Algeria, Referendum of 28th November 1996* (Algiers: Ministry of Justice, 1996), Article 29.

[3] "Order No. 70-86 of 15th December 1970 setting out the Nationality Code" (Ministry of Justice), Article 6.

[4] *Women's Human Rights—Algeria: Steps Towards Change or Empty Promise?* (New York: Amnesty International [AI], 15 September 2003), http://www.amnestyusa.org/women/document.do?id=BE58192FE056415380256D7F0051E54B.

[5] *Constitution . . . of Algeria,* Article 44: "A citizen entitled to his civil and political rights has the right to choose his place of residence and to move about on the national territory. He is guaranteed the right of entry and the right to leave the territory."

[6] A study on the degree of attachment to egalitarian values among the Algerian population shows that this is the major taboo mentioned by women. *Degré d'adhésion aux valeurs égalitaires au sein de la population algérienne,* "Synopsis" (Algiers: UNIFEM and Collectif 95 Maghreb Egalité, 2002), 15.

[7] Family code, Article 39: "The wife is required to: 1) obey her husband and show him the respect due to him as head of the family..."

[8] "Consideration of Reports Submitted By States Parties Under Article 18 of the Convention on the Elimination of All Forms of Discrimination Against Women, Initial reports of States parties, Algeria" (New York: UN CEDAW/C/DZA/, 1 September 1998), http://www.un.org/womenwatch/daw/cedaw/cedaw20/algeria.htm.

[9] Rassemblement Contre la Hogra et Pour les Droits des Algériennes [RACHDA], *Femmes contre l'oubli* (New York: UN Population Fund [UNFPA], 2002), 15.

[10] *Algeria: Steps Towards Change. . . ?* (AI).

[11] There are no reliable statistics on the number of women subjected to rape, abduction, and murder during the internal conflict.

[12] *Femmes contre l'oubli* (UNFPA), 37.

[13] "Algeria: Briefing to the Committee on the Elimination of Discrimination Against Women" (AI, December 2004).

[14] *Rapport sur l'Enquête nationale. Violence à l'encontre des femmes* (Algiers: Ministry of Health, Population and Hospital Reform, Institut nationale de la Santé publique, and UNFPA–UNIFEM, 2004), to be published.

[15] Ibid.

[16] Family code, Article 53.

[17] Family code, Articles 126 to 183. There is an exception however, for paternal grandparents, who inherit equal parts.

[18] *Degré d'adhésion aux valeurs égalitaires au sein de la population algérienne,* "Synopsis" (Algiers: UNIFEM and Collectif 95 Maghreb Egalité, 2002), 12.

[19] Table 26, "Gender inequality in education," in *Human Development Report 2004: Cultural Liberty in Today's Diverse World* (New York: United Nations Development Programme [UNDP], 2004), 225-228. http://hdr.undp.org/reports/global/2004/.

[20] *Enquête qualitative sur la santé de la famille–2002, Rapport principal* (Algiers: Ministry of Health, Population and Hospital Reform and National Statistics Office, July 2004).

[21] Statistical data (Ministry of National Education, 2000), in Algerian Union of Democratic Women, *Masculin/Féminin, égalité et mixité à l'école* (Algiers: UNFPA, 2003).

[22] *Stratégies visant à renforcer le statut social, économique et politique des femmes dans le processus de développement: Rapport relatif à l'état des lieux.* Vol. 2 (Algiers: UNDP Ministry of Foreign Affairs [MAE], July 2002).

[23] Société nationale des hydrocarbures: the largest state-owned company.

[24] *Violence, salariat, socialization: trois facettes du destin social féminin* (Algiers: UNFPA and Algerian Union of Democratic Women, 2003), 42.

[25] *Stratégies visant à renforcer le statut . . . . Rapport relatif à l'état des lieux,* Vol. 2 (UNDP MAE, July 2002), 123.

[26] Electoral Law, Article 5.

[27] "Women in Parliament in the Arab World" (New York: Carnegie Endowment for International Peace).

[28] In August 2004, out of 40 ministers the Minister for Culture, the Secretary of State for Emigration, the Secretary of State for Research, and the Secretary of State for Women's Affairs were women.

[29] Fatima Zohra Sai, "Les Algériennes dans les espaces politiques, quelle perspective?" *Revue Algérienne des sciences juridiques, économiques et politiques* (Université d'Alger Faculté de Droit, 2003), and interview with Maître Nadia Aït Zaï, Algiers, August 2004.

[30] According to *l'Enquête qualitative sur la santé de la famille–2002.*

[31] *Degré d'adhésion . . .* (UNIFEM), 7.

[32] "Algeria's Reply to the Questionnaire to Governments on Implementation of the Beijing Platform for Action (1995) and the Outcome of the Twenty-third Special Session of the General Assembly" (New York: United Nations, 2000).

[33] "Algeria: Briefing to the Committee on the Elimination of Discrimination Against Women" (AI, December 2004).

[34] According to *"Algeria: Steps Towards Change . . . ?"* (AI), since 1992 more than 100,000 people have been killed in murders, fighting, massacres, and bombings. About 7,000 people are reported as missing.

[35] Cherifa Bouatta, "La pratique psychologique au temps du trauma, L'expérience traumatique," *NAQD (Revue d'Etudes et de Critique Sociale)* 18 (Algiers, winter 2003): 98.

[36] "Algeria: Briefing to the Committee on the Elimination of Discrimination Against Women" (AI, December 2004).

[37] Ibid.

[38] "Algeria's Reply to the Questionnaire to Governments on Implementation of the Beijing Platform for Action (1995) and the Outcome of the Twenty-third Special Session of the General Assembly" (New York: United Nations, 2000).

[39] *"Stratégies visant à renforcer le statut . . ."* (UNDP MAE), 103.

[40] This is an advertisement for Danone in which a young girl is slapped by her younger brother, who then takes away her yogurt (August 2004).

[41] According to *"Algeria: Steps Towards Change . . . ?"* (AI), around 8,000 members of armed groups are still operating in the country.

Bahrain

by Sabika al-Najjar

Population: 700,000
GDP Per Capita (PPP): $17,170
Economy: Capitalist-statist
Ranking on UN HDI: 40 out of 177
Polity: Traditional monarchy
Literacy: Male 91.5% / Female 84.2%
Percent Women Economically Active: 34.2%
Date of Women's Suffrage: 2002
Women's Fertility Rate: 2.6
Percent Urban/Rural: Urban 87% / Rural 13%

Country Ratings for Bahrain
Nondiscrimination and Access to Justice: 2.2
Autonomy, Security, and Freedom of the Person: 2.3
Economic Rights and Equal Opportunity: 2.9
Political Rights and Civic Voice: 2.1
Social and Cultural Rights: 2.8
(Scale of 1 to 5: 1 represents the lowest and 5 the highest level of freedom women have to exercise their rights)

Introduction

Bahrain gained its independence from Britain in August 1971 and adopted its first constitution on December 6, 1973. In August 1975, Emir Isa ibn Salman al-Khalifa dissolved Bahrain's National Assembly and suspended its constitution. For the next 25 years, the citizens of Bahrain lived under the State Security Law and the Emergency Law. Legislation issued during this period, such as the penal code, the Associations Law, and the Criminal Procedures laws, was poorly implemented due to the executive authority's control over the judiciary system. The regime banned political parties and trade unions, suspended civil liberties, and imprisoned political activists and political opponents.

Under Bahrain's 2002 constitution, the king is the head of all three branches of Bahrain's monarchical government. After the death of Emir Isa in 1999, his son Hamad bin Isa Al Khalifa took power and began to implement various political and economic reforms. By the end of the year 2000, general

51

amnesty was granted to political prisoners and exiles, the State Security Law and State Security Court were abolished, and women obtained previously denied political rights. On February 14, 2001, Bahraini citizens overwhelmingly approved the National Action Charter that would establish a partially elected legislature, a constitutional monarchy, and an independent judiciary. A bicameral parliament now exists with a 40-seat appointed upper house, the Shura Council, and a 40-seat elected lower house, the House of Deputies. Despite these positive steps, political parties remain banned in Bahrain, the media are constrained, and NGOs face extensive restrictions.

The small island nation of Bahrain is a rich, tax-free country with a per capita income of $17,170. Migrant workers and expatriates, predominantly from Asia, comprise about 38 percent of Bahrain's population of 700,000. Most immigrants are employed in industries, construction, or domestic work. The majority of the population of Bahrain is Muslim, mostly Shi'as;[1] while the government is predominantly Sunni. Poverty ratios are high among the Shi'a population.

The government of Bahrain encouraged women to run for office in the 2002 parliamentary and municipal elections and has initiated work on family law aimed at regulating women's rights in areas such as divorce, marriage, and child custody. In 2001, the government established the Supreme Council for Women, an umbrella organization devised to oversee women's rights–related work in Bahrain. The number of NGOs devoted to women's issues has grown over the last three years.

Despite the recent attention directed toward women's rights, the government has failed to adopt any viable policies that would positively affect women's status in Bahrain. The law obliges women's NGOs in Bahrain to obtain permission before organizing national-level meetings on critical issues regarding women's rights. Moreover, they are not allowed to receive independent funds from abroad. The government of Bahrain ratified the UN Convention on the Elimination of All Forms of Discrimination Against Women (CEDAW) in 2002, but with reservations on articles concerning family law, equality, freedom of movement, and residence. Women still encounter numerous social and legal obstacles such as arbitrary divorce, gender-based violence, and discrimination in the workplace. Gender discrimination remains a problem in Bahrain; the UNDP *Human Development Report* ranked Bahrain 66th out of 177 countries on the status of gender empowerment measures in 2004.[2]

Nondiscrimination and Access to Justice

On February 14, 2002, the king issued the Constitution of the Kingdom of Bahrain, replacing the constitution of 1973. According to Article 5/B of the constitution, the state shall maintain the balance between family obligations and women's work and also help to maintain women's equal status with men in political, social, cultural, and economic life, without jeopardizing the *Shari'a* laws. The constitution also ensures all citizens the right to education at all levels, health care, property, housing, work, the right to defend the country, and the right to engage in economic activities.[3] Although the constitution does not discriminate between people based on their gender, nationality, or belief, there are no laws that make discrimination illegal.

Bahraini Nationality Law establishes the right of Bahraini men to pass their nationality on to their foreign-born wives and the children of these marriages. On the other hand, the law forbids Bahraini women to transfer their nationality to their children or foreign-born husbands.[4] However, in April 2004, the parliament agreed to allow Bahraini women to sponsor their foreign spouses and children, enabling adult children and husbands to work in the country without an employment sponsor.[5]

Bahrain's judicial system and its constitution stipulate that both men and women should have equal access to justice and the right to a fair trial. In reality, practical guarantees against gender discrimination do not exist. It is not uncommon for judges to demonstrate prejudice against women in court.[6] Women may also face numerous obstacles during Shari'a court proceedings, which are male dominated and extremely complex. Lengthy court procedures, particularly in cases of divorce, are just one example of the hardships placed on women seeking justice. Men are free to divorce their wives at any time, but women are required to appeal to Shari'a courts in order to be granted a divorce.

A woman is recognized as a full person before the court in Bahrain; a woman's testimony is equal to that of a man's, and a woman can file a complaint and represent herself in all legal matters. The Shari'a courts, however, state that a valid witness should be two men, or two women and one man. In cases of domestic violence against women, Shari'a courts do not accept the testimony of close relatives or of just one woman. Considering that most domestic violence occurs in the home, where witnesses are usually mothers or close relatives, victims have little chance of proving their cases. Moreover, female victims of spousal abuse are often subject to blackmail or threats by the police and judges during investigations or trials. In some cases, the families pressure victims to remain silent and deter them from seeking justice.

In an attempt to reform the Shari'a courts, on March 10, 2004, the Supreme Judicial Council appointed to the Shari'a four male judges known to be impartial and judicious with regard to family issues.[7] Although this is considered a positive step toward women's rights, the judicial system is still in need of fundamental reform.[8]

Bahrain's penal code contains numerous gender-specific laws. Some articles in the penal code are devised to protect women from violence by punishing such crimes as assaults on pregnant women, rape, and sexual harassment. Article 344 of the penal code states that any person who has sexual intercourse with a female against her will shall face life in prison.

While Bahrain's criminal and penal laws do not discriminate against women criminal defendants, some laws actually discriminate against women who are victims of crimes. Article 353 states that no penalty shall be inflicted upon a person who rapes an unmarried woman, as long as he then marries the victim. Article 333 of the Bahraini penal code specifies a life sentence or death for the crime of murder; but Article 334 provides a reduced sentence (unspecified length) for a man who surprises his wife in the act of adultery and proceeds to murder or assault her. Such laws often allow criminals to escape punishment, as families and victims often accept these unjust verdicts or fail to report the crimes altogether in order to avoid social disgrace and shame. Bahraini law does not penalize the sexual violation of spouses. According to social norms and local understanding of religious traditions, it is the obligation of the wife to satisfy her husband sexually.

The constitution prohibits arbitrary arrest, detention, exile, and the stripping of citizenship, with the exception of cases involving grand treason.[9] In practice, non-citizens such as foreign workers and female domestic helpers often face arbitrary detention and deportation as a result of disputes with their sponsors or due to lack of work permits.[10] Some sponsors take advantage of this situation and deport domestic workers without paying them their salaries.[11]

The Bahraini government ratified the Convention on the Elimination of All Forms of Discrimination Against Women (CEDAW) on March 2, 2002, but included a number of reservations. Reservations were applied to the following articles: Article 2, on the basis that its implementation would conflict with the Shari'a; Article 9, which addresses equality in nationality rights; Article 15, paragraph 4, which relates to freedom of movement and residence; and Article 16, which deals with family law and equality within the family.[12] These reservations have served to basically nullify the treaty's fundamental aims and functions.

While women's status has somewhat improved since the ratification of CEDAW in areas such as political rights and increased representation in the Shura Council, the government of Bahrain has made almost no effort to review and amend the existing national laws and policies to bring them into conformity with CEDAW standards. Moreover, it has not signed the Optional Protocol on CEDAW that allows women to register complaints with the CEDAW committee if they cannot achieve justice in their own country.

The number of NGOs devoted to women's issues increased from 5 in 2001 to 14 at the close of 2003.[13] Women are active in political societies[14] as well as in NGOs that advocate for the recognition of women's rights under CEDAW. Women's groups also serve to educate women on their rights under the Shari'a and Bahrain's laws. However, NGOs have done little to promote a review of or changes in existing legislation that negatively impacts women's lives.

In addition to the organizational and financial challenges confronting women's NGOs, Bahrain's Societies Law, which regulates all of Bahrain's NGOs, imposes severe restrictions on their work. Bahrain's NGOs are prohibited from engaging in political activity, and the law permits the Ministry of Labor and Social Affairs to intervene in their internal affairs and activities. According to the Societies Law, the Ministry of Labor and Social Affairs has the right to access NGO files, suspend their executive boards, and terminate their licenses. NGOs must also obtain permission to organize a national meeting or international conference to address such topics as family law or violence against women.

RECOMMENDATIONS

1. The government and National Assembly should amend national laws in order to bring all legislation in conformity with principles of non-discrimination.
2. The Supreme Judiciary Council should reform Bahrain's judiciary system so that women do not face discrimination from judges and other court officers, particularly in Shari'a courts.
3. The Supreme Council for Women (SCW) should assist women's rights NGOs to conduct media and public outreach programs to inform women of their legal rights under Bahrain's existing laws.
4. The government should remove all reservations to CEDAW and take steps to implement it locally by bringing national laws in conformity with CEDAW.

Autonomy, Security, and Freedom of the Person

Bahrain has made progress in achieving both civil and personal freedoms since the start of the political reforms of 2001. However, laws that restrict freedom of the press raise skepticism about the sustainability of these rights.

Article 22 of the constitution states that, "Freedom of conscience is absolute. The State guarantees the inviolability of worship and the freedom to perform religious rites and hold religious parades and meetings in accordance with the customs observed in the country." Bahrain's citizen population is 98 percent Muslim, but Christians, Jews, Hindus, and other religious adherents are able to practice their religions freely in their churches and temples.[15] The same freedom holds true for Shi'as, who constitute two-thirds of the indigenous population.[16] Conversion between the Sunni and Shi'a sects is not favorably regarded in Bahrain, and converting from Islam to another religion or declaring oneself a non-believer is not tolerated.

While there are no direct legal restrictions on women's freedom of movement, women's rights may be limited by socially imposed restrictions such as requiring a woman to request permission from the head of the household in order to travel abroad. Islamic fundamentalists in Bahrain support this practice, in that they consider it to be a part of a woman's religious obligation. In some cases, women are obliged to request permission to leave their residence to visit friends or family.

It is not socially acceptable for a single woman to live on her own, especially if she still has a living parent. According to the now-outdated practice of *bayt al-ta'a* (literally, "house of obedience"), a woman could be forced by the police to reside with her husband against her will. This procedure is no longer implemented in Bahrain but the law still exists. The Shari'a courts in Bahrain consider a wife who refuses to live with her husband to be *nashiz* (disobedient)[17] and can deprive her of a *nafaqa* (an allowance from her husband).

Family law is not yet codified in Bahrain. Despite efforts by the government and women's NGOs, the family law agenda is frequently sidelined, often as a result of opposition from both Shi'a and Sunni religious leaders. Some legislators are calling for a unified law, while others prefer two Islamic codes to accommodate the demands of both the Sunni and the Shi'a populations. The absence of a family law has rendered women vulnerable to individualistic, patriarchal, and often contradictory interpretations of the Shari'a by Bahrain's all-male judges.

The marriage contract in Bahrain has remained unchanged since it was adopted some 75 years ago. With the exception of the *mahar* (dower, a sum of money given to a wife by her husband at the time of marriage), this contract does not provide both parties equally with the opportunity to stipulate conditions or negotiate their rights. In some cases, a wife can stipulate that she would like to continue working after marriage or to remain in Bahrain if the husband lives abroad.

In Bahrain, a Sunni bride is required to have a *wali* (guardian) who will represent her during the marriage proceedings. A wali is most often a father, brother, or uncle. If a woman does not have a wali, the judge will represent her in completing the marriage formalities. Conversely, a Shi'a woman can sign her own marriage contract, but Shi'a women tend not to have as much independence in selecting their marriage partner and are often heavily influenced by their family's choices. When a marriage contract is completed, a husband will pay his wife the mahar, which will usually become the property of the wife. If the wife requests a divorce, she is expected to pay the mahar back to her husband.

Bahrain lacks anti-trafficking laws and does not fully comply with international standards on the elimination of trafficking in persons. Foreigners, mostly from South Asia and other Arab countries, constitute approximately

38 percent of Bahrain's total population.[18] Many female domestic workers and expatriates in Bahrain are victims of trafficking and indentured servitude. Some female domestic workers and women employees of restaurants and hotels reportedly experience practices such as forced 12- to 16-hour workdays, rape, sexual harassment, and forced prostitution. Some of these problems may be linked to the sponsorship system, which places expatriate workers under the control of their sponsors.[19]

Bahraini law prohibits torture or cruel, inhuman, or degrading punishment. Credible reports indicate that prisoners, including female prisoners, are not subject to systematic torture in the Bahraini prisons.[20] Female criminals are held separately from men, and women are not required to have a male custodian in order to be released. Foreign workers, particularly domestic workers, on the other hand, often face torture, humiliation, and degrading treatment at the hands of their sponsors. Courts have looked into torture allegations of domestic workers, but female victims often tend to drop their cases due to fear, isolation, and lengthy court procedures, opting to return to their home countries instead of prosecuting the perpetrators.[21]

The penal code of Bahrain addresses violence and harm to the physical safety of men and women, as well as gender-based violence such as rape, sexual harassment, and physical abuse. However, there are no legal protections against domestic violence. Women in Bahrain tend not to report domestic violence until it reaches intolerable levels. A study conducted by Dr. Banna Bou Zaboon revealed that of the 712 cases of violence recorded by the Bahrain Defense Forces Hospital in 2001–02, 281 were cases of women who had been abused by their husbands.[22] While a few victims of domestic abuse are granted divorce, Shari'a judges often regard acts of violence against women by close relatives such as fathers, brothers, or husbands as a right guaranteed to the relatives by religion and laws.[23]

While Bahrain's labor laws do not address sexual harassment in the workplace, Articles 350 and 351 of the penal code specify punishment for any indecent act in public or by telephone. Article 350 states that any person who commits an act of indecency with a female should be liable for punishment even when the act is not committed in public. Many women are embarrassed to file complaints of this nature for fear of damaging their reputations or professional careers. These same laws are also implemented to punish women, specifically unmarried females who engage in consensual sexual activity, which is considered a crime in Bahrain's customary law and the Shari'a.

Women's societies and other NGOs in Bahrain have not yet been able to convince victims of violence to break their walls of silence. Two women's societies in Bahrain have established legal and social counseling centers, but these groups currently work to address the impact of violence rather than its prevention.

RECOMMENDATIONS

1. The government should enact family laws that are non-discriminatory and expand women's human rights.
2. The government should criminalize domestic violence and adopt procedures to allow women, including foreign women and domestic workers, to report violence.
3. The government should enact the necessary laws to prosecute those who traffic in persons and ensure that victims of trafficking are not criminalized and have access to supportive services, rehabilitation, and legal aid.
4. The government, the Supreme Council for Women, and independent NGOs should monitor women's working conditions in both the public and private sectors and appoint female labor inspectors.

Economic Rights and Equal Opportunity

Bahrain's economy is geared toward the diversification of national income through the development of small- and medium-size industries. The free economic environment has encouraged small entrepreneurs, including women, to enter the business marketplace for the first time. Nevertheless, a number of factors work to create a hostile business environment for women. The monopolization of the market by a few individuals and large companies, social beliefs that private business is a male's domain, and women's lack of familiarity with and access to the intricacies of commercial and industrial procedures all pose obstacles to women's progress in Bahrain's economic sphere.

Women can legally own, sell, and rent land, real estate, and property in Bahrain. However, women often authorize a male relative such as a father, brother, or husband to take charge of and manage their properties. The male-dominated nature of the real estate business, combined with the time-consuming and burdensome procedures involved in managing property are often influential factors that weigh on a woman's decision to pass on this responsibility to a male. Women often have additional family responsibilities placed upon them by society that limit their time.

The Islamic Shari'a in Bahrain commits the husband to support his wife and family financially. Women in Bahrain can open their own bank accounts and manage their income. In most households women generally administer the domestic budgets; however, there are also cases in which working wives hand over their salaries to their husbands out of fear of divorce. Working wives or daughters often contribute to family living expenses. Despite a woman's financial contributions, social customs and a lack of economic policies that benefit women dictate that the house is most often registered in the husband's name. These conditions tend to place women, particularly wives, in a position of financial insecurity and disadvantage in matters of divorce.

Women inherit from their husbands, fathers, and brothers in accordance with the interpretation of Shari'a. Non-Muslim women cannot inherit from their Muslim husbands, while Shi'a wives may inherit movable items but not land. In Shi'a practices in Bahrain, daughters without brothers inherit everything from their deceased father, while a Sunni relative from the father's lineage will share the inheritance with the Sunni daughters if there is no son.

Statistics on the proportion of businesses in Bahrain owned by women demonstrate a noticeable increase recently, from 24.30 percent in 2001 to 30.60 percent in 2002.[24] The number of female members of the Bahrain Chamber of Commerce and Industry reached 1,785 in 2003.[25] Even though some women administer their own businesses, men still manage the majority of female-owned firms. This is partly due to the time required to administer a business, as well as the fact that Bahraini men often want to circumvent the law that prohibits employees in the public sector from owning private businesses. Men who work in the public sector will often register their private business under the name of a female relative but manage it themselves.

A free education system is provided in Bahrain through the secondary level, and a new education law making education compulsory for six to fifteen year olds was approved by parliament in May of 2004. The number of girls enrolled in intermediate and secondary schools during the 2001–02 school year exceeded that of boys.[26] In fact, women outnumber men in most of the colleges in Bahrain, with the main exception being the college of engineering (3,079 males and only 1,337 females).[27] Women do not have the same opportunities as men in vocational education, which trains workers in such fields as industry, mechanical maintenance, and carpentry, among others. Bahrain's labor market does not openly accept women in these occupations, and social customs and traditions often impede women from pursuing such careers.

Female students in Bahrain tend to specialize in fields that enable them to work as teachers. Government jobs with daily shifts that permit women to maintain a balance between careers and family are also popular. Competition and over-qualification are contributing to an increase in the unemployment rate among female graduates;[28] the public sector cannot absorb more employees, and the private sector prefers to hire men.

Bahrain's labor laws do not prohibit or provide protections against gender-based discrimination in the workplace. Hiring discrimination is evident in Bahrain's private sector, where employers may be reluctant to shoulder the financial responsibility of maternity leave, which women employees are guaranteed under the labor laws. The Bahrain Human Rights Society reported that in 2001–02, a number of female graduates who had specialized in mechanical engineering had been discriminated against because of their gender and were not employed in factories in the private sector.[29] The government has not taken any action against employers guilty of gender discrimination.

In addition to discrimination in hiring, Bahraini female employees are also subject to unequal wages for equal work. Female workers often fail to receive equal job training opportunities and are trained in marginal skills that are not in demand in the labor market.[30] Furthermore, women are not guaranteed equality in promotion opportunities. This disparity is exemplified in the industrial sector, where only one woman holds a decision-making position and just three women fill supervisory roles.[31] Women are also absent in senior management positions in the academic field even though they comprise the majority of teachers.

Under Bahrain's labor laws, women in the public sector are entitled to 45 days of maternity leave starting with the day of delivery. This provision does not meet International Labor Organization standards. Female public employees are allocated one hour per day for four months to breast-feed their babies. Women in the private sector receive 45 days' maternity leave and 15 days' leave without pay, plus a daily one-hour break to breast-feed their babies for two years. Moreover, Article 63 of the labor law declares that a female employee in the private sector may not be fired as a result of marriage, pregnancy, or maternity leave.

Labor laws regulating private-sector employment tend to have a larger number of gender-based provisions. For instance, women in the private sector are prohibited from working between the hours of 8 P.M. and 7 A.M., with the exception of hospital employment. Women are also not allowed to work in hazardous places (undefined) that might jeopardize their health and/or the health of their baby (Article 60).

With the help of Almostkbal (a women's NGO), women in the ready-made garment industry can belong to an established trade union that protects the rights of female workers. This union is one of the first of its kind in Bahrain. Furthermore, women's groups have helped to secure jobs for low-income women through job training. In 1998, the UNDP and the government of Bahrain initiated a project, now implemented by the Awal Women's Society and the Child and Mother Welfare Society, to grant small loans to some 10,000 low-income women to start their own micro businesses.[32]

RECOMMENDATIONS

1. The Ministry of Trade, working with the Bahrain Businesswomen's Society, women's rights NGOs, and the Bahrain Chamber of Commerce and Industry, should encourage more women to establish their own businesses and work with banks to facilitate loans and financial training for women.
2. The National Assembly should amend the labor laws to prohibit gender-based discrimination at the workplace and violence against domestic workers, appoint labor inspectors to monitor the working conditions of domestic workers, and establish complaint mechanisms for women to report violations.

3. The Ministry of Education should work to eliminate all gender discrimination in education and permit the enrollment of women in vocational schools.

Political Rights and Civic Voice

While women were prohibited from participating in the country's first democratic elections in 1973, both the National Charter, approved in February 2001, and the 2002 Constitution guarantee women's suffrage and political participation. Article 1, Paragraph E, of the Constitution of the Kingdom of Bahrain now clearly states, "all citizens, both men and women, are entitled to vote and to stand for elections, in accordance with this constitution and in the conditions and principles laid down by law. No citizen can be deprived of the right to vote or to nominate oneself for elections except by law." With the dissolution of the National Assembly in August 1975, parliamentary elections were not held again until 2002.

Bahrain's constitution guarantees freedom of expression and opinion and the right to associate freely.[33] Over the last few years, the state-owned Bahrain Radio and Television has diversified its programming and has covered a broader spectrum of topics, including women's issues, violence against women, and women's political rights. By the end of 2003, Bahrain had four Arabic-language and two English-language newspapers. The number of female journalists has steadily risen in recent years. Women's organizations also conduct seminars and lectures to discuss women's rights.

Since the beginning of 2001, women have participated overtly in a variety of demonstrations and political, cultural, and social activities. On October 14, 2002, women held a demonstration in front of the Ministry of Justice to call for a unified family law. Women are active members in Bahrain's political societies.

Despite advances toward liberalization, the 1989 Societies Law of Bahrain still remains in effect. This law acts to prohibit all NGOs from engaging in politics and provides the Ministry of Labor and Social Affairs extended authority over NGOs. The ministry continues to deny a license to the Bahrain Women's Union, a federation of women's NGOs whose aim is to advocate for women's rights and to pressure the government and legislators to issue regulations in accordance with international standards and CEDAW principles.

The enhancement of women's rights was an important by-product of recent political reform. Both the National Charter and Bahrain's constitution now fully guarantee the right of all citizens, men and women, to be involved in the public affairs of the country, including the rights to vote, participate in elections, and run for office. The government supported and encouraged women to take part in the 2002 elections. While women participated as both voters and candidates in the municipal council elections of May 2002 and the October 2002 parliamentary elections, no women were elected to either of these bodies.

Women candidates faced many challenges in the 2002 elections, including those from Islamists who argued that women are created to be mothers and wives, but not politicians. Some female voters were heavily influenced by male family members to vote only for male candidates.

While many Bahraini women specialize in law, and there are no laws to prohibit women from serving as judges, Bahrain's judges are all men.[34] However, six women currently participate in the justice system through their appointments by the king to the office of the attorney general.

Appointments of women to government positions have increased in the last few years. Sheika Haya Al-Khalifa was appointed Ambassador to France in December 1999. In November 2001, Lulwa Al-Awadi received ministerial rank as General Secretary for the Supreme Council for Women. The king's appointment of six women to the Shura Council (upper chamber) also provided women with access to legislative authority.[35] Despite these advances, little progress has been made toward the appointment of women to lower decision-making posts of the government. There are only three women at the assistant under-secretary level today, and 31 women out of 286 directors of departments in the various ministries.[36]

Due to a governmental ban on political parties, political societies have flourished in Bahrain. Women's participation in political societies varies from 9 percent to 50.8 percent, but only 7 out of 13 political societies have elected women to their executive boards. Recently, three women won election to the executive boards of two Islamic political societies. Religious public meetings and meetings in private *majalis*,[37] on the other hand, tend to be gender-segregated. No political societies are currently working for the rights of non-Bahraini citizens, immigrants, or foreign workers. However, trade unions represent non-Bahraini labor issues, and human rights groups work to defend the rights of Bahrain's immigrants.

Despite women's active participation in Bahrain's political societies, women's issues do not feature prominently in the agendas of these groups. In reality, the majority of women in Bahrain are not aware of their political rights, as they lack access to information. Information sources on women's human rights are scarce and are not always available in public libraries or in native languages. NGOs that educate women on their rights also fail to reach a large majority of Bahrain's local and rural women.[38]

RECOMMENDATIONS

1. The ruling authorities in Bahrain should allow political parties to operate legally and participate in competitive elections, lift all remaining restrictions on freedom of expression and association, and actively encourage women's participation in public life.

2. The government should provide support, training, and assistance to female politicians and political workers from all political parties on a nonpartisan basis.
3. The government should appoint female judges to all courts in Bahrain, including the Shari'a courts.
4. The government should develop a gender integration plan to increase the number of women in senior decision-making positions in both the private and public sectors.

Social and Cultural Rights

The maternal mortality rate in Bahrain is very low (0.22 per 1000 live births).[39] Medical care, including primary health and maternity services, is provided free of charge in public hospitals and health centers. The high rate of education and the relatively high standard of living in Bahrain has helped to produce a high level of health awareness. Girls enjoy the same access to health care as do boys.[40]

Health and reproductive health services, including guidelines for maternity care and birth control, are provided free of charge to all women. Health centers do not require a husband's consent in order to provide women with family planning services, with the exception of the procedure of sterilization.[41] In practice, it is uncommon for a woman to seek birth control services without the permission of her spouse.

Harmful traditional practices such as female genital mutilation (FGM) are reportedly no longer practiced in Bahrain. Polygamy is practiced by a small number of Islamic fundamentalists and by older generations in Bahrain's villages. Some Shi'a also practice *muta'a* (short-term marriages), which are allowed in some Shi'a communities. A woman marrying for the first time is expected to be a virgin, but virginity tests are no longer conducted.

Shari'a courts in Bahrain consider a man to be the head of household. A Bahraini woman can own government-supplied housing only in the event of the death of the male head of household or in cases in which the woman gains custody of the children after divorce. The house will still often be registered under the family name rather than the name of the female beneficiary.

Women face many challenges in their efforts to gain influence in community life. The complete lack of female representation on the local municipal councils tends to place women's priorities and needs low on the community agenda. The councils have not shown much initiative in communicating with women's organizations, nor have they undertaken studies to assess women's needs.

The number of female journalists and columnists has increased in Bahrain's national press, but they tend to focus on political issues rather than women's rights. Very few women work in programming in Bahrain's radio or television,[42] and most media outlets fail to report on the progress achieved by Bahraini women. Negative stereotypes of women are often perpetuated in the media, and violence against women is an accepted norm on many radio and television programs.

While many of Bahrain's media outlets have failed to address women's issues, some radio and television programs do provide their audiences with interviews and discussions led by well-known women's rights leaders. The few programs that do succeed in addressing women's issues, such as violence against women and the need for a family law, do not have a large audience base.

No concrete information exists on the incidence of women's poverty in Bahrain. According to the United Nations Economic and Social Commission for Western Asia (ESCWA), 5 percent of Bahrain's population is poor.[43] It is difficult to infer from these statistics whether women in Bahrain are disproportionately affected by poverty as a result of their gender.

Assisting low-income women has been one of the main priorities of women's NGOs. The Awal Women's Society and the Child and Mother Welfare Society are two of the NGOs that provide assistance to low-income women through micro-credit programs. In addition, women's NGOs and social centers run by the Ministry of Labor and Social Affairs train women in traditional crafts and help them to start their own small businesses. However, few of these groups operate as women's human rights establishments; they tend to function more as charities.

While women do not face explicit legal obstacles in defending their economic rights, social traditions, customs, and the domination of conservative concepts do hinder women's advocacy. Advocacy for gender equality is sometimes viewed as a western concept. Many women's rights groups have been accused by extremist elements of working against Islam. Additionally, women's NGOs must contend with a lack of financial and human resources. Few actually receive substantial funding from the Ministry of Labor and Social affairs. The strict laws that govern the activities of NGOs also hinder the work of women's groups. The private sector does not support women's rights activities, and the NGO law prohibits NGOs from receiving any financial support from abroad.

RECOMMENDATIONS

1. The government should provide NGOs more freedom to work and eliminate government interference in their affairs, including removing any restrictions on NGOs receiving funds from international donors.
2. The Supreme Council for Women should train members of women's NGOs in cooperation with international organizations.
3. The Supreme Council for Women and civil society groups should work with women in rural areas and poor communities and with foreign women, particularly domestic workers.

4. The government, the Supreme Council for Women, and women's NGOs should conduct public advocacy campaigns to promote women's rights and to reverse the negative stereotyping of women in the media.

AUTHOR: Dr. Sabika Mohammed Al-Najjar lives and works in Bahrain. She has a PhD in social science and has worked on women's rights and human rights issues for more than 25 years. She is the Secretary General and a founder of the Bahrain Human Rights Society, as well as a founder of the Awal Women's Society in Bahrain.

Notes

[1] Some studies indicated that Shi'as form 70 percent of the Bahraini population, but no official statistics have been published on this regards.

[2] Table 25, "Gender empowerment measure," in *Human Development Report 2004: Cultural Liberty in Today's Diverse World* (New York: United Nations Development Programme [UNDP], 2004), 221-224. http://hdr.undp.org/reports/global/2004/.

[3] Jalila Ahmed Mahmood Al-Sayed, *Women in Bahraini Legislation* (Manama: Nov. 1995), 2.

[4] "Declaration No. 8 on Bahraini Nationality Law, 16 Sept. 1963, and its amendment as of the law No. 12, 1989" (Manama: Government of Bahrain).

[5] "Supreme Council for Women Agrees that a Bahraini Married to a Foreigner Can Sponsor Him and Her Children" *Alayyam*, Bahrain, 8 April 2004.

[6] Hana Almahroos, "Important Recommendation for Situation of Women Workshop," *Akhbar Al-Kaleej*, 27 April 2004, 10.

[7] According to the Judicial System Law in Bahrain, judges are appointed for life. Their service stops only for illness, voluntary resignation, and death.

[8] Fatima Al-Hijri, "Looking for Fundamental Reform in the Judicial System," *Alwasat*, 27 April 2004, 2.

[9] Articles 17, 19.

[10] *The Working Group on Arbitrary Detention, Report on Visit to Bahrain* (New York: UN Economic and Social Council, 2 March 2002), 31.

[11] The Philippine embassy has established a shelter for its citizens abused as workers in Bahrain.

[12] Decree No. 5/2002, 2 March 2002 (Bahrain: National Gazette, No. 2520, 6 March 2002).

[13] Author obtained information by telephone from Ministry of Labor and Social Affairs.

[14] Because political parties are prohibited in Bahrain, political societies (NGOs) have been formed. They fall under the Societies Law of 1989.

[15] *International Religious Freedom Report 2003– Bahrain* (Washington, D.C.: U.S. Dept. of State, Bureau of Democracy, Human Rights, and Labor, 18 Dec. 2003), http://www.state.gov/g/drl/rls/irf/2003/c10269.htm.

[16] It should be noted here that the discrimination against Shi'as is political.

[17] A *nashiz* woman is a married woman who refuses to live in the *bayt al-ta'a*. This woman may live all her life separated from her husband without divorce, unable to re-marry. If she succeeds in obtaining a divorce, then she must repay her husband the ma-har paid to her, in addition to a *khula* (a certain amount of money to buy her freedom).

[18] *International Religious Freedom– Bahrain* (U.S. Dept. of State).

[19] *Annual Report on Human Rights in Bahrain 2003* (Bahrain: Bahrain Human Rights Society, 2004), 24.

[20] *Annual Report, Jan. 2001–Dec. 2002* (Bahrain: Bahrain Human Rights Society, 2003), 19.

[21] *Trafficking in Persons Report 2003* (Washington, D.C.: U.S. Dept. of State, Office to Monitor and Combat Trafficking in Persons, 11 June 2003), http://www.state.gov/g/tip/rls/tiprpt/2003/21275.htm.

[22] Banna Bou Zaboon, *The Impact of Violence Against Wives on Children in Bahraini Society*, 6.

[23] Article 16 of the penal code states, "Nothing is an offense which is done in exercise of a right justified by law or custom."

[24] Afnan Alzayani, *Women and the Arab Economy: The Bahrain Experience* (Bahrain: Business Women's Association), 13–14.

[25] Ibid.

[26] *Educational Statistics 2001/2002* (Bahrain: Ministry of Education), 83.

[27] *The Annual Report 2001/2002* (Bahrain: University of Bahrain, 2003), 120.

[28] *Country Profile Bahrain* (Beirut: UN Economic and Social Commission for Western Asia [ESCWA], Centre for Women).

[29] *Human Rights Reports 2001/2002* (Bahrain: Bahrain Human Rights Society, 2003), 30.

[30] Munira Fakhro, "Promotion of the Equal Access of Girls and Women to Technical and Vocational Education in Bahrain" (Seoul: UNESCO, 1995), 5.

[31] Fowzia Al-Saleh, "Women in the Decision-Making Positions" (Riyadh: 2004), 15.

[32] Author obtained information by telephone from Child and Mother Welfare Society and Awal Women's Society.

[33] Articles 23, 27, and 28 of the Constitution of the Kingdom of Bahrain.

[34] There is no educational institution for judges in Bahrain. The Supreme Judiciary Council nominates judges and sends them abroad for training.

[35] The legislative body in Bahrain is composed of two chambers: the Shura Council (40 members), appointed by the king, and the Council of Deputies (40 members), chosen in a general election.

[36] *Draft of the Shadow Report on CEDAW* (Bahrain Young Ladies Association, unpublished).

[37] A *majlis* (plural *majalis*) is a place attached to the house of a sheik or wealthy person where he meets with his male guests. Some merchants and members of the opposition open their weekly majlis to discuss different public issues. These majalis are attended by men. One woman, supported by her political NGO, has opened a majlis in her residence. This majlis is attended by women, who discuss issues related to women more than political issues.

[38] There are two reasons behind this: First, women's NGOs do not have enough human and financial resources. Second, Muslim clergy, who have full authority over women in both rural and urban areas, can block the advocacy activities of women's NGOs.

[39] *Medical Statistics 2002* (Bahrain: Ministry of Health), Table 1.7, 1–13.

[40] Doctors working in hospitals and public and private clinics confirmed this fact.

[41] Fahkhriya Dairi, "Reproductive Health," in *Population Problem in Bahrain* (Bahrain: Bahrain Socialists Association, 2003), 144–45.

[42] Radio and television in Bahrain are owned by the government. The press is independent, but it reflects official views and existing social norms.

[43] Abdulla Al-Sadiq, *Poverty and Social Security: Present Situation and Challenges* (Manama: Bahrain Centre for Studies and Research, 2004), 5. Also see *Human Development Report, Bahrain, 2001* (Bahrain: UNDP, 2001), 56–57; and *Achievement and Challenges of Human Development* (Bahrain: UNDP, 1998), 79–80.

Egypt

by Amira El-Azhary Sonbol

Population: 72,100,000
GDP Per Capita (PPP): $3,810
Economy: Mixed statist
Ranking on UN HDI: 120 out of 177
Polity: Dominant party (military-influenced)
Literacy: Male 67.2% / Female 43.6%
Percent Women Economically Active: 35.7%
Date of Women's Suffrage: 1956
Women's Fertility Rate: 3.5
Percent Urban/Rural: Urban 43% / Rural 57%

Country Ratings for Egypt
Nondiscrimination and Access to Justice: 3.0
Autonomy, Security, and Freedom of the Person: 2.8
Economic Rights and Equal Opportunity: 2.8
Political Rights and Civic Voice: 2.7
Social and Cultural Rights: 2.4
(Scale of 1 to 5: 1 represents the lowest and 5 the highest level of freedom women have to exercise their rights)

Introduction

Egypt is a republic that gained its formal independence from Great Britain in 1922 and acquired full sovereignty following the end of World War II. The country's constitution, adopted in 1971 under President Anwar al-Sadat, established a strong presidential political system. Egypt is ruled by the president, who serves as chief of state; the prime minister, who is the head of government; a presidential-appointed cabinet; the majority-elected People's Assembly (*Majlis al-Sha'b*); and the partially elected Consultative Council (*Majlis al-Shura*). Following the assassination of al-Sadat in 1981, Hosni Mubarak became president and declared a state of emergency, which he has since renewed every three years. Lack of competitive elections and the continuation of emergency laws constrain the rights of all Egyptians, including women.

The majority of Egypt's population of 72.1 million[1] is Muslim, while an estimated 6 percent follow the Christian Coptic Church. Together with pov-

69

erty, overpopulation is the greatest challenge to development. The United Nations estimates that 16.7 percent of Egypt's population live below the poverty line and that its population increases by 1.8 percent each year. While the country experienced high economic growth in the late 1990s, the economy and foreign direct investment have dropped over the last few years. Since the September 11, 2001, attacks on the United States, Egypt has experienced declines in some of its principal sources of income, such as the tourism industry, Suez Canal tolls, oil sales, and expatriate remittances. Approximately 30 percent of the population work in the almost entirely privately owned agriculture sector.

Freedom of the press is limited, and the right of assembly and association is severely restricted. In 2003, a new law went into effect that regulates the actions of nongovernmental organizations (NGOs). The National Democratic Party (NDP) has dominated the country's political system since its establishment in 1978. While the state allows for multiple parties, political parties are required to seek the approval of the Political Parties Committee (PPC), an NDP-controlled body affiliated with the Consultative Council.

Egyptian women have made advances during the last few decades through the work of an active civil society, women's rights advocates and organizations, and the dedication of the president's wife, Suzanne Mubarak. Highlights of recent achievements include the passing of the *khul'* law, which permits women to divorce without a husband's consent; the establishment of a family court; and the revisions to Egypt's nationality law, which now extends nationality rights to the children of Egyptian mothers married to non-Egyptian fathers. Egyptian women have enjoyed nearly two centuries of education,[2] and today women constitute an important part of public and private employment and labor. Egypt has a woman judge at the Constitutional Supreme Court level and a gender-ombudsman office to which women victims of gender discrimination can send confidential complaints. In two years, the office has received 7,000 complaints.[3]

While women's status has improved to some degree, women's empowerment in Egypt has faced many obstacles, including the country's political and economic conditions, its patriarchal social environment, and the efforts of religious extremists. While women have had full and equal suffrage since 1955, the strong legal basis for women's human rights in Egypt is often limited by a lack of proper implementation mechanisms to ensure women's equal access to justice and the law. Egyptian women also have limited influence at the national and community levels, despite their having filled leadership positions as ministers, ambassadors, media heads, MPs, and university professors. The state encourages groups that advocate for women's rights but is not as supportive of groups that associate women's rights with the call for greater participation in the political system.

Nondiscrimination and Access to Justice

Egypt has the structure of an independent judiciary, with courts of varying degrees and judicial review by a Supreme Constitutional Court and Council of State. The country's laws are based on French, English, and Islamic legal codes.

The 1971 constitution guarantees equality to all citizens without prejudice based on gender; it confirms women's rights to inherit and own property, have freedom of movement, and have access to education, employment, and pay.[4] Article 40 of the 1980 amended Egyptian constitution states, "All citizens are equal before the law. They have equal public rights and duties without discrimination between them due to race, ethnic origin, language, religion, or creed."[5] Nevertheless, advances in laws to ensure gender equality are often offset by their lack of full implementation and the absence of protection mechanisms against gender discrimination at all levels.

Two recent Egyptian laws advanced efforts to eliminate legal gender discrimination and fulfill Egypt's obligations under the UN Convention on the Elimination of All Forms of Discrimination Against Women (CEDAW), which it ratified in 1981. First, in January 2000, the Egyptian National Assembly passed Law No. 1, granting women the right to a no-fault divorce within three months without a husband's consent. Then, in July 2004, an amended nationality law extended nationality rights to children of Egyptian women married to non-Egyptian husbands. However, the nationality law failed to give nationality rights to foreign husbands and forbade the children of these marriages from holding government positions, even though the law extends such rights to foreign wives and children of Egyptian fathers. At present, many women also lack identity cards because they were not registered at birth. The National Council for Women is working to rectify this serious situation in order to assure all women their civil rights.

Most Egyptian women have equal access to justice, and a woman's testimony is equal to that of a man's in court.[6] However, complaints about male court officials and judges exhibiting patriarchal attitudes are quite common in Egypt. The problems women face in courts are mostly shared by all Egyptians: overburdened dockets, overworked judges, bureaucratic corruption that prevents execution of court decisions, and endless delays in a system badly in need of overhaul. Women do, however, face gender discrimination in the courts in cases involving property disputes, particularly over agricultural land, due to traditions favoring greater male inheritance. The creation of family courts in 2004 and the plan to include women judges are welcomed steps by women activists.

While Egypt's criminal and penal codes do not explicitly discriminate against women, women may face unequal treatment from the police, society, and their families when accused of crimes of adultery or culturally inappropriate behavior. Promiscuity is considered unacceptable behavior for both genders within Egyptian culture. However, while men or boys may be reprimanded, women or girls may be severely punished, or in extreme cases, killed for "dishonorable" acts. While "honor crimes," or the killing of women in the name of family "honor," are not prevalent in Egypt and are not specifically addressed within the law, these crimes do occur. Article 17 of the Penal Law gives the judge the right to mitigate a penalty of death to a life-sentence. Unfortunately, this article is sometimes unequally applied in favor of men and is used to discriminate against women, especially in cases involving "honor crimes."[7]

Another problem is the reporting and investigating of an "honor crime." Police officials, especially at the local level, often do not investigate such cases with the same rigor as they might for other crimes. Families and villages may collude by not informing or assisting police. Local authorities often close investigations of "honor crimes" by labeling them as accidents or crimes perpetrated by an unknown person.

Contradictions and inconsistencies in Egyptian laws contribute to a continuation of violence against women. When applied correctly, the law is severe toward convicted abusers, ranging from three years to life imprisonment for rape, with an added death sentence for the abduction and rape of a woman.[8] On the other hand, the law does not seriously address violence against women in the home. Marital rape and emotional and verbal abuse are not considered crimes, and wife beating meets with condemnation only when it leads to serious injury.[9]

The Egyptian government plays an active role in global conferences on women. The country ratified the UN Convention on the Elimination of All Forms of Discrimination Against Women (CEDAW)[10] in 1981, albeit with a number of reservations. Nevertheless, a number of Egypt's national laws still do not adhere to universal standards on women's human rights or non-discrimination issues.

Egypt has an active and effective women's rights movement. Egyptian civil society activists from various walks of life have been working for decades and have achieved some success through their challenges to patriarchal systems. They have succeeded in changing Egyptian laws and have improved women's access to justice and citizenship rights.

RECOMMENDATIONS

1. The government should amend all laws in order to bring all legislation in conformity with the principles of non-discrimination.
2. The government should revise the nationality and citizenship laws to be in accordance with the Egyptian constitution, which guarantees equal rights to all citizens.

3. The government should remove all reservations to CEDAW and take steps to implement it locally by bringing national laws in conformity with CEDAW.

Autonomy, Security, and Freedom of the Person

Egyptian law guarantees full enjoyment of civil liberties to all citizens, and the country's institutions are legally prohibited from discriminating against women. In practice, however, women face gender discrimination in many aspects of their lives, and their personal security is threatened by both state and non-state actors.

Changes in Egyptian law now provide Muslim women the right to divorce without a husband's consent—the right of *khul'*. Khul' law is drawn from Islamic *Shari'a* and basically grants a woman the right to divorce by court order on condition that the woman forgoes many of her financial entitlements.[11] The inclusion in the Personal Status Law of Article 20 that grants women the right of khul' was considered a significant accomplishment by Egypt's women's rights activists.

Some have criticized Egypt's khul' laws as harmful to women's financial rights because they force a wife to give up her *mahr*[12] (dower payment), alimony, and any gifts provided by the husband during the marriage. Returning the dower and losing alimony are hardships poor women can ill afford, given the overall poverty rates in Egypt, particularly in rural areas. This is, however, a complex issue that involves culture, the law, and the integral financial balance between husband and wife in Egyptian marriages. Traditionally, a husband is expected to pay an advance dower, support his wife and children during the marriage, and pay the wife's delayed dower, alimony, and compensation if he unilaterally divorces her. Similarly, because khul' divorce is a divorce without a husband's consent, it is believed that the wife should accordingly relinquish the dower and alimony to her husband.

Egypt does not have a unified personal status code. Consequently, different laws govern women from different religions. Most often, male religious leaders select a community's religious laws; women followers of a faith or women's rights advocates are rarely included in such negotiations with the government. Egypt's new family courts are expected to help safeguard the human rights of women and children and improve upon some of the complications women face due to conflicting laws.[13]

Egyptian law prohibits the marriage of girls below the age of 16, but the law is not always implemented, particularly in rural areas. The median age for women to marry is 19 years.[14] The Coptic Church does not recognize any marriage outside the church. Egyptian Muslims, on the other hand, permit men to marry non-Muslim women, but Muslim women are forbidden from marrying outside the religion. While Christian leaders in Egypt opted to follow Islamic inheritance laws, divorce options open to Muslim men and women are not available to Christians. The Coptic Orthodox Church permits divorce only in specific circumstances, such as adultery or conversion of one spouse to another religion.[15] Christian men, like Muslim men, can sue their wives for lack of obedience (*ta'a*), which if successful, allows the husband to ignore his financial responsibilities to support his wife. Christian women, who have no right to khul', lose their right to financial support when the courts deem them disobedient. Such multiple codes are particularly discriminatory against Christian women.

Violence against women is a serious problem in Egypt. Women victims of violence most often suffer within the home at the hands of family members, such as husbands, fathers, or brothers.[16] Egyptian families and government authorities, such as the police, often ignore violent acts against women. Domestic violence and marital rape are not considered crimes in Egyptian law, and women victims of rape and incest have tremendous difficulties prosecuting their perpetrators. Spousal abuse is grounds for a divorce, but the victim is required to produce medical reports of bodily harm as proof. The Center for Egyptian Women's Legal Assistance conducted a survey that reported that 67 percent of women in urban areas and 30 percent in rural areas had been involved in some form of domestic violence at least once during a set period between 2002 and 2003. Less than half of those women who had been beaten sought help.[17] The Ministry of Social Affairs have opened 150 family counseling centers to help victims of domestic violence, but many women victims still have limited access to supportive legal, psychological, and social services.

Women also face various forms of violence outside the home, ranging from verbal harassment to physical and sexual abuse and rape. The harassment of women in public is a serious problem in Egypt; more serious punishments for verbal harassment should be instituted and enforced. Current statistics on the prevalence of rape, domestic abuse, and "honor killings" in Egypt are rare. Crime pages of daily newspapers show that rape is quite widespread, even if most incidents are not reported or legally prosecuted by the state, victims, or their families. After decades of advocacy, Egyptian feminists succeeded in getting the government to abolish the laws that had previously allowed for the forgiveness of rapists if they married their victims. However, the new law is often undermined by the police, who continue to encourage the marriage of a woman and her rapist and the dropping of charges against the man.

RECOMMENDATIONS

1. The government and civil society organizations should initiate a national public education media campaign on the problems of domestic violence, incest, and rape.

2. The government should criminalize all forms of violence committed against women within the family and create supportive services for victims of family violence.
3. The government should establish procedures to inform the public of new laws affecting women's rights, such as khul' divorce.
4. The government should facilitate public discussion on issues of women's security and freedom in the context of Islamic and Christian traditions.

Economic Rights and Equal Opportunity

According to Egyptian laws, women can own, inherit, and independently use land and property. While no longer prevalent, it is still preferable practice for male heirs to own land so that outsiders cannot inherit through marriage. The Egyptian government does not provide women with legal aid services to help them better understand or protect their land rights. Buyouts, exchange of assets, and outright usurpation are additional factors that contribute to the serious discrepancy between the numbers of women and of men with land tenure.[18] The Egyptian government estimated that there were 8,417,962 male landowners and only 341,905 women landowners in 1999/2000.[19]

Egypt's land-tenure system is based on *shuyu'*, a collective-property arrangement by which heirs own shares of a property.[20] Egypt's system tends to complicate and delay inheritance until all heirs agree to a division or to the alienation of marked-out pieces of land for registration.[21] This process can sometimes span generations and tends to favor men. Methods of proving land tenure require documents (i.e. official registration, payment of taxes, delivery of crops, or registration with the local village association in the case of rented property), which are usually issued in the name of the male head of household. Therefore, even though the whole family may rent, work, or buy a piece of land, it will be registered under the father's name. When the father dies and leaves younger children, the wife usually assumes rights over the land, but if there is an older son, sometimes from an earlier marriage, the son's rights to the land supersede those of the wife.

The same system of shuyu' applies to all forms of real estate. Most often, women are neglected, denied, or bought out by the male head of family. Despite some positive steps, the government has made very little progress in addressing the problems of women, especially rural women, in regard to land and property ownership. There is a serious need to overhaul Egypt's property system.

According to international human rights standards, Egyptian inheritance laws, which are derived from Islam, discriminate against women; Muslim female heirs receive half of a male heir's share. Christian widows of Muslims have no inheritance rights.[22] While inheritance laws allocate unequal shares for men and women, the system is supposed to balance the traditional financial responsibilities of males and females. The male may inherit more, but it is the male who must pay his wife's dower and provide financial support to his family, parents, younger siblings, and in some cases, grandparents. This model, however, is not without flaws. Considering the current decline in economic conditions and the increase in women's workforce participation, this model is increasingly problematic and outdated; today, both married and unmarried women contribute their income to the home and family. Furthermore, the government has not made sufficient efforts to invest in a social welfare system to take care of women, children, and the elderly in vulnerable conditions.

Egypt has a long history of women's education in arts and sciences,[23] and other than due to economic and practical limitations, there is little resistance to educating girls. Education at all levels is free for Egyptians and is compulsory up to 15 years of age; however, there is a general lack of enforcement. Wealthy families traditionally send their children to private foreign-language schools and universities, while poor families often need the income from a daughter's labor and prefer to educate sons in hopes that they will later support the family. Early marriage in rural areas is a large contributor to female school dropout rates.[24]

In 2002, women's literacy rate of 43.6 percent lagged behind men's rate of 67.2 percent, but this is still quite an improvement from women's rate of 38.8 percent in 1995.[25] Women's literacy is expected to improve still further as women today constitute nearly half of the students in Egypt's 13 public universities.[26] Nevertheless, wide discrepancies persist between the illiteracy rates of rural and urban women.[27]

World Bank data show a marked improvement in female student enrollment in Egyptian primary and secondary schools from 1980 to 2000, rising from 61 percent in 1980 to 93 percent in 2000 for primary school and from 39 percent to 82 percent in 2000 for secondary school (compared with 88 percent for males).[28] Nevertheless, the quality of Egypt's educational system has deteriorated significantly as a result of overpopulation.

Considering the number of female students graduating from Egypt's universities and the percentage of women in the workforce, the representation of women in leadership positions is very poor. Patriarchal discrimination is at the heart of the disequilibrium. Promotion in government is based on date of hiring, merit being secondary, up to the leadership level, where selection is left to the ministers, who often exclusively select males. For example, male and female university professors follow similar hiring, tenure, and promotion procedures, with selection of deans and presidents being left up to the Minister of Higher Education. With the exception of the rare symbolic appointee, there are almost no female deans or presidents. Such selection procedures have a direct impact on gender power relations at the very level of the educational system, where there should be absolute equality of opportunity.

During the period 1995 to 2000, 35 percent of women in the workforce were employed in agriculture, 9 percent in industry, and 56 percent in services.[29] Working women in Egypt come from different economic and social backgrounds. Women in the higher economic classes are active as modern professionals, including doctors, lawyers, engineers, architects, scientists, and university teachers. Women open businesses, invest money, manage shops, work in retail, and own housing. A few women manage successful international consultancies, clothing manufacturing, and textile workshops. Particularly active in the informal market, many women are penny-capitalists investing small outlays of funds. Most women in this class have their own private transportation, such as a personal car.

According to the UN (FAO), more than 50 percent of rural women are actively involved in tasks such as fertilizing, weeding, harvesting, sacking, marketing, and storage of crops. About 70 percent of women's working time in agriculture is devoted to animal husbandry.[30] Rural women are industrious and, when able, will take out loans to invest in raising cattle or chickens or rent small patches of land to grow cash products. NGOs help women through micro-finance projects, but these NGOs have limited outreach, resources, and capital.

While the constitution guarantees equal hiring, firing, and pay for men and women, serious discrepancies exist in reality. There are large gender gaps in income and a basic trend of feminization of unemployment.[31] According to UNDP estimates, in 2000 the average earned income of women was US$2,003, while that of men was US$5,227.[32] The majority of women workers in the second and third income groups do not have health care, pensions, or other state-provided or subsidized benefits. Labor laws require employers of 100 women or more to provide a nursery, maternity leave at full pay, two daily breaks to breastfeed a child for two years after birth, and the right to take two years off from work to care for the family. Employers often react to such laws by placing a glass ceiling on promotions for women, hiring women on a temporary basis, or firing them when they marry or become pregnant in order to avoid these costs. The private sector is not in favor of hiring women.[33] There are no sexual harassment laws that protect working women in Egypt, even though sexual harassment exists at all levels of labor.

Women's employment and education have served as focal points for women's rights and civil society groups, particularly in villages and low-income areas. Women's civil groups are encouraged by the state to work on these issues and to work in cooperation with government agencies.

RECOMMENDATIONS

1. The government should provide low-interest loans, financial management training, and equal opportunities to women engaged in small businesses.

2. The government should hire personnel to assist and advise women on the legalities of inheritance, land registration, and other agricultural land and real estate issues and make loans available for women to cover land registration and legal fees in property cases.
3. The government should overhaul the educational curriculum and remove gender stereotypes from textbooks.
4. The National Assembly should enact a sexual harassment law for enforcement at all levels in the public and private sectors.
5. The government should facilitate public debates through the media, syndicates, and universities on women's legal rights, including inheritance rights.

Political Rights and Civic Voice

Many contradictions exist between Egyptian law and its implementation in the field of political and civil rights. While in theory, Egyptians can freely elect their representatives, in practice, men and women have very limited access to the country's political process and structure. Egypt's political system itself is seriously flawed. The emergency laws in effect since 1981 and the government's slow reform strategy exacerbate its undemocratic nature.

While the system appears outwardly multi-party and democratic, it is actually a clone of Egypt's earlier Arab Socialist Union, in which interrelated combines controlled all politics. In reality, Egypt's political system is closed and contradictory; all state facilities and powers rest with the National Democratic Party (NDP). The NDP dominates the People's Assembly and Shura Assembly, the civil service, provincial authorities, and the public industrial sector. Opposition parties have little say in the political process. Any possible future opposition can be curbed by law and by security forces that have license over the activities of Egypt's press, NGOs, and citizens in the name of national security.

While freedom of speech is guaranteed in the constitution, in practice, certain subjects are taboo, such as criticism of the president and the military and views considered anti-Islamic. Article 48 guarantees freedom of the press and also states, "Censorship of newspapers is forbidden as well as notifying, suspending or canceling them by administrative methods. In a state of emergency or in time of war a limited censorship may be imposed on the newspapers, publications and mass media in matters related to public safety or purposes of national security in accordance with the law."[34] Government permission is needed to open or publish a newspaper.[35] The government and its committees (including the religious committee of the al-Azhar) may forbid particular types of journals and close newspapers through executive action.

Women have little say in the political process and have limited access to participation in the political structure. While women have had full suffrage

since 1956, the political system tends to work against their efforts to run successfully or win election to public office. In many cases, women are unable to
afford the high costs required to mount a political campaign. The proportion
of registered voters who were women in 2003 was just 37.4 percent.[36]

The patriarchal structure of the political system is reflected in the number
of women who participate or who are selected to be included in the system.
Women's participation in the People's Assembly is just 11 out of 454 elected
representatives. The number of female parliamentarians is just 2.2 percent
in the First House and 5.7 percent in the Second House.[37] The cabinet has
only two female ministers, with no women serving in any significant way in
the crucial ministries such as defense, economic, or the interior. The Ministry of Foreign Affairs, on the other hand, does include a large percentage of
women, who hold positions as ambassadors and who work in such locations
as New York and Tokyo.

One female judge now sits on the Supreme Constitutional Court, and the
government has indicated that it plans to place two more women in the family
courts. Nevertheless, women's opportunities for advancement within Egypt's
judicial system are highly restricted. Graduates of law schools enter into the
legal bureaucracy of the Ministry of Justice and are promoted through the
system based on date of hiring and merit. Both men and women rise in the
system, but whereas men are promoted to be district attorneys and judges,
women are not. Some years ago, two women sued the government for the
right to be promoted to district attorneys, but their efforts continue to be
blocked in Egypt's courts under various pretexts.

The state encourages the establishment of NGOs; an estimated 17,000 organizations are active and involved in social and educational programs, human
rights, micro-finance, and other issues. The activities of NGOs, however, are
strictly controlled by the state. An NGO law that became effective in 2003
acts to restrict NGO activity through licensing, security regulations, and the
interference of the Ministry of Social Affairs. The Ministry of Social Affairs
now has the authority to dissolve NGOs by decree and has the right to put
its own representatives on the NGOs' boards.

Egyptian human rights groups have condemned the new NGO regulatory laws, but the state continues to use what it calls security reasons to limit,
constrain, and ultimately control all activities that focus on women's human
rights or political rights and civil liberties. A select few women currently wield
the hegemonic power to determine the agenda of women's rights advocates,
the formation of and membership in civil groups, and their access to government financing and international aid.

The NCW was established in 2000 as a government institution with the
aim of advancing the status of Egyptian women. By registering, as required by
the new law, women's NGO's are virtually forced to accept the hegemony of

the NCW and the Ministry of Social Affairs. Those groups who refuse to conform are denied registration, as was the case with The New Woman Research Center (NWRC). The NWRC, active since 1984, was denied registration on security grounds, but took the matter to the administrative court and won a judgment against the ministry in late 2003.[38] However, the ministry has yet to comply with the court's orders even though the judiciary has declared the 2003 NGO laws to be in direct conflict with Egypt's constitution.

Women's ability to access information has improved with the expanding diversity of media programs in Egypt resulting from the growth of satellite television. Greater literacy programs have also increased women's awareness of their rights.

RECOMMENDATIONS

1. The government should abolish the Emergency Law to ensure that national security interests do not override fundamental rights guaranteed under the constitution.
2. The government should permit open, direct elections with free competition between political parties to increase participation and to give Egyptians, both men and women, a stake in the country's politics and future.
3. The government should promote more women to judgeships and district attorney positions and open all positions currently closed to women within the legal system.

Social and Cultural Rights

Many women in Egypt suffer from a basic lack of access to adequate health services and health insurance. While government hospitals theoretically provide free services, available health facilities are poorly equipped. Top-quality hospitals can be found in major cities but tend to be very expensive and serve only the rich, or particular sectors like the army, air force, or police. Egypt's wealthy, who can afford such hospitals, prefer to travel overseas for better-quality medical services. Together with the United States Agency for International Development (USAID), Egypt launched a successful campaign to improve health facilities in 1975, and infant mortality declined by 65 percent between 1976 and 1997.[39] Nevertheless, demographic and health surveys published in 2000 revealed that while there was an overall improvement in maternal care, postpartum care services are not widely utilized. Maternal mortality rates outside metropolitan areas are almost double those in metropolitan areas.[40]

Studies prepared by USAID indicate that 96 percent of women live within 5 kilometers of a source of family planning.[41] Contraceptive use increased from 24 percent to 56 percent between 1980 and 2000, and the Ministry of Health began addressing the reproductive health of adolescents for the first time in 2003.[42] Articles 260 to 262 of the Egyptian penal code prohibit all abortions, with the exception of abortions performed to save a mother's life. Despite the laws, abortions are frequently performed in hospitals for the rich and at home for the poor.

Perhaps the most harmful traditional practice experienced by a majority of Egypt's women, Muslim and Christian alike, is female genital mutilation (FGM). This practice was outlawed in 1996 and is forbidden under articles 241 and 242 of the penal code, which punish the deliberate infliction of bodily harm.[43] FGM, as practiced in Egypt, commonly involves either Type I (commonly referred to as clitoridectomy) or Type II (commonly referred to as excision).[44] Popularly known as *tahara* (purification), the practice is viewed as a positive physical cleansing for women and is most often performed on girls between the ages of 7 and 10 years.[45] Egyptians widely believe FGM to be an Islamic practice, even though it is also performed by Egyptian Christians and is not practiced in most Muslim countries outside the Nile valley. While the leadership of the *al-Azhar*, the central authority on Islam in Egypt, condemned the inaccuracy of this information, clergymen continue to confirm FGM as religiously mandated, which is one reason for its continuation. Both the state and NGOs have made serious efforts to eradicate the harmful practice. The National Council for Childhood and Motherhood launched an extensive program to combat FGM in 2003.[46]

Most Egyptian families rent small apartments or continue to live with grandparents. Owning a house is a dream for the millions of homeless poor families who live in places of refuge like Cairo cemeteries or as squatters in garages.[47] Poverty has led many families to exploit the labor of their female members. Daughters and sisters may be sent to work in urban homes or in other countries while families directly pocket their earnings. Fear of violence and laws that place daughters under the power of male family members tend to perpetuate these conditions.

Female-headed households are more likely to be disadvantaged than male-headed households. Government services, including social security and welfare, are available to women, but the numbers of homeless children, abandoned newborn babies, beggars, and destitute elderly of both genders are increasing, and shelters are hardly adequate. It is estimated that while educated women hold 25 percent of senior government and managerial bank positions, 12 million women live in slums. Social class must be the focus of any effort to end gender discrimination in Egypt, for women are the first to suffer from poverty.[48]

While social security and pensions do not discriminate between men and women as a matter of law, women experience discrimination in their implementation. Widows represent a forgotten group in discussions of gender discrimination; rural women lose tenure rights to land leased in their husband's name, and widows of white-collar employees suffer incredible hardship upon their husband's death. Pensions are tied to the cost of living and are rarely adequate for subsistence. Inherited pensions are divided according to Islamic law, with a widow receiving no more than one-quarter or one-eighth of the pension if there are children. Wives in polygamous marriages must share this one-quarter or one-eighth with the other wives, often resulting in a life of severe impoverishment. Furthermore, the government becomes the beneficiary of pensions not paid out.[49] In contrast to women, the husband always receives his full share of the wife's pension, as legally she is not allowed to have other husbands.

Social security is an aspect of a modern state system whose regulations can easily be changed by the state. Social security is not an inheritance but a system of benefits into which a person pays while he/she is alive. Assigning Islamic inheritance laws to social security is one way of denying widows and women what they desperately need and deserve. Yet, in this case, Islamic laws of inheritance are not even fully applied. Unlike social security benefits, under Islamic inheritance law, women may still inherit past the age of 21 and after they are married, and relatives are eligible to inherit in cases in which there is no longer an immediate family. Under social security regulations the government is the beneficiary in these cases.

Female journalists and TV producers have some influence on the content of media programs, but overall media content is predominantly male-controlled, particularly Egypt's political and news programs. Independent TV channels, on the other hand, present excellent programs on which women lead courageous discussions of women's rights issues. While steps are being taken to improve the image of women in the media,[50] programs emphasizing polygamy, the roles of dominant men and submissive women, and the virgin/whore dichotomy dominate public television and perpetuate societal patriarchy. The NCW has created a Media Watch Unit to monitor the content of media messages relating to women and to recommend corrective measures to further enhance the status of Egyptian women.[51]

Many domestic and international groups of men and women are currently involved in rethinking women's issues. The success of the campaign on the khul' law in Egypt was partly due to open discussions about the law in the media and dialogue among the public. Increased advocacy and information on the seriousness of the problems facing women seeking to leave abusive marriages, as well as the other complications involved in divorce, helped to make the law more acceptable to the majority of Egyptians, notwithstanding the organized opposition. Continuing research is needed to tie today's struggle for women's rights to the Islamic teachings of equality.

The most effective argument that has been used by conservative forces to block women's rights in Egypt has been the employment of religious discourse as an instrument of confinement for women and of empowerment for men. The use of Islam to discriminate against women contradicts the universality of Islam and Islamic dogma, which emphasize the equality of all people. This contradiction needs to be tackled directly so that principles of equality can be established from within an Islamic framework and universal principles of human rights can gain acceptability among Egyptians.

RECOMMENDATIONS

1. The government should appoint monitors to ensure that women have non-discriminatory access to pension and social security benefits. Special measures should be adopted to protect single mothers, widows, rural women, and women living in extreme poverty.
2. The government should prioritize women's access to health care services by allocating needed resources and providing health facilities for women, especially women living in rural areas.
3. The government should encourage policies to change the negative portrayal of women in the media and expand its public education campaigns against FGM and other harmful traditional practices.

AUTHOR: Amira El-Azhary Sonbol is Professor of Islamic Law, History, and Society at The Edmund G. Walsh School of Foreign Service of Georgetown University, Washington D.C. She specializes in women's history, Islamic history and law, and history of modern Egypt. Her publications include Women, the Family and Divorce Laws in Islamic History *(editor);* Beyond the Exotic: Women of the Islamic World and the Deconstruction of Patriarchy *(editor);* Women of the Jordan: Islam, Labor and Law; The New Mamluks: Egyptian Society and Modern Feudalism; *and* Creation of a Medical Profession in Egypt: 1800–1922.

Notes

[1] *Freedom in the World:* Egypt (New York and Washington, D.C.: Freedom House, 2004).

[2] Starting from before the 19th century in mosque-schools and in the home and later in government-run specialized schools (the School of Hakimas, graduating women doctors, was opened in 1832) and primary/secondary education beginning in the 1870s. See Nelly Hanna, *In Praise of Books* (Syracuse, NY: Syracuse University Press, 2002) and Amira Sonbol, *Creation of a Medical Profession in Egypt 1800–1922* (Syracuse, NY: Syracuse University Press, 1991) for details about Egypt's educational system since the Ottoman period.

[3] "Member States' Responses to the Questionnaire on Implementation of the Beijing Platform for Action (1995) and the Outcome of the Twenty-third Special Session of the

General Assembly, 2000," (Cairo: National Council for Women [NCW] and New York: United Nations), http://www.un.org/womenwatch/daw/Review/responses/EGYPT-English.pdf.

[4] The Constitution of the Arab Republic of Egypt, Articles 8, 11, 13, 14, 18, 33, 34, 36, 40, 41, 46, 47, 50, 68.

[5] The Constitution of the Arab Republic of Egypt, after the Amendments Ratified in the May 22, 1980, Referendum, http://www.sis.gov.eg/eginfnew/politics/parlim/html/pres0303.htm.

[6] *Country Reports on Human Rights Practices – 2003:* Egypt (Washington, D.C.: U.S. Dept. of State, Bureau of Democracy, Human Rights, and Labor, 18 December 2003).

[7] "Honor Crimes" (Cairo: Center for Egyptian Women's Legal Assistance), http://www.cewla.org/en/case/04/honor.html.

[8] *Country Reports . . . :* Egypt (U.S. Dept. of State, 2003).

[9] See, for example, Muhammad Azmi al-Bakri, *Mawsu`at al-fiqh wal-qada' fi al-ahwal al-shakhsiyya* vol. 1 (Cairo, 1991): 683–690, for explanation and court cases based on Law 209 of Egypt's personal status law, which allows "a husband to punish his wife, light punishment, for every disobedience for which there is no specified punishment. But he has no right to beat her excessively even if he has reason."

[10] *The United Nations Human Rights Treaties* (Chapter IV.3, Multilateral Treaties Deposited with the Secretary-General), Reservations and Declarations, Egypt, http://www.bayefsky.com/./html/egypt_t2_cedaw.php.

[11] Maria Tadros, "Khul' law passes major test," *Al-Ahram* Weekly Online, No. 617, 19–25 December 2002, http://weekly.ahram.org.eg/2002/617/eg11.htm.

[12] A *mahr* is an amount of money agreed upon before a marriage, of which a Muslim woman will receive a portion from her husband upon marriage, and the rest if he divorces her unilaterally, i.e. against her wishes, or at the time of his death.

[13] "Member States' Responses . . . " (NCW), http://www.un.org/womenwatch/daw/Review/responses/EGYPT-English.pdf.

[14] "Country Profiles" (Beirut: UN Economic and Social Commission for Western Asia [ESCWA], http://www.escwa.org.lb/divisions/ecw/profile/egypt/main.html.

[15] *Country Reports . . . :* Egypt (U.S. Dept. of State, 2003).

[16] Al-Majlis al-qawmi li'l-mar`a and UNIFEM, *Taqrir `an al-awda` al-ihsa'iyya l'il-mar'a al-misriyya* (Cairo: National Committee for Women, 2002), 114.

[17] Ibid.

[18] Ibid., 60. Average size of landholding for men was 1.8 acres and 1.6 acres for women.

[19] Al-Majlis al-qawmi li'l-mar`a and UNIFEM, *Taqrir `an al-awda` al-ihsa'iyya l'il-mar'a al-misriyya* (Cairo: National Committee for Women, 2002), 60.

[20] A unit of property is always divided into 24 karats, and each karat is divided into 24 sahm.

[21] Inheritance becomes more complicated when a death occurs among the heirs and the process has to begin all over again to take into consideration those who are to inherit from the deceased. It should be noted that according to Islamic law, the extended family beyond the children inherit; for example, father, mother, grandparents. If any of these family members are deceased, then those who are eligible extends further.

[22] *Country Reports . . . :* Egypt (U.S. Dept. of State, 2003).

[23] See note 2, above.

[24] "Member States' Responses . . . " (NCW), http://www.un.org/womenwatch/daw/Review/responses/EGYPT-English.pdf.

[25] Table 24, "Gender-related development index," in *Human Development Report 2004: Cultural Liberty in Today's Diverse World* (New York: United Nations Development Programme [UNDP], 2004), 217-220. http://hdr.undp.org/reports/global/2004/ and USAID, http://www.usaid-eg.org/arabic/detail.asp?id=2.

[26] Government of Egypt, Ministry of Education.

[27] "Country Profiles" (ESCWA), http://www.escwa.org.lb/divisions/ecw/profile/egypt/main.html.

[28] "Gender Stats: Education" Egypt (Washington, D.C.: The World Bank Group, 2002), http://genderstats.worldbank.org/genderRpt.asp?rpt=education&cty=EGY,Egypt,%20Arab%20Rep.&hm=home2.

[29] "Country Profiles" (ESCWA), http://www.escwa.org.lb/divisions/ecw/profile/egypt/main.html.

[30] "People, Gender and Development, Egypt" (Rome: Food and Agriculture Organization of the United Nations [FAO], Sustainable Development Department [SD], 1994), http://www.fao.org/waicent/faoinfo/sustdev/WPdirect/WPre0016.htm.

[31] "Member States' Responses . . . " (NCW), http://www.un.org/womenwatch/daw/Review/responses/EGYPT-English.pdf.

[32] "Country Profiles" (ESCWA), http://www.escwa.org.lb/divisions/ecw/profile/egypt/main.html.

[33] "Member States' Responses . . . " (National Council for Women), http://www.un.org/womenwatch/daw/Review/responses/EGYPT-English.pdf.

[34] Ibid.

[35] Egypt's publications include 518 diverse periodicals: 64 national papers, 40 opposition party papers, 7 private newspapers, 252 specialized publications, 142 scientific journals, and 67 local publications. *Country Reports* (U.S. Dept. of State).

[36] "Member States' Responses . . . " (NCW), http://www.un.org/womenwatch/daw/Review/responses/EGYPT-English.pdf.

[37] Ibid.

[38] Maria Tadroz, "A Battle Half Won,"*Al-Ahram* Weekly Online, No. 662, 30 October–5 November 2003, http://weekly.ahram.org.eg/2002/617/eg11.htm.

[39] "USAID/Egypt: Programs" (Cairo: USAID), http://www.usaid-eg.org/detail.asp?id=14.

[40] "Member States' Responses . . . " (NCW), http://www.un.org/womenwatch/daw/Review/responses/EGYPT-English.pdf.

[41] "Country Profiles" (ESCWA), http://www.escwa.org.lb/divisions/ecw/profile/egypt/main.html.

[42] "Member States' Responses . . . " (NCW), http://www.un.org/womenwatch/daw/Review/responses/EGYPT-English.pdf.

[43] In 1996, doctors were forbidden to perform FGM, and in 1997 the Higher Administrative Court confirmed the decree, http://weekly.ahram.org.eg/print/2003/644/eg7.htm.

[44] "Egypt: Report on Female Genital Mutilation or Female Genital Cutting" (Washington, D.C.: U.S. Dept. of State, Office of the Senior Coordinator for International Women's Issues, June 2001).

[45] Ibid.

[46] "Member States' Responses . . . " (NCW), http://www.un.org/womenwatch/daw/Review/responses/EGYPT-English.pdf.

[47] Azza Khattab, "The Months News in Figures," *Egypt Today: the Magazine of Egypt* 25, 7 (July 2004), http://www.egypttoday.com/article.aspx?ArticleID=1746.

[48] The richest 20% of the population are said to earn 39.0% of total income, while the poorest 20% earn 9.8% of total income. The national poverty rate is estimated to be 22.9%, with the urban population constituting 22.5%. *Earth Trends Country Profiles*, http://earthtrends.wri.org/pdf_library/country_profiles/Eco_cou_818.pdf.

[49] For example, in cases where there are no children, the children have reached 21 years of age, or the daughters are married.

[50] The first activity of the NCW was a conference on how to better present the image of women in the media.

[51] "Member States' Responses . . . " (NCW), http://www.un.org/womenwatch/daw/Review/responses/EGYPT-English.pdf.

Iraq

by Amal Rassam

Population: 24,200,000
GDP Per Capita (PPP): N/A
Economy: Transitional
Ranking on UN HDI: N/A
Polity: Transitional
Literacy: Male 55.9% / Female 24.4%
Percent Women Economically Active: N/A
Date of Women's Suffrage: 1980
Women's Fertility Rate: 5.4
Percent Urban/Rural: Urban 68% / Rural 32%

Country Ratings for Iraq
Nondiscrimination and Access to Justice: 2.7
Autonomy, Security, and Freedom of the Person: 2.6
Economic Rights and Equal Opportunity: 2.8
Political Rights and Civic Voice: 2.2
Social and Cultural Rights: 2.1

(Scale of 1 to 5: 1 represents the lowest and 5 the highest level of freedom women have to exercise their rights)

Introduction

Editor's note: This survey assesses developments up until December 31, 2003. It therefore does not include 2004 events, when insurgency and violence dominated certain areas of Iraq. Nevertheless, in the Sunni-majority sections of Iraq, developments in 2004 represented a continuation of trends from the previous year.

Formerly part of the Ottoman Empire, Iraq was established as a League of Nations mandate in 1921 and gained formal independence in 1932. In 1958, a military coup toppled the British-installed Hashemite monarchy, and Iraq was declared a republic. A series of military coups ensued, until the Ba'ath Party assumed power in 1968 under the leadership of Ahmad Hassan al-Bakr. Al-Bakr resigned from the presidency in 1979 in favor of Saddam Hussein, the Ba'athist regime's de facto strong man. A ruthless dictator and a shrewd politician, Saddam managed to embroil Iraq in a series of disastrous wars that exhausted and traumatized the Iraqi people and ruined their country.

The year 2003 was a watershed in the modern history of Iraq. The military occupation of Iraq by a United States–led coalition in March of 2003 brought a sudden end to 35 years of the Ba'ath regime and 25 years of Saddam Hussein's dictatorial rule. It also brought chaos, political instability, and insecurity to a country reeling from 20 years of wars and 12 years of severe economic sanctions that were imposed by the UN Security Council following Saddam's invasion of Kuwait. The state of chaos continues today, as Iraq is scheduled to hold national and provincial elections in 2005, which will lead to the drafting of a new Iraqi constitution by the new assembly.

Given this context and the continually evolving developments in Iraq, the assessment of women's rights can only be tentative and contingent. This is most true in the key area of laws and legislation. For example, in May 2003, the Coalition Provisional Authority (CPA) suspended the Iraqi constitution of 1970. The CPA, which was established one month after U.S. and coalition forces took control of Baghdad on April 9, 2003, was created with the aims of restoring conditions of security and stability, of enabling Iraqi people to fully determine their own political future, and of facilitating economic recovery, sustainable reconstruction, and development.[1] On May 6, 2003, U.S. President George Bush appointed Ambassador L. Paul Bremer III as a special envoy and civil administrator of Iraq and head of the CPA. In essence, Ambassador Bremer, who reported directly to U.S. Secretary of Defense Donald Rumsfeld, was the de facto ruler of Iraq. But whereas the Iraqi constitution was suspended, the Iraq Civil Code of 1953 and all other state laws and decrees remained valid unless Ambassador Bremer specifically repealed them. Needless to say, this state of affairs, in which people did not know which laws were in effect and which had been abrogated by the CPA, was a major source of confusion.

Iraq's population was an estimated 24,200,000 in 2003, with Arabs comprising 75 percent to 80 percent of the population, Kurds 15 percent to 20 percent, and additional ethnic groups such as Turkmen and Assyrians constituting the remaining 5 percent. Iraq's Sunni Muslims, who constitute about 35 percent of the population, are made up of Sunni Kurds, Sunni Arabs (who dominated political and economic life under the Ba'ath Party), and a small number of Sunni Turkmen. Shi'a Muslims, on the other hand, who comprise around 60 percent of the population, were marginalized and often severely persecuted under the old regime.[2] Iraq's economy was always dominated by the oil sector; however, the military occupation in March 2003 and the sabotage of pipelines that followed, resulted in the shutdown of much of the central economic administrative structure. Unemployment soared as a result of the CPA's early de-Baathification decrees, which left around 35,000 civil servants out of work and disbanded Iraq's 400,000-man army.

Until the mid-1980s, women were guaranteed equal access to education and employment opportunities under the Ba'ath regime; Iraqi women achieved significant strides in the political, economic, and educational spheres. The Iraq–Iran war, the Kuwait war, and the economic sanctions imposed by the UN on Iraq in the early 1990s, however, severely affected the educational and economic status of women. Today, women suffer from high rates of illiteracy and unemployment. In 2003, illiteracy rates reached 75.6 percent for women and 44.1 percent for men.[3]

While women's abilities to organize and advocate for their rights and for greater representation increased with the fall of Saddam's regime, women's freedom of movement and personal security have been limited by the state of lawlessness and insecurity that has accompanied the 2003 U.S. military occupation. In addition, many women's groups and human rights activists are concerned that conservative Islamists may act to rescind or abolish Iraq's relatively progressive Personal Status Law and replace it with a fundamentalist version of *Shari'a* law, thus increasing discrimination against women. While it is difficult to predict which laws will be in effect by the end of 2005, it is clear today that Iraqi women's freedom and social and political status hang in the balance, suspended between the shadow of the past and the uncertainty of the future.

Nondiscrimination and Access to Justice

It is difficult to assess the status of women's rights at this transitional period in Iraq. On March 8, 2004, the Iraqi Interim Governing Council (IGC), with the approval of the CPA, signed an interim constitution (the Transitional Administrative Law), to be effective until a permanent constitution is written following national elections in 2005.

The 2004 interim constitution guarantees women equal rights with men and 25 percent representation in the National Assembly. Article 12 declares that "All Iraqis are equal in their rights without regard to gender, sect, belief, nationality, religion, or origin, and they are equal before the law. Discrimination against an Iraqi citizen on the basis of his gender, nationality, religion, or origin is prohibited." Article 30 of the interim constitution also states, "The electoral law shall aim to achieve the goal of having women constitute no less than one quarter of the members of the National Assembly." The extent to which these guarantees will be translated into practice, however, remains to be seen.

In 1970, two years after seizing power, the Ba'ath regime drafted a new constitution, the Iraqi provisional constitution. This constitution remained in effect until its suspension by the CPA in April 2003. Article 19 of the 1970 constitution guaranteed women equal rights with men and stated that all citizens of Iraq are equal before the law regardless of gender, language, religion, or social origin. This applied across the religious and ethnic spectrum of the country, and the secular courts of Iraq made no differentiation between citizens, whether they were male or female, Arab, Kurd, or Turkmen.

Prior to 2003, Iraqi courts were secular and administered by the Ministry of Justice. The judges and other court functionaries were civil servants paid by the state. Women were legally considered adults in Iraq and were fully capable of representing themselves in court; they had the same recourse to justice as men. However, given the patriarchal nature of Iraqi society and the prevalence of tribal organization, women have been less likely than men to resort to the court system. This has been particularly true in cases of domestic disputes, which tend to be settled through mediation by family elders and religious leaders. Nevertheless, the law encourages women to represent themselves and plead their cases in court; this is true today, as it was before 2003.

Iraq was one of the first Muslim countries to ratify the Convention on the Elimination of All Forms of Discrimination Against Women (CEDAW) in 1986, albeit with reservations. Reservations were applied to Articles 2(f), 2(g), 9, and 16, which address women's rights in the private sphere, such as marriage and family relations. The state argued that the existing state laws, which were based on progressive interpretations of Islamic law (Shari'a), should continue to regulate these domains. Moreover, whereas CEDAW's Article 9 guarantees a woman the right to confer her own nationality upon her child, Iraqi Nationality Law (43/1961) states that only the father has the right to confer nationality on the child.

Iraqi women achieved significant strides in the political, economic, and educational spheres throughout the 1970s. These achievements were underwritten by state-sponsored laws that were, on the whole, liberal and nondiscriminatory. The ideologically secular and socialist Ba'ath regime introduced social and economic reforms that in many ways benefited women, who were specifically targeted to spearhead Iraq's modernization. Legal reforms included government-issued decrees that outlawed a Muslim husband's ability to verbally divorce his wife and limited the authority to grant divorce strictly to the courts. Reforms to Iraq's Law of Personal Status also forbade a husband to take a second wife without the permission of his first wife and made it easier for women to gain custody of their children in cases of divorce or separation.

In December of 1972, the government established the General Federation of Iraqi Women (GFIW) to raise women's awareness and to ensure their participation in the economic and social development of the country. The GFIW, which was in effect an implementing arm of state policies, managed to play an important role in promoting the general welfare of Iraqi women. The GFIW ran more than 250 rural and urban community centers that offered job training, literacy programs, and legal advice to women. Moreover, the GFIW provided the means for women activists to attain high political positions that allowed them to lobby effectively for legal reforms on behalf of women, especially in areas of personal status (marriage, divorce, child custody, and inheritance). By utilizing radio and television, the GFIW educated women on their legal rights and provided them with practical advice on how to pursue these rights in the courts.

In the mid-1970s, newly introduced laws mandated that boys and girls must attend primary school. Women were encouraged to pursue higher education and join the work force. By the late 1970s, it was estimated that women made up about 60 percent of the Iraqi civil service. However, the advance in women's status was not uniform throughout all sectors of Iraq's society. The religiously conservative and tribal circles continued to maintain patriarchal traditions that called for the restriction of women to domestic duties within the household.

The gains that women achieved in the 1960s and 1970s began to unravel with the onset of the Iraq–Iran war, which started one year after Saddam assumed power in 1979. Triggered by long-standing territorial disputes, the war lasted eight years and ended in 1988 with a UN-arranged ceasefire treaty. Iraqi war casualties were estimated to number anywhere between one-quarter and one-half million people. War expenses depleted Iraq's $35 billion in foreign reserves and incurred a debt of over $80 billion. The massive loss in human life and the economic cost of the war, together with the lower oil prices of the 1980s, combined to undermine the capacity of the Ba'ath regime to sustain the social welfare state it had started to build in the 1970s. Shortages of food and medicine, rampant inflation, and degraded health care services took a heavy toll on the Iraqi population; women, a large number of whom were widowed heads of households, particularly suffered.

In an attempt to bolster his faltering regime and stem the growing tide of opposition, Saddam took measures to appease and gain the support of the conservative religious and tribal leaders. He issued decrees that suspended or reversed a number of progressive laws that had raised the ire of the conservative elements in Iraq. In 1982, for example, he issued decrees that forbade Iraqi women from marrying foreigners. In 1988, in order to make room for the demobilized soldiers, women were discouraged from working in offices and factories and encouraged to take early retirement and return to "the home."

In 1990, Article 111 was introduced into the Iraqi penal code; the decree reduced prison sentences from eight years to no more than six months for men who kill their female relatives and plead family "honor" as justification, thus reviving the practice of "honor killings," which had been on a decline in Iraq.[4]

Legal restrictions were also placed on women's freedom of movement during this time; women were forbidden to travel outside Iraq without being accompanied by a male relative. In 1993, Saddam reversed one of his own earlier decrees with a new presidential decree that allowed Iraqi men to marry a second and third wife without the consent of the first wife. Compulsory education for women was all but ignored so that by the end of 2000, less than 25 percent of Iraqi adult women were literate.[5]

Iraqi women's involvement in civic activities dates back to the early 1940s, when women's charitable and educational organizations participated in the national struggle for independence from the British. Prior to the Ba'ath party regime, Iraqi women, particularly the educated urban elite in Baghdad, Mosul, and Basra, were active participants in a dynamic civil society. As a measure of control, the Ba'ath party acted to dismantle many of Iraq's civil society organizations, including women's literary and charitable organizations; soon after, the regime established the General Federation of Iraqi Women (GFIW) to help implement the state's agenda on women's issues.

After a long period of state-imposed restrictions on political rights and civil liberties, women today are taking advantage of increased freedom of expression and the ability to organize by lobbying actively for better representation in the political process. A large number of women's NGOs, by some accounts 80 in Baghdad alone, have formed in Iraq. Iraq's women activists and NGOs include educated upper and middle class Iraqi women who had been living abroad before the toppling of Saddam's regime, Kurds with 12 years of experience working with international NGOs and human rights groups, and women who were active members of the Iraqi Communist Party and who had worked for women's rights in the past. In addition, several Iraqi women from poor neighborhoods have been trained by international NGOs since 2003 and are now committed advocates for women's rights. The diversity of NGOs ranges from groups that advocate for a secular and liberal government to those who call for an Islamic state governed by Shari'a.

RECOMMENDATIONS

1. The government should ensure that women are included in the process of drafting the new Iraqi constitution.
2. The government should include a nondiscrimination clause in the new constitution to guarantee women's equal status as citizens.
3. The government should remove all reservations to CEDAW and take steps to implement it locally by bringing national laws in conformity with CEDAW.

Autonomy, Security, and Freedom of the Person

In addition to Iraq's strong tradition of patriarchy, the rise of religious extremism has had a direct impact on women's lives. Several customs and traditions place real limits on women's personal freedom and autonomy. Culturally, individual rights are subordinated to the welfare of the large extended family, which remains a strong institution in Iraq. Patriarchal tribal values tend to be more dominant in the rural areas, where concern about family "honor" and reputation often result in early marriage for females and women's confinement to the household.

Iraq's cultural mosaic comprises various linguistic, ethnic, and religious groups that have a long history of mutual accommodation. Iraqi citizens, men and women, have mostly enjoyed the freedom to practice their religion. However, the Shi'a population was not always free to participate in the political affairs of the country under Saddam's regime. Since the U.S. invasion of Iraq, religious tensions, factionalism, and religious militancy have been on the rise.

No laws have forbidden Iraqi women to drive or be alone in public, but a 1988 presidential decree prohibited women under the age of 45 from leaving the country without a male relative. While the Iraqi interim government repealed this decree in 2003, the state of lawlessness and the breakdown of order that followed the U.S. occupation have resulted in everyday restrictions on women's movement, with increased incidents of abduction, sexual assault, and rape. Many women are reluctant to leave their homes for work or shopping without the protection of a male relative. Many women who work with foreign organizations operating inside Iraq have been harassed or have had their lives threatened, and in some cases, have been killed.

The *Qanun Al-Ahwal Al-Shakhsiyya Al-Muwahhad* (Unified Law of Personal Status) regulates the domestic life of Iraqi men and women. It was first codified in 1959 and has since gained 12 amendments. Its principles are based on the Muslim Shari'a, as interpreted by the Ja'afari (Shi'a) school of jurisprudence. Most of the amendments, which were introduced by the secular Ba'ath regime, granted more rights to women than those provided under the 1959 law in areas such as divorce, inheritance, and the custody of children. For example, the Personal Status Law was amended to provide authority to Iraqi judges to grant divorced women custody of their children until the age of 10 (previously it was 7 for boys and 9 for girls), at which time, the judge can decide to extend the custody until the age of 15.

Early marriage is still a problem, however. Despite Iraqi law that forbids marriage of girls under the age of 15, girls as young as 12 years old are routinely married off to cousins or other relatives, in both the cities and the villages of Iraq. Most girls in early marriages do not have the freedom to refuse the marriage.

In December of 2003, the Coalition-appointed IGC took a major step backward on women's rights when, after hasty deliberations in a closed session, it passed Resolution Number 137. In one stroke, this resolution acted to void the liberal and secular Iraqi Law of Personal Status by replacing it with Islamic Shari'a law, including some of the most conservative interpretations of

Islamic text. The resolution declared that in matters of personal status, each religious community should be governed by its own religious laws. Among other things, the resolution gave self-appointed, all-male, conservative clerics total power over matters of marriage, divorce, inheritance, and child custody, signaling an erosion of the rights previously guaranteed to women under the national law that equally applied to all citizens.[6]

Women's organizations and human rights activists, both inside and outside Iraq, actively and immediately condemned Resolution 137. Ambassador Bremer did not sign the resolution into law, and when the IGC repealed Resolution 137 two months later by a vote of 15 to 10, several council members left the meeting in protest. This incident, among other things, is a forceful reminder that women's rights and freedoms in Iraq remain hostage to the whims and dictates of any group that is in power.

No specific laws protected women from torture under Saddam's regime; torture was used against both men and women by the state. In most cases, women, like men, were fired from their jobs, put in prison, and often tortured not because of their gender, but because of their political views and activities or their relationships with alleged enemies of the regime.

No cases of slavery have been reported in Iraq. However, a pre-existing problem with human trafficking that resulted from the UN Economic Sanctions and the 1991 Gulf War has intensified due to the breakdown in law and order, unemployment, and decreased social welfare that followed the 2003 war. These conditions have expanded the opportunities for organized networks of human trafficking and increased prostitution, as well as the exploitation of children, many of whom now live on the streets in Baghdad.

The post-conflict breakdown in public order in 2003 resulted in increased violence directed at civilians, especially women. Daily reports of harassment, abduction, and rape, as well as the rampant violence connected with common criminals and terrorist groups, have kept women confined to their homes. Families are afraid to send their daughters to school without male escorts; universities and colleges report a sharp decline in the attendance of female students. Increasingly large numbers of women are choosing to wear the veil, or *hijab*, not necessarily out of religious conviction but as a way to avoid harassment and to protect themselves in public. Iraqi women who worked for the Coalition forces found themselves threatened by conservative religious clerics who used the Friday sermon and street pamphlets to warn women that they would be maimed or killed if they worked for the "military occupiers and the infidels." Several women were, in fact, targeted and murdered en route to work in the Green Zone[7] or to a military base.

Domestic violence does occur, but there are no published statistics on its prevalence.[8] The stigma attached to rape and domestic violence in Iraq, and the fear of retaliatory violence by male family members, prevents an overwhelming majority of women from reporting these incidents or seeking legal redress. In spring of 2003, the CPA, along with the Ministry of Labor and Social Affairs, announced plans to open a shelter in Baghdad for female victims of domestic violence; a few shelters already exist in the Kurdish region that were established by Kurdish NGOs.

RECOMMENDATIONS

1. The United Nations and other international groups should provide immediate training and financial support to local Iraqi women's NGOs to create awareness of protections for women against violence, to establish shelters, and to provide counseling and support services to victims of sexual violence and domestic abuse.
2. The Iraqi Ministry of Justice should institute a standing Committee of Experts, comprised of legal experts who specialize in women's human rights, to safeguard the rights of women in the Personal Status Law of Iraq.
3. The international community should provide technical assistance to the Iraqi government to assist in the drafting of a law that protects women from all forms of violence, including domestic violence.

Economic Rights and Equal Opportunity

Women's access to economic rights in Iraq over the last 50 years has been greatly influenced by the country's overall political, economic, and social environment. While the Ba'ath regime's social and economic reforms of the 1960s and 1970s helped to improve the legal status of women, the country's wars and imposed sanctions, as well as Iraq's patriarchal attitudes and traditions, have heavily impacted women's lives and have limited their economic opportunities and rights.

In Iraq, a woman's right to own, buy, and sell property; lend and borrow money; enter into contracts; and run her own business is underwritten by state laws. The court respects these laws, and many Iraqi women are known to sue brothers and ex-husbands in court over property disputes. Iraqi businesswomen enter into business contracts, hire and fire employees, and represent themselves in court.

A married Muslim woman is under no legal obligation to support her family with her income. A Muslim husband, on the other hand, is legally obliged under Iraq's laws to support his wife and children. In general, wage-earning women are free to dispose of their incomes as they choose. How a woman spends her income or uses her assets varies with each case in Iraq, generally having little to do with religion or law.

Women have the right to inherit property and can bequeath their personal property to their children under Iraq's Personal Status Law. Women's inheritance is regulated by a strict quota system that is in accordance with the Shari'a, as interpreted by the Ja'afari school of jurisprudence in Iraq. Under Iraq's laws, men receive a larger share of inheritance than women, which is in accordance with men's legal obligations to financially support their families. Specific circumstances and exceptions do exist, however, particularly among the Iraqi Shi'a, who permit an only daughter to inherit her father's full property and the family house. In some cases, non-Muslim Iraqi women married to Muslim Iraqi men may face problems in claiming the family assets if their in-laws decide to dispute the widow's claims. Court officials, however, tend to side with the widows.

In 1976, a Compulsory Education Law (118) mandated that all children between the ages of 6 and 10, regardless of their gender, must attend primary school; after the age of 10, girls may be withdrawn from school if their parents so desire. New colleges and universities were established throughout the country during this time, and women were encouraged to pursue higher education. In 1979, additional legislation was passed requiring all illiterate Iraqis between the ages of 15 and 45 to attend reading classes provided free at literacy centers operated by the GFIW. These centers specifically targeted women and as a result, the literacy gap between men and women narrowed significantly by the mid-1980s. By the early 1990s, female literacy rates in Iraq were the highest in the region.[9]

The 1970 Iraqi constitution and subsequent legislation granted women the right to work outside the home. Article 4 of the Unified Labor Code[10] established the right to equal pay, while Articles 80 to 89 charged the state with the protection of women from harassment in the work place. In 1971, a maternal law was enacted that provided working women six months' paid maternity leave with the option for an additional six months of unpaid leave.

The massive increase in oil revenues in the early 1970s[11] led the government to undertake large-scale development projects and expand its health and education programs. Faced with labor shortages to meet these new demands, the Iraqi government opened its doors to foreign workers and encouraged Iraqi women to join the work force. The state provided subsidized nurseries for the children, free transportation to the work place, and subsidized housing. These facilities were mainly provided to professional women who were working in the public sector in the urban areas.

Women who graduated from the newly established universities, including those in the provinces, were all guaranteed employment by the state. In 1976, the Iraqi Bureau of Statistics reported that women constituted approximately 40 percent of teachers, 30 percent of doctors, 50 percent of dentists, 25 percent of lab technicians, 15 percent of accountants, and 15 percent to 20 percent of civil servants. Nevertheless, women were still victims of gender discrimination with respect to promotions and access to positions of authority, which were, and continue to be, the reserve of men. It is interesting to note that while women's increased participation in the workforce in the 1970s provoked little opposition from the more conservative constituents of society, some of these same groups had earlier opposed women's education.

The economic downturn following the Iraq–Iran War and the economic sanctions imposed on Iraq after the 1990 Gulf War had a disproportionate effect on women, many of whom were widowed and had become de facto heads of households. To win the support of the tribal and conservative religious leaders, Saddam ordered the gender segregation of high schools and discouraged women from competing with men for jobs. Saddam made speeches to the effect that a woman's national responsibility was to make room for Iraqi men in the labor field and that they should return to their "sacred" duty as mothers. Many women during this time were either fired from their jobs or driven out by low wages.

In 1977, Iraq reported that women constituted 12 percent of the total working population. In 1997, this figure had dropped to 9.7 percent. These figures, however, only account for the percentage of those employed in the formal sector as wage earners and do not include agricultural workers and the many women who worked in the informal sector. A UN/World Bank Needs Assessment survey conducted in the summer of 2003 noted that women comprised no more than 23 percent of the formal work force, mostly "as mid level professionals in the public and service sectors and in rural areas as seasonal agricultural workers." This survey, however, included agricultural and service workers. Needless to say, there are little to no reliable statistics at this time concerning women's present status in the labor field. At the time of the UN/World Bank survey, it was estimated that more than 50 percent of the labor force was unemployed or underemployed.

When schools reopened in 2003 after the U.S. occupation, women principals and teachers went back to classes. Despite the new CPA-established pay scales that were nondiscriminatory toward women, many women professionals were reluctant to return to their place of employment, preferring to wait for wide-scale looting of offices and buildings, insecurity, and general chaos to subside.

RECOMMENDATIONS

1. The United Nations and international NGOs should help the government of Iraq to review its labor laws and gender policies to ensure that all laws and procedures protect women's rights to work without discrimination and harassment.
2. The government of Iraq, in cooperation with the UN, World Bank, and other international organizations, should train women in entrepreneurial skills, legal rights, and labor laws so that they can actively compete in the post-conflict economy.

3. Governmental and nongovernmental organizations should provide vocational computer and other technical skills training to women students in high school and college, as well as in public community centers, to help them gain practical skills for future jobs.
4. The Ministry of Labor and Social Affairs should initiate income-generating training programs, including small credit programs, to help women, particularly widows and those living in rural areas, earn money independently.

Political Rights and Civic Voice

Although the 1970 constitution formally guaranteed women equal rights with men, Saddam Hussein's repressive regime served to deny men, women, and children almost all political rights and civil liberties. The authoritarian nature of the Ba'ath regime prohibited the expression of any political views that deviated from the one party line and imposed particularly harsh restrictions on the freedoms of Iraq's ethnic minorities such as the Kurds and religious groups like the Shi'as.

Iraqi citizens were not able to exercise any political rights under Saddam's regime. With the exception of a small circle of high-ranking party members and Saddam's own tribal supporters, Iraqis lived in a "Republic of Fear," subject to the whims of a ruthless dictator and his sycophants. No political parties were allowed under Saddam, and the Ba'ath party strictly controlled the country's professional associations. No groups were in a position to promote and protect the rights of women, or any other Iraqi citizen.

Despite the deteriorating security conditions that have accompanied the fall of the regime, Iraqis are free today to talk openly, to assemble peacefully, to organize themselves into political groups and parties, to publish newspapers, and to access news and information via satellite dishes that were forbidden under Saddam. Taking advantage of this new freedom, and cognizant of the rising postwar power of extremist Muslim groups, Iraqi women activists lobbied the progressive elements of Iraqi society and the CPA to protect and defend their rights. Many women have been concerned that fundamentalist religious groups, Sunni and Sh'ia alike, will succeed in introducing legislative controls on women's lives and undermine their long-established freedom to make personal decisions such as whether or not to veil, to drive, to vote, to work outside the home, to hold political office, and to preside as judges, among other rights.

As far back as the 1950s, Iraq has had a cadre of trained women lawyers. Graduates of the College of Law in Baghdad also work as court clerks and public prosecutors. However, very few women have served as judges due to a cultural resistance to women serving in high posts. In 2003, a U.S military commander in Najaf appointed an Iraqi woman lawyer as the first female judge in the conservative city of Najaf. Her appointment brought protests from lawyers, both men and women, and from conservative Shi'a clerics who issued *fatwas*, rulings on Islamic law, claiming that Islam forbids women judges; this led to her forced resignation.

In the 1980 parliamentary elections, women won 16 out of 250 seats on the National Council; in the following elections in 1985, women won 33 council seats, representing 13 percent of the total body. However, these were party-controlled elections that did not represent any democratic process and therefore had little lasting impact on women's political representation or women's political rights.

The Coalition's stated goal in 2003 to promote women and protect their rights did not immediately translate into viable programs or action. While it is generally recognized that women make up anywhere from 54 to 60 percent of the Iraqi population, only three women were appointed to the 25-member IGC, which was formed in July 2003. No women were included in the nine-member rotating presidential council or in the drafting committee of the Transitional Administrative Law (interim constitution). Again, in August of 2003, a 25-person interim cabinet was selected and only one position, the Minister of Municipalities and Public Works, was allocated to a woman. The CPA did not appoint any women as governors in any of the 18 provinces.

In 2003, the U.S. allocated $27 million dollars to support women's programs in Iraq. Under the guidance of CPA advisers and gender experts, the U.S. and other foreign sources funded Iraqi women to organize a number of national women's conferences and to support newly formed local NGOs that focus on women's issues. It is too early to assess the overall impact of such limited initiatives; by early 2004, only a small portion of the funds for women's programs had been spent, and only one of nine planned women's centers had been established in Baghdad.

Newly formed women's organizations, such as The Iraqi Women's League, The Iraqi Higher Council for Women, and The Organization of Women's Freedom, among others, are actively working for women's full representation in the political process and to ensure that the women's rights agenda does not get marginalized in the country's slow and painful road to a new democratic Iraq. These groups have organized national and regional conferences, held open public meetings to discuss the status of women in Iraq, and presented their cases in international meetings. In 2003, Iraqi women activists lobbied both the CPA leadership and the Iraqi Governing Council for a 40 percent quota for women in the National Assembly and any subsequent legislative bodies; the result was a 25 percent minimum representation in the National Assembly.

Kurdish women in Iraq's three northern provinces have enjoyed a relatively privileged status over the last 13 years. In 1991, following a failed Kurdish uprising against the government of Saddam Hussein, allied troops forced the withdrawal of the Iraqi army from the region and established a safe haven zone in the Kurdish region of Iraq. This soon led to the creation of a politically autonomous Kurdish state in northern Iraq that was completely independent from the rest of Iraq; the Kurds had their own government and international aid. Under allied protection and with the help of international organizations, Kurdish women leaders succeeded in establishing dozens of well-organized, well-financed, and effective women's NGOs. Kurdish women successfully lobbied for a law against crimes against women perpetrated in the name of "honor" and increased women's representation in the regional administrative system.

RECOMMENDATIONS

1. The international community should ensure that Iraqi women are able to participate fully in all aspects of political life in Iraq.
2. The international community should train Iraqi women political activists and their NGOs to monitor women's participation in decision-making posts at all levels.
3. The new government of Iraq should take affirmative steps to enact laws and set up implementing mechanisms that ensure women's appointments to high-level decision-making posts in all governing and administrative institutions.
4. International women's rights and human rights organizations should develop networks and joint projects with Iraqi women's rights organizations to support their advocacy efforts to increase women's representation in Iraqi politics.

Social and Cultural Rights

Massive oil revenues in the 1970s enabled the Ba'ath regime to establish the early foundations for a socialist, welfare-oriented society. In the 1960s and 1970s, Iraq had a quality health care system, with decent access to medical service, well-equipped hospitals and clinics, and subsidized medicine. Conditions began to decline in the mid-1980s however, and by the 1990s, Iraq's health care system was in crisis. Lack of investment and insufficient upkeep led to the physical deterioration of hospitals and clinics, as well as a lack of equipment and qualified staff. The years of war and economic sanctions, and the rampant corruption that permeated all state institutions, took the greatest toll on Iraq's most vulnerable groups - the elderly, women, and children.

In the 1980's, the government initiated a pro-natal policy to spur population growth during the Iraq-Iran war; they encouraged women to have more children and offered modest subsidies for families. However, the deterioration in health services meant higher risks for women, who suffered from malnutrition and who had limited access to prenatal care and hospitals. Women's health care during this time often took low priority behind the needs for family food and medical care for men at war.

While the situation improved somewhat after the introduction of the Oil-For-Food program in 1996, a reproductive health survey conducted by Physicians for Human Rights in July of 2003 found the maternal death rate in Iraq to be 292 per 100,000. A UN/World Bank Joint Needs Assessment report in the summer of 2003 revealed that general insecurity and gender-based violence prevented many women from seeking health care for themselves and their children. Current plans to phase out food rations in the midst of severe inflation and a chaotic transition to a market economy is likely to further jeopardize the health of poor female heads of households and their children.

A woman's ability to make autonomous decisions about family planning varies according to the family's level of education, religious beliefs, and social standing, as well as additional socio-cultural factors. However, given the strong patriarchal bias of Iraqi society, women's sexuality and reproductive choices remain within the confines of marriage and family life. The pronatal Ba'ath government had made abortion illegal.

Early marriage for girls is still practiced in the rural parts of Iraq, especially in areas that retain a strong tribal organization; but widows are not traditionally forced to marry against their wishes. Female virginity is highly prized, and brides are expected to be virgins; virginity tests may be carried out in certain cases, but little research has been done on this topic. While there are no statistics on the prevalence of female genital mutilation (FGM) in Iraq, it is not believed to be a general problem. However, studies have shown that FGM is practiced in the southern half of Iraqi Kurdistan and is most prevalent in rural areas.[12]

Iraq does not have any laws that discriminate against women and their rights to housing; women may own their houses independently of their husbands. Subsidized housing is accessible to most unmarried or widowed women employed by the government. While there are no known laws that forbid a woman from living alone, social pressures may discourage it.

A woman's influence, in general, is limited to the household and rarely extends to the community unless she happens to be in public office. While women constitute the majority of school principals in Iraq, even women doctors, who are highly respected in society, have not been able to extend their influence in the community in any organized way. Iraqi women have no role in tribal decision making, which remains strictly a male domain. Yet, Iraqi women who worked in international groups in Iraq during 2003 were able to help organize and recruit women to municipal advisory councils, which have begun to play an important role in the community and even city-wide affairs.

Before 2003, Iraqi women were well represented in the media. They worked as sound engineers, producers, and program presenters. While Iraqi women, at this time, are both eager and wary of pushing their way into the public arena, by the end of 2003, a large number of Iraqi women were again working in various newspapers, radios, and local and international television.

The economic depression of the 1990s and the Gulf War had a particularly drastic effect on the large and increasing number of widows in Iraq who are heads of households. The by-products of the 2003 war, such as shortages of electricity, clean water, cooking oil, and gasoline, coupled with a high rate of unemployment, poverty, and rampant inflation have also further exacerbated the plight of Iraq's women, especially the widows. In the first years of the Iraq–Iran war, the regime paid handsome stipends to the widows of war heroes, but by the late 1980s, the government stopped these subsidies. Another social by-product of the wars has been the large number of unmarried women in Iraq today; some attribute this new phenomenon to the unbalanced gender ratio, among other things.

Many Iraqi women are discouraged by the prevailing state of insecurity and the resulting harm to the already weak social services sector. Restoration of security in Iraq will greatly help women and all citizens of Iraq. Another major obstacle to women's social and cultural rights protection is the general lack of awareness of women's rights in Iraqi society due to the country's prolonged isolation from the outside world. There is an urgent need for nationwide civic awareness campaigns on basic human rights, citizenship rights, and women's rights.

Due to decades of living under authoritarian rule and state restrictions on civil society activity, the NGO movement in Iraq is new and inexperienced, lacking organizational capacity and the needed skills to work locally, nationally, and regionally. Civil society groups, particularly women's groups, need urgent training and support in advocacy methods, organizational management skills, networking, information technology, and civic participation issues, along with training and information on women's human rights and basic human rights. In order for these programs to be successful, Iraqi women must also be provided with quality education, vocational training, adequate health care, and effective social welfare programs. These efforts should be long-term and locally sustainable. There is no doubt that this is a critical juncture for Iraqi women; unless they remain active and vigilant, they risk the erosion and loss of their recently gained political rights and civic voice.

RECOMMENDATIONS

1. Iraqi health care providers, government service agencies, and women's rights groups should design long-term programs to provide mental health care services to Iraqi women.
2. International organizations and funding agencies should work closely with Iraqi journalists and women's rights advocacy groups to help them develop radio and television programs devoted to women's needs and priorities.
3. International donors, the United Nations, and international NGOs should work closely with Iraqi women's groups to design specific projects to empower widows and women with disabilities.
4. International human rights organizations and USAID should provide financial assistance and training in advocacy, media, and communication skills to Iraqi women's rights groups and women leaders.

AUTHOR: Amal Rassam is an Iraqi-American who was born and raised in Iraq. She received a Ph.D. in Anthropology from the University of Michigan. A retired professor of anthropology who taught at the City University of New York, Professor Rassam works in development as a consultant on gender issues and civil society, with focus on the Middle East. She is co-author, with Daniel Bates, of Peoples and Cultures of the Middle East, *a book published by Prentice Hall.*

Notes

[1] *Report to the Congress Pursuant to Section 1506 of the Emergency Wartime Supplemental Appropriations Act, 2003 (Public Law 108-11)* (Washington, D.C.: U.S. Office of Management and Budget, 2 June 2003), 2.

[2] *International Religious Freedom Report 2003– Iraq* (Washington, D.C.: U.S. Dept. of State, Bureau of Democracy, Human Rights, and Labor, 18 Dec. 2003), http://www.state.gov/g/drl/rls/irf/2003/c10269.htm.

[3] "Country Profiles: Iraq" (Beirut: UN Economic and Social Commission for Western Asia [ESCWA], 2003), http://www.escwa.org.lb/divisions/ecw/profile/iraq/main.html.

[4] In 2000, after strong lobbying by Kurdish women's rights organizations, the administration of the semi-autonomous regions of Kurdistan in northern Iraq suspended Article 111 of the penal code.

[5] "Occasional Paper: Situation of Women in Iraq" (U.N. Office of the Humanitarian Coordinator for Iraq [UNOCHR], 28 May 2003).

[6] While the Law of Personal Status applies to all citizens, special cases are referred to courts set up to address issues pertaining to non-Muslims.

[7] The International Zone (formerly known as the Green Zone) is the heavily guarded area of closed-off streets in central Baghdad where U.S. occupation authorities live and work.

[8] *Country Reports on Human Rights Practices – 2002:* Iraq (Washington, D.C.: U.S. Dept. of State, Bureau of Democracy, Human Rights, and Labor, 2002).

[9] "Country Profiles: Iraq" (Beirut: UN Economic and Social Commission for Western Asia [ESCWA], 2003), http://www.escwa.org.lb/divisions/ecw/profile/iraq/main.html.

[10] Law 151/1970, later replaced by Law 81/1987.

[11] In 1975, Iraq's annual income from oil averaged $8 billion.

[12] Nicholas Birch, "Genital Mutilation Is Traditional in Iraq's Kurdistan," *Women's eNews*, 1 August 2004, http://www.womenenews.org.

Jordan

by Reem Abu Hassan

Population: 5,500,000
GDP Per Capita (PPP): $4,220
Economy: Mixed capitalist
Ranking on UN HDI: 90 out of 177
Polity: Traditional monarchy and limited parliament
Literacy: Male 95.5% / Female 85.9%
Percent Women Economically Active: 27.6%
Date of Women's Suffrage: 1974
Women's Fertility Rate: 3.7
Percent Urban/Rural: Urban 79% / Rural 21%

Country Ratings for Jordan
Nondiscrimination and Access to Justice: 2.4
Autonomy, Security, and Freedom of the Person: 2.4
Economic Rights and Equal Opportunity: 2.8
Political Rights and Civic Voice: 2.8
Social and Cultural Rights: 2.5
(Scale of 1 to 5: 1 represents the lowest and 5 the highest level of freedom women have to exercise their rights)

Introduction

The Hashemite Kingdom of Jordan is a constitutional monarchy that gained independence from Britain in 1946. King Hussein ruled the country from 1952 until his death in 1999, at which time his son, Abdullah II, ascended the throne. King Abdullah II, along with his council of ministers, holds broad executive powers and may dissolve the bicameral National Assembly at his discretion, as he did in 2001; he reinstated it in 2003. The central government appoints the upper house of the National Assembly, the regional governors of the 12 governorates, and half of the municipal council members. The National Assembly's lower house and the other half of the municipal council members are elected through universal adult suffrage. The king serves as head of the judiciary.

Jordan has a population of an estimated 5.5 million, a substantial number of whom are Palestinian.[1] A number of Jordanians live in rural areas, although rural–urban migration is on the rise. Islam is the state religion;

105

more than 95 percent of Jordanians are Sunni Muslims. Religious minorities are relatively free to practice their religions.

Under King Abdullah II, Jordan has embarked on a course of economic reform, acceding to the World Trade Organization and working closely with the International Monetary Fund, as well as signing free trade agreements with the United States and the European Union. Nevertheless, Jordan continues to lack significant supplies of water and oil. The country has a GDP per capita of $4,220.

The Jordanian government limits freedom of expression. It owns a majority of broadcast media, has wide discretionary powers to close print publications, and often censors potentially offensive articles. Freedom of assembly is also somewhat restricted. A substantial number of nongovernmental organizations (NGOs) operate within the country on a broad range of social and political issues, but professional associations have come under pressure to abstain from engaging in political activities.

The status of Jordanian women is currently undergoing a historic transition, with women achieving a number of positive gains and new rights. While much room for progress remains, Jordanian women enjoy equal rights with respect to their entitlement to health care, education, political participation, and employment. Nevertheless, women in Jordan continue to be denied equal nationality and citizenship rights with men. Women also face gender-based discrimination in Jordan's family laws and in provision of government pensions and social security benefits. Violence against women remains a serious problem in Jordan, and protection mechanisms for women victims of violence are inadequate.

The government has taken several steps to improve women's status in recent years, including the appointment of women to government ministries and high-level posts. In November 2003, King Abdullah II appointed 7 women to the 55-seat upper house of the National Assembly.

A significant number of NGOs work for the promotion and protection of women's rights in Jordan. Women's NGOs have had much success in breaking the silence on the issue of domestic violence by lobbying high political offices to denounce domestic violence and by increasing debate on the issue in the media. Despite the parliament's rejection of several decrees and draft legislation aimed at providing women greater equality, Jordanian women's rights advocates have made great strides in placing women's rights at the center of national political debates.

Nondiscrimination and Access to Justice

Jordanian law is a blend of Napoleonic code (inherited from the Ottoman and Egyptian legal systems), Islamic *Shari'a*, and influences of tribal traditions. The Jordanian Personal Status Law (JPSL) (No. 61 of 1976) is derived from Shari'a, and includes various opinions from a number of jurisprudential schools; in the absence of a provision in the law, the Jordanian courts refer back to the most authoritative opinion in the Hanafi school. The JPSL is applied in all personal status matters related to the Muslim family such as inheritance, child custody, marriage, and divorce.

Article 6(1) of Jordan's constitution states: "Jordanians shall be equal before the law. There shall be no discrimination between them as regards their rights and duties on grounds of race, language or religion." Article 6(2) of the constitution further stipulates: "The Government shall ensure work and education within the limits of its possibilities, and it shall ensure a state of tranquility and equal opportunities to all Jordanians." While the constitution refers to the right of "every Jordanian" in numerous articles, it fails to prohibit gender discrimination. Nevertheless, women's rights advocates frequently cite this article as verification of the constitution's intention to guarantee full equality between men and women, even though it does not explicitly specify gender.[2]

While Jordan's laws are not overtly discriminatory, women are treated unequally in a number of statutes. Gender-discriminatory language can be found in provisions that regulate economic rights such as retirement and social security, as well as laws that govern the family. In cases that fall under the jurisdiction of Shari'a, Jordanian women are not provided the same rights as male citizens and endure unequal treatment in their right to divorce, custody, and inheritance.

In the absence of a constitutional court, the available legal means to contest the constitutionality of laws include bringing a case before the High Court of Justice and submitting an ancillary challenge in a case before the courts.[3] The National Center for Human Rights[4] deals with gender discrimination cases through its complaints unit but does not have the legal capacity to file such cases before the courts.

Gaps in Jordanian laws also fail to provide protections for women's rights and equality. For example, no law specifically defines or criminalizes domestic violence, and there are no enforcement mechanisms to ensure the implementation of laws to promote and protect gender equality.

The actual implementation of Jordan's laws is often influenced by factors such as a lack of training of police and court officials, patriarchal cultural norms and customs, and male domination of the public sphere. Many women internalize these social norms and practices, leading them to believe that the discrimination they face is a normal part of life. Offenses committed against women are often justified in terms of cultural beliefs. In addition, the state tends to favor the interests of its male citizens by continuing to enact laws that reflect certain social beliefs, value systems, and attitudes discriminatory against women.

Despite the challenges to the advancement of women's rights, the Jordanian government has taken steps to update Jordan's laws and bring them in line with international standards. From 2001 to 2003, after the king dissolved the parliament and much of the government, King Abdullah and the Council of Ministers issued a number of provisional laws that promoted women's rights. These provisions included amendments to the Personal Status Law (No. 82 of 2001), the criminal code (No. 86 of 2001), the Civil Status Law (No. 9 of 2001), and the Provisional Passport Law (No. 5 of 2003). Nevertheless, when the House of Representatives came back into session in the summer of 2003, it rejected many of the provisional laws.

Article 3(3) of Jordan's Nationality Law (No. 6 of 1954) declares, "Any child born of a father with a Jordanian nationality shall be Jordanian wherever born." A Jordanian woman is allowed to retain her nationality after marrying a non-Jordanian; however, Jordanian women married to non-Jordanians are not permitted to confer their citizenship on their children. Furthermore, the Law of Residency and Foreigners' Affairs (No. 24 of 1973) does not facilitate residency for foreign men married to Jordanian women nor to their children, even though this law grants foreign wives of Jordanian men preferential treatment.

Women have the right to be plaintiffs and defendants in Jordanian courts and may appear before the police, the public prosecutor, the courts, and administrative tribunals as witnesses or as experts. The testimonies of men and women in Jordan's civil courts are afforded equal weight, as they are in non-Muslim (Christian) tribunals. In Shari'a courts, however, the testimony of two Muslim women is equal to that of one man.

Social norms and traditions sometimes deter a woman from seeking justice from the courts on the premise that she is disobeying her family. While the Bar Association Law (No. 11 of 1972) states that one of its objectives is to provide legal aid to financially incapable citizens, in practice this does not include equal access for women. A number of civil society organizations provide legal aid for women, but most groups are based in Amman, and rural women have limited access to such services.

The Jordanian penal code (No. 16 of 1960) provides certain gender-specific concessions to women who are pregnant or mothers. According to Article 27, if a married couple is sentenced to prison for more than a year and have children under the age of 18, then such sentences are consecutively applied. Article 17 also substitutes the death sentence with life imprisonment and hard labor for pregnant women. At the same time, the Law of Criminal Procedures (No. 9 of 1961) seems to contravene Article 17; it states that the death sentence for a pregnant woman should be delayed for three months after she gives birth.

Certain articles of the Jordanian penal code also discriminate against women. Article 340 provides reduced penalties for any man who surprises his wife or a female relative during the act of adultery, in any location, and proceeds to kill or injure the woman and/or her partner. While a wife who injures or kills her husband or his lover during the act of adultery may also receive a reduced penalty, the adulterous act must have been committed in the matrimonial home.

Article 98 of the penal code also mandates penalty reductions for a perpetrator who commits a crime in a fit of anger in reaction to an unlawful or dangerous act on the part of the victim. Although this article is gender-neutral in language, it is most often applied by the court in favor of men. Courts sometimes cite this article to justify more lenient treatment in cases of alleged "honor crimes," in which a male family member kills a female family member based on the suspicion of fornication.

Family-based violence against women in the name of family "honor" is a serious problem in Jordan, and men and women receive different legal and social treatment based on their gender. Although the Jordanian Law of Criminal Procedures contains a number of principles that guarantee the right of the accused,[5] these principles are often jeopardized by other laws and regulations that contradict the rule of law. The Crime Prevention Law contains some preventive measures that empower the administrative governor to place persons who may constitute a danger to the community in administrative detention. In the case of "honor crimes," women whose lives are threatened by their families are placed in prison pursuant to this law for their own protection. However, the release of such women from detention is conditional upon the consent of a male relative.

The penal code outlines the standards of proof for adultery cases, one of which is conclusive documentary evidence that a crime has been committed. In practice, the police will submit a request to the forensic medical department to carry out an examination of a woman accused of adultery by a forensic physician. Women will usually consent in writing to such an examination in order to prove their innocence.

Women victims of sexual violence in Jordan face numerous gender-specific legal and social obstacles. Societal customs often serve to pressure the guardians of a female victim to waive personal claims and drop charges to avoid social stigma, particularly in cases of sexual assault, rape, and homicide. Waiving the personal claim by the guardian allows the court to use its discretion, which often leads to lenient sentences for perpetrators. In most cases, a perpetrator of rape or molestation will avoid punishment if he marries his victim in accordance with Article 308 of the penal code. This provision is always justified on the basis of conferring protection on the female victim from social stigma. There are no clear procedures to ensure the victim's consent to such a marriage.

Jordan signed on to the UN Convention on the Elimination of All Forms of Discrimination Against Women (CEDAW) in 1992, with reservations on articles[6] chiefly concerning women's nationality and housing rights. The reporting system of CEDAW encourages Jordan to eliminate gender-discriminatory legislation; however, for CEDAW to affect Jordanian laws, the convention must be approved by the parliament in accordance with Article 33(2) of the constitution.[7] Debates on the compatibility of CEDAW and Islam are frequent in Jordan, and a number of civil society groups have called for the removal of Jordan's reservations to CEDAW, particularly Article 15(4) concerning freedom of movement and choice of residence. The Jordanian National Committee for Women (JNCW) monitors Jordan's compliance with CEDAW.

Women's rights groups and civil society actors in Jordan are working to promote the status of women's freedoms in all aspects of life. Their activities include lobbying for legal reforms and better rights protections, providing services such as counseling and legal aid for women, and implementing numerous advocacy projects. The government is engaged in a dialogue with women's rights groups that has helped to advance women's rights as a key component within Jordan's overall strategy for political development.

RECOMMENDATIONS

1. The government should amend the nationality law and the law of residency to ensure that Jordanian women and men have equal nationality rights as citizens.
2. The government and civil society organizations should expand legal aid and education programs to foster social values that reject gender-based discrimination and violence against women.
3. The Jordanian parliament should revise and repeal discriminatory clauses in the criminal and penal codes to ensure women's equal access to justice.
4. The government should remove all reservations to CEDAW and take steps to implement it locally.

Autonomy, Security, and Freedom of the Person

Article 14 of the constitution guarantees freedom of religion, provided that religious practices are consistent with "public order and morality." Islam, Christianity, and Judaism are the only state-recognized religious faiths. However, while the Druze and Baha'i faiths are not officially recognized, their practice is not prohibited. According to the constitution, *waqf* (religious community trusts) and matters of personal status such as marriage, divorce, child custody, and inheritance, fall within the exclusive jurisdiction of Shari'a courts for Muslims and separate, non-Muslim tribunals for the other state-recognized religious communities. The small Druze and Baha'i communities do not have their own courts to adjudicate personal status and family matters, and their cases are heard in Shari'a courts.

Jordanian law provides citizens the right to travel freely within the country and abroad except in designated military areas. Unlike Jordan's previous law (No. 2 of 1969), the current Provisional Passport Law (No. 5 of 2003) does not require women to seek permission from their male guardians or husbands in order to renew or obtain a passport. Nevertheless, in several recent cases mothers reportedly could not depart abroad with their children because authorities complied with requests from fathers to prevent their children from leaving the country. Social norms continue to play a major role in maintaining restrictive measures on women's freedom of movement.

The Personal Status Law is applied in all matters relating to family law that involve Muslims and the children of Muslim fathers. Non-Muslim tribunals apply their own personal status laws, which are not published in the official gazette. However, many Christians elect to apply Islamic legal provisions regarding inheritance.

Jordanian Muslims are required to marry according to Islamic marriage law. According to Article 19 of the Personal Status Law, a woman can stipulate conditions in the marriage contract provided that the conditions are not unlawful and do not affect the right of any other person. In practice, however, many women are unaware of this right and it is therefore rarely exercised. Some Jordanian women's advocates have suggested attaching a list of the possible conditions to the actual marriage contract in order to inform women of their full rights.

Welaya (guardianship) is a system in Jordanian law whereby a person is appointed to act on behalf of and in the interests of a minor or any other person of limited legal capacity. In Jordan, such a guardian has the authority to require that his female dependent be under his supervision if the woman is unmarried and under the age of 40 or previously married. If such a woman rebels against her guardian, she will no longer be entitled to her financial maintenance.

Islamic legal principles allow women to be the legal guardian of their children, but the Personal Status Law in Jordan does not provide women with this right; only the father is designated as the guardian of his children.

Recent amendments to Jordanian laws have raised the minimum age of marriage to 18 years, but the chief justice retains discretion to permit the marriage of anyone who is at least 15 years old if it is deemed to be in his or her interest. While the Hanafi school of Islamic law, dominant in Jordan, does not require a male guardian to conclude a marriage contract on behalf of an adult Muslim woman, the Jordanian government elected to adopt the position of the Maliki school in this matter. The consent of a Shari'a judge is required to conclude the marriage if the woman's guardian opposes the marriage without lawful justification.

Article 66 of the Personal Status Law is derived from Islamic Shari'a and obligates the husband to provide maintenance for his wife including food, clothing, housing, and medical care. This entitlement is viewed as a wife's lawful right, irrespective of her wealth or religion, and is interlinked with the husband's role as a provider and as the head of the matrimonial household.

In the case of a wife who works outside the home, amendments in Jordanian laws protect her right of maintenance provided that her husband views her work as legitimate and has agreed to it either explicitly or implicitly. The condition regarding a husband's approval stems from the argument that a wife should obey her husband, which some Jordanian jurists interpret as the husband's right to confine a woman to the home. In practice, the legal and social hardships that some women encounter while recovering their maintenance diminishes the positive aspects of this right.

While polygamy is allowed in Jordan for Muslim men, amended laws obligate the judge to verify that the husband has the financial means to maintain his new wife. In addition, the courts are now required to inform the second wife of the first marriage and notify the first wife of her husband's second marriage. If a man can satisfy all such financial and legal requirements, he can be legally married to up to four wives at one time.

Women do not have the same rights as men to marriage and divorce in Jordan. The most common divorce procedure is the *talaq* (arbitrary divorce), which is exclusively a right of the husband to divorce his wife without providing any legal reason. The law recognizes the wife's right to financial compensation after an arbitrary divorce. Recent amendments have increased this amount to equal the wife's maintenance, compensated for no less than one year and no more than three years. The wife also has the right to keep her dower amount and the maintenance accumulated during the *iddat* period, a compulsory waiting period for a woman following a divorce to ensure that she is not pregnant by the husband with whom she is getting a divorce. Although there is increasing social resistance in Jordan to men's arbitrary right of divorce, there are currently no legal restrictions on this practice.

A woman seeking a divorce in Jordan, on the other hand, must sue under the *Khula*[8] divorce proceeding. The Khula divorce was recently introduced through amendments in Jordanian law that enable a wife to appear before the court and request a dissolution of the marriage by stating that "she does not want to continue her marital life, is afraid of disobeying God's rulings, and gives up all marital rights." This method does not require the woman to prove her claims; she simply states her desire, and the court will order the dissolution of the marriage. However, this method of divorce favors financially affluent women and does not take into consideration the circumstances of poor women who will have trouble giving up their financial marital rights to dissolve the marriage.

There are no specific provisions or laws in the penal code that criminalize domestic violence, and there are no restraining orders for cases of abuse.

Cases of domestic violence in Jordan are prosecuted under the penal code's general laws on assault and battery.[9] Although assault and battery are accepted as valid reasons for initiating a judicial divorce, it is often very difficult for a woman to prove such a case. Shari'a courts require the testimony of two male witnesses in these circumstances; the testimony of the wife alone is not accepted as sufficient evidence.

The law obligates members of the medical profession to report cases that may involve a possible felony or misdemeanor; however, underreporting is common. The police will not pursue cases in which the inflicted injury causes an inability to work for ten days or less without a complaint by the injured party. Women victims of violence are often discouraged from reporting their abuse to police because of the social stigma and shame associated with such crimes. A battered woman may also be pressured by her family to drop the charges.

Although the Family Protection Department[10] and the Ordinance of Shelters for Family Protection (No. 48 of 2004) represent major advances in services rendered to victims of domestic violence, the shortage of shelters for battered women has prevented the Family Protection Department from delivering sufficient assistance to victims of physical and spousal abuse. Only one temporary shelter for battered women is in operation; it was set up by the Jordanian Women's Union, a nongovernmental organization.

Women's rights groups and civil society actors in Jordan are working to promote the status of women under the family law and to address issues of gender-based and domestic violence. The government is also working in cooperation with civil society to combat these problems.

RECOMMENDATIONS

1. The government and parliament should amend the Jordanian Family Law to remove articles that do not ensure women equal rights with men within the marriage.
2. The government and civil society organizations should expand their efforts to raise public awareness of the problems of family violence and the need to support women victims of violence.
3. The government and parliament should amend the penal code to provide clear and explicit penalties for instances of domestic and family violence and abuse.
4. The government should take steps to fully implement the 2004 Ordinance of Shelters for Family Protection Number 48 in honor killing cases.

Economic Rights and Equal Opportunity

Jordanian law recognizes a woman's right to own property without restrictions. Women do not need the approval of their husbands or guardians to dispose of their property. Nevertheless, a recent report by the United Nations Fund for Women (UNIFEM) states that only 10 percent of land and property owners in Jordan are actually women.[11] Social norms, especially in rural areas, hinder women's ability to obtain economic resources, particularly for land ownership and finance.

There are no legal restrictions on the right of Jordanian women to enjoy their income and assets independently. However, it is the accepted norm for single working women, who represent the highest percentage of economically active women, to contribute to the family income by giving their salaries to their families. Working wives, on the other hand, often use their salaries to pay for family expenses directly.[12]

Women are guaranteed the right to inheritance under Islamic law as applied in Jordan, but in certain cases the woman will inherit half the share of the man. In addition, social constraints impede women's rights to inheritance. Societal customs place emphasis on confining family property to the males of the family, exerting pressure on women to waive their portions of inheritance, especially property, in favor of their brothers. There are no set procedures in Jordanian Shari'a courts to protect women from being forced to waive their inheritance rights and no guarantees that they will be compensated.

According to UNIFEM's 2004 report, it is common practice in Jordan for the head of the family to transfer his real assets legally to his sons during his lifetime to prevent women from receiving their inheritance share.[13] If a father dies before making such a legal transfer, no laws can prevent a daughter from receiving her share as calculated under the Shari'a system. However, many women in rural areas may not be aware of such legal rights or know how to litigate such claims.

Women can freely enter into business and finance-related contracts and activities at all levels, and they enjoy full legal competence in the field of business. Women represent 70 percent of all beneficiaries of micro-finance projects in Jordan, with many of these programs exclusively targeting women. Micro-finance projects are being extended to many regions of Jordan. However, a study conducted by the ministry of agriculture and the United Nations Food and Agriculture Organization (FAO) on the status of women in agriculture in 2001 demonstrated that women obtained only 20 percent of the total amount of agricultural loans, the value of which did not exceed 12 percent of the total amount of loans for that year.

Article 20 of the Jordanian constitution declares elementary education compulsory for all Jordanians and free for all students in government schools. There is no legal gender discrimination, and social norms encourage families to enroll their children in schools and universities. At the national level the gross education enrollment rate is now higher for females than for males (76.1

percent for women as compared to 71.9 percent for men), and 85.9 percent of women age 15 and above are literate.[14]

The Jordanian constitution recognizes the basic principles of the right to work and equal opportunity for all its citizens in Articles 22 and 23.[15] Workers and employees are described in gender-neutral ways in both Article 2 of the Labor Law, which defines the worker as "each person, male or female, who performs a job in return for wages," and the Civil Service Ordinance.[16] However, no provisions specifically prohibit gender discrimination in labor opportunities or in the workplace, and no provisions stress equal salaries for men and women who hold the same positions.

Social discrimination against women is common in the field of labor and stems from popular notions that women need to be protected. Another popular belief in Jordan is that women who enter the job market are doing so to supplement and increase their family's income rather than to become economically independent or to individually support their family.

Laws and regulations in Jordan place certain conditions on the professions women can choose to pursue. As a result, women's economic participation is concentrated in the socially accepted professions for women, such as nursing and teaching.

According to Article 23 of the constitution and Article 69 of the labor code, the minister of labor issues decisions specifying the industries and economic activities that are off-limits for women workers, as well as the hours during which women are prohibited from working.

Women are prohibited from working in quarries (stone, limestone, phosphate, and other hazardous environments) and are not allowed to work between 8 at night and 6 in the morning, except in some professions in hotels, theaters, restaurants, airports, offices of tourism, hospitals, clinics, and some transportation industries. Exceptions are also made for jobs requiring yearly inventories and jobs preparing for beginning- and end-of-season retail sales, as well as jobs that involve a fear of financial loss. Generally, these regulations tend to cater to market interests rather than the protection of women. Evening work for women is limited to 30 days per year and a maximum of 10 hours a day. In reality, these restrictions serve to limit the competition between men and women in favor of men.

According to the Civil Service Ordinance of Jordan, the department for civil service does not differentiate between applicants based on gender; employment is determined by the application number and the results of exams and personal interviews. However, the Civil Service Ordinance does discriminate against women by unequally distributing certain benefits for men, such as the family allowance and cost-of-living allowance, which are not equally provided for women.

Within the Jordanian legal, cultural, and religious value system, women technically have the right to be maintained by their husbands, as husbands are required to support their wives financially. Based on this premise, the Jordanian state does not recognize women's rights to retirement and social security benefits[17] unless certain conditions are met. Gender plays a key role in determining eligibility for benefits based on: the length of employment needed to become eligible for retirement benefits; when the benefits become available; who is eligible to receive benefits; and the conditions under which benefits are provided in the event of the death of an employee.

Article 14 of the Civil Retirement Law and Article 45(a) of the Social Security Law encourage women to resign from their jobs by allowing them to retrieve their entire retirement fund, giving them incentive to quit their jobs during times of family financial trouble. Working women are also encouraged by such legal provisions to leave their jobs when they marry. The law awards an end-of-service bonus to a bride that she would normally receive only at retirement.

Article 52 of the Social Security Law deems beneficiaries as, "those family members of the insured ... who fit the following [categories]: a) his widow; b) his children and those of his brothers and sisters whom he supports; c) his widowed and divorced daughters; d) the husband of the deceased insured [woman].

Whereas a widow and dependents of a deceased male employee need only to prove their relationship with him and that he is in fact deceased, the requirements for the family of a deceased female employee make it extremely difficult for the family to receive any of the retirement benefits due her by law. According to Article 56 of the Social Security Law, the family must prove that the husband is incapacitated or that the woman was the sole provider for the family. The state justifies such discrimination on the premise that women are usually the secondary providers for the family, which contradicts the requirement that women workers pay the same share for such benefits as men.

Many women work in sectors not governed by the labor law and therefore cannot enjoy the protection or benefits afforded by the law. Article 3 of the labor law states that it does not apply to, "domestic labor (servants), gardeners, cooks, and those in the same capacity, as well as members of the owner's family who work in his projects without receiving pay." Foreign women workers, who work primarily as domestic help or maids, receive no protection from gender-based discrimination under these laws.

Women have specific protections in the workplace, including the right to a 10-week maternity leave for the purpose of childcare, of which 6 weeks must be allowed immediately following the birth of the child.[18] An employer who employs 20 or more women must provide a childcare facility for working mothers' children under the age of four in cases in which at least 10 children need care. Furthermore, a working mother is allowed to take a year of absence without pay to raise her children, and a mother is entitled to paid breaks to breast-feed her child during the first year after birth.

Sexual harassment in the workplace or any other public area is not explicitly defined or forbidden in Jordanian legislation. The Working Women Department at the ministry of labor in Amman receives complaints from working women, but these complaints are usually related to the misapplication of the labor law concerning payment of wages. Women workers are told to file complaints of sexual harassment with the Family Protection Department, as the ministry of labor does not document such complaints. There are no statistics on sexual harassment in the workplace and no specific records at the family protection department on this matter.

RECOMMENDATIONS

1. The government and parliament should pass legislation banning gender-based discrimination in all stages of employment and benefits and establish enforcement mechanisms so that women have recourse to file complaints and receive justice.
2. The government and parliament should pass legislation banning sexual harassment in the workplace and establish procedures for receiving complaints, collecting statistics on cases of sexual harassment, and providing support services for women.
3. The labor ministry should establish a department to monitor the application of relevant laws and to ensure nondiscrimination against women in areas such as minimum wage and equal wages with their male counterparts, with particular focus on the situation of foreign workers, part-time workers, seasonal or temporary workers, and micro-enterprises.

Political Rights and Civic Voice

According to Article 3(a) of Jordan's Law on Public Gatherings, all Jordanians have the right to hold public gatherings and to organize marches provided that prior written approval is obtained from the administrative governor. The request must be submitted at least three days before the date of the gathering and must include the names of the applicants, their addresses, signatures, and the purpose, time, and place of the gathering.

Women are free to express their opinions and discuss gender issues in public and in the media within the confines of Jordan's general restrictions on free speech and the media. Freedom of speech and freedom of the press are guaranteed in Article 15 of the constitution; however, the Press and Publications Law (No. 8 of 1998) imposes a number of restrictions on these rights. According to the law, all publications must be licensed by the government. The government is given discretionary powers to issue fines, withdraw licenses, and order media shutdowns, enabling the state to control the editorial content of newspapers. State intimidation encourages journalists to use self-censorship, as citizens may be prosecuted for slandering the royal family, the state, or foreign leaders and for "sowing sedition."

The constitution and a number of Jordan's laws guarantee the rights of citizens, both men and women, to vote and run for elections. Women face no legal barriers in their right to participate in local assemblies and other institutions. The state has taken some steps to encourage women's participation in the public sphere, with the appointment of 3 women ministers, 94 municipal council members, 7 members of the senate, and 2 ambassadors. In 2001, Jordan also established a quota for women in the House of Representatives, reserving 6 out of 110 seats for women candidates.[19] However, the application of this quota is conditional on the approval of the Council of Ministers, who can apply it in consecutive elections if it is deemed in the public interest. The quota system was introduced in the 2003 elections through a legislative amendment; as a result, six women were elected to the lower house of parliament.

More than two-thirds of state-appointed seats in the municipal government are held by men, while women hold about 27 percent. Women can also run and vote in municipality elections, although women have generally showed less interest in these elections in comparison to the parliamentary elections. In 2003 local elections, female candidates represented a mere 2.4 percent of all candidates (winning less than 1 percent of the seats), whereas nearly 7 percent of candidates in the parliamentary elections were women. The only requirement placed on candidates running for municipal and national elections is a fee, which is stipulated in Article 12 of the election law. Nevertheless, this nonrefundable deposit serves to discourage some women from participating as candidates.

While the law does not prohibit women from joining the judiciary, there are currently no female judges in the Court of Cassation, the Court of Grand Felonies, or Jordan's Shari'a courts. In 2003, women constituted less than 3 percent of Jordan's 608 judges, and no women served as public prosecutors.

Women are also underrepresented in senior civil service positions. Only about 4 percent of employees in the highest levels[20] of the civil service system are women. The percentage of women increases in the third class of the civil service, in which women constitute nearly 54 percent of the total number of employees.[21] Overall, women constitute 39 percent of civil service employees.

Women's participation as ambassadors in the diplomatic field continues to be limited. Women generally do not hold high-ranking positions such as minister plenipotentiary or counselor, and only 4 percent of ambassadors are women.

Article 4 of the Political Parties Law (No. 32 of 1992) grants Jordanians the right to form and join political parties; conditions for membership, as listed in Article 5, do not discriminate against women. Women participated in the founding bodies of 28 of Jordan's 31 political parties, representing 7 percent of the total number of members of such founding bodies.

Women are generally free to participate in civic life. Laws governing Jordan's 12 professional associations do not discriminate against women. However, women are underrepresented in these associations, constituting about 22 percent of the total membership. Only two professional associations have women serving on their board of directors.[22] Women fill an estimated 25 percent of positions in the administrative bodies of voluntary organizations and constitute 25 percent of the founders. A 1996 survey by the general statistics department on living standards in Jordan showed that one-third of men over the age of 15, and one-tenth of women, oppose women's participation in voluntary work.

RECOMMENDATIONS

1. The government should appoint more women as judges, senior officials in Jordan's diplomatic corps and civil service, ministers of government, senators, and members of municipal councils.
2. Professional associations should take steps to ensure that women have full and equal opportunities to participate as members and leaders in their organizations.
3. The government and parliament should amend the election law to help women become more competitive candidates in elections.

Social and Cultural Rights

A noticeable divide between Jordan's public and private domains greatly affects the advancement of women's rights and explains many of the gender inequalities that prevail. In this divide, Jordanian women are often limited to the private sphere, while men enjoy the public sphere. Additionally, a broad societal perception of a tension between women's rights and family obligations continues to impede advancement of the status of women. Some Jordanians fear that women's equality and independence might lead to the destruction of the family unit. As a result of these dominant cultural attitudes and the public–private divide, Jordanian women face particular challenges in obtaining full social and economic rights.

A woman is not legally required to inform her husband or obtain his approval concerning her choice of contraception. However, service providers ensure the consent of the husband and wife during the counseling and the selection of contraceptive methods. A husband's written consent is also needed by service providers for a tubal ligation. Of Jordanian women who do not use contraceptives, 58 percent attribute this decision to their husband's opposition, while 28 percent of women claim that not using contraception is a personal choice. Of the married women who use contraceptives, 79 percent state that the decision is a mutual one shared by both partners, while 18 percent of married women using contraceptives stated that it was a personal decision that was made without the interference of their husbands.[23]

According to prevailing customs in Jordan, women generally do not visit the doctor or a health unit on their own, especially if they are unmarried. This is partly because a majority of women do not have independent financial means, and their ability to receive medication depends on being supported by their husbands or fathers. In most cases, health insurance for women is a benefit provided by the husband or father's employer, particularly in the case of women who do not work. Obtaining coverage for medical expenses is a problem for a large percentage of women in Jordan; particularly for divorced and widowed women.

A woman's right to housing is connected to her status as a wife or a daughter. According to Article 36 of Jordan's personal status law, "The husband prepares a residence which includes the living necessities in accordance with his abilities and in his domicile and place of work." The wife has the right to obtain housing in the event of divorce, but only if she is nursing or has been given custody of the children. Social traditions discourage women from living alone, particularly when they are single.

The Law of Owners and Lessees (No. 11 of 1994) declares that property intended for purposes other than residence should be transferred to the heirs (ancestors and offspring) of the deceased and to his wife. However, a widowed woman will lose this property if she remarries. The wife and children of an arbitrary divorce or an ecclesiastical separation (the husband abandons the leased property) have the right to continue to occupy the property as original lessees, provided that a final judgment is issued from a competent court.

Groups most affected by poverty in Jordan are the elderly, the sick, widowed women, the disabled, and those without family support. These groups commonly have low educational attainment, poor-quality housing, and inadequate income, and are dependent on cash assistance and welfare services.[24] However, some victims of poverty are unable to gain access to welfare assistance and must depend on relatives, friends, or charity groups. Official statistics show that Jordanian women have a high chance of becoming widowed or abandoned after the age of 55.[25] Widows, divorcees, abandoned women, and girls over 18 years with no provider are categorized as eligible for aid under the Law of the National Aid Fund (No. 36 of 1986). Jordanian women married to non-Jordanians are also eligible but on an individual basis. In addition, emergency aid is provided for families whose financial provider has died, was imprisoned, or is ill.

Women are able to advocate openly for the promotion and protection of women's human rights in Jordan; there are no legal restrictions on their efforts. While some issues such as "honor crimes," women's reproductive rights, and sexual harassment are regarded with skepticism and doubt, women activists continue to lobby for advances in these areas. Women's overall participation in nongovernmental sectors is on the rise, and women's NGOs are engaging in issues such as domestic violence and women's political participation. However, the percentage of women working in nongovernmental organizations outside the capital remains low, as does women's representation in Jordan's media, particularly in upper decision-making positions.

Gender issues and women's participation are key components of any attempt by the government to pursue sustainable development. While recent advances in Jordan are encouraging, the state needs to take further steps toward gender equality. To progress further, the government and women's rights activists should reframe women's rights issues out of the current cultural context and adopt a rights-based argument—a move that would shift the terms of the debate, advance women's rights, and promote Jordan's overall development.

RECOMMENDATIONS

1. The government should amend the legal provisions that discriminate against women in housing, including the Law of Owners and Lessees, to ensure gender equity.
2. The government and media leaders should provide training to journalists on women's rights issues and facilitate the research capabilities of more women in order to encourage further assessment of social policies from a gender perspective.
3. The government should ensure that women, particularly those divorced, abandoned, or widowed, have full access to a basic level of health care and housing.

AUTHOR: Reem M. Abu Hassan is a lawyer in Jordan who specializes in family protection and women's legal issues, and serves as the Vice President of the Jordanian Society for Protecting Victims of Family Abuse. Ms. Abu Hassan has conducted extensive research on "honor crimes" and violence against women in Jordan.

Ms. Widad Adas, a human development expert based in Amman, contributed to the social science research aspect of this report.

Notes

¹ *Freedom in the World 2004* (Washington, D.C. and New York: Freedom House, 2004), 295.

² The general consensus among Jordanian legal experts is that gender equality is mandated by the Jordanian constitution. The term "Jordanians" refers to men and women. In Arabic, the male form of the adjective includes males and females. (Author's note.)

³ There are no precedents; judgments can vary, which leads to instability in court rulings. This acts as a deterrent, especially for women, to employing this method as a way to contest the constitutionality of gender-discriminatory laws. (Author's note.)

⁴ The provisional law for the National Center for Human Rights is No. 75 of 2002; the center began operations in June 2003.

⁵ These rights include, among others: the right to be presumed innocent, the right to counsel and legal representation, and the right not to be detained except in certain crimes.

⁶ CEDAW, Articles 9(2), 15(4), 16(1c, d, g).

⁷ Article 33(2) of the constitution: "Treaties and agreements which involve financial commitments to the Treasury or affect the public or private rights of Jordanians shall not be valid unless approved by the National Assembly."

⁸ Also known as "Khul."

⁹ Articles 333, 334, 335 of the Jordanian penal code.

¹⁰ The Family Protection Department is part of the Public Security Directorate; it is a specialized police center assigned to deal with cases of violence against women and children.

¹¹ *Jordan Human Development Report 2004: Building Sustainable Livelihoods* (Amman: United Nations Development Program [UNDP], 2004), http://www.undp-jordan.org/jordan_hdr/JHDR_2004.pdf.

¹² Under the personal status law, a husband should provide for his wife. Therefore, any payments made by her to the household are voluntary and she is not entitled to reclaim them in a divorce.

¹³ *Jordan Human Development Report 2004: Building Sustainable Livelihoods* (Amman: United Nations Development Program [UNDP], 2004), http://www.undp-jordan.org/jordan_hdr/JHDR_2004.pdf.

¹⁴ Table 24, "Gender-related development index," in *Human Development Report 2004: Cultural Liberty in Today's Diverse World* (New York: United Nations Development Programme [UNDP], 2004), 217–220, http://hdr.undp.org/reports/global/2004/.

¹⁵ Article (22) of the constitution states: "(i) Every Jordanian shall be entitled to be appointed to public offices under such conditions as are prescribed by law or regulations. (ii) Appointment to any government office or to any establishment attached to the Government, or to any municipal office, whether such appointment is permanent or temporary, shall be made on the basis of merit and qualifications."
Article (23) states: "(i) Work is the right of every citizen, and the State shall provide opportunities for work to all citizens by directing the national economy and raising its standards. (ii) The State shall protect labor and enact a legislation therefore based on the following principles:...(d) Special conditions shall be made for the employment of women and juveniles."

¹⁶ The Labor Law (No. 8 of 1996) governs labor relations in the private sector, while the Civil Service Ordinance (No. 55 of 2002) governs civil service employment in the public (government) sector.

[17] The laws governing such benefits in the private sector are the Social Security Law (No. 19 of 2001) and the Civil Retirement Law (No. 34 of 1959).

[18] The Civil Service Ordinance gives a 90-day maternity leave, of which only 15 days are allowed before the birth of the child.

[19] Article 3 of the Ordinance for the Division of Electoral Districts and Seats (No. 42 of 2001).

[20] This level includes employees of the higher administration such as legislators, chairmen of legislative councils, the prime minister, chiefs of administrative divisions, as well as government employees at high levels, such as general managers and chief executives of institutions with special mandates.

[21] The legal requirement for holding a job in the third class is to have a high school certificate.

[22] These include the 11 female members of the board of directors of the Bar Association and the 10 members of the board of directors of the Pharmaceutical Association.

[23] *The Status of Jordanian Women: Demography, Economic Participation, Political Participation and Violence* (Amman: United Nations Development Fund for Women [UNIFEM], 2004), http://www.unifem.org/global_spanner/index.php?f_loc=arab.

[24] *Jordan Human Development Report 2004: Building Sustainable Livelihoods* (Amman: United Nations Development Program [UNDP], 2004), http://www.undp-jordan.org/jordan_hdr/JHDR_2004.pdf.

[25] Ibid.

Kuwait

by Haya Al-Mughni

Population: 2,400,000
GDP Per Capita (PPP): $16,240
Economy: Capitalist-statist
Ranking on UN HDI: 44 out of 177
Polity: Traditional monarchy and limited parliament
Literacy: Male 84.7% / Female 81.0%
Percent Women Economically Active: 36.4%
Date of Women's Suffrage: No women's suffrage
Women's Fertility Rate: 4.0
Percent Urban/Rural: Urban 100% / Rural 0%

Country Ratings for Kuwait
Nondiscrimination and Access to Justice: 1.9
Autonomy, Security, and Freedom of the Person: 2.2
Economic Rights and Equal Opportunity: 2.9
Political Rights and Civic Voice: 1.4
Social and Cultural Rights: 2.8
(Scale of 1 to 5: 1 represents the lowest and 5 the highest level of freedom women have to exercise their rights)

Introduction

Kuwait is a constitutional hereditary monarchy with an appointed Cabinet (Council of Ministers) and a National Assembly (parliament) that is elected every four years. The parliament in Kuwait serves as a legislative body with the power to overturn the decrees issued by the Emir—the head of state. The Al-Sabah family tribe has presided as the ruling authority in Kuwait for over 200 years. The country gained its independence from Britain in 1961 and adopted a new constitution in 1962. In July 2003, Kuwait held its tenth elections since independence for its 50-member National Assembly. While the 1962 constitution provides men and women with equal rights in most areas, only men 21 years and older are allowed to vote or run for office. Women cannot vote in Kuwait.

Kuwait is a small, rich country with a $16,240 per capita income and approximately 98 billion barrels of crude oil reserves.[1] Islam is the state religion;

roughly 70 percent of Kuwait's inhabitants are Sunni, while 30 percent are Shi'as. Kuwaiti nationals comprise an estimated 45 percent of the country's population of 2.4 million. The remaining 55 percent, non-nationals, are predominantly foreign workers and their families who originate from surrounding Arab countries and South Asia. An estimated 125,000 *bidun* (stateless citizens) reside in Kuwait. Foreign communities are able to establish their own schools and practice their religious faiths.

Public gatherings in Kuwait require governmental approval, and the state imposes restrictions on the right to peaceful assembly. Formal political parties are banned. While there is some degree of freedom of expression, the Cabinet retains the authority to suspend Kuwait's press outlets. Kuwaiti NGOs, controlled and funded by the state, do not operate freely. An advisory body to the National Assembly, the Human Rights Defense Committee, works to review and propose amendments to national legislation to ensure conformity with human rights principles. The committee examines individual complaints of human rights abuses, including women's rights cases and those brought by foreign women seeking justice for employment-related grievances.

Kuwaiti women have experienced some advances in recent years. Opportunities for education and employment opened up for women in the early 1960s, and Kuwaiti women now attend universities, participate in the labor force, and have access to affordable and quality health care. The Kuwaiti government ratified the UN Convention on the Elimination of All Forms of Discrimination Against Women (CEDAW) in 1994, albeit with reservations affecting nationality and political rights for women.

At the same time, women suffer from discrimination and inequality in law, practice, and custom in many areas of life. Women enjoy limited political and civil rights. Among other things, they are prohibited from serving as judges or elected officials and are forbidden to join the military. Women are relegated to an unequal status in marital relations; they are not allowed to pass their nationality on to their foreign-born husbands or children. While advocacy concerning these issues is visible and growing, it has proved largely ineffective due to state-imposed restrictions on the creation, structure, and management of women's organizations.

Nondiscrimination and Access to Justice

Article 29 of Kuwait's constitution declares, "All people are equal in human dignity, and in public rights and duties before the law, without distinction to race, origin, language or religion." While the constitution does not explicitly discriminate on the basis of gender, a number of laws adopted under the constitution ensure the unequal treatment of women. There are few protections against gender discrimination. Kuwait's laws and policies, such as the

Personal Status Law, Welfare Law 22/1987, and Decree Law 1116 on Housing Care, define Kuwaiti women as dependents of men and not as individuals with equal rights and responsibilities. The Election Law issued in 1962 limits voting rights to Kuwaiti men and denies women the right to vote and to be elected to public office.

Kuwait has three courts: courts of first instance, the high court, and the Supreme Court. Specialized courts exist for administrative, military, and constitutional cases. Personal matters, including marriage, divorce, and inheritance, are governed by Islamic law but handled in the state's court system.[2] In October 2003, the government approved the establishment of the Shi'a Court of Cassation to handle Shi'a personal status and family law cases.

Kuwait's state laws and policies allow for differential gender treatment with respect to citizenship rights. Kuwait's Nationality Law denies Kuwaiti women the legal right to confer their nationality on their foreign-born husbands or the children of these marriages, while Kuwaiti men are permitted to exercise these rights. Foreign-born husbands and children are considered and treated like expatriates; they have no legal rights to remain in the country unless they have valid residency permits, which are only granted to the employed. By contrast, the law does not require Kuwaiti men to pay residency fees for their non-Kuwaiti wives. The wife of a Kuwaiti man is granted immediate residency by virtue of her marriage, and she can become a Kuwaiti national after 10 years of marriage—or less if she is a citizen of the Gulf.

An estimated 12,000 Kuwaiti women are married to non-Kuwaiti men, most of whom originate from Arab countries.[3] In 1991, many families suffered when the government deported all Arabs from countries that supported the Iraqi invasion of Kuwait, such as Palestine, Jordan, Yemen, Sudan, and Iraq.

Kuwait's refugee policy and strict naturalization requirements have contributed to the large population of residents who do not hold Kuwaiti citizenship. Between 1992 and 2002, an estimated 6,909 Kuwaiti women married non-Kuwaiti men, of whom 20 percent were bidun.[4] The bidun—or *ghayr muhadad al jinsiya* (people "of undetermined nationality")—are lawful residents of Kuwait who have not enjoyed the rights of citizenship or nationality since the 1980s. The bidun have lived in Kuwait for many generations; some were Bedouins and people who migrated from Iraq, Saudi Arabia, and Iran. Kuwait's population of bidun was estimated to be over 125,000 in 2000.[5]

The penal procedures code provides for the right of all residents, regardless of their nationalities, to gain equal access to courts and to have a court-assigned lawyer and/or interpreter if needed. However, most foreign-born domestic workers are not aware of their legal rights and are reluctant to bring charges if they have suffered a serious offense or violence at the hands of their employers.

Adult women are recognized as full persons before the court and are not barred from testifying in the secular courts. However, *Shari'a* law, which is interpreted in family court, deems the testimony of one man to be equal to that of two women.

In most cases, women are treated equally under Kuwait's penal code and criminal laws. In principle, all perpetrators of murder, rape, or violence against women are subject to severe penalties such as life imprisonment or execution. However, in cases of "honor killings," the penalties are reduced for men. According to Article 153 of the penal code 16/1960, a husband who murders his wife and/or her partner during an adulterous act will be sentenced to a maximum of three years in jail.

While Kuwait practices the death penalty, death sentences are not carried out on pregnant women or mothers of dependent children. Women are housed in a separate prison from men, and those who are pregnant are exempted from prison work and receive special care in terms of food and rest.

Women continue to suffer instances of gender-based and discriminatory arbitrary arrest, detention, and exile. Non-Kuwaiti nationals, men and women, may be expelled from the country if they are unable to renew their work and residence permits. In the late 1990s, following Islamists' (political activists who cite religion as their authority) pressure to increase social control and moral discipline in society, women became victims of harassment and were arrested at checkpoints. Sexual relations outside marriage, in particular prostitution, are considered moral crimes. Those engaging in such activities are susceptible to arrest, and foreign women may face imprisonment and deportation.

In 1994, Kuwait ratified CEDAW but adopted reservations on articles dealing with citizenship and voting rights. Reservations were also adopted on articles that call for equal rights concerning guardianship and the adoption of children.

The Kuwaiti National Assembly's Human Rights Committee can receive individual rights complaints from women, as well as complaints from foreign women seeking justice for employment-related grievances. Yet, in general, women's rights groups and the Human Rights Committee have not effectively dealt with the issues of gender discrimination and women's unequal access to justice.

RECOMMENDATIONS

1. The government should amend national laws in order to bring all legislation in conformity with the principles of non-discrimination established in the constitution.
2. The government should amend the Kuwait Nationality Act of 1959 (specifically Article 2) to ensure that Kuwaiti women have the same rights as Kuwaiti men to transfer nationality to foreign-born spouses and children.

3. The government should remove all reservations to CEDAW and take steps to implement it locally by bringing national laws in conformity with CEDAW.

Autonomy, Security, and Freedom of the Person

Women in Kuwait have few restrictions on the right to practice their religion and beliefs. Since the 1980s, religious observance among women has been on the rise. An increasing number of Kuwaiti women are now choosing to wear the *hijab*, pray in the mosques, and perform the pilgrimage rituals. Non-Muslim women also have the freedom to practice their religions. There are seven churches in Kuwait that serve the needs of the Christian community: Roman Catholic, Anglican, Greek Orthodox, Armenian Orthodox, Coptic Orthodox, Greek Catholic, and National Evangelical. Minority religious groups such as Sikhs, Hindus, Buddhists, and others are free to practice their religion in private homes or on the premises of the recognized churches.[6]

Social norms and official policies remain a major hurdle to women's freedom of movement in Kuwait. By custom, Kuwaiti women must request permission from their male guardians or parents to travel abroad or visit friends at night. However, police generally do not arrest and return a woman to her home if she is found to be traveling alone. Under Article 15 of the Passport Law 11/1962, a married Kuwaiti woman cannot apply for a passport without the written approval of her husband, but an unmarried woman over 21 years of age can directly obtain her passport. However, many large businesses send their female employees abroad for business or conferences, and it is uncommon for women to face problems in their employment due to gender-related travel restrictions.

There are two different sets of active family laws in Kuwait: a Sunni Family Law, which was drawn up in accordance with the Maliki interpretation of Islam, and the Shi'a Family Law (the Jaafari laws). The Sunni Family Law affects the majority of Kuwaiti women, as Sunni Muslims constitute the majority of the population.

The Sunni Family Law, as interpreted in Kuwait, legitimizes male control over women. However, while Sunni Family Law requires husbands to support their wives and children, it does not provide the husband with the absolute right to *ta'a* (obedience). Article 89 of the Sunni Family Law specifies that a husband should not forbid his wife from working outside the home unless the work negatively affects "family interests." But the law does not clearly define family interests. The phrase can thus be interpreted as referring to the stability of the marriage or the upbringing of the children. The very notion that women have a right to work has been stigmatized by a commonly held view in Kuwait, that women's neglect of domestic duties has led to a rise in divorce rates, juvenile delinquency, and drug addiction among Kuwaiti youth.

A husband is permitted to have more than one wife under both Sunni and Shi'a family laws. A man can marry a second wife without the permission of his first wife, and in some cases, without her knowledge. A wife may not petition for divorce on the grounds that her husband has taken another wife. If a man remarries, his second wife is expected to share the same house with his first wife, unless the husband has the means to provide his second wife with a new home. Under Sunni Family Law, a divorced woman will retain custody of her children until her sons reach 15 years of age and her daughters are married. If the mother remarries, she forfeits the right to custody.

While Sunni Family Law in Kuwait provides husbands with the unconditional right of divorce, women do not have the same rights and are unable to petition for divorce. However, women do have some form of protection against arbitrary divorce and mistreatment. A woman is owed financial compensation equal to one year of maintenance if her husband divorces her without her consent. Women also have the right to seek divorce if they are deserted in the marriage or subjected to *darar* (violent treatment that leads to physical injury). However, proof of injury is required in such cases. This is often difficult for many women, because they tend not to file complaints with the police and do not report causes of injury to doctors. Unsupportive and untrained police and doctors who examine abuse cases also hinder the gathering of evidence. According to reports, some husbands even try to bribe police to ignore charges of domestic violence.[7]

The most discriminatory aspect of the Sunni Family Law in Kuwait involves the marriage rights of women. The Sunni Family Law deprives a woman of the right to conclude a marriage contract without the presence and consent of her *wali* (guardian). The wali is usually the woman's father, or in his absence, her brother, uncle, or other close male relative. In other words, a woman cannot marry the partner of her choice without the prior approval of her family. Yet, in cases in which the father of a Kuwaiti woman has refused her choice of husband, the Sunni Family Law grants a woman the right to appeal the decision of her wali in family court.

Some women opt to marry outside Kuwait to circumvent the marriage restrictions. Nevertheless, a marriage contracted outside Kuwait is not legally recognized within the country; the head of the bride's family has the right to ask the court to annul the marriage. The minimum legal age for marriage is 15 for girls and 17 for boys. Within the urban community, it is rare for girls to be married at an early age or forced into marriage. However, arranged marriages between families of similar social standings are still the norm. A woman can refuse to marry altogether and remain single, but the social burden placed on aging single women is so high that most women prefer an unhappy marriage to facing the social stigma of the spinster label.

Kuwait's penal code prohibits the practice of all forms of slavery, torture, cruelty, or degrading punishments against any person regardless of age, gender, religion, or nationality. Slavery-like practices such as forced marriages and forbidding a person to leave the home are rarely reported. There are no forms of protection against these practices.

Kuwait's labor laws specify that a working day should be restricted to eight hours, yet female domestic workers are often underpaid and forced to endure long working hours. Employers have been known to confiscate the passports of domestic workers, making it difficult for them to leave their jobs and/or the country. There are also reports of abuse of domestic workers and foreign women in the workplace.

Domestic workers can take legal recourse against their employers by filing complaints directly with the Dasma police station—the main center for dealing with employer abuse cases, or with Kuwait's administrative courts. Kuwait has been drafting a new labor law to protect the rights of domestic workers.[8] Yet by the end of 2003, the law had not been finalized.

While domestic violence is a concern in Kuwait, the lack of comprehensive data and research on this issue makes it difficult to assess the severity of the problem. No known NGO or government office efficiently works to collect such statistics. The scarcity of analyzed data on domestic violence in Kuwait is partly due to the social belief that this issue is a family affair. Victims of abuse are often reluctant to file complaints with the police due to fear and shame, and little effort has gone into providing assistance or protection to the victims. There are no laws against domestic violence, and there are no shelters, support centers, or free legal services to aid female victims.

Rape and sexual assault outside marriage tend to receive more attention from the police and the press than incidents of domestic violence. There have been reports of the physical abuse of female detainees under police custody, but no monitoring mechanism is in place to record such violations on a regular basis. By law, anyone found guilty of sexual violence and/or rape may receive a jail sentence or the death penalty, depending on the severity of the case.

Women's groups have not been able to work effectively to promote and actualize women's rights surrounding autonomy and personal freedom in Kuwait. In 2003, issues of domestic violence and the exploitation of domestic workers did not feature highly in the campaigns of Kuwaiti women's rights groups and received only sporadic coverage in the press.

Kuwaiti women's groups did advocate for amendments to a number of articles that curtail women's rights within marriage, including the right to choose one's husband and an increase in the minimum age of marriage for girls.

RECOMMENDATIONS

1. The government should amend the age of marriage laws to increase the minimum age of marriage to 18 years for both boys and girls.
2. The government should amend the marriage contract laws under the family law to allow Kuwaiti women over 18 the right to marry the partner of their choice.
3. The government should start gender-sensitive, women's rights–oriented training for police and/or hire female police officers to investigate cases of violence so that women will feel more comfortable when reporting incidents of abuse.
4. The government and women's rights organizations should also organize public awareness campaigns on the problems of domestic violence.

Economic Rights and Equal Opportunity

Kuwaiti women are entitled to own and have full and independent use of their land, property, income, and assets. A woman's right to inheritance, as defined in the family law and in accordance with Islamic Shari'a, stipulates that a brother should receive double his sister's share.

Kuwaiti women are freely able to enter into business and financial contracts and activities at all levels. Women have the right of ownership and the right to dispose of assets, as well as the legal right to undertake civil and commercial transactions, conclude contracts, and engage in commercial and financial transactions. It is not necessary for a woman to obtain the consent of a husband or father to exercise these rights. By law, any Kuwaiti over 21 years of age may conduct any commercial activity in Kuwait provided that he or she is not affected by a personal legal restriction, such as a criminal record.

All Kuwaiti citizens, men and women, are guaranteed free and equal access to the education system, from primary school through the university level. Students are also provided with equal opportunities to study abroad. However, Kuwaiti women are required to seek the permission of their male authority figures to accept study-abroad scholarships. Kuwaiti women comprise almost two-thirds of university-level students and more than half of the student population of the Public Authority for Applied Education and Training. Women are enrolled in all major subjects and graduate at higher rates than men.

In the mid-1990s, Kuwait University introduced different GPA requirements for the admission of female and male students, with the goal of reducing the percentage of female students in certain academic fields. Female students are now required to have a 3.3 GPA to be admitted to the engineering department, while male students need only a 2.8 GPA. Women must possess a 3.5 GPA to be admitted to the field of medicine, while men need only a

3.3 GPA. A rationale for such policies is the dilemma presented by the right of a woman's male guardian or husband to restrict her right to work outside the home. Because of instances in which women graduates of professional schools have been forbidden to work, some believe that admitting a woman to medical school may ultimately be a waste of that seat, as after graduation she may not be able to pursue the profession. A male student, by contrast, has no such constraints. Thus the odd logic that while a male student may be less qualified than a woman, he will certainly work as a professional after graduation, while the woman may not be able to do so.

Women's access to education began in the 1960s and has since provided Kuwaiti women with opportunities that have enabled them to become financially independent and pursue diverse careers. Women's contributions to the Kuwaiti labor force increased from 20 percent in 1985 to 40 percent in 2003,[9] with the majority of the increased number of female employees filling positions within the public sector. Women can be found in most professional fields including engineering, architecture, medicine, and law. Yet, they do not have full freedom to choose their professions; women are prohibited from working in the police, the army, and the judiciary.

Women in Kuwait generally receive equal pay for equal work in the public and private sectors. According to labor laws, a woman who performs the same work as a man must be paid equal remuneration. If a woman feels that she has been discriminated against, she may file a complaint directly to the administrative court or to the National Assembly's Human Rights Committee.

There are no laws prohibiting sexual harassment in the workplace. Women workers, particularly foreign women and domestic employees, are in urgent need of such laws.

Standard working hours for men apply equally to women, with the exclusion of night work. With the exception of a few professions and places of employment, women in Kuwait are forbidden to work at night, or in some cases after midnight. Employers are obliged to arrange transportation for women who work at night. These labor restrictions apply to both private and government offices, as well as jobs within the informal sector.

All working women are entitled to maternity leave for up to two months at full pay. They may receive an additional four months at half pay, provided they present a medical certificate declaring that their illness was a result of the pregnancy. Day care facilities for children aged three to six years are widely available and affordable in all parts of Kuwait; some are provided by the Kuwaiti government, others are privately run.

Advocacy on such concerns as the right to education, inheritance, and employment is strong. At the same time, groups of conservative Islamists have also been demanding that women "return to the household." Since 1990, in coalition with conservative tribalists, Islamists have successfully opposed all parliamentary initiatives to expand women's rights. They have blocked the passage of a women's suffrage bill and the admission of women to the military. In 1996, Islamists succeeded in passing a bill that obligates Kuwait University and post-secondary colleges to incorporate building changes to ensure gender segregation.

RECOMMENDATIONS

1. The government should ensure greater employment opportunities for all women in the labor market and allow Kuwaiti women to work as judges in the courts.
2. The government should set gender-specific hiring targets for government jobs.
3. The government should establish a mechanism to allow Kuwaiti women to file gender-based discrimination complaints against public or private actors and institutions.
4. Women's rights groups should be allowed to advocate on all issues related to women's economic rights and equal opportunity, including protection for domestic workers.

Political Rights and Civic Voice

Kuwait is a constitutional monarchy with a Cabinet and a National Assembly that is elected every four years. The parliament serves as a legislative body with the power to overturn the decrees issued by the Emir—the head of state. Males who are 21 and over and have been citizens for at least 20 years and are not members of the military are granted the right to vote and seek election to the National Assembly. This means that suffrage is restricted to 14 percent of the population.[10] There are no formal political parties; instead, there are quasi-political groups of Islamists (extreme conservatives) and liberals, who operate within voluntary organizations (NGOs) and are active in the National Assembly.

According to Kuwaiti Election Law 35/1962, women are not permitted to vote or run for election in the national legislature. Women are also forbidden to run for office or vote in the municipal council elections. In recent years, the Emir of Kuwait and the Cabinet have attempted to integrate women into the political system. In May 1999, during an interregnum between parliaments, the Emir promulgated a decree granting women the right to run for office and to vote in parliamentary and municipal elections. Yet, in November 1999, the parliament voted down the decree. In July 2003, Kuwaiti Prime Minister Shaikh Sabah Al Ahmed Al Sabah promised to submit to parliament a new bill to amend electoral laws. In October 2003, the government approved a bill that would grant women the right to vote and run in municipal council elections. However, the bill was rejected during the same year by the parliament.

Since the 1990s, Kuwaiti women have used every opportunity to bring their demands for political rights to the attention of the National Assembly. They have organized and held public demonstrations to protest against gender discrimination and have marched to the polling station to protest their lack of equal political rights during parliamentary elections.

While women's right to assemble is moderately respected by the Kuwaiti government, women's rights groups face structural restrictions on their ability to create and manage their organizations. Requests to establish NGOs must be made directly to the Ministry of Social Affairs and Labor. According to Association Law 24/1962, the ministry has full authority to license or terminate associations, as well as dissolve their elected boards. Voluntary associations are required to have an elected board, a written constitution, and a dues-paying membership. In 1993, the government dissolved all unlicensed associations. The Kuwait Human Rights Society, who had been waiting for a license since 1992, was finally officially licensed in August 2004. A license is required before an NGO can open an office or formally discuss rights issues with the government.[11]

Kuwaiti women have limited freedom of expression. The Printing and Publications Law 3/1961 deems it a criminal offense to criticize the Emir, publish materials offensive to Islam, or publish material that may incite violence, hatred, or dissent. Stiff penalties for violations of the press laws have contributed to increased self-censorship and an avoidance of controversial issues. In January 2000, charges were brought against two female authors for writing novels that allegedly contained improper and immoral language.

Women are not represented in Kuwait's judiciary. While they may hold positions as investigative judges, women are not permitted to serve as judges in court. However, Kuwaiti women do hold relatively senior positions within the ministries of Kuwait.

Formal political parties are banned in Kuwait, but political groups often operate informally as political organizations. The most prominent political groupings are the National Democratic Forum (NDF), the Islamic Constitutional Movement (ICM), and the Islamic Popular Alliance (IPA). Kuwaiti women are involved in all major political groups and occasionally serve as founding members or contributing board members. Women are not invited to fill leadership positions in Islamic organizations. They are active, however, in promoting these groups' ideologies and visions of an Islamic order—calling for the implementation of the rules of Shari'a and gender segregation in public places.

Kuwaiti women are involved in civic life issues and participate in mixed-gender professional clubs and societies as both members and board members.

Women also have the right to join unions and local cooperative stores, where they can vote and hold office.

While Kuwait does not have a freedom of information act, women do have some freedom to gain access to and use information to empower themselves in both their civil and political lives. Internet usage has increased among young women and is easily accessible for many at home, in offices, and in public cafes. The Internet has provided Kuwaiti women with a forum to air their views and freely communicate with others on a variety of issues.

RECOMMENDATIONS

1. The government and the parliament should amend Election Law 35 of 1962 to allow Kuwaiti women to vote and run for office in parliamentary and local elections.
2. The government should guarantee the right of political parties to exist, compete in elections, and conduct their internal affairs independent of the state.
3. The government should amend its Printing and Publications Law to allow greater freedom of expression and withdraw the provisions that allow for the criminal prosecution, imprisonment, and fining of authors and journalists.
4. The government should remove obstacles to the registration of nongovernmental organizations and permit them to work and advocate for democratic reforms and human rights, including women's rights.

Social and Cultural Rights

Kuwait has an extensive welfare system. The state also offers up-to-date health care services to all residents at minimal cost. Citizens are free to participate in community life and non-Kuwaitis enjoy the right to form their own cultural associations openly.

Women have some freedom to make independent decisions about their health and reproductive rights. While Kuwait does not have a government-sponsored family planning program, research has shown that the contraceptive needs of the majority of married women are adequately met.[12] Contraceptives are easily available and affordable; birth control pills and the IUD are available through government health services, and private pharmacies offer birth control pills without a prescription. Contraceptive use is significantly higher among educated Kuwaiti women. Those who disapprove of contraception in Kuwait tend to believe that family planning is forbidden by Islam.[13]

Abortion is prohibited and constitutes a criminal act. Under the penal code, any person "who supplies, or is instrumental in supplying a pregnant or non-pregnant woman with drugs or other harmful substances, with or without her consent, or who uses force or any other means to induce an abortion shall be liable to a penalty of up to 10 years' imprisonment." Doctors are often reluctant to perform abortions, even in cases in which the pregnancy is a serious threat to a woman's life, due to the strict penalties under Kuwait's penal code. The United Nations Human Rights Committee has recommended that the Kuwaiti government amend this law and make provisions for the protection of the right to life of pregnant women.[14]

Women have full and equal access to health care. Health care services at government-run clinics and hospitals are generally provided free of charge or at a low cost for all residents of Kuwait, including Kuwait's non-citizens and migrant workers. Since the mid-1990s, the government and women's groups have launched campaigns to raise women's awareness about female health issues like breast cancer and osteoporosis.

Although there are no reliable data available, women seem to be protected from harmful practices such as virginity tests and female genital mutilation. Early marriage has grown uncommon and cross-cousin marriages are no longer widely practiced.

Unmarried sons and daughters, regardless of their age, are expected to live with their families. Unlike foreign-born women who reside in Kuwait, a single Kuwaiti woman cannot rent her own dwelling. While such a policy is not enshrined in law, landlords often refuse to rent apartments to Kuwaiti women unless they can provide proof of marriage.

Housing is a serious problem for Kuwaiti women, particularly divorced women from low-income groups. Women are excluded from Kuwait's low-interest loan policy, which is an initiative provided to married men to encourage them to build their own homes. Kuwait's housing law also forbids Kuwaiti women from owning government-supplied or subsidized housing that is available to Kuwaiti men by virtue of their positions as *rab al'usra* (heads of families). The only exception to this law is for divorced women with children who can claim a rent allowance if they do not intend to remarry and have no one to support them. However, divorced women are expected to share the government-subsidized housing with their former husbands, who often force them to move out.

The government has been reluctant to address the problem of housing for women and has failed to offer satisfactory solutions. The state has constructed special apartment buildings to house divorced women and childless couples, but this has resulted in the isolation and marginalization of female heads of households.[15] Efforts to integrate divorced women into the society remain limited and lack a women's human rights perspective. In 1982, Kuwaiti women married to non-Kuwaiti men lost the right to own government housing; the National Assembly rejected a proposal that would have overturned this law in October 2003.

In recent years, Kuwait has witnessed an increase in the number of impoverished female heads of households. Many divorced women and Kuwaiti women married to bidun struggle to make ends meet, largely as a result of the discriminatory components of the state's welfare system. Kuwaiti women are entitled to welfare assistance in the form of monthly income support and rent subsidies, but only when they are able to provide evidence that they have no one to support them and are unemployed.[16] The state allocates child support benefits to the husband in divorce cases even when the mother has been granted custody of the children. Many men refuse to give financial support to their former wives even though the law requires it.

The media provide adequate coverage of women's concerns, and many women are employed in both print and electronic media. Growing numbers of Kuwaiti women work in the media as journalists, reporters, and editors. Women in Kuwait use the media as an influential tool to introduce change and to promote new roles for themselves. Liberal newspapers such *Al-Qabas,* *Al-Siyassah,* and the weekly political magazine *Al-Talia,* devote considerable space to the activities of liberal women's groups and their efforts to gain political rights. Islamist women's activities and views are covered more extensively in *Al-Watan* and *Al-Anba'.* Despite the increasing presence of both liberal and Islamist women in the press, women's images continue to be stereotyped in the media and in educational materials. Yet, overall, the media have contributed to the normalization of an ever-broadening range of public roles for women and to the rise of female public figures.

Women's rights activists have some freedom to advocate openly about the promotion and protection of women's rights in Kuwait. While Kuwaiti women's groups are able to work with international and regional organizations and organize and attend international conferences on women's rights, there are some limitations. Five licensed women's groups currently operate in Kuwait; all receive government subsidies for their running expenses. Women's NGOs cannot refuse funds from the government and cannot receive funds from donors outside the country. Membership is restricted to women; the groups largely comprise elite and professional women from the upper and middle classes. The economic and social problems of divorced and widowed women, as well as the plight of female migrant workers, are not often addressed in the groups' campaigns. Kuwait's government has to a great extent succeeded in co-opting women's groups, in the process transforming them from an independent voice for women's rights to a progovernment support network.

RECOMMENDATIONS

1. Government agencies responsible for law and order and health services should receive in-depth training on violence against women and children so that they are positioned to provide assistance and protection to victims of violence.

2. The government should protect the rights of divorced mothers and Kuwaiti women married to non-Kuwaiti men, to ensure that adequate social assistance is provided when needed.
3. The government should promote positive women's representation and participation in the media and reduce gender stereotypes in educational materials.

AUTHOR: Haya Al-Mughni is a Kuwaiti sociologist based in Kuwait. She is the author of Women in Kuwait: The Politics of Gender. *Ms. Al-Mughni currently works for a mobile telecommunications company in Kuwait.*

Notes

[1] *The World Factbook: Kuwait* (Springfield, VA: U.S. CIA, 2003).

[2] See Nathan J. Brown, "Kuwait (country)" (Microsoft Encarta Online Encyclopedia, 2004), http://encarta.msn.com.

[3] "Statistics of Kuwaiti Women Married to Non-Kuwaiti Men" (Kuwait City: Al-Qabas, Center of Information and Studies, file no. 1044035, 2003).

[4] Ibid.

[5] For more details on the status of *bidun* in Kuwait, see "Promises Betrayed: Denial of Rights of Bidun, Women, and Freedom of Expression," *Human Rights Watch* 12, 2(E) (October 2000): 25; see also, Mary Ann Tétreault and Haya al-Mughni, "Gender, Citizenship, and Nationalism in Kuwait," *British Journal of Middle Eastern Studies* 22, 1 & 2 (1995): 64–80.

[6] *Country Reports on Human Rights Practices–2003:* Kuwait (Washington, D.C.: U.S. Dept. of State, Bureau of Democracy, Human Rights, and Labor, 25 Feb. 2004), http://www.state.gov/g/drl/rls/hrrpt/2003/27931.htm.

[7] Ibid.

[8] *Arab Times*, 26 May 2004, 1.

[9] *Handbook of Statistics of the Population and Labor Force*, 24th ed. (Public Authority for Civil Information [PACI], 30 July 2003).

[10] *Country Reports on Human Rights Practices–2003: Kuwait* (U.S. Dept. of State).

[11] Ibid.

[12] See Nasra M. Shah, Makhdoom A. Shah, and Zoran Radovanovic, "Patterns of Desired Fertility and Contraceptive Use in Kuwait," *International Family Planning Perspectives* 24, 3 (August 1998), http://www.agi-usa.org/pubs/journals/2413398.html.

[13] Ibid.

[14] "Promises Betrayed," Human Rights Watch, op. cit.

[15] See Mary Ann Tetreault and Haya al-Mughni, "Modernization and Its Discontents: State and Gender in Kuwait," *Middle East Journal* 49, 3 (1995): 403–417.

[16] Ibid. and Haya al-Mughni and Mary Ann Tétreault. "Citizenship, Gender and the Politics of Quasi-States," in Suad Joseph, ed., *Gender and Citizenship in the Middle East* (New York: Syracuse University Press, 2000), 237–60.

Lebanon

by Zeina Zaatari

Population: 4,200,000
GDP Per Capita (PPP): $4,360
Economy: Mixed statist
Ranking on UN HDI: 80 out of 177
Polity: Presidential-parliamentary (military and partly foreign-occupied)
Literacy: Male 92.4% / Female 81.0%
Percent Women Economically Active: 30.3%
Date of Women's Suffrage: 1952
Women's Fertility Rate: 2.4
Percent Urban/Rural: Urban 88% / Rural 12%

Country Ratings for Lebanon
Nondiscrimination and Access to Justice: 2.8
Autonomy, Security, and Freedom of the Person: 2.9
Economic Rights and Equal Opportunity: 2.8
Political Rights and Civic Voice: 2.9
Social and Cultural Rights: 2.9
(Scale of 1 to 5: 1 represents the lowest and 5 the highest level of freedom women have to exercise their rights)

Introduction

Lebanon was established as a French mandate in 1920 and gained its independence in 1943. A long series of conflicts began in 1975,[1] with a civil war that continued erratically until after the 1989 Taif Peace Accord.[2] In 1976, the president of the republic invited Syrian forces to enter Lebanon as a peacekeeping mission to help expedite an end to the civil war, and Syria has since retained a military presence. Israel invaded Lebanon in 1978 and again in 1982. After partial withdrawal in 1985, Israel continued to occupy a portion of South Lebanon, "the Occupied Strip," until the resistance movement forced its evacuation in May of 2000.[3] Syria redeployed and withdrew some of its troops from Lebanon in 2004.[4]

Lebanon is a parliamentary republic in which the president, who is chief of state, governs the country's affairs, along with the prime minister, who acts as head of the government, and an executive cabinet. A unicameral National Assembly of 128 deputies is elected every four years by the people. The president is formally elected by the parliament every six years; the current incumbent, Emile Lahud, has been in office since November 24, 1998.

The French mandate government (the French High Commission) officially recognized 17 religious sects in 1936.[5] Today, Lebanon has 18 officially recognized religious sects[6] and 15 personal status codes and court systems that officiate over personal and family matters. Lebanon's political structure is sectarian, or consociational, in which particular quotas of religious sects inform the divisions of power. This practice was solidified in the constitutional amendments of the Taif Accord in 1990.[7] Each of the 18 officially recognized religious sects is represented in parliament and in the ministries. By custom, the president of the republic is Maronite Christian, the prime minister is Sunni Muslim, and the speaker of the house is a Muslim Shi'a. The division of power and the quota system are supposedly in accordance with a census conducted by France in 1932,[8] which resulted in special rights for the Maronites, who were allied with France. The current political structure is not capable of adapting to changes in demographic or power relationships.

The population of Lebanon is estimated to be 4.2 million but many argue that the numbers are much higher. Lebanon's population includes a significant number of Palestinian refugees, as well as Armenians and minority Kurds. While most Kurds and Armenians have been granted Lebanese citizenship, the majority of Palestinians maintain refugee status.

Most of the country's infrastructure was destroyed during Lebanon's many wars; a reconstruction/rehabilitation project has been under way since the end of the civil war. However, 15 years of efforts to rebuild and recreate Lebanon's early days as a tourism and commercial hub, led by Prime Minister Rafiq Hariri, have resulted in a $40 billion foreign debt.[9] Lebanon has a GDP of 19 billion and ranks 80 out of 177 countries on the Human Development Index.[10] Increasing gaps between a rich minority and an increasingly poor majority have diminished the middle class and perpetuated the migration of young adults seeking employment. In 1999, an estimated 28 percent of the population was living below the poverty line, with an overall unemployment rate of 20 to 25 percent.[11]

While Lebanon's constitution guarantees equality to all citizens, the country's laws are multifaceted and tend to discriminate against women in practice. General patriarchal attitudes in Lebanese society also make it difficult for women to obtain upper-level positions in the public and private sectors and challenge women's efforts to advance their overall status. Nevertheless, women are active in most—including the economic, political, and social—aspects of Lebanese life. Women's associations and nongovernmental organizations (NGOs) advocate for the greater participation of women in the government and society, as well as lobby for increased human rights and nondiscriminatory laws and protections. NGOs also work to hold the government accountable to its obligations under CEDAW and other international treaties to which it is a signatory.[12] While the president and prime minister attend many women's conferences, their commitments to women have yet to evolve into material changes or actual implementation. The government has not made noticeable, practical efforts to assist rural women who suffer disproportionately from poverty and have little awareness of their rights due to a high rate of illiteracy.[13]

Nondiscrimination and Access to Justice

Article 7 of Lebanon's constitution asserts, "All Lebanese are equal under the law, enjoying equally civil and political rights, and performing duties and public responsibility without any discrimination among them."[14] While the spirit of Lebanon's constitution guarantees women's equality before the law, no article or clause explicitly prohibits gender discrimination. As a result, many laws adopted under the constitution fail to ensure protections against gender discrimination, and women are denied equal rights. For example, earlier governments restricted women's political rights until women successfully organized and petitioned for equality—resulting in the decree of December 1952. The Women's Political Rights Agreement now ensures that, "women have the right to vote in all elections and under conditions that equate them to men without any discrimination."[15] Lebanon's labor laws are an exception, in that they clearly indicate that discrimination based on gender is unacceptable and punishable by law.[16]

Citizenship Law No. 15 and the Nationality Law govern Lebanese citizenship. The first article of the citizenship law states that citizenship is inherited through the father or acquired by birth on Lebanese territory.[17] Citizenship laws prioritize patrilineal decent, and a Lebanese woman who marries a foreign national cannot pass her citizenship on to her husband or the children of this union. A Lebanese man, on the other hand, can pass his nationality on to his foreign wife and children.[18] A naturalized wife retains the right to pass Lebanese citizenship on to her children only in the event of the death of her husband or if the child's father is unknown or does not possess a nationality.[19] This limit on transference of citizenship affects the children's rights to work, own property, and access governmental resources. Such limitations can be detrimental to a woman's well being, especially in cases of divorce or widowhood.

Lebanon's judicial system is made up of four courts of cassation, a Constitutional Council that rules on the constitutionality of laws, and the Supreme Council. Most women have equal access to all levels of the courts and are entitled to equal representation. However, due to the country's consecutive wars and the dominance of family structures, women's overall access to the judicial system is occasionally restricted. Women's access to justice can be limited by a variety of factors, including socioeconomic status, education, patronage ties, nationality, age, or gender.

A woman's testimony in civil court is generally considered equal to that of a man's;[20] this is not the case in the Sunni and Shi'a religious courts, where the testimony of two women is required to match the value of one man's testimony. While women have the right to bring lawsuits in both the civil and religious courts,[21] women are prohibited from serving as lawyers and judges within the religious court system.

Women and men are treated equally in most sections of the Lebanese criminal and penal codes, with the exception of laws that address adultery, violence against women in the name of "honor," abortion, rape, and prostitution. Articles 487 to 489 criminalize adultery but discriminate between men and women in terms of the conditions of the crime, proof, and sentencing. A woman can be found guilty of adultery if the act takes place inside or outside her home, whereas the man will only be punished for adulterous acts that take place inside his home or when his adulterous relationship is public knowledge. While a man's sentence ranges from one month to a year, a woman's sentence for adultery is three months to two years' incarceration. A woman is required to have the testimony of witnesses to prove her innocence, whereas a man can be proven innocent based on lack of material evidence, such as incriminating letters or documents. In general, however, few adultery cases are actually handled in the courts. Lebanese law is different from public sentiment; adultery is seen as a moral crime, not a legal crime punishable in a court of law. Adultery may lead to divorce, family quarrels, and disagreements, and in a few cases, the murder of the woman in the name of family "honor."

Law No. 562 allows for a man to receive a lighter sentence in the event that he surprises his wife, sister, or any female relative in the act of adultery or unlawful copulation (mostly sex without marriage) and proceeds to (or attempts to) kill or injure one or both of the participants without prior intent.[22] Before the amendments of March 20, 1999—largely due to the advocacy efforts of women's and human rights groups—this law had allowed for lighter sentencing for any man who committed a crime of "honor" against a woman. While the amended law no longer allows for premeditation and now requires the element of surprise and emotion, the law remains discriminatory against women. The current wording of the law still enables lawyers to manipulate the defense, does not equally guarantee similar rights for women who commit the same crime, promotes violence against women, and contradicts both the Lebanese constitution and CEDAW.

Lebanon ratified the Convention on the Elimination of all Forms of Discrimination against Women (CEDAW) on April 21, 1997, with reservations on Articles 9 (2), 16 (1) (c) (d) (f) and (g) and 29 (2).[23] Article 9 of CEDAW addresses equal rights for men and women with respect to citizenship and nationality, and Article 16 commits the state to eliminate discrimination against women in matters of the family and marriage.

A large number of women's groups are active in Lebanon. While a few are government-associated entities, the majority of women's groups are nongovernmental organizations (NGOs) that operate nationally and regionally within the country. The National Committee on Lebanese Women (NCLW)[24] is a national organization, under the control of the government, which was created by a governmental decree on December 12, 1996, to further implement the Beijing Platform for Action. This entity consists of a board of directors appointed by the cabinet, with the president directly appointed by the president of Lebanon. Since its inception, the position of committee president has been occupied by the country's first lady, while the wife of the head of parliament has held the position of committee vice president. The NCLW has no legislative or executive powers, however, and much of its work is restricted to conferences and presenting recommendations to government officials. The Women's Affairs Bureau, an office in the Department of Family Affairs that is housed in the Ministry of Social Affairs, is the only other governmental entity that addresses women's issues.

As a result of the country's history of conflict and wars, many women's NGOs have prioritized their missions toward the economic and social needs of women in rural areas and women with little access to resources. These organizations work toward achieving women's rights on the ground. A large number of women's organizations also focus on lobbying and aim to research and publish their findings on women to influence policy makers and the judicial system. The Lebanese Women's Council (LWC), established in the 1950s, serves as an umbrella entity for more than 140 organizations. Other organizations work to monitor Lebanese women's status, such as the NGO Committee for the Follow-up to Beijing, the League for Lebanese Women's Rights, and the Institute for Women's Studies in the Arab World.[25] These organizations have helped to raise gender awareness through conferences, media campaigns, and articles in national newspapers. Several Palestinian women's groups operate outside and within refugee camps; they focus their work largely on eradicating poverty, raising awareness, and vocational training of women and men.

The Lebanese government generally supports women's entities. Organizations are licensed with relative ease, and government officials attend and participate in their conferences. The Ministry of Social Services works rather closely with some of the organizations, specifically those groups involved with day care or elementary schools.[26] Nevertheless, while the government does not obstruct the work of women's groups, it does not provide any initiatives, funding,[27] resources, or material encouragement. Reports of the Ministry of Treasury indicate that spending on entities that could positively impact women's lives is minimal.[28] While women's organizations operating in Beirut are usually well connected with other UN entities and to international sources of funding, those working in rural areas increasingly face problems securing funds for their projects.

RECOMMENDATIONS

1. The government should amend the constitution to include a clause that ensures gender equality in all rights and obligations under the constitution.
2. The government should repeal all discriminatory clauses within the criminal and penal code, particularly laws dealing with adultery and crimes against women in the name of "honor," to ensure women's equal treatment before the law.
3. The government should amend citizenship and naturalization laws to enable children of any Lebanese man or woman to receive their right to citizenship.
4. The government should remove all reservations to CEDAW and take steps to implement it locally.

Autonomy, Security, and Freedom of the Person

The Lebanese constitution guarantees the freedom of creed to all its citizens. Article 9 of the Lebanese constitution (1926) states, "There shall be absolute freedom of conviction. While acknowledging the Most High, the State respects all creeds and religions. It guarantees and protects the free exercise of all forms of worship, on condition that public order is not interfered with. It also guarantees that the personal status and religious interests of the entire population are respected."[29]

All Lebanese citizens are assigned to the religious sect of their father upon birth, which they can change at a later age if they so wish. While groups are permitted to practice religions other than the 18 officially recognized religions, they must officially be in accordance with the rules of one of the 15 personal status codes in order to engage in such procedures as marriage, divorce, inheritance, or burial. Therefore, individuals and religious groups may face restrictions on their right to practice their religion freely; religious groups who believe in equal status between men and women, for example, may be forced to conform to a court's gender-discriminatory laws.[30] Civil marriage is not allowed in Lebanon. However, Lebanon does recognize civil marriages that have taken place outside the country; in the case of disputes relating to such marriages, the laws of the particular country in which the ceremony took place will be applied to resolve the marriage, divorce, and/or custody details.[31]

Women's freedom of movement is not legally restricted in Lebanon but may be restricted in practice. While married women are not legally required to obtain their husband's permission in order to get a passport or travel abroad, a husband or father can petition immigration authorities, airport officials, or court officials to stop his wife or daughter from leaving the country. Social customs and cultural traditions also affect women's freedom to travel outside the country or to fill employment positions that require late hours or living away from their families. A woman's family will often collectively make the decisions regarding her movement. Age and socioeconomic background are additional factors that may contribute to a woman's degree of personal freedom and autonomy. There are no legal avenues for men or women to file complaints against restrictive family decisions regarding their movement.

It is difficult to assess or generalize women's treatment under Lebanon's personal status codes, with 15 separate codes and court systems officiating over personal and family matters. Personal status codes in Lebanon preside over marriage, divorce, guardianship, child custody, adoption, and inheritance. However, Lebanon's religious courts lack executive powers to implement their decisions, and inefficient police may not always enforce court decisions favorable to women.

Gender differentiation, and in some cases gender discrimination, can be found in most, if not all of the personal status codes that govern Lebanese lives. Some personal status codes consider the testimony of one man to be equal to that of two women. Muslim inheritance laws in Lebanon also discriminate on the basis of gender, providing two shares to the male heir and one share to the female heir. Men and women also receive differential treatment in the courts in matters of marriage. The accepted, or minimum age of marriage varies, but all courts agree that this age should be different for males and females.[32] In the Druze personal status codes,[33] the minimum age for marriage is 18 for males and 17 for females (with the absolute minimum of 16 for males and 15 for females accepted only by an official statement from the court). In the Eastern Catholic personal status codes,[34] Law 75 indicates that the minimum age for marriage is 16 for males and 14 for females.[35] The minimum marriage age for Shi'a is puberty, or with judicial permission, 15 for girls and 9 for boys.[36]

All personal status codes in Lebanon require the consent of both parties in marriage, even in cases in which a guardian has been appointed. While it is not customary, a woman and a man can marry without a guardian, as long as they are of maturity (18 years or older). The religious judge is required to hear verbal consent from both parties and receive the signature of the couple, along with their guardians and witnesses. Couples can agree to place conditions into the marriage contract within the Muslim courts, which may include agreements on monetary compensation, a wife's right to work outside the home, divorce, and custody rights. Legally, the husband has no right to forbid his wife from working; however, some Christian courts in Lebanon hold that the man must approve his wife's decision to work.[37]

Some of the laws in Lebanon's Personal Status Codes actually work to a woman's advantage. Lebanon's Personal Status laws that are applied in Muslim courts clearly state that a woman's property and earnings are her own and she is not required to spend them on the household or the family. As the husband is perceived to be the breadwinner of the family, his inability or refusal to financially provide for his family is grounds for divorce. Lebanon's personal status laws that are applied in Christian courts indicate that it is the mother's duty to nurse her child. For instance, the Armenian Orthodox court indicates, "a mother has the obligation to nurse her child from the moment of his birth and up to two years."[38] Muslim courts in Lebanon, on the other hand, recognize that this is a privilege, and a mother is entitled to compensation or pay for these services from the father.

Men and women are also treated differently under the various personal status codes in matters of divorce. Many of the Christian courts do not allow divorce, while those that do, permit it only under specified conditions. These conditions usually require proof of adultery or abuse. The Greek Orthodox personal status code, for example, declares that divorce will be granted only under conditions in which the husband can prove in court that his wife was not a virgin when he married her, that she destroyed a pregnancy willfully (either by contraceptive methods or through actual abortion), disobeyed him and left the house to visit associates without his knowledge, or refused to live in her husband's home.[39] A woman married under Muslim laws in Lebanon faces hardships and years of litigation if she seeks a divorce against her husband's wishes. On the other hand, under the same laws, a Muslim man can divorce his wife easily, verbally, and without needing to provide any reasons.

For the most part, kinship, family, and religion tend to play a greater role in governing the lives and affairs of Lebanon's residents than the country's laws and courts. Many individuals are not aware of the laws that govern their unions or individual rights. It is only in such cases as a troublesome marriage or a death without a will in a conflict-ridden family that people are faced with dilemmas that require the intervention of the law. Families will often attempt to resolve disputes through kin networks, informal channels, and mediators before taking the issue to a court of law. It is even general practice within Sunni and Shi'a religious courts for the judge to mandate a period of mediation, requiring the litigants to try, through relatives and friends, to resolve a conflict or reach an acceptable compromise. Only after all these procedures are exhausted will a religious judge issue a sentence. This process of justice sometimes benefits women who may receive help from their relatives, but it can also be a disadvantage if a woman's conflict stems from her family or if she is unable to seek outside help as a result of her family's constraints.

It is both illegal and socially unacceptable for women to be held in slavery or slavery-like conditions. It is, for example, very difficult for parents to marry off their daughters without their consent or to keep them hidden behind closed doors. Lebanese law protects both men and women from being detained or held against their will. Article 8 of the constitution guarantees personal freedom under the law, making it unlawful for anyone to be imprisoned or arrested except within the boundaries of the law. Article 569 of the penal code addresses the deprivation of liberty of any individual.[40] Nevertheless, the trafficking of women does occur. Women from Ethiopia, Sri Lanka, and the Philippines are contracted for employment as domestic workers in Lebanon. These women may be subjected to extreme working conditions or physical abuse. Women from Russia, Romania, Ukraine, Moldova, and Bulgaria are also trafficked into the country for commercial sexual exploitation, but in smaller numbers.[41] The Lebanese government has taken some preventive measures to combat trafficking, but it has not made sufficient efforts to prosecute traffickers or protect women victims.

Article 14 of the Lebanese constitution states that the home is a sacred space, and no one is allowed entry except through legally prescribed instruments. While this law intends to protect a family's right to privacy, its implementation can have negative repercussions for women. The general sentiment in Lebanon, which is reflected in the implementation of this law, is that the state has no right to interfere in matters of the home or in conflicts between a husband and wife; therefore, a woman is left totally unprotected by the law in her own home. This law can also affect other family members and non-family members who reside in the home, such as domestic workers. There are several concerns surrounding the freedom of mobility and travel of female foreign domestic workers.[42] Research indicates that violations of human rights and abuses are common, yet the state has not established mechanisms to protect victims and prosecute offenders.

The penal code guards against torture and unlawful arrest and detention of all subjects of the state. Article 513 punishes employers, prison guards, and officials for crimes committed against prisoners, detainees, or any of their family members.[43] Despite the laws, violations against both women and men in prisons and detention centers do occur. There is no evidence however, to indicate differential gender treatment between men and women regarding arrest, detention, or exile.

Domestic violence has increasingly become a topic of discussion in conferences and the media over the last eight years.[44] Both Muslim and Christian courts in Lebanon recognize a husband's physical abuse of his wife as grounds for divorce or separation. While some still consider the topic to be taboo, spaces are continuing to open for women to discuss, organize, and seek help for domestic violence. A first-of-its-kind open forum session, the Women's Court, was held in Beirut in 1995 for women to discuss the issue of domestic violence and to give their personal testimonies as victims. The forum was organized by several local and regional women's NGOs as one of the follow-up steps to the Beijing platform. Another NGO, the Lebanese Council to Resist Violence Against Women (LCRVAW),[45] was founded in Beirut in March 1997 to monitor violence against women, disseminate information, network with other organizations, provide free legal aid and counseling, and lobby the government. They managed to install the first domestic violence hotline, and in 1996, successfully established The Permanent Arab Court to Resist Violence Against Women, a symbolic popular court where women victims of violence could present testimonies.

The Lebanese government, on the other hand, has not taken any major or concrete steps to change the laws or policies that govern the issue of domestic violence against women, and it has failed to provide resources or funding to agencies that work to promote domestic violence awareness. According to 1997 police statistics, 1,302 incidents of violence against women were reported in the country, although the percentage of abuse cases that could be classified as domestic was not available.[46] Reporting of domestic abuse is still relatively low.[47] Various NGOs counsel women victims of violence and a few have set up shelters.

Lebanese laws that criminalize rape tend to be lenient toward men and do not apply to marital relationships.[48] Marital rape is not considered a crime in Lebanon. Women's groups are actively advocating for changes to laws that provide weak sentences for perpetrators of sex crimes, such as Article 522, which declares that the state will not prosecute a rapist and will nullify his conviction if the rapist marries his victim. The sentence for rape, according to Article 503, is forced labor for at least five years or for at least seven years if the victim is under 15 years of age.[49] Article 518 sentences a man who seduces a virgin into intercourse with the intent of marriage and then recants to six months in jail and/or a fine. Little research has been done on the prevalence of rape or marital rape in Lebanese society.

RECOMMENDATIONS

1. The government should amend all laws that do not currently protect women from all violence, including eliminating legal provisions that allow reduced sentences for abusers who marry their victims or claim honor as justification for their crimes.
2. The government should enact a law against domestic violence and take concrete steps to ensure implementation.

3. The government and women's NGOs should work to create broader societal awareness about women's legal rights, including the rights of foreign domestic workers and the elimination of violence against women.

Economic Rights and Equal Opportunity

Economic conditions in Lebanon have continued to deteriorate since the end of the civil war in 1990, and high rates of migration for employment and education among Lebanon's youth have been reported. While women have full access to educational institutions under the law, as well as full rights to engage in business and own property, they continue to be poorly represented in the labor force due to social customs and gender discrimination.

Act No. 380 of 1994,[50] provides married and single women, 18 years and older, the full capacity to engage in commerce and to own and dispose of property at will.[51] Most of Lebanon's personal status codes allow for the wife to keep all assets acquired prior to the marriage, as well as have independent ownership and usage of her assets during the marriage. In 1959, an equal inheritance law was passed that requires all citizens, with the exception of the Muslim sects, to abide by equal inheritance provisions for males and females. The inheritance laws of the Sunni and Shi'a religious sects of Lebanon usually designate one share for daughters and two shares for sons.[52]

Education remains a very important avenue for social mobility in Lebanon and is emphasized by families across the socioeconomic, sectarian, and regional divides. Elementary education in Lebanon was made compulsory and free in 1998 under Law 34/59.[53] In accordance with the Department of Statistics (1997), the percentage of both boys and girls enrolled in elementary and middle school is high, and there is little variation between genders.[54] The years of war and conflict, however, have left their mark on the public educational system, which generally benefits the lower socioeconomic level of the population. Private schooling provides students with a greater competitive edge in gaining access to higher education and employment. In 2004, 81 percent of women age 15 and above were literate, compared to 92.4 percent of men in the same age category.[55]

War and economic crises tend to increase families' needs for working hands. It is common for boys in the intermediate level of school to leave education in search of work or vocational training. Girls who stay in school tend to continue their education as an alternative to early marriage, which is common among poorer families. Palestinian refugees, especially those residing in refugee camps, generally attend United Nations Relief and Works Agency (UNRWA)–funded schools, whose standards have been on the decline. The government has not taken any measures to ensure that students stay in school, and there are no specific laws that address gender discrimination within the educational system. Various women's organizations are working to improve literacy rates through adult literacy workshops and classes for females in rural areas where the need is greatest.

Women's participation in Lebanon's labor force has generally been on the rise (from 16.2 percent in 1990 to 20.3 percent in 2000).[56] Many economists attribute the increase in women's employment to harsh economic conditions and the dire need of their families, although more single women are in the work force than married.[57] Social customs and traditions in Lebanon seem to be more influential than economic restrictions on women's career choices. At the university level, higher rates of females enroll in what are considered to be more traditionally female fields, such as the social sciences and humanities, while men tend to enroll in more traditionally male fields, such as engineering. While the participation of women in some labor fields, like construction, is less socially acceptable, no fields at the university level or in the labor force are off limits to women. In fact, gender crossover seems to be on the rise within many professions.[58]

On May 26, 2000, Article 26 of Lebanon's Labor Law was amended,[59] largely due to the advocacy efforts of women's groups and unions. Article 26 now states that it is forbidden for the employer to discriminate based on gender between female and male workers in terms of type of work, salary or wage, employment, promotion, progress, professional rehabilitation and training, or dress code.[60] While women may now sue their employers for gender discrimination, lawsuits of this type are rare. Women will often seek alternative avenues for help or justice, such as appealing to employment heads or governmental officials with whom they have connections, rather than the courts.

Lebanese labor laws provide women with a number of gender-specific protections in the workplace. Article 28 specifies that private sector employers are required to give an expectant mother seven weeks of maternity leave with full pay, and Article 38 was amended to provide women employees in the public sector with 60 days' maternity leave.[61] It is not permissible for employers to fire a mother who is on maternity leave, and a termination of work notice cannot be rendered to a pregnant employee starting from the fifth month of her pregnancy or during her maternity leave.[62] Female employees are entitled to equal compensation with men for termination of service. Labor laws also ensure certain family benefits for employees. Employee compensation[63] is provided for every child, regardless of the employee's gender. However, inequalities in employment benefits do exist. Male employees are always entitled to compensation for their non-working wives, but female employees are only entitled to such compensation if their husbands are deceased or suffer from an illness that prevents them from working.

Public awareness of sexual harassment in the workplace has increased, as the topic has received more coverage in Lebanese television programs and newspapers. While there are laws to address physical violence against women outside the home, no specific laws protect women from harassment in the workplace. Women's NGOs are working to pressure the government to create these needed laws.

Lebanon has a large number of Palestinian refugees residing within its territory.[64] The majority of refugees live in camps dispersed throughout Lebanon, with a higher concentration in the south and in the suburbs of Beirut. Lebanon's Palestinian population increasingly lives under extreme circumstances of poverty and economic duress.

Palestinian women in Lebanon are very active and have created organizations to help support their families and advocate for their rights. Some of these groups, such as the General Union of Palestinian Women, work to promote vocational training, social and medical awareness, and economic development among Palestinian refugee women.[65] However, since the Oslo Accord, these organizations and the larger refugee population have suffered additional economic setbacks as a result of a lack of funding and support from Arab and foreign nations.

Lebanese laws that refuse citizenship, or provisional citizenship, to Palestinian refugees have served to restrict Palestinian efforts to gain employment. In addition to a lack of citizenship, Palestinian refugees face further impediments to employment, with government-imposed fees on both the institutions that attempt to hire Palestinians and the workers themselves. Workers are required to pay large fees for a work permit, as they are considered foreign subjects in Lebanon. One effect of state-imposed labor restrictions has been that Palestinian women have been pushed into the informal sector of the economy.

Several women's organizations in Lebanon actively work to promote women's labor rights. One such organization is the Association of Working Women of Lebanon and Women's Rights Committee. Their work focuses on advocacy and social awareness campaigns to ensure that Lebanon complies with its commitments to CEDAW and ILO treaties. Women participate as members of unions and labor associations but rarely fill leadership positions. While union membership laws do not discriminate against women, unions do not have initiatives to encourage women's participation in union organizing or in the labor force. Lebanon's unions also lack initiatives that call for gender-specific laws[66] and policies to protect the rights of women workers.

RECOMMENDATIONS

1. The government should create a monitoring body to record and research gender discrimination in the labor market.

2. The government should enable the judiciary and executive system to prosecute those who discriminate against women in the private and public
sectors.
3. The government should address the rights of Palestinian refugees to have
decent living and employment opportunities.
4. The government should enact and implement laws to ensure that foreign
women workers are not trafficked or abused.

Political Rights and Civic Voice

Political and civic rights in Lebanon are guaranteed by the constitution. However, violations of these rights do occur, often under the cover of new laws
and decrees. A ban on public demonstrations,[67] for example, was put in place
in 1996 by the government and was aimed at weakening labor union organizing.[68] Curtailment of freedom of speech and new restrictive media laws
enacted in the 1990s led to the arrest of several journalists who had addressed
taboo topics such as Syria's involvement in Lebanese domestic affairs. Syria
plays a significant role in Lebanon's internal and external politics.

Lebanon's constitution guarantees freedom of assembly and expression.
Article 13 states: "Freedom of speech and of writing, freedom of the press,
freedom of assembly and freedom of association shall be guaranteed within
the limits laid down by law."[69] Women have equal rights to peaceful assembly
and can freely advocate for any cause. Since 1997, the Lebanese Council to
Resist Violence Against Women has organized several marches on International Women's Day. Women's groups such as the Lebanese Women's Council
have also successfully organized national and regional conferences. While
women have the right to assemble and to organize, the government provides
little aid in terms of resources or funding for these efforts.

Lebanon's history of conflict has resulted in a political arena that is almost
exclusively dominated by a small population of elite families. This political
exclusivity, in combination with restrictive societal norms and beliefs concerning women's gender roles, has resulted in a low percentage of women
politicians. While women have the right to vote and run for elections, a glass
ceiling exists for female employment in both elective and appointive public
office. To address the low rate of women's participation in politics and government, the Lebanese Women's Council (LWC) organized a conference in
1998. Along with other women's NGOs, the LWC proposed a quota system
to the government to ensure women's equal representation in elections. The
government has yet to follow up on this recommendation.

In the year 2000, 68 female judges served in Lebanon's judicial courts out
of a total of 364, while women filled 6 of the 35 positions in the Administrative and Supreme courts.[70] Only one female judge, in the Anglican court,

served among the numerous religious courts in Lebanon, as the position of judge is primarily restricted to men in the religious circuits.

Representation of women in the ministries and parliament is low. Only 26 women competed in parliamentary elections between the years 1953 and 2000.[71] Currently there are 3 women in parliament out of a total of 128 members, 2 female ambassadors out of 53, 3 directors-general out of 22, 2 women mayors, and 2 women ministers.[72] Women also hold less than 1 percent of total municipal council seats. However, recent municipal elections (2004) witnessed an increase in the number of women running for office independently and on coalition lists. The Lebanese Women's Council has tried to promote and support women candidates running for election but with little success. One leading belief within Lebanese society is that politics are a dirty business, involving men fighting for power and control and thus not a very appropriate place for women.

Women are members of political parties in Lebanon but rarely achieve decision-making positions or leadership roles. Despite heavy constraints on their access to upper-level positions, however, Lebanese women have found many alternative avenues through which they have participated in building their society, impacted social change, and fulfilled their desires for activism. For example, women have ample space for participating in civil society. The plethora of women's organizations, as well as women's participation in other groups focused on such issues as the environment, development, children and the family, and poverty eradication indicate women's interests and deep commitments toward the improvement of their society. Even within conservative circles, women can easily extend their mother/nurturer role from the domain of the interior or the home to the domain of the exterior or the civil sphere.[73]

Women generally have access to information in order to empower their lives and decisions. This access, however, may be affected by their location (rural or urban) and their socioeconomic and educational background, as well as the type of information they may need.

RECOMMENDATIONS

1. The government should establish an independent monitoring body of experts to help formulate policies and procedures that ensure women's equitable representation in elections, political parties, and state appointments.

2. The government should provide special funds and assistance to women politicians and women's NGOs to increase women's participation in public life.

3. The government should support and facilitate civil society groups and the media to initiate public education campaigns that would increase social acceptance of women's involvement in politics and civil society.

Social and Cultural Rights

Women and men have equal access to available health care in Lebanon. The country has both private and public medical institutions, with many free or low-cost clinics that are run by either private entities or by the Ministry of Social Services. Community health clinics and Family Planning Association centers are available to women in rural and urban settings. Women are not required to seek permission from their husbands for any medical procedure.[74]

Lebanon's Family Planning Association works in conjunction with the Ministry of Social Services and has centers in various parts of the country, both rural and urban. It provides women with information on how to plan their families, as well as information on contraceptives. Several fertility studies[75] have demonstrated that women in Lebanon are aware of various contraceptive methods, even if they do not use them. There are many social taboos[76] surrounding the use of contraceptives for single women, as high value is placed on a woman's virginity. The prevalence of contraceptive use among married women seems to be heavily influenced by the couple's religious beliefs, level of education, and urban or rural status. Some reports indicate that single motherhood is becoming a choice on the rise in Beirut.[77]

Abortion is generally permitted only under specific circumstances in which it is necessary to save the mother's life. According to Article 541 of the penal code, self-aborting a fetus or consensually having an abortion is considered a misdemeanor, which can carry a sentence of six months to three years' imprisonment. Performing an abortion without a woman's consent is considered a crime, and an abortion that leads to the woman's death is considered a felony.[78] Despite the laws, an investigative report for *The Daily Star*[79] claims that abortion is available on demand in an underground industry that involves an unofficial network of doctors, where women have little difficulty tapping into its resources.[80] There are no available statistics on either the number of abortions that actually take place in Lebanon or the health risks involved for women.[81]

Women have the right to own housing and the right to choose their place of residence. Traditionally, both male and female children live with their parents until they are married. However, with increasing numbers of students moving to Beirut to attend universities or to gain employment, the number of single males and females who rent their own housing has increased. While this pattern is gaining social acceptance, it is often easier for sons to convince their families of this housing choice than it is for daughters.[82] Cohabitation[83] between unmarried couples, particularly in Beirut, is another increasing trend among the younger generation; however, social acceptance is limited, and living together before marriage tends to occur only in urban areas. There are no restrictions on women's abilities to rent or buy housing in large cities. Nevertheless, some landlords choose not to rent to unmarried couples or single women.

Women actively participate in Lebanon's community life through both established organizations and informal social networking systems with family and neighbors. Women influence policy through their memberships in women's associations and civil associations, as well as through their participation in local municipal committees, religious associations, and teachers' unions. Rural women often participate in church groups and *Husainiyyat*[84] as a form of community involvement. While women's abilities to influence major decisions are often restricted as a result of their gender, older women, especially those who have passed their childbearing age, can have significant power and influence in rural communities.

Women's groups have launched brief campaigns against the objectification of women in the advertising industry, but little else has been done to improve women's overall representation in Lebanon's media. Women's opportunities to fill key production and decision-making positions in the media are limited. According to the National Committee on Lebanese Women (NCLW), large numbers of females are graduating in media studies, but they comprise only 33.3 percent of those employed in the field.[85] Mona Ziade, news editor at *The Daily Star* in Lebanon, has commented that women's coverage of politics and other serious issues is fairly recent and continues to raise male suspicions.[86]

Lebanese media tend to be dominated by political analysis and game shows, with very little focus on women's issues. However, increasing numbers of local TV stations (like NTV, LBC, and *Al-Manar*), newspapers (like *An-Nahar* and *As-Safir*), and Arab satellite channels (including *Al-Jazeera*, NBN, and *Al-Arabiyya*) are broadcasting programs that directly address women's issues.[87] The all-male National Council for Media was created in 1996. It does not provide any gender-specific guidelines or policies for Lebanon's media institutions.

Women disproportionately suffer from poverty in Lebanon.[88] According to the Department of Statistics, the proportion of female-headed households in Lebanon was estimated at 12.5 percent in 1998.[89] The number of such households is on the rise due to the large numbers of men needing to migrate for work. The poorest of the female heads of households are widows. The government does not provide any kind of financial, legal, or social help to households that have lost the male income provider due to death or desertion and has done little to help rural women meet their needs. The disparity between the working wages of men and women is significant, with the largest wage gap existing between men and women in the agricultural field; women are not often recognized as farmers or peasants but as unpaid helpers. The average income of women working in agriculture was found to be about half of the average income of a male in the same field (1998).[90]

Women's organizations and other human rights groups are working in all parts of the country to improve women's status and to increase women's empowerment. Several changes have occurred in Lebanon's society and laws as a result of the advocacy of women's groups. Nevertheless, NGOs have the ability to organize and work freely but not always effectively. Competition for foreign funding and media attention often forces women's groups to compete rather than collaborate on projects, thus deflecting energies away from effective advocacy for women's rights.

RECOMMENDATIONS

1. The government should take steps to ensure equal gender representation within government-run media outlets and modify media regulations to ensure women's equal participation in private media companies.
2. The government should compile gender-disaggregated statistics on the problem of poverty and work to strengthen economic opportunities for impoverished women.
3. The government should investigate violations of labor laws in the agriculture sector and their adverse effects on women farmers.
4. The government should increase public spending on health and work to provide equal access to health care for all women.

AUTHOR: Dr. Zeina Zaatari is from South Lebanon. She received her Ph.D. in Anthropology at the University of California at Davis and was a lecturer at the University of California at Davis and at the Women's Studies Program at California State University, San Francisco. Dr. Zaatari has conducted field work in South Lebanon and is currently working on her manuscript, Women Activists of South Lebanon: Nationalism, Motherhood and Subjectivity. *Dr. Zaatari works as the Program Officer for the Middle East and North Africa Region at the Global Fund for Women in San Francisco.*

Notes

[1] The beginnings of the civil war pitted a coalition of Lebanese Muslim and leftist militias aligned with Palestinian guerrilla groups against an array of Maronite-oriented, right wing militias bent on preserving Christian political privileges. In its later years the war lost much of its sectarian character, with the bloodiest outbreaks of fighting taking place mainly within the Shiite, Christian, and Palestinian communities.

[2] The Taif Accord (a plan put forward by the Arab League) was signed by Lebanese parliamentarians at a meeting in the city of Taif in Saudi Arabia to put an end to the civil war, disarm militias, and create basic changes in the political structure.

3 Israel continues to occupy several villages of Lebanon (Shib'a Farms) deemed to be of strategic military significance until today.

4 15,000 Syrian troops remain in Lebanon and Syria has considerable weight in Lebanese affairs.

5 Amal Abu Rafeh, *Women in the Lebanese Legislation: Theory and Practice* (Beirut, American University of Beirut Press, 1999), 2.

6 The Muslim sects are Sunni, Shi'a, Alawite, and Druze. (In the Lebanese confessional political system, the Druze are considered a Muslim sect.) The Christian sects include Maronites, Eastern Catholics, Anglicans, Syrian Orthodox, Syrian Catholics, Roman Orthodox, Roman Catholics, Armenian Orthodox, Armenian Catholics, Protestants, Chaldeans, Assyrian Orthodox, Copts, and Baha'is.

7 The Taif Accord includes a commitment to a transition to a nonsectarian political structure within 10 years, but this path has not yet been pursued.

8 No new census has been undertaken by any of the governments ruling Lebanon. Most surveys and population counts are actually estimates.

9 According to Abu Khalil's "Lebanon One Year After the Israeli Withdrawal" (Washington, D.C.: Middle East Research and Information Project [MERIP], 2001), foreign debt had increased from $3 billion to $30 billion with Hariri's rebuilding plan. Estimates today put the figure at $40 billion.

10 Table 1, "Human development index," in *Human Development Report 2004: Cultural Liberty in Today's Diverse World* (New York: United Nations Development Programme [UNDP], 2004), 139-142. http://hdr.undp.org/reports/global/2004/ ; "Lebanon Data Profile" (Washington, D.C.: The World Bank Group, 2003), http://devdata.worldbank.org/external/CPProfile.asp?SelectedCountry=LBN&CCODE=LBN&CNAME=Lebanon&PTYPE=CP.

11 *The World Factbook* (Springfield, VA: U.S. Central Intelligence Agency [CIA]), 2003.

12 Lebanon is a signatory to The Universal Declaration of Human Rights, CEDAW (1997), and two ILO Conventions (Equal Remuneration Convention No. 100, 1951, and Discrimination Convention No. 111, 1958).

13 "Official Report on Follow-up of the Implementation of the Beijing Platform for Action (1995) and the Outcome of the Twenty-third Special Session of the General Assembly (2000)" (Beirut: National Commission for Lebanese Women [NCLW], 2004).

14 Shafiq Jiha (ed.), *al-dustur al-lubnany: tarikhuhu, ta'dilatuhu, nasuhu al-haliyy 1926–1991 [The Lebanese Constitution: History, Amendments and Current Text 1926–1991]* (Beirut: Dar Al-ilm Lil-malaiyyn, 2000), 38.

15 Mona Qamar Murad, *musharakat al-mar'a fi al-hayat al-siyassiyya fi lubnan [Women's Participation in Political Life in Lebanon]* (Tunisia: Conference on Women and Politics, paper, 31 May–1 June 2001), 5.

16 Article 26 prohibits discrimination by gender under any circumstances.

17 Ghada Hamdan, *al-mar'a wa al-qanun fi al-jumhuriyya al-lubnaniyya [Women and Law in the Lebanese Republic]* (National Committee on Lebanese Women [NCLW], paper, in Arabic) 6, http://www.nclw.org.lb/textfile/ghadahamdan.doc.

18 Jessy Chahine, "Women Discuss Sexist Citizenship Law: Children of Non-Lebanese Fathers Do Not Have Right to Nationality," *The Daily Star,* 10 October 2003.

19 "Denial of Nationality: The Case of Arab Women" (Beirut: Collective for Research and Training on Development, Gender, Citizenship and Nationality Programme, Summary of Regional Research, February 2004).

[20] "Consideration of Reports Submitted by States Parties under Article 40 of the Covenant" (Beirut: Institute for Human Rights in Lebanon, Human Rights Committee, 1996), 2: "According to the legislation governing the organization of the land register, which dates back to 1922 and 1926, the two parties to a property transaction must, when they appear before the land register officer, be accompanied by two witnesses 'of the male sex' to testify to their identity before the contract is concluded. The words 'of the male sex' were deleted by Act. No. 275 of 4 November 1993. Women now have the same capacity as men to act as witnesses." This specification of a male witness previously applied only to land registers and religious courts but was sometimes incorrectly applied to other areas as well.

[21] Women have the right to approach the religious courts at all times. The grounds on which anyone can bring a lawsuit are defined by the particular doctrines adopted by the 15 religious courts in Lebanon. For example, the grounds for a lawsuit vary according to the plaintiff's gender, relationship to the defendant, age, and the religious court.

[22] Seeta Krichikian, "at-tamiyyz dida al-mar'a fi qanun al-'uqubat al-lubnani [Discrimination Against Women in the Criminal Law of Lebanon]," *Qadaya* (publication of Beirut Bar Association Human Rights College) 5 (2001): 1.

[23] Article 29 (2) of CEDAW declares that Lebanon is not bound to paragraph (1), which requires that any dispute between two or more states parties concerning the interpretation or application of the convention that is not settled by negotiation shall be submitted to arbitration.

[24] NCLW's Web site: www.nclw.org.lb.

[25] The latter's Web site is: http://www.lau.edu.lb/centers-institutes/iwsaw.html.

[26] For example, the Women's Progress Association (WPA) of Nabatiyeh in South Lebanon has raised funds to create a Dar al-Farah, a day care center, a nursery, and an elementary school, which serve low-income families. The Ministry of Social Affairs cooperates with the WPA by paying the salaries of the employees, while other expenses are covered by fundraising activities of the association.

[27] Entities registered with the Ministry of the Interior as nonprofit receive a nominal contribution from the government that rarely covers even such expenses as telephone costs.

[28] Spending on social affairs, education, population and social services amounted to 3 percent in 2001, 5.97 percent in 1997 and 5.95 percent in 1996 of the government's budget. See Mona Shemali Khalaf, *Evaluating the Status of Lebanese Women in Light of the Beijing Platform for Action* (Beirut: UNIFEM, Regional Office for the Arab World, 2002), 73.

[29] Shafiq Jiha (ed.), *al-dustur al-lubnany [The Lebanese Constitution]* (Dar Al-ilm Lilmalaiyyn), 39.

[30] When certain groups gain political power and are large enough in numbers, they can lobby to become an official sect in the country (the Copts became the 18th sect in Lebanon several years ago).

[31] Cyprus is a favorite destination for many young Lebanese couples who prefer a civil marriage as a personal choice or due to the fact that they are of different religions and do not wish to convert. Once they return, their marriages are registered in the Ministry of the Interior and the laws of Cyprus take effect in terms of divorce, custody of children, and inheritance. There have been several movements calling for optional civil marriage to come into effect in Lebanon. Currently various religious groups appear to be resisting this alternative.

[32] See "Women's Rights in Arabic" (Beirut: Institute for Human Rights Lebanon, Beirut Bar Association), http://www.humanrightslebanon.org/arabic/WRights.htm#Y1917. The age of maturity under Lebanese law is actually 18.

[33] Law issued 24 February 1948.

[34] Law issued 22 February 1949.

[35] Lebanon signed on to the Convention on the Rights of the Child in June 1991.

[36] "Family Laws" (Bethesda, MD: Women's Learning Partnership), http://learning-partnership.org/legislation/family_law.phtml.

[37] "Women's Rights in Arabic" p. 8, http://www.humanrightslebanon.org/arabic/Wrights.htm#Y1917.

[38] Ibid.

[39] Amal Abu Raheh, *Women in the Lebanese Legislation* (American University of Beirut Press), 4.

[40] "Consideration of Reports Submitted by States Parties under Article 40 of the Covenant" (Beirut: Institute for Human Rights in Lebanon, Human Rights Committee, 1996), 4.

[41] "Trafficking in Persons Report, IV. Country Narratives: Near East" (Washington, D.C.: U.S. Dept. of State, Office to Monitor and Combat Trafficking in Persons, 14 June 2004), http://www.state.gov/g/tip/rls/tiprpt/2004/33195.htm.

[42] For more on this particular issue see Ray Jureidini, *Migrant Workers and Xenophobia in the Middle East* (Beirut: United Nations Research Institute for Social Development, Identities, Conflict and Cohesion Programme Paper Number 2, November 2003) and Ray Jureidini, *Migrant Women Domestic Workers in Lebanon* (Beirut, International Labour Organisation, 2001).

[43] "Women's Rights in Arabic" (Beirut: Institute for Human Rights Lebanon, Beirut Bar Association), 14, http://www.humanrightslebanon.org/arabic/WRights.htm#Y1917.

[44] "LBC's Domestic Abuse Story Stirs up Trouble," *The Daily Star,* 29 February 2004.

[45] LCRVAW Web site: http://www.lebanesewomen.org/index.html.

[46] Mona Shemali Khalaf (ed.), *Evaluating the Status of Lebanese Women* (UNIFEM), 45. Of the 1,302 cases, 66 are rape, 52 are rape of a minor girl, 62 are murders, 110 are attempted murders, and 1,011 are abuse and other kinds of physical violence.

[47] Majdoline Hatoum, "The Pervasive Problem of Domestic Abuse Against Women," *The Daily Star,* 17 February 2004.

[48] Nada Raad, "Women Unequal under Law: New Report from Amnesty International," *The Daily Star,* 6 March 2004.

[49] Seeta Krichikian, "at-tamiyyz dida al-mar'a fi qanun al-'uqubat al-lubnani [Discrimination Against Women in the Criminal Law of Lebanon]," *Qadaya* (publication of Beirut Bar Association, Human Rights College) 5 (2001): 3.

[50] Prior to 1994, the Lebanese Code of Commerce specified that a married woman in Lebanon could not engage in commerce without a written authorization from her husband.

[51] See "Consideration of Reports Submitted by States Parties under Article 40 of the Covenant" (Institute for Human Rights in Lebanon, Human Rights Committee, 1996), 2.

[52] Different provisions in the Quran and in the various schools of Muslim jurisprudence interpret and specify the distribution of inheritance among members of the family depending on the circumstances (all female children, no remaining spouse, etc.). (Author's note)

[53] Mona Shemali Khalaf (ed.), *Evaluating the Status of Lebanese Women* (UNIFEM), 15.

[54] Male percentage enrollment is: 95.6% (5–9 yrs), 94.8% (10–14 yrs), 67.6% (15–19 yrs) and 28.1% (20–25 yrs). Female percentage enrollment is: 95.3% (5–9 yrs), 93.2% (10–14 yrs), 61.2% (15–19 yrs) and 25.6% (20–25 yrs). Ibid.

[55] Table 24, "Gender-related development index," in *Human Development Report 2004: Cultural Liberty in Today's Diverse World* (New York: United Nations Development Programme [UNDP], 2004), 217-220. http://hdr.undp.org/reports/global/2004/.

[56] Mona Shemali Khalaf (ed.), *Evaluating the Status of Lebanese Women* (UNIFEM), 57.

[57] Ibid., 58–59.

[58] In 1997, the numbers of females in some professions were as follows: 1,654 engineers, 1,180 doctors, 592 dentists, 1,474 pharmacists and 1,722 lawyers. National Committee on Lebanese Women, *Facts on Lebanese Women, 1970–1995* (Beirut: La Sourous Institute, 1997), 65.

[59] It was amended by Law No. 207.

[60] "Labor Laws, Women's Section (in Arabic)" (Beirut: Institute for Human Rights Lebanon, Beirut Bar Association), http://www.humanrightslebanon.org/arabic/LLaw.html#WL.

[61] "Official Report on Follow-up . . ." (NCLW).

[62] Articles 29 and 52.

[63] Compensation refers to a sum of money that is given to the male employee to help support his non-working wife and his children. Employees of the government receive this money from the state, while private sector employees receive their compensation directly from the company depending on its size.

[64] The estimates of the number of Palestinian refugees currently living in Lebanon vary tremendously based on political positions. According to 2003 UNRWA statistics, the number is 391,679.

[65] For more on the Palestinian Women's Movement and Palestinian women's organizing see writings by Rosemary Sayigh and Julie Peteet.

[66] See Ghada Hamdan, *al-mar'a wa al-qanun fi al-jumhuriyya al-lubnaniyya [Women and Law in the Lebanese Republic]* (NCLW), 12, http://www.nclw.org.lb/textfile/ghadahamdan.doc. Also see Mona Qamar Murad, *musharakat al-mar'a fi al-hayat al-siyassiyya fi lubnan [Women's Participation in Political Life in Lebanon]* (Conference on Women and Politics), 16–17.

[67] See http://www.clhrf.com/humanrights/human.rights.in.lebanon.2002htm.htm.

[68] This was a strategy by the Hariri government to weaken the power of unions. In effect this led to the replacement of an elected and united national labor union by an appointed one.

[69] Shafiq Jiha (ed.), *al-dustur al-lubnany: tarikhuhu, ta'dilatuhu, nasuhu al-haliyy 1926–1991 [The Lebanese Constitution: History, Amendments and Current Text 1926–1991]* (Beirut: Dar Al-ilm Lil-malaiyyn, 2000), 40.

[70] Ghada Hamdan, *al-mar'a wa al-qanun fi al-jumhuriyya a-lubnaniyya [Women and Law in the Lebanese Republic]* (NCLW), 8, http://www.nclw.org.lb/textfile/ghadahamdan.doc.

[71] Mona Qamar Murad, *musharakat al-mar'a fi al-hayat al-siyassiyya fi lubnan [Women's Participation in Political Life in Lebanon]* (Conference on Women and Politics), 17.

[72] Recent Cabinet formed in 2004 saw the appointment of 2 women ministers (one as the Minister of Economy and the other without specification).

[73] On political participation see writings by Suad Joseph, Dissertations by Zeina Zaatari and Lara Deeb.

[74] According to Lebanese labor laws, "the woman is able to receive medical care including family planning without the consent or approval of her husband." Ghada Hamdan, *al-mar'a wa al-qanun fi al-jumhuriyya al-lubnaniyya [Women and Law in the Lebanese Republic]* (NCLW), 11, http://www.nclw.org.lb/textfile/ghadahamdan.doc.

[75] On fertility studies see work by Huda Zurayk and Joseph Chamie.

[76] Daryl Champion and Jessy Chahine, "Women would rather risk their lives than be seen in a pharmacy: They say the stigma of seeking birth control is more than they can bear," *The Daily Star*, 25 February 2004.

[77] Jessy Chahine, "For Some, Being a Single Parent Makes Perfect Sense," *The Daily Star*, 20 April 2004.

[78] Ghada Hamdan, *al-mar'a wa al-qanun fi al-jumhuriyya al-lubnaniyya [Women and Law in the Lebanese Republic]* (NCLW), 3, http://www.nclw.org.lb/textfile/ghadahamdan.doc.

[79] *The Daily Star* is a local English-language newspaper.

[80] Daryl Champion and Jessy Chahine, "Abortion is Illegal in Lebanon, but Available," *The Daily Star*, 27 February 2004.

[81] Jessy Chahine, "Abortion, Still a Major Taboo in Society: All Religious Groups Condemn the Procedure," *The Daily Star*, 24 October 2003.

[82] Jessy Chahine, "More Single Women Opt to Live Away from Home," *The Daily Star*, 8 March 2004.

[83] Jessy Chahine, "Cohabitation Among Couples on the Rise in Lebanon," *The Daily Star*, 11 February 2004.

[84] A Husainiyya is a religious center associated with Shi'a Islam where people meet to pray, organize, and hold commemorative events as well as funerals.

[85] Mona Shemali Khalaf (ed.), *Evaluating the Status of Lebanese Women* (UNIFEM).

[86] Magda Abu-Fadil, "Globalization of the Media: A Bicultural Woman's View" (Abu Dhabi: Fourth Forum of the Arab Women's Summit on Arab Women and the Media, paper, 1–3 February 2002), 1.

[87] A recent weekly show called Lil-Nisa'i Faqat (For Women Only) on Al-Jazeera TV deals with women's issues. Another show on Syrian Satellite is called Qadaya Nisa'iya (Women's Issues).

[88] Mona Shemali Khalaf (ed.), *Evaluating the Status of Lebanese Women* (UNIFEM), 1–13.

[89] Ibid., 12.

[90] Ibid., 10.

Libya

by Alison Pargeter

Population: 5,500,000
GDP Per Capita (PPP): $7,570
Economy: Mixed statist
Ranking on UN HDI: 58 out of 177
Polity: One party (presidential dictatorship)
Literacy: Male 91.8% / Female 70.7%
Percent Women Economically Active: 25.6%
Date of Women's Suffrage: 1964
Women's Fertility Rate: 3.7
Percent Urban/Rural: Urban 86% / Rural 14%

Country Ratings for Libya
Nondiscrimination and Access to Justice: 2.3
Autonomy, Security, and Freedom of the Person: 2.1
Economic Rights and Equal Opportunity: 2.3
Political Rights and Civic Voice: 1.2
Social and Cultural Rights: 1.8

(Scale of 1 to 5: 1 represents the lowest and 5 the highest level of freedom women have to exercise their rights)

Introduction

Libya gained independence in 1951 and was ruled by King Idris until Colonel Muammar al-Qadhafi took power in a bloodless coup in September 1969. He has retained complete control ever since. In the 1970s, Qadhafi developed what he termed the *Jamahiriyah* (State of the Masses), which was based on his political, economic, and sociological ideas as laid out in his famous *Green Book*. The Jamahiriyah is a unique form of popular Arab socialism that in theory enables every citizen to participate in the political process through a complex hierarchy of people's committees and congresses. However, in reality, Qadhafi is in complete control and runs an authoritarian centralized state that relies heavily on the security apparatus to maintain control.

Libya's population is currently estimated to be around 5.5 million, with GDP in 2002 at $19.1 billion.[1] Libya's economy is heavily state centralized and based primarily on the hydrocarbons sector. Private sector activity remains

165

extremely limited, as it has been strongly discouraged by the regime, and at certain times outlawed. As a result, the bloated state sector is the largest employer. However, public sector wages have been more or less frozen since the early 1980s and most people have had to take on two jobs in order to survive. Unemployment levels are estimated to be around 30 percent,[2] and this affects the youth in particular. There is also a large parallel economy that developed especially during the 1990s when Libya was under international sanctions.

Around 97 percent of the population is Arab or Berber[3] (although the regime denies the existence of its Berber minority), and the vast majority of the population follows the *Maliki* school of Sunni Islam. Libya was largely isolated for much of the 1990s but is currently in the process of restoring its relations with the international community. Despite this new opening, the regime appears to be doing little to loosen its grip domestically. Due to the authoritarian nature of the regime, there are no genuinely independent women's organizations, and anyone permitted to work on behalf of women's rights must do so within the framework of the state and of what it terms "advancing the revolution." As a result, women's groups are tightly linked to the state and are permitted to cooperate only with international women's organizations that have been sanctioned by the regime.

Since coming to power, Qadhafi has repeatedly claimed to have improved the status of women by introducing legislation aimed at eliminating discrimination, by attempting to improve women's access to education and employment, and by encouraging women to participate in Libya's political, social, and economic life. However, in reality, women have not made many inroads into what is still essentially a male-dominated society, and they continue to suffer gender-based discrimination. This is largely associated with the fact that Libyan society remains extremely conservative, and patriarchal religious values and tribal cultures prevail. Moreover, despite the rhetoric of the regime, it has done little to try to overcome social and cultural hindrances to improving women's status.

It should be noted that the regime does not produce statistics on the status of women in the country on a regular basis.

Nondiscrimination and Access to Justice

Men and women are generally treated as equals under Libyan legislation. However, in some areas inequalities and discrimination persist, especially in those laws related to family issues, in which certain Islamic interpretations are followed. Officially, women have access to justice equal with that of men, but in reality they still find themselves at a disadvantage.

Libya has no constitution as such; instead, it has a series of declarations that form the basis of Libyan legislation. The most important are the New

Constitutional Declaration (1969), which asserts the equality of all citizens before the law, and the Declaration of the Establishment of the Authority of the People (1977). The latter was based on Qadhafi's *Green Book*, which outlines his vision for the Libyan state and asserts, "Woman and man are equal as human beings. Discrimination between man and woman is a flagrant act of oppression without any justification."[4] However, the text also stresses the biological differences between men and women, concluding, "man and woman cannot be equal."[5]

There are laws and policies that include clauses aimed at protecting women from discrimination in various aspects of life. One of the most important is the Great Green Charter of Human Rights in the Age of the Masses (1988), which states, "men and women are equal in everything which is human. The distinction of rights between men and women is a flagrant injustice which nothing justifies."[6] These charters and declarations, written in Arabic, are widely distributed by the regime as propaganda tools.

The most important legislation to date that relates to women's status is the Charter on the Rights and Duties of Women in Libyan Arab Society. Drafted in 1997 by the regime, the charter asserts that women should participate in the General People's Congresses and Committees (equivalent of the parliament and associated bodies), defend their country, enjoy independent financial status, and assume leadership positions.

Women have the right to full and equal status as citizens and enjoy the same rights as men regarding the right to acquire, change or retain their nationality, or replace it with another nationality. A woman forfeits her nationality only if she wishes to adopt her husband's nationality. However, Libyan women do not have the same rights as Libyan men to transfer their nationality to their foreign-born spouses or children. While children of a Libyan father and non-Libyan mother are given Libyan nationality, children of a Libyan mother and a non-Libyan father are not and require visas to enter the country.

Under existing legislation, Libyan women officially have the same access to justice as men. Qadhafi abolished the dual court system after the revolution and merged civil and *Shari'a* courts.[7] There are four levels of courts—summary courts, courts of first instance, appeal courts, and the Supreme Court. Civil courts now employ Shari'a judges who sit in regular courts of appeal and specialize in Shari'a cases, i.e. family cases. At the top of the judicial structure is the Supreme Court of Libya, which has five separate chambers, one each for civil and commercial, criminal, administrative, constitutional, and Shari'a cases. The Supreme Council for Judicial Authority is the administrative authority of the judiciary, which handles matters of appointment, transfer, and discipline.[8] People's or revolutionary courts were set up to try political and certain economic offenses, although Qadhafi declared in 2004 that these were to be abolished.

Both men and women have the right of recourse to the judiciary.[9] Women are free to pursue legal proceedings, and any woman subjected to discrimination on the basis of sex has the right to submit complaints to the court, although there is no information available as to whether any such case has been brought to trial.

Despite this legislation, however, many women find themselves at a disadvantage when seeking legal redress. This is due to the traditional nature of a society that expects a woman to consult with her husband or male relatives before taking any form of legal action. Moreover, the accepted practice is for legal action to be taken by a male on a woman's behalf, although women of a higher social class have more freedom in this respect.

The penal code and criminal legislation apply equally to men and women. However, women and men are treated differently in some cases such as adultery. Although both sexes are liable to a punishment of 100 strokes of the whip for adultery, Article 375 of the penal code allows for a reduced punishment for men who kill a female relative for committing adultery. Furthermore, if a man inflicts bodily harm against the female relative, the prison sentence is limited to a maximum of two years. Beating or light injury is not penalized. There is no such legislation relating to women, and they do not have similar rights.[10] The killing of women in the name of family "honor" (or "honor killings") is not thought to be widespread in Libya. However, there is little information available about the extent of the problem.

Women suspected of engaging in oppositional political activity are subject to arbitrary arrest, detention, and exile. Although it is generally assumed that women do not engage to any significant extent in such activities, those suspected face the same penalties as men. However, the regime tends to be more cautious about imprisoning women, as families and tribes view the imprisonment of one of their women as an insult to the "honor" of the family.

An adult woman is recognized as a full person before the court and is equal to a man throughout all stages of litigation and legal proceedings.[11] However, in practice, women are generally not considered to be as authentic witnesses as men. Islamic principles that are followed in Libya assert that one male witness is equivalent to two females.

The Libyan government acceded to the UN Convention on the Elimination of All Forms of Discrimination Against Women (CEDAW) in 1989. However, it maintains reservations to Articles 2 and 16(c) and (d) on the grounds that they are imcompatible with Islamic Shari'a law, especially Libya's personal status code. It appears that the Libyan government has attempted to implement some of the CEDAW stipulations, largely through introducing legislation aimed at eliminating discrimination in various sectors. However, as already stated, the gap remains between legislation and reality on all of these measures, due primarily to the conservative nature of society. In reality, women continue to face discrimination at all levels.

A number of women's groups are operating in Libya, such as the Libyan Midwife Association for Mother and Childhood Care and the Al Wafa Association for Human Services. However, little information is available about what these groups are engaged in and the extent of their activities. Moreover, as everything in Libya is done through the state, there are no genuinely independent groups or civil society actors. Anyone who tries to initiate such activities would be in a very dangerous position and liable to harassment, imprisonment, and other forms of mistreatment.

RECOMMENDATIONS

1. The government should implement a nationwide program to provide legal literacy to girls and women through media, schools, community centers, and public events.
2. The government should make printed copies of laws, policies, and statistics readily available so that open discussion on problems women face can take place.
3. The government should appoint women's rights monitors in all government ministries to ensure integration of women's rights into the work of all government agencies.
4. The government should remove all reservations to CEDAW and take steps to implement it locally by bringing national laws in conformity with CEDAW.

Autonomy, Security, and Freedom of the Person

Women have some degree of autonomy and independence under Libyan legislation. However, due to the authoritarian nature of the Libyan state, both men and women suffer limitations on their freedoms and are vulnerable to the arbitrary nature of the security apparatus. Women suffer from additional restrictions due to social pressures that deter them from acting independently. They are also vulnerable to violence and abuse that go unreported due to the social stigma attached to taking any incident beyond the confines of the family. Any woman who tries to do so is generally considered to be disloyal to her family, and as such, is likely to be ostracized by the community and regarded with disdain.

Islam is the declared state religion, and Libya broadly follows the Maliki school of Sunni Islam. The state controls mosques as well as the content of the *Khoutba* (weekly sermon) at Friday prayers. After coming to power, Qadhafi devised his own particular interpretation of Islam, and Libyans who do not adhere to this interpretation may find themselves in a dangerous position. Women, like men, are generally unlikely to face harassment solely because of their religion. However, if they engage in any religious activity that is deemed to have a political dimension, they are likely to be persecuted by the state. Although there appears to be an increasing tolerance of women wearing the *hijab* (head cover) in recent years, wearing the *niqab* (complete covering of a woman's body and face) is likely to attract suspicion because of fears about Islamist opposition. The government is broadly tolerant of other faiths, largely because they do not represent a threat. However, a non-Libyan man must convert in order to marry a Muslim Libyan woman, whereas a non-Libyan woman is not required to convert if she marries a Muslim Libyan man.[12]

Officially, women have freedom of movement and do not need to request permission to travel abroad. However, due to the overtly patriarchal nature of Libyan society, most women will not travel unless accompanied by a husband or male relative. Those who choose to travel alone or with other women are generally members of the elite and are still expected to secure the permission of their families in order to do so. Traveling inside Libya also presents difficulties for Libyan women if they wish to stay in hotels, as rooms are generally not rented to unaccompanied women due to cultural traditions.

Libyan women are also restricted in their local environment. Due to social pressures, women rarely walk in the streets in the evenings unless accompanied by a male family member or another female. Furthermore, unlike her male siblings, an unmarried woman is expected to provide her family with details of any excursion outside the home. Restrictions are generally stronger in rural areas or small towns.

The family code in Libya is partly based on the Maliki school of Sunni Islam. Women do not receive equal treatment with men under certain parts of the family laws. While not particularly widespread, polygamy is still permitted, although Qadhafi has tried to dissuade people from engaging in the practice by speaking out against it. In order to take a second wife, the man must secure prior judicial permission based on grounds of financial and physical capacity. He must also obtain the written agreement of the first wife, although authorization may be given by a court in exceptional circumstances. A man has the right to divorce his wife by law, though he must petition the court in order for it to be valid and the divorce has to be agreed by a legislator. Judicial divorce is also available to women if the husband is deemed unable to maintain his wife, is absent without justification, or is impotent.

The court will decide for a couple if both parties do not mutually agree to divorce and cannot be reconciled. If the woman is deemed the cause of the divorce, then not only is she denied any outstanding *mahar*[13] (dower payment), but in addition, the custody of her children is given to the husband. In some cases, she is also ordered to pay compensation. If the court decides that the divorce is the fault of the husband, he is ordered to pay compensation as well any outstanding mahar. After a divorce has been granted, the law imposes on the husband a duty to maintain his wife for a certain period regardless of how wealthy she may be. However, in practice it seems that this is not enforced and that divorced women face many difficulties if they do not have family to fall back on.

Custody is a right of both parents with a married status. If a couple separates based on mutual agreement, the mother has the right of custody, followed by her mother, then the child's father and his mother. However, a child who is in the custody of its mother must be supported financially by its father unless the child has its own private assets.

By law, women are able to negotiate their marriage rights. The Promotion of Freedom Act No. 20 (1991) stipulates, "Every male and female citizen has the right to form a family based on a contract of marriage concluded with the consent of both parties." Officially a guardian may not force a ward of either sex into marriage or prevent a ward from marrying. However, according to tradition, women cannot marry without the consent of their father or male guardian. Marriage is generally a family affair, especially in rural areas, and partners are often designated from birth and are dependent upon family and tribal ties.

The minimum marriage age for women is 20 (the age of majority is 18), although they can marry earlier if a court grants permission.[14] There are cases, especially in rural areas, where women are married at a much earlier age. Educated women tend to marry later but find it more difficult to meet husbands. This is partly due to the tradition that dictates that once females pass a certain age, they are less marriageable. These women are often regarded with suspicion and disapproval by much of society, which is an added challenge for older women in search of a spouse. Women still often marry older men, but it is considered shameful for a man to marry a woman who is older than he.[15] In any marriage in Libya, the man is considered to be the head of the household.

Slavery is prohibited under the penal code[16] and does not appear to be a problem. However, women are subject to torture and other forms of intimidation and abuse. Those who are suspected of belonging to or being sympathetic to outlawed opposition groups are at risk. There were, however, no known cases of women being tortured during 2003. Women are included in the Collective Punishment Law of 1997 that rules that if a member of a family or tribe commits a crime, the entire family or tribe is liable for punishment. Women are sometimes denied the right to leave the country in order to join family members who are suspected of involvement in opposition or political activities outside the country.

The penal code prohibits the trafficking of women for the sex trade. Yet, women—mainly from sub-Saharan Africa—are sometimes trafficked across

Libya into Western Europe.[17] In 2003, Italy and Libya signed an agreement to jointly patrol their territorial waters to curb trafficking.[18] The extent of the problem, however, and the state's actions to address this problem, remain unclear due to the paucity of information provided by the state.

Domestic violence remains a problem, yet there is no law that declares domestic violence or marital rape a crime in Libya. Domestic violence is therefore handled under Libya's general criminal law. Article 63 of the penal code stipulates that there must be evidence of inflicted damage in order for the perpetrator to be punished.[19] Little detailed information is available on the extent of the violence, as it often goes unreported, largely because the issue is still considered taboo and shameful. Furthermore, in some parts of Libyan society, hitting one's wife is not considered unacceptable. Cases of incest or rape occurring in the home are also not generally reported or prosecuted, as this too is considered a private matter and also carries much social stigma.

Rape that occurs outside the home is generally not reported or discussed. Problems are sorted within the family, as most families want to conceal any violation of "honor." According to Libyan legislation, if a man rapes a woman, then he is expected to marry his victim to "save her honor." The woman is supposed to agree to the marriage, but in reality, under social pressures, the victim has no option but to marry. In view of the shame associated with matters of violence, and especially sexual violence, there is no support system to assist the victims.

Women who choose not to wear the hijab are sometimes subjected to verbal abuse, intimidation, and sexual harassment. Women who walk unaccompanied may also face some forms of intimidation, as they are considered to be morally loose and targets for male attention. Divorced women are also viewed as shameful by society. They are subject to verbal harassment and more likely to be vulnerable to sexual harassment and abuse. There is no state provision or legislation to protect women from these types of abuse.

No genuinely independent rights groups or civil society actors are working to improve the situation of violence against women, as none are permitted to exist in Libya. Any activity outside that sanctioned by the state is prohibited. The state itself is not known to have initiated any women's groups to work on such issues, which may be because the state, for political reasons, has chosen to accommodate certain traditional and cultural norms.

RECOMMENDATIONS

1. The government should introduce laws criminalizing domestic violence and rape, including rape within families.
2. The government should initiate support networks, create counseling and legal and financial services, and establish shelters for women who are victims of violence.

3. The government should implement public awareness campaigns addressing domestic violence, rape, incest, and sexual harassment of women and girls to bring these issues into the open and reduce the taboos surrounding them.
4. The government should allow independent women's rights groups to work freely and openly to promote women's human rights, including advocacy around women's autonomy and personal freedom.

Economic Rights and Equal Opportunity

Despite the regime's encouragement and Qadhafi's repeatedly stressing that women should undertake jobs, females continue to be underrepresented in the workforce primarily due to social pressures. Socially, a woman's place is still generally considered to be in the home and her primary role to be caring for her family. However, some members of the elite have chosen to pursue a career. Women are entitled to their economic rights, but in reality men continue to hold most of the purse strings.

Under the revolutionary system in Libya, private ownership is limited. However, women have the same rights as men to ownership and have full and independent use of their land and property. They have the right to bank loans, mortgages, and other forms of financial credit. Nevertheless, due to the dominant social tradition, land and property ownership is still considered a male's domain.

Under Libyan legislation, women have full and independent use of their income and assets. They are also free to use banking services, and banks do not require the consent of a husband in order to provide loans to the wife. Yet in reality, social traditions dictate that males generally control the income and finances. Even if a loan is secured in a woman's name, the money usually goes to the husband. This is not always the case for women of higher social class, especially those who are single.

While women are legally able to enter into business and economic activities at all levels, this area is still dominated by men in practice. There is a system in Libya that allows people to set up private partnership schemes if they apply for a license. However, women are not granted as many of these licenses as men, largely because fewer women choose to apply, as this is considered to be a male's domain. Furthermore, some women who have been granted licenses choose to hand them over to a male relative to run the partnership, a more socially acceptable arrangement.

Women fare unfavorably under Libyan inheritance laws, which are based on interpretations of Islamic principles; they inherit only half of that which is due to their brothers. For the minority Tuareg population, however, it is believed that inheritance should be through the female line, although there is no accurate information available on this issue.[20]

Education is free and open to all Libyan citizens. The regime has taken numerous steps to improve women's education, including making it compulsory up to the intermediate level. However, this requirement is rarely enforced. The number of women taking advantage of educational opportunities has increased over the past few decades, but girls continue to lag behind boys. Furthermore, while urban women have relatively good access to education, a significant proportion of rural women still do not attend school. The UNDP recorded that in 2004, 29.3 percent of Libya's females over the age of 15 were illiterate.[21]

According to the Libyan government's National Committee for Information and Documentation, the number of males and females receiving education is almost equal. In the 2000–01 academic year, 131,529 women attended university out of a total female population aged between 20 and 24 of 346,130. In the same year, 151,390 men were attending university out of a total population for the age group of 346,130.[22] At the other end of the scale, for the age group of 6 to 14 year olds, 534,425 girls were attending school, out of a total population of 556,693, as opposed to 560,029 boys out of a total population of 571,458.[23] The Libyan National Committee for Information and Documentation reported that in 2001, 16 percent (41,336) of the female work force had a university degree or above and 48.3 percent (125,398) had a secondary school certificate.[24] All academic fields are open to women, although they tend to shy away from subjects that have traditionally been considered the male domain, such as engineering.

The regime has specifically encouraged women to join the workforce. The Resolution of the General People's Committee (1988) states that work is a duty for every woman who is capable of working. The Consolidation of Freedoms Law 20 (1991) stipulates that men and women are both free to choose the work that suits them. However, by law, women are prevented from undertaking heavy labor or dangerous work, and they are not to be made to work more than 48 hours per week.

According to the UNDP, women comprise 22 percent of the Libyan labor force.[25] However, women continue to work mainly in the service sectors, especially in education and health.[26] Large numbers of women, especially in rural areas, undertake unpaid work, including agriculture or traditional or cottage industries.

In 2003, women were permitted to enter the traffic police for the first time, and Qadhafi called on Libyan women to fight for their country again. In fact, the regime has encouraged women to undertake military training and there are special female police forces, bodyguards, and military academies. However, this is generally looked upon as something shameful by much of Libyan society, which views it as contrary to cultural and religious tradition.

Despite the regime's attempts to increase female employment, decisions relating to a woman's employment are generally influenced by her father while she is unmarried and her husband after she is married.[27] Considerations such as the distance of employment from a woman's home play a part in the decision-making process, as women are generally expected to choose work that is close to their home. Moreover, families still tend to prefer their daughters to work in traditionally female jobs, such as education, nursing, and cleaning. For those women who continue to work after marriage, their jobs are generally considered to be of secondary importance to their husband's job.

Libyan labor legislation rules that employers must pay equal wages to men and women if the nature and conditions of their work are the same. However, in reality, women are often paid less than their male counterparts. According to the latest available figures from the National Committee for Information and Documentation, more than 50 percent of women earned between 150 and 199 *dinars* per month in 2001, as opposed to only 27.4 percent of men, and very few women earned more than 250 dinars per month.[28]

Furthermore, there is still considerable discrimination in the job market, as employers often see women as unreliable, less competent than men, and likely to leave their employment once they are married. There is also still significant resistance to the idea of a woman's holding a position that involves having authority over men. In a survey of Libyan students, only 29 percent of men asked whether women should be employed in jobs that give them authority over men accepted the idea, while 63 percent of women accepted it.[29] There is no legislation to protect women from sexual harassment in the workplace.

Libyan legislation provides for maternity leave of three months, during which time 100 percent of earnings are payable. The woman must have worked for her employer for a minimum of six months in order to qualify. Women are also eligible for a maternity grant from the fourth month of pregnancy until confinement. They are legally permitted two half-hour breastfeeding breaks per day that are considered to be part of their working hours. Any employer who employs more than 50 workers in one place should provide a nursery. However, in reality, childcare is still considered a responsibility to be taken on by the extended family.

RECOMMENDATIONS

1. The government should invite education experts and women's rights advocates to study the levels of gender-stereotyping and discrimination against women in school materials and textbooks and use the findings to introduce positive role models of women.
2. The government should revise existing labor laws to abolish policies that discriminate against women and establish a gender-discrimination office where women can send confidential complaints.
3. The government should allow independent women's groups to work openly to highlight the obstacles facing women and to present suggestions on how

women can more easily access business opportunities and income generation programs.

4. The government should draft laws that protect women from sexual harassment in the workplace in both the public and the private sectors.

Political Rights and Civic Voice

Due to the authoritarian nature of the Libyan regime, men and women have
no political or civic rights outside those sanctioned by the state. Political
parties are banned and membership in such entities is punishable by death.
Libya has a unique political system comprising a complex hierarchy of people's
congresses and committees in which, in theory, all citizens can participate.
However, in practice, all decisions are in the hands of the leader and his immediate circle. Anyone trying to engage in political or civic activity is liable
to severe penalties including arrest, detention, and possible torture.

The regime does not tolerate any unauthorized assembly. Women are permitted to take part in gatherings and demonstrations orchestrated by the state
but are prohibited from any type of gathering that has not been sanctioned in
advance. Assemblies, strikes, sit-ins, and demonstrations are all banned under
Law 45 of 1972. A General Women's Union is responsible for implementing
social programs on behalf of women and children. However, all activities of
this nature remain heavily regulated by the state. The state regularly organizes
conferences on women's issues, but they are little more than large-scale propaganda exercises to promote the regime.

The oppressive nature of the regime acts to limit freedom of expression, which
is prohibited in Libya. The state has a multi-layered security apparatus; any man
or woman daring to express any opinion contrary to that of the Jamahiriyah
will be in an extremely dangerous position. Due to social pressures, women
are further expected to refrain from expressing their opinions. The regime denies the existence of minorities in Libya, including Berbers, and it is illegal for
parents to give their children Berber names. The authorities refuse to register
children with such names and will deny them access to schooling.[30]

Women have been allowed to participate in Libya's judiciary since the
beginning of the 1990s and have been free to work as judges, public prosecutors, and case administrators under the same conditions as men. A number
of female judges have been appointed by the state, although they remain
underrepresented in comparison to men. Libyan women are able to work as
lawyers, but information on independent women lawyers or women's lawyer
groups working for human rights is not available.

In theory, executive structures of government are open to women. However, in practice, men almost exclusively fill these positions. Very few women
have been appointed to the General People's Committee (cabinet), and in

the cabinet reshuffle of June 2003, no women ministers were appointed. The number of women appointed to the secretariats of the General People's Congresses is extremely limited, although in 2003, one woman was appointed as the Secretary of Social Affairs of this body. A General Secretariat for Women's Affairs that was established in 1992 has a series of offices under it. In January 2003, a Libyan woman was appointed by the Libyan government to chair the annual session of UN Commission on Human Rights in Geneva. Libya has also appointed a small number of women ambassadors.

Women are encouraged to participate in the Basic People's Congresses, where every citizen can come to discuss and make decisions on policies, although they continue to be dominated by men. In an attempt to encourage more women to participate, the regime set up separate women's congresses to appeal to the conservative elements of Libyan society. However, while this means more women may attend, it in fact serves to reinforce the idea of gender segregation. There are also women's revolutionary committees—these are paralegal organizations set up to "defend the revolution" and spread regime propaganda.

Overall, despite narrowly defined attempts by the regime, it is still socially difficult for a woman to take a position in politics. Social attitudes continue to be resistant to the idea of women participating in politics. In a survey carried out among Libyan students, only 38 percent of men were in favor of women playing a political role, but 72 percent of women were in support.[31]

Access to information is generally limited in Libya; most foreign newspapers and publications are banned. Women increasingly use the Internet for information, but it is partly censored. For example, the websites of Libyan opposition groups based abroad have been disabled. Women also have access to some satellite television stations. Nevertheless, due to the repressive nature of the state, the possibilities for women to use information to empower themselves are extremely limited.

RECOMMENDATIONS

1. The government should allow free and competitive elections to take place, and should take concrete steps to ensure that Libyan women have equal participation at all levels of the political process.
2. The government should allow independent political parties to operate freely and mandate the reservation of seats in political bodies for women.
3. The government should allow independent civil society organizations to operate freely in all parts of the country and cooperate with international women's groups.
4. The government should establish mechanisms to ensure that women are not discriminated against in the hiring policies of government structures and to ensure that women are promoted to senior positions within all branches of the government.

Social and Cultural Rights

Women have limited social and cultural rights due primarily to the dominance of traditional values. In the past, Libya was largely a Bedouin society, but it is increasingly urbanizing. Despite these changes, Libya remains very conservative. Religion and tribal affiliation are the main driving cultural forces in Libya. Women find themselves at a disadvantage in many areas. The state has tried to promote women's social rights through legislation and through Qadhafi's repeated encouragements for women to play a more active role in society. However, this has not fundamentally changed perceptions, and women continue to face discrimination.

Women have limited abilities to make decisions about issues relating to their reproductive health, which in most cases is considered a family affair. While contraception is available in Libya, little information is available in the public domain, and it therefore remains a taboo subject. According to the UN, there is no government support to assist women with contraceptive use; the latest available figures suggest that in 1995, the proportion of married women using modern contraception was only 26 percent.[32] Female genital mutilation is not widely practiced in Libya, although it is still thought to occur in a number of remote rural areas.[33]

Abortion is illegal and punishable under the penal code. Anyone who procures an abortion is liable to imprisonment, although if it is deemed that the reason behind the act was to preserve the family "honor," i.e. in the case of rape, then the penalty is halved. If a woman procures her own abortion, the punishment is imprisonment for at least six months. However, illegal abortions are carried out in Libya, or some Libyan women who can afford it are thought to travel to Tunisia, where the procedure is more readily available.

Every Libyan citizen is entitled to free health care, and women have the same access as men. However, due to the poor standards of health care inside Libya, those who can afford it travel abroad for treatment. Considering that women are expected to be accompanied by a male relative during travel, the cost of being treated abroad increases, and the expense may prevent some women from traveling in order to receive higher quality treatment.

Libya has a limited private housing market due to the peculiarities of a political system that discourages private sector activity. Women do have the right to own and use housing, but the tradition dictates that a woman's home is generally in the husband's name if she is married. Single women are expected to live with their parents or relatives, as it is deemed shameful by society for a young woman to live alone. The government does not provide accommodation or hostels to assist working women.

Women are able to work in the media. However, all forms of media are strictly controlled and neither women nor men are free to influence media content. Only those women with the necessary connections are able to secure employment in this field. The print media frequently publicize the promotion of women in society, but this is primarily pro-regime propaganda. For example, International Women's Day is celebrated and widely reported in the media, but this attention is generally focused around praising achievements of the regime. Many stereotypes appear in the media that emphasize a woman's role as mother and housewife.

Women are adversely affected by poverty, especially those who are illiterate. Under the social security law, widows are entitled to welfare payments in the form of a percentage of their deceased husbands' pension. They are allotted between 30 percent and 75 percent of the pension regardless of age.[34] However in practice, due to bureaucratic inefficiencies, these payments appear to be difficult for women to collect, and the amount is often insufficient for survival. Women who are divorced face particularly acute challenges. Those who are widowed or divorced and unable to work are expected to rely upon their families for survival.

Women are not free to participate in or influence community life, policies, and/or social development at the local level unless sanctioned by the state. However, older women tend to be given more respect and are consulted about decisions that affect the family, such as marriage and other domestic affairs.

Genuinely independent women's rights groups do not exist in Libya; as a result, women are not able to carry out advocacy work to promote and protect women's social and cultural rights. Any activity in this regard must be sanctioned by the state.

RECOMMENDATIONS

1. The government should take concrete steps to reduce the taboos associated with contraception and reproductive health through countrywide information campaigns and increased education for women, especially those living in rural areas.
2. The government should work with schools and community centers to encourage and provide sports facilities for girls and women.
3. The government should establish women's centers throughout the country to provide clear and simple information to Libyan women about their legal rights, government services, and access to complaint mechanisms and legal services.
4. The government should create support networks for the most vulnerable groups of women in society such as widows, disabled women and girls, women in prison, and unmarried women who become pregnant.

AUTHOR: Alison Pargeter is a Research Fellow at the International Policy Institute at Kings College London. She works primarily on security issues in North Africa with a particular focus on Libya. She has conducted several research projects on Libya that have entailed fieldwork, and has also published numerous articles on the country.

Notes

[1] "Libya Data Profile," in *World Development Indicators database* (Washington, D.C.: The World Bank, August 2004), http://devdata.worldbank.org/external/CPProfile. asp?SelectedCountry=LBY&CCODE=LBY&CNAME=Libya&PTYPE=CP.

[2] *The World Factbook:* Libya (Springfield, VA: U.S. Central Intelligence Agency [CIA], 2004), http://www.cia.gov/cia/publications/factbook/geos/ly.html.

[3] Ibid.

[4] Muammar al-Qadhafi, *The Green Book* (Tripoli: World Centre for the Study and Research of the Green Book, 1983).

[5] Ibid.

[6] Great Green Charter of Human Rights in the Age of the Masses (1988), http://www.geocities.com/Athens/8744/grgreen.htm.

[7] *Legal Profile: Libya* (Atlanta, GA: Emory Law School Islamic Family Law Project, undated), http://www.law.emory.edu/IFL/legal/libya.htm.

[8] "Judiciary: Libya" (New York: UNDP Programme on Governance in the Arab Region, undated), http://www.pogar.org/countries/judiciary.asp?cid=10.

[9] "Libyan Arab Jamahiriyah" (New York: United Nations CEDAW Second Periodic Reports of States Parties, 15 March 1999), http://www.un.org/womenwatch/daw/cedaw/reports.htm#l.

[10] "Nahwa ufq awsa wa musahama fa'ala lilmarra al-libya [Moving Towards A Greater Horizon and Effective Contribution for Libyan Women]," *Al Beit* magazine, undated.

[11] Conversation between the author and a Libyan lawyer based in the UK, May 2004.

[12] *International Religious Freedom Report 2003: Libya* (Washington, D.C.: U.S. Dept. of State, Bureau of Democracy, Human Rights, and Labor, 18 Dec. 2003), http://www.state.gov/g/drl/rls/irf/2003/c10269.htm.

[13] *Mahar* is an Arabic term for the dower payment that a Muslim woman has the right to receive from her husband at the time of her marriage.

[14] *Libyan Arab Jamahiriyah,* Second Periodic Report of States Parties Due in 2000 (New York: United Nations, Committee on the Rights of the Child, CRC/C/93/ Add.1, 19 Sept. 2002), http://www.unhchr.ch/tbs/doc.nsf/(Symbol)/CRC.C.93. Add.1.En?OpenDocument.

[15] Mustafa Attir, "Mulahathaat hawla audaa ashabaab fi Libya [Notes on the Situation of Libyan Youth]," (undated), www.moattir.com.

[16] *Country Reports on Human Rights Practices–2003: Libya* (Washington, D.C.: U.S. Dept. of State, Bureau of Democracy, Human Rights, and Labor, 25 Feb. 2004), http://www.state.gov/g/drl/rls/hrrpt/2003/27933.htm (hereafter cited as *Country Reports* (U.S. Dept. of State)).

[17] *2002 Human Rights Report on Trafficking in Persons, Especially Women and Children:*

Libya (Washington, D.C.: Johns Hopkins University, The Protection Project, March 2002), http://209.190.246.239/ver2/cr/Libya.pdf.

[18] *Trafficking in Persons Report* (Washington, D.C.: U.S. Dept. of State, Office to Monitor and Combat Trafficking in Persons, 14 June 2004).

[19] Abdel Salam Bashir al-Duwaiby, "Al Unf al-Ahili: Al Aba'at al-Silbiya wal Ijra'at al-Wikaiya (Al-Mustama al-Arabi al-Libi Kanamuthej) [Family Violence: The Negative Dimension and Prevention and Treatment Procedures— Arabic Libyan Society as a Sample]" (undated), http://www.amanjordan.org/studies/sid=21.htm (in Arabic).

[20] The Tuareg are a nomadic tribal group located in the deserts of the southwest of Libya that are thought to number around 10,000. They adhere to a form of Sunni Islam but incorporate non-orthodox elements. However, as the regime denies the existence of minorities in Libya, it is extremely difficult to find information about them or the status of Tuareg women.

[21] Table 24, "Gender-related development index," in *Human Development Report 2004: Cultural Liberty in Today's Diverse World* (New York: United Nations Development Programme [UNDP], 2004), 217-220. http://hdr.undp.org/reports/global/2004/.

[22] "The Distribution of the Libyan Population Aged between 6 and 24 in Education According to Gender for the Academic Year 2000–01" in *Al Khitab al-Ahsai [Statistics Book]* (Tripoli: Libyan National Committee for Information and Documentation, 2002), www.nidaly.org.

[23] Ibid.

[24] "Educational Level of the Workforce According to Gender, 2001," op. cit., www.nidaly.org.

[25] "Libya: Women in Public Life" (New York: UNDP Programme on Governance in the Arab Region, 2004), http://www.pogar.org/.

[26] "Educational Level of the Workforce According to Gender, 2001," See Appendix III, op. cit.

[27] M. Attir, op. cit.

[28] "Breakdown of Libyan labour force according to income and gender 2001," op. cit., www.nidaly.org (in Arabic only); see Appendix II.

[29] A. Obeidi, *Political Culture in Libya* (Richmond, Surrey, UK: Curzon Press, 2001), 185.

[30] "Al-Zawari li Al-Tawalt [Al-Zawari speaks to Al-Tawalt]," www.tawalt.com/letter (in Arabic).

[31] A. Obeidi, op. cit., 187.

[32] *World Contraceptive Use 2003* (New York: United Nations, Department of Economic and Social Affairs, Population Division, 21 April 2004), http://www.un.org/esa/population/publications/contraceptive2003/WCU2003.htm.

[33] *Country Reports* (U.S. Dept. of State).

[34] *Social Security Programs Throughout the World—Libya Report: 2002–03* (Washington, D.C.: Social Security Online, 2003), http://www.ssa.gov/policy/docs/progdesc/ssptw/2002-2003/africa/libya.pdf.

Morocco

by Rabéa Naciri

Population: 30,400,000
GDP Per Capita (PPP): $3,810
Economy: Capitalist-statist
Ranking on UN HDI: 125 out of 177
Polity: Traditional monarchy and limited parliament
Literacy: Male 63.3% / Female 38.3%
Percent Women Economically Active: 41.8%
Date of Women's Suffrage: 1963
Women's Fertility Rate: 2.7
Percent Urban/Rural: Urban 57% / Rural 43%

Country Ratings for Morocco
Nondiscrimination and Access to Justice: 3.2
Autonomy, Security, and Freedom of the Person: 3.2
Economic Rights and Equal Opportunity: 3.1
Political Rights and Civic Voice: 3.0
Social and Cultural Rights: 3.0
(Scale of 1 to 5: 1 represents the lowest and 5 the highest level of freedom women have to exercise their rights)

Introduction

Morocco became a hereditary monarchy headed by King Mohammed V after gaining independence from France in 1956. King Hassan II ascended the throne five years later upon the death of his father. Morocco's constitution, which was adopted in 1962, provides for multiparty democratic institutions, fundamental freedoms, and the principle of separation of powers. Successive revisions to the constitution created a Constitutional Council in 1992 and a bicameral legislature in 1996. The king continues to maintain supreme executive power under the 1996 constitution and has the duty of appointing the prime minister and the cabinet. The bicameral parliament consists of a lower house, the Chamber of Representatives, which is directly elected, and an upper house, the Chamber of Counselors, whose members are indirectly elected for nine-year terms.

After the death of King Hassan in July 1999, the throne was passed to his son Mohammed, who upon assuming power launched an extensive program of economic and political liberalization. Elections have become more transparent, and several mechanisms have been put in place to strengthen the constitutional state and reduce corruption. The king also released thousands of prisoners and allowed exiled opposition figures to return to Morocco. Nevertheless, while respect for public freedoms has improved both in law and in practice, press freedoms and freedom of association remain somewhat restricted.

Morocco's population in 2003 was an estimated 30.4 million. More than half of Moroccans live in cities (57 percent), and the country has an average annual growth rate of 1.5 percent. Close to 99 percent of Moroccans are Sunni Muslim; in addition, there are small populations of Jews and Christians who are free to practice their religions.

In spite of recent progress in the political realm, Morocco still faces a number of economic and social challenges. The country has a market-based economy with a growing manufacturing sector, a sizable services sector, and a diverse agricultural and fisheries sector. However, a low rate of economic growth of 2.6 percent on average, combined with high illiteracy, low school attendance rates, and poor access to basic social services,[1] has resulted in extreme poverty and unemployment. About one in five Moroccans live below the poverty level, and the national unemployment level is estimated at 12.5 percent.

Significant measures have been taken to improve the status of women in Morocco in recent years. Efforts to reduce gender discrimination within the legal system produced changes in the country's criminal code, labor code, and code of personal status (CSP). The CSP, also known as the *Mudawana* and based on the *Malikite* school of Islamic law, governs the status of women under civil law. The revised CSP now upholds the principle of equality between men and women and confirms joint responsibility for the family. Women's representation in decision-making positions has also improved. In 2002, women held 10.8 percent of the seats in the Chamber of Representatives. Some demographic changes have also benefited women's health, such as a decline in fertility rates and a rise in the age of women contracting their first marriage. Nevertheless, women continue to face violence and societal discrimination in many aspects of their lives. Multiple inequalities persist between men and women and between Morocco's urban and rural populations in terms of access to education, employment, and health care.

It is still too soon to evaluate the impact of recent legislative reforms. Positive legislative changes, however, will only become truly significant if they are incorporated into the day-to-day lives of Morocco's millions of women and girls. This remains a major challenge for a society in the middle of an incomplete transition toward democratization, integration into the global economy, and urbanization—not to mention a country torn between the forces of regression and the forces of progress.

Nondiscrimination and Access to Justice

Morocco's legal system is based on both Islamic law, as inspired by the Malikite school of jurisprudence, and the French and Spanish civil law systems. Family courts adjudicate family issues such as marriage, divorce, inheritance, and child custody for Muslim citizens. The promulgation of the new family law in 2004 marked historic changes in family laws, much to the credit of the growing activism of civil society, in particular Moroccan women's nongovernmental organizations (NGOs).

Despite recent progress, many Moroccan laws and policies still discriminate against women and deny their equality. While Article 8 of the constitution of 1996[2] guarantees women equal political rights with men, the constitution does not provide women with the equal enjoyment of civil rights. Furthermore, Article 8 of the constitution provides for equality of citizens "before the law," rather than "in law," a subtle but important distinction that in no way guarantees equal rights for women and men.

Morocco's laws are progressively becoming less discriminatory toward women and more protective of human rights and public freedoms. Although the gender perspective has not yet fully been integrated into all government policies, the government machinery has generally become more sensitive to the needs of its women and girl citizens. In 1998, the government created a ministerial department responsible for the status of women. The state has also established programs over the past six years to improve young women's access to education, decrease maternal mortality, improve women's health, and combat violence against women. In practice, however, the application of positive measures is subject to several constraints.

Women are still not considered full citizens in many sectors of the law. For example, traditional notaries still require male witnesses for some documents, such as establishing proof of marriage or paternity. Additionally, Moroccan women do not have the same rights to citizenship as Moroccan men. According to Section 6 of the nationality code of 1958, unlike Moroccan men, Moroccan women married to foreigners cannot automatically transfer their nationality to their children. A Moroccan woman married to a foreign man can transfer her nationality to her children only in cases in which the father is unknown or is stateless, or if the child is born in Morocco and he/she declares Moroccan nationality two years prior to reaching the age of majority. Moreover, while the foreign wife of a Moroccan man can easily obtain Moroccan citizenship, the foreign husband of a Moroccan woman does not benefit from the same conveniences and must resort to the normal naturalization procedure (a long process with uncertain outcomes).

Significant measures have been taken over the past few years to facilitate women's access to the justice system. Section 336 of the code of criminal procedure (CPP), repealed in 2002, had required a woman wishing to bring a complaint against her husband to obtain authorization from the courts. Additional measures to increase women's access to justice include: free court costs for women who are divorced and/or are abandoned by their husbands;[3] the creation of a fund to guarantee payment of support pursuant to an enforceable judgment; and the creation of family courts and the training of family court judges, in connection with the new CSP.

Revisions to Morocco's criminal code in 2003 also helped to improve women's legal status by eliminating unequal sentencing in adultery cases. Article 418 of the penal code had granted extenuating circumstances to a husband who murders, injures, or beats his wife and/or her partner, when catching them *in flagrante delicto*. While this article has not been repealed, the penalty for committing this crime is at least now the same for both genders. Furthermore, revisions to Article 491 of the penal code now permit the state to sue either a husband or a wife guilty of adultery while the spouse is out of the country. Previously, only an unfaithful wife could be sued in these circumstances.

A newly added provision to the penal code now provides for heavier sentences in cases in which one spouse voluntarily inflicts blows and wounds on the other spouse, including cases of recidivism. Furthermore, Article 446 has been revised to authorize health care professionals to bypass professional secrecy in cases of violence between spouses or violence against a woman.

Nonetheless, a number of laws under the penal code still discriminate against women. Article 475, paragraph 2, stipulates that in cases in which a minor girl has been abducted, all legal proceedings and the enforcement of sentences will cease if the abductor and the girl subsequently marry. The abductor can be prosecuted only on the basis of an action brought by persons who have the capacity to request annulment of the marriage, and he can be convicted only after the marriage has been annulled. Additionally, while not provided for by law, victims' families may offer rapists the opportunity to marry their victims in order to preserve family "honor."

Articles 494 and 496, which were not amended during the 2003 penal code revisions, specify punishments for anyone who hides or abducts a married woman. However, the law does not take into account conditions under which a woman might choose to hide or leave her husband, such as domestic abuse. In such a case, those who give an abused wife shelter also become liable under this provision of the law. Sentences under these articles range from two to five years' imprisonment. Such laws serve to reinforce women's inferior status and continue to support the power of husbands over their wives in the social and legal systems of Morocco.

The criminal code provides for severe punishments for rape and other forms of sexual violence; however, due to the difficulties in establishing proof of rape and the taboos surrounding this issue, women tend not to report these crimes. In Moroccan criminal law, rape is regarded as indecent assault or public indecency, not as a crime against the person. In some cases, the courts have treated rape committed against minor girls as corruption of a minor or as sexual relations outside marriage. Marital rape is not considered a crime under Moroccan criminal law. On the other hand, sexual relations outside marriage are penalized by Article 490 of the penal code, which imposes a one-month to one-year sentence for such an act; such relations can only be proven by confession or if the person is caught in the act. Nevertheless, an unmarried woman's pregnancy is proof of sexual relations and criminal prosecution of pregnant unmarried women remains on the books. The law does not establish the fault of her male partner, however.

Any citizen may normally avail himself or herself of remedies before all jurisdictions, including Morocco's administrative tribunals. These tribunals are responsible for examining disputes resulting from arbitrary decisions made by an administrative authority, as well as complaints of discrimination and requests for compensation. However, many Moroccan women lack awareness of such legal mechanisms and the ways in which they can gain access to these remedies.

Morocco ratified the Convention on the Elimination of All Forms of Discrimination Against Women (CEDAW) in 1993 but adopted reservations on Articles 2, 9(2), 15(4), 16, and 29. Article 2 commits state parties to condemn discrimination against women in all its forms and agree to pursue a policy of eliminating discrimination against women. Morocco's additional reservations to CEDAW concern women's equal rights with men with respect to the nationality of their children; equal rights under the law relating to the movement of persons and the freedom to choose their residence; and the state's commitment to take all appropriate measures to eliminate discrimination against women in all matters relating to marriage and family relations.

Morocco's reservations to CEDAW serve chiefly to nullify the convention's objectives and purpose. While Morocco has ratified most international conventions related to women,[4] it has not adopted the Optional Protocol to CEDAW. The Optional Protocol would allow Moroccan women who had exhausted all domestic remedies to file complaints of discrimination with an international committee of CEDAW experts.

Moroccan women's rights groups and NGOs are free to advocate for women's rights, create associations, and receive foreign funding without state control. The first association for the defense of women's rights, the Democratic Association of Moroccan Women (ADFM), was established in 1985. Several other Moroccan women's NGOs that started as advocacy organizations in the second half of the 1980s have become pressure and proposal groups, forming broad coalitions with unions, human rights organizations, and the media. Women's NGOs repeatedly prod the government to drop its reservations to

CEDAW by preparing evaluative reports of state progress in implementing CEDAW, issuing public statements, and organizing press conferences and women's rights training sessions and seminars.

RECOMMENDATIONS

1. The government should amend the constitution to include the principle of equality between men and women in all rights and responsibilities.
2. The government should provide judges, police personnel, and medical personnel with more rigorous training on the country's new legal provisions related to women's rights.
3. The government should abolish the prosecution of unmarried pregnant women, amend its penal code to criminalize marital rape, and abolish laws that criminalize those who assist married women.
4. The government should remove all reservations to CEDAW and take steps to implement it locally by bringing national laws in conformity with CEDAW.

Autonomy, Security, and Freedom of the Person

The Moroccan constitution establishes Islam as the official state religion and designates the king as Commander of the Faithful and Defender of the Faith. Article 6 of the constitution guarantees freedom of worship for all, and the government for the most part respects this right. However, in practice, some restrictions do exist. Moroccan Muslim citizens who convert to other religions or adopt an Islamic tradition other than the Malikite rite generally face social ostracism. The Moroccan CSP places further restrictions on Moroccan Muslim women, who, unlike Muslim men, are forbidden to marry a non-Muslim.

Regulatory provisions that prohibited women from traveling or having a passport without authorization from their husbands/guardians were repealed in 1994. However, in reality, women's freedom of movement remains inhibited by social limitations and traditions. Many government officials still require a woman to seek her husband's authorization to obtain a passport. Government passport authorities sometimes oblige unmarried women who have reached the age of majority to produce a "certificate of good conduct" or authorization from their father in order to travel.

Since the promulgation of a series of family laws in 1957 and 1958, the CSP has governed the status of Moroccan women in civil law. While some minimal reforms of the code were adopted in 1993, it has only been after 20 years of mobilization by the women's movement that revisions of the CSP in 2004 finally enabled Morocco to take a significant step forward in the direction of democracy and modernity.

A major development in the CSP is the granting of equality between men and women in terms of family responsibility; the family is now placed under the joint responsibility of the husband and the wife. The rights and duties of spouses under the older version of the CSP had obliged a husband to provide for his wife, while a wife was responsible for taking care of the household, breast-feeding the children, remaining faithful, obeying her husband, and respecting his family. The new CSP abolishes all these provisions and replaces them with a single article that provides for the rights and duties of both spouses without discrimination. A woman's duty to obey her husband was eliminated in favor of equality of rights and duties between the spouses.

Additional changes to the CSP increased the minimum age for marriage for women from 15 to 18 to equal that of men. Furthermore, matrimonial guardianship has been made optional for women of the age of majority. In other words, the marriage will still be valid without the presence of a matrimonial guardian.

Although polygamy is still allowed under the new code, it is now subject to draconian legal conditions and a judge's authorization. New restrictions stipulate that a man's first wife must be informed of her husband's intention to take another wife, and the latter must be informed that her future husband is already married. A woman also now has the right to ask her future husband not to take another wife and to give her the right to have the marriage dissolved if this agreement is not respected. Polygamy is forbidden in cases that might result in unfair treatment between the wives, and a court will only authorize polygamy if it is proven necessary and if the husband possesses sufficient resources to support both families and guarantee all rights, including household allowance, lodging, and equality, to both wives.

Divorce under the new code has been regulated in such a way as to limit abuses resulting from the husband's exercise of repudiation. All types of divorce are subject to a reconciliation procedure by a judge and must be decreed within six months. The most important new changes, however, are the options for consensual divorce and divorce due to irreconcilable differences, which allow women to divorce under the same conditions as men.

Nevertheless, problems remain in the family laws for women and with the *khul'* divorce, whereby a woman must provide financial or other compensation to her husband. This form of divorce, maintained under the new 2004 laws, has become a means for blackmailing women seeking a divorce. New changes in 2004 stipulate that in cases in which the spouses cannot agree on the amount of the compensation, the judge must decide.

Women's custody rights under the new family laws guarantee that a Moroccan mother no longer automatically loses her custody rights if she remarries or moves to a town other than the town where her husband resides. However, a mother may still lose custody of her children over the age of seven if she

remarries and her husband requests custody; she may obtain legal guardianship of her minor children only in cases in which the father is deceased or
legally incompetent.

Slavery no longer exists in Morocco, but some categories of women and
girls live or work under conditions that may be likened to slavery. Morocco is
a country of origin, transit point, and destination for trafficked persons who
originate from sub-Saharan Africa, the Arab region, and Asia. Some Moroccan victims are lured into Europe and then forced into drug trafficking,
coerced labor, and sexual exploitation.[5] Moroccan women are also trafficked
to the Gulf region. Internal trafficking also exists, with child domestics and
underage girls sold into marriage.

The employment of young girls as domestic workers continues to be a
serious problem. For example, 3.6 percent of households in the Casablanca
region employ a minor domestic girl, and nearly 60 percent of them are under
15 years of age.[6] A 2001 study performed by the Moroccan League for the
Protection of Children and UNICEF reported that 45 percent of household
employees under the age of 18 were between the ages of 10 and 12, and 26
percent were under the age of 10. The legal age for employment was only
recently raised from 12 to 15 in January of 2002. Parents have been known
to contract their daughters as maids and retain their earned salaries.[7]

The Moroccan government enacted new anti-trafficking laws in 2003 and
prohibited the selling of child brides under the new CSP, but it has not yet
signed or ratified the 2003 Protocol to Prevent, Suppress and Punish Trafficking in Persons, Especially Women and Children, supplementing the UN
Convention against Transnational Organized Crime.

Violence against women remains a problem in Morocco and is sometimes
justified in social or even religious terms. While the Ministry of Justice is
working to publish annual reports on violence against women based on the
cases heard by the courts, these incidents represent only a small percentage
of the overall number of cases. The lack of data on violence is exacerbated
by the silence of the victims. The obligation imposed on victims to produce
medical certificates and witnesses hinders victims of domestic violence from
coming forward, due to the fact that this form of violence often does not
involve the presence of eyewitnesses. The government has pursued a policy
of neglect on this issue, failing to ensure that enough people in the medical
professions, police, and judiciary are adequately prepared to address cases
of violence against women. However, some large hospitals in major cities
such as Casablanca and Rabat have begun to set up units to help women
victims of violence.

A study conducted[8] within NGO-operated victim assistance centers revealed
that eight out of ten cases of violence against women who come to the centers
are perpetrated by individuals close to the victims. Law enforcement officials

reportedly do not respond adequately to complaints of domestic violence and continue to view domestic violence as a private matter.[9] A poll taken of 1,500 people[10] reported that 45.3 percent of respondents found it legitimate for husbands to use violence against their wives in certain circumstances.

From 2000 to 2002, the Ministry of Women's Affairs worked with government departments and Moroccan women's NGOs to draw up a national strategy against violence. While changes to criminal legislation have strengthened some protections for women against violence, violent practices against women in the public and private sphere continue to be tolerated, including sexual harassment, violence against domestic workers (especially young girls), and violence against unmarried mothers and their children.

Taboos on openly discussing violence against women have declined, however, as the problem is increasingly being addressed and debated in the media and within society. Moroccan women's NGOs have helped to break the silence surrounding violence and other degrading treatment suffered by women by organizing symbolic courts and radio campaigns on violence against women. Several Moroccan and international NGOs advocate for the prevention of violence against women and for the protection of women victims. Centers provide support services, legal aid, and information.

RECOMMENDATIONS

1. The government should reform laws that remain discriminatory towards women, in particular the nationality code that currently does not allow women married to foreigners to confer Moroccan nationality to their children or to their husbands.
2. The government should eliminate discriminatory legal provisions that place the burden of proof entirely on female victims of violence, and ensure perpetrators of violence against women do not escape prosecution.
3. The government should work with women's NGOs to develop appropriate remedies and services for women who suffer from trafficking, exploitation, and violence.
4. The government should initiate awareness campaigns to ensure that the public knows about and understands new laws such as the revised 2004 Family Law.

Economic Rights and Equal Opportunity

Moroccan legislation provides women with the right to dispose of their property freely and enjoy full and independent use of their incomes; the new CSP's elimination of a wife's obligation to obey her husband further reinforces these rights. In practice, however, conflicts in the home do arise over this issue that often lead to divorce. A national survey revealed that 60.7 percent of rural women reported that their husbands or guardians appropriated their income.[11]

According to the Maliki Muslim laws as interpreted in Morocco, sisters inherit less than half of their brothers' share of inheritance. If there is no male heir, the daughter still does not get the full inheritance, and part of her parents' estate goes to her uncles and aunts. The only changes regarding inheritance in the 2004 revision of the CSP concern the rights of the children of a deceased mother to inherit from the maternal grandparents in the same way as children of a deceased father. Laws that forbid a non-Muslim Moroccan wife from inheriting from her Muslim husband remain intact. Discrimination against women in matters of inheritance is exacerbated by cases in which women, particularly rural women, are excluded from receiving their inheritance altogether. The government has not addressed this issue, and the access of rural women to their rightly deserved land and credit continues to be restricted.

The 1995 revisions of Morocco's commercial code and its obligations and contracts code provided women with the right to start a business and enter into a contract of employment without a husband's authorization. In spite of these advances, women owners of businesses or commercial enterprises represent only 0.8 percent of the total female workforce (compared to the 4.6 percent of the male workforce who own businesses). Women employers likewise represent only 5 percent of all employers and are concentrated in agriculture (30 percent) and in the crafts and services sector (20 percent).[12] Personal and family capital is the main source of financing for 77 percent of woman-run businesses, and only 12 percent of them use bank loans. In rural areas, a major obstacle to the creation of woman-run businesses is the difficulty of gaining access to land and to loans.[13]

Many Moroccans have limited access to education, and women's rates of participation and literacy lag behind those of men. An estimated 49 percent of Morocco's population of 15 years of age and older[14] are illiterate; 61.7 percent of women are illiterate, compared to 36.7 percent of men.[15] Rural women's opportunities for education are among the most restricted, with nearly 8 out of 10 rural women unable to read.[16] It was only in the year 2000 that elementary school education became mandatory. While the rate of participation at the elementary school level (children 6 to 11 years of age) increased from 68.6 percent in 1997 to 90 percent in 2002,[17] improvements have not absorbed the deficit in the schooling of girls in rural areas; an estimated 22 percent of rural girls do not receive any formal education.

The government has undertaken efforts to promote gender equality in the educational system with its National Program to Promote Human Rights Culture in Schools. The National Charter of Education and Training of 1999 also stipulates that the principles and rights granted to men, women, and children shall be respected in any delivery of education and training services. The government, however, has not taken any actions against parents who do not send their daughters to school. Moroccan human rights NGOs are also working to address gender inequalities in education through projects to support the schooling of girls in rural areas and by conducting qualitative surveys on discrimination, violence, and sexual harassment in schools.

Article 13 of the constitution guarantees women the right to employment. This right is also now reinforced in the new labor code of 2003, which emphasizes equality in the workplace with regard to employment and salaries. However, specific civil service regulations prohibit women from pursuing some careers such as firefighters, territorial administration officials, and active service in the army. At the national level, the most common occupations for working women are in agriculture or the fishing industry (52.4 percent of working women, compared to 24.6 percent of men).

Moroccan women have made significant progress in the field of labor, and the overall quality of women's employment has improved. More women are in wage-earning positions (24.7 percent of women report being at the level of paid employment),[18] the number of women in managerial positions has increased, and a larger proportion of women in the workforce have an advanced degree or diploma. However, while women wage-earners in urban areas are significantly better educated than men, women still tend to work in occupations that lack status, such as family helpers, home workers, or cleaning staff.[19] The social protection system, associated with the formal sector, excludes most women workers in these types of jobs.

Some surveys have shown that the wage disparity between men and women varies between 30 percent and 40 percent in the industrial sector (including textiles and garments),[20] and that on average, a woman worker makes only 50 percent of the guaranteed minimum wage.[21] Moreover, 32.8 percent of women in the industrial sector live below the poverty line, compared to 22.6 percent of men.[22] Disparities in wages are often a consequence of a hiring process that tends to place women in lower-level secretarial posts and promotion practices that make it more difficult for women to achieve higher positions.

Unemployment affects nearly 12.5 percent of the workforce and primarily occurs in cities, where 83 percent of the unemployed live. However, it is difficult to assess unemployment rates in rural areas, because many rural women who are not paid for their work may not describe themselves as unemployed. Women city dwellers are more affected by unemployment than men living in cities (24.7 percent versus 18 percent), and women with a higher degree or diploma are one of the largest groups affected by unemployment (35 percent compared to 21.8 percent for men).

The 1958 civil service regulation provisions guaranteed women maternity leave and time for breast-feeding, established limits on women's night work, and in some sectors, banned employers from dismissing women employees for pregnancy, maternity, or marital status. The administrative reform of 1993 granted women additional benefits such as the option of early retirement with 15 years of seniority instead of 21 years. In June 2003, the advocacy efforts of Moroccan women's NGOs resulted in significant advances in the country's new labor code. Nondiscrimination between men and women regarding pay, employment, and promotions is now codified for the first time. However, the terms and conditions for implementing nondiscrimination remain vague.

Additional changes in the new labor code include an increase in paid maternity leave from 12 weeks to 14 weeks for women salaried staff in the public and private sector. The 2003 labor law also requires day-care centers in businesses with more than 50 female employees; however, very few companies respect this law. Women wage-earners, obliged to find their own solutions to day-care needs, resort primarily to domestic workers who are often very young, poorly paid, and without status or social protection.

Section 4 of the 2003 labor law provides for the establishment of a special system to define hiring and employment conditions specific to domestic workers and to the agricultural sector, which employs the majority of women workers. Despite these changes, the status of domestics is still not codified; the labor code applies only to salaried workers and stipulates that the status of non-salaried workers should be covered by a separate code.

Sexual harassment in the workplace is now a criminal offense under Article 503-1 of the revised 2003 penal code, which stipulates that "Any person who abuses the authority conferred upon him by his position, to harass another using orders, threats, coercion or any other means in order to obtain sexual favours is guilty of sexual harassment and is punishable by one to two years imprisonment and a fine." However, this measure, which is very vague, has little chance of reducing the prevalence of this problem, as women workers have not been fully informed of the new law or how to take advantage of it. Women are likely to continue to stay quiet about sexual harassment—fearing loss of employment or judgment by their family or society—thus providing their harassers with total impunity.

Despite positive advances within Morocco's labor code, employers continue to discriminate against women regarding financial allowances. When both spouses are government employees and are in a position to receive a family allowance, that allowance continues to be paid exclusively to the husbands as "head of the family" and not to wives. Considering women's advancements within the labor field, this anachronistic practice serves only to reinforce the social stereotype that women are subordinate to men within the household.

A coalition of women's NGOs and trade union members carried out lengthy advocacy campaigns to make sexual harassment in the workplace a criminal offense, to increase maternity leave, and to codify the work of domestics. Much of the success of the coalition's advocacy is apparent in the new labor code; however, women's NGOs continue to advocate for the codification of the labor of domestic workers and those employed in the agricultural sector. The coalition is also examining practical ways in which to implement the new legislation on sexual harassment in the workplace, and to disseminate information about the rights of women workers under the revised labor code.

RECOMMENDATIONS

1. The government should review legislation on inheritance to ensure strict equality between men and women and work in cooperation with women's NGOs to inform women of their rights under inheritance laws.
2. The government, working in cooperation with teacher's organizations and women's NGOs, should increase efforts to combat illiteracy among women and girls.
3. The government, in consultation with women's NGOs, should review and revise education methods and materials to ensure that women are presented in a positive and equal way and not negatively stereotyped.
4. The government should adopt measures to encourage the practice of nondiscrimination in the hiring and promotion of women in the public and private sectors and regulate the working conditions of women, particularly those who work in the agricultural sector and as domestic workers and family helpers.

Political Rights and Civic Voice

The Moroccan constitution guarantees free elections and universal suffrage. The country's electoral code was completely revised in 2002, introducing a proportional list system and a national list of 30 seats reserved for women in the 2002 house of representatives for the parliamentary elections. Since Morocco's independence in 1956, the country's successive constitutions have granted women political rights and the right to participate in all aspects of political and public life. However, these rights began to be truly implemented only in the late 1990s, when Morocco started taking steps to reform its political system.

Legislative reforms have led to advances in public freedoms for both men and women, with few restrictions in practice, at least in the large cities. Progressive acts by the state in recent years have included rescinding the 1935 royal decree that had prohibited demonstrations contrary to public order, in addition to revising the code governing the creation of associations. However, the interior ministry requires permits for public gatherings, and the police have forcibly dispersed demonstrations in the past. Furthermore, nongovernmental organizations must receive government permission to operate legally.

There is no discrimination between men and women in regard to freedom of expression. However, while Morocco's press laws were revised in 2002, cases still exist in which freedom of the press is attacked. The law still provides for jail sentences and fines for journalists found guilty of libel, and several foreign and domestic publications have been confiscated in recent years. Despite some advances and openings in the print media, broadcast media remain under state control.

Women have the right to take part in elections, which in Morocco are based on a multiparty system. However, all women are not freely able to exercise their right to vote and participate in fair elections, as some candidates exploit the poverty and illiteracy of the poorest women to buy their votes. Government authorities are also known to intervene and direct the voting process, especially in rural and semi-urban areas; nevertheless, these practices, which were widespread in the past, are on the decline.

In 1998, there were 391 women judges serving in Morocco's trial courts, appeal courts, and the Supreme Court. A woman was appointed to the Constitutional Council for the first time in June 1999.[23] Morocco has nearly 1,065 women lawyers out of a total of 6,400; 8 women serve as counsel for the prosecution at the Supreme Court, and 5 women are deputies of the Attorney General. Although women have a significant presence in the judicial hierarchy, no woman presides over a chamber of the Supreme Court or a public prosecutor's office, and there are no female examining magistrates. Women are also absent from the higher judicial division of the army court.

Women first became part of the Moroccan government in 1997, when one was made Secretary of State. Since that time, however, the number of women ministers has remained limited. Women generally receive portfolios as secretaries of state or junior ministers and tend not to be given strong institutional mandates with significant human or financial means.

While women vote as much, if not more, than men, very few women run as candidates for office. The number of female elected representatives at the local, regional, and national levels remains insignificant. To address the low level of women's representation in government, women's NGOs have called for a quota system of 25 percent within the leadership of political parties and among candidates in elections at different levels of representation. In February 2002, the government adopted a national list of 30 seats reserved for women for the legislative elections in September 2002.[24] This measure facilitated the access of 30 women who gained seats as a result of the national list, as well as 5 who won seats in their local districts. The proportion of women in the Chamber of Representatives therefore increased from less than 1 percent to nearly 10.8 percent. Furthermore, at present, a woman from the Progressive and Socialist Party (PPS) is president of a parliamentary group, and a woman from the Popular Movement (MP) is vice president of the Chamber of Representatives.

Moroccan women's NGOs pressed the government to implement mechanisms, such as financial incentives or sanctions,[25] to accompany the list voting system in order to guarantee women's representation. Nevertheless, the quota system was not institutionalized and was not used in the local elections of 2003. As a result, the proportion of women elected as local representatives remained unchanged at 0.6 percent.[26]

Information on women's participation in political parties is scarce, yet a national survey indicates that only 1 percent of women are members of a political party.[27] Another survey showed that a majority of women (89.2 percent) did not belong to a political party, trade union, or associative organization.[28] The national survey reported that 6 in 10 urban women felt that they had not been informed of the existence of political parties and associations.[29]

Many Moroccan women do not have full access to information or resources with which to empower their civic or political lives. The country's audiovisual means are still not adequately adapted to meet women's informational needs. To meet the deficits in information available to Moroccan women, NGOs are increasing the number of radio campaigns, posters, meetings, and training sessions for women, to encourage them to stand for office in elections and to vote for candidates who are likely to consider women's agendas.

RECOMMENDATIONS

1. The government should ensure free, competitive, and democratic elections that are open to all parties, with the full and equal participation of women at all levels of the political process.
2. The government should institutionalize mechanisms and affirmative measures to promote women to positions of senior-level responsibility and decision-making, both in the civil service and in the private sector.
3. The government should create a quota system for female candidates in political parties to ensure that women are able to run as candidates.
4. International donors and the Moroccan government should offer technical and financial support to Moroccan NGOs in the women's political rights field, to help increase access to information for all Moroccan women, particularly rural women.

Social and Cultural Rights

Morocco's high levels of illiteracy, poor access to health care and education, high rates of unemployment, and extensive poverty are exacerbated by stark inequalities between the country's male and female populations and between the rural and urban populations. Women are more affected by poverty and poor economic conditions than men, and women's access to social and cultural rights are often severely restricted.

Glaring inequalities exist between rural and urban areas, and among the various regions of the country in terms of access to health care. Maternal mortality remains high (228 per 100,000 live births nationally and 307 in rural areas), and assistance and follow-up for childbirth remains very low nationally (45.6 percent), with very significant discrepancies between urban areas (75.2 percent) and rural areas (26 percent). There are no programs of systematic screening for breast and cervical cancer; only women from the upper social strata can afford these tests.

Overall progress in women's health is evident however, due partly to the government's policy to reduce the birth rate and partly to women's health education initiatives. The sale of contraceptives is unrestricted and encouraged by the official media; in 1997, the prevalence of contraceptive use had increased to 65.8 percent in urban areas and 51.7 percent in rural areas. Furthermore, women's fertility rates have significantly declined; the fertility index has changed from 5.9 children per woman in 1980 (7.04 for rural women) to 2.7 in 2003.[30]

Voluntary termination of pregnancy is forbidden under the criminal code; abortion is authorized only in cases in which the pregnancy places the mother's life in danger. However, anecdotal evidence suggests that women do have abortions but must pay high prices or may experience the termination in conditions that are dangerous to their health or to their lives. There is limited data available on the incidence of illegal abortions in Morocco.

According to 2001 statistics, sexually transmitted infections (STIs) have become a real public health problem in Morocco, with 250,000 new cases reported per year. Women are particularly vulnerable to STIs and HIV/AIDS due to their lack of power over decisions regarding their reproductive health, such as the use of contraceptives for effective prevention and protection.[31] While it is believed that HIV/AIDS is still relatively limited in Morocco,[32] women are becoming as vulnerable as men. The subject of HIV/AIDS, however, is no longer taboo, and the Ministry of Health and health-specialized NGOs have organized several awareness programs. Nevertheless, the efforts of government and civil society to combat HIV/AIDS are often challenged by the activism of conservative political groups opposed to consciousness-raising and sexual education programs.

Some gender-based traditional practices that are harmful to women's health exist in Morocco. Social preference for women to give birth at home, the use of traditional medicines, and consultations with unlicensed doctors can be detrimental to women's safety and well-being. Although these practices are widespread, they are not effectively recorded or addressed by the government.

Another harmful gender-based practice is the use of the virginity test. Young women are often compelled by their parents to take a virginity test in order to prove their virginity before marriage. Virginity is highly valued by society—a woman who has lost her virginity before marriage is considered to have brought dishonor on her family and may not be able to marry. Unmarried mothers and their children, who usually come from disadvantaged backgrounds, are often subjected to inhuman treatment by society, and the mothers may be threatened with imprisonment for having sex outside marriage. The loss of virginity and/or pregnancy outside of marriage, combined with societal mores, lead many young women to commit suicide, abandon their children, or engage in prostitution. While several associations work to care for these women, their resources are inadequate to meet the women's needs due to the high number of cases. The government seems to have adopted a policy of ignoring the problem, yielding to pressure from extremist religious groups.

There are no legal restrictions on women's right to own property in Morocco, and housing is guaranteed as one of the rights of the child when parents divorce under the new CSP. Therefore, mothers with custody of their children—who were previously turned out into the street—are now entitled to housing. However, in practice, widespread poverty, which is attributable mainly to rapid urbanization, complicates the issue of women's housing. The government has initiated many affordable housing programs to help the most disadvantaged members of society but has been unable to meet the needs of many Moroccan women.

Poverty affects nearly one in five Moroccans[33] and is more prevalent in rural areas. While both men (18.9 percent) and women (19.1 percent) suffer from poverty,[34] women are more likely to be exposed to poverty and to be poor at every age. Select factors make some female populations more vulnerable to poverty than others. Widows and divorcees in urban areas[35] are more exposed to poverty (34.3 percent). Women-headed poor households are likely to be larger than poor households headed by men; in urban areas, 16.9 percent of poor people live in households headed by women, compared to only 5 percent in rural areas. Women in rural areas encounter a number of additional problems connected with poverty, such as: widespread illiteracy; poor access to and retention in the education system; poor access to health care; isolation; impoverished social structures; and poor access to resources such as land, water, domestic energy, bank credit, training, and information.

In recent years, women have gained a strong presence in Morocco's two public television networks, the country's various radio stations, and print journalism. The media in general, and especially the press, have contributed to and influenced positive changes in the status of women in Morocco. The women's press has recently experienced remarkable growth. The leaders of the women's movement are regularly asked by Moroccan media to contribute comments, and their activities are generally well covered. A woman was recently appointed head of the senior institute of journalism, and another woman holds a high position in the management of a public network. Moreover, women journalists have recently formed an association with the aim of promoting women in the profession and their image in the media.

Moroccan women's NGOs and human rights groups in the country have intensified initiatives to promote better conditions and improve the status of women and the most vulnerable populations. NGOs are directing the most important programs for women in the areas of literacy education, microfinancing and microcredit. Moroccan NGOs have also set up many centers where women can obtain information and legal aid. Campaigns to increase awareness of diseases such as HIV/AIDS and sexually transmitted infections, as well as campaigns to promote the schooling of young girls, have become widespread. NGOs are also conducting projects to rehabilitate schools and other shared infrastructures. Nevertheless, government efforts to support women's economic rights remain limited in scope and depth. The government's annual development budget is far from ideal and fails to address the key issues facing women in rural areas.

RECOMMENDATIONS

1. The government should work in cooperation with NGOs to make contraception and information on reproductive health more accessible in vocational training centers, national mutual aid centers, and literacy education courses.
2. The government should allocate more funds for women's healthcare in all parts of Morocco.
3. The government and NGOs should work together to prevent the spread of STIs and HIV/AIDS.
4. The government should implement a specific strategy to help women who are most exposed to social marginalization and poverty, through support services, credit, financial literacy, and employment skills.

AUTHOR: Rabéa Naciri is President of the Association Démocratique du Femmes du Maroc (ADFM/Rabat) and former Executive Director of the Collectif 95 Maghreb Egalite, a network of women's associations and women researchers from Algeria, Morocco, and Tunisia committed to preventing violence against women. Ms. Naciri was also a Professor in the Faculté des Lettres et Sciences Humaines at the University of Rabat in Morocco.

Notes

[1] Less than half of all households are connected to the drinking water system, and scarcely more are hooked up to the electrical system.

[2] The most recent constitutional revision was in 1996; references to the constitution in this report refer to the 1996 constitution unless otherwise indicated.

[3] Finance Act, Section 22.

[4] The exceptions being the Convention on the Nationality of Married Women (1954) and the International Convention on Consent to Marriage, Minimum Age for Marriage and Registration of Marriages (1962).

[5] "Trafficking in Persons Report" (Washington, D.C.: U.S. Dept. of State, Office to Monitor and Combat Trafficking in Persons, 14 June 2004).

[6] "Statistical survey of girl domestics under 18 years of age in the administrative district of Casablanca" (Ministry of Economic Forecasting and the Plan, Regional Delegation of Greater Casablanca, with support of UNICEF and UNFPA).

[7] *Country Reports on Human Rights Practices–2003:* Morocco (Washington, D.C.: U.S. Dept. of State, Bureau of Democracy, Human Rights, and Labor, 25 February 2004).

[8] Rabéa Naciri, "Gender-based violence in Women and men in Morocco. Analysis of the situation and of changes in discrepancies in a gender perspective" (Rabat: Kingdom of Morocco, Ministry of Economic Forecasting and the Plan, Statistics Directorate, UNIFEM, UNDP, ESCWA, publication in progress).

[9] Carin Benninger-Budel, "Violence Against Women in Morocco" (New York: UN Committee on the Elimination of Discrimination against Women [CEDAW], report for 29th session, 2003).

[10] "Equality between men and women: viewpoint of the Moroccan population. Report analyzing the results of the opinion poll" (Rabat: Democratic Association of Moroccan Women, July 2004).

[11] *ENBTF, Women's use of time in Morocco,* "Summary report," Vol. 2 (Ministry of Economic Forecasting and the Plan, Statistics Directorate, 1997–1998).

[12] Benninger-Budel (CEDAW) 18.

[13] Ibid., 19.

[14] Nearly 10 million individuals.

[15] Table 24, "Gender-related development index," in *Human Development Report 2004: Cultural Liberty in Today's Diverse World* (New York: United Nations Development Programme [UNDP], 2004), 217-220. http://hdr.undp.org/reports/global/2004/.

[16] Recensement General de la Population et de l'Habitat [*RGPH*] 1994; and *National survey of the standard of living of households (ENNVM)* (Rabat: Statistics Directorate 1998-1999).

[17] "School Statistics: Report on the class of 2001–2002" (Rabat: Ministry of National Education (MEN), May 2002).

[18] *Workforce participation, employment and unemployment 2002,* "Summary Report" (Rabat: Kingdom of Morocco, Office of the High Commissioner of the Plan, Statistics Directorate).

[19] Aziz Ajbilou, "Economic activity, vulnerability to poverty and inequalities between men and women," Workshop on men and women in Morocco: analysis of the situation and changes in disparities, from a gender perspective (Rabat: Kingdom of Morocco, Statistics Directorate, UNIFEM, UNDP, ESCWA, 18–19 March 2003).

20 Saad Belghazi, "Employment of women and Morocco's competitive advantage" (Geneva and Rabat: UN Research Institute for Social Development [UNRISD]/ Centre d'Etudes et de Recherches Aziz Belal [CERAB], 1995).

21 At present, the guaranteed minimum wage set by the government for the industrial sector is nearly US$185 per month.

22 Benninger-Budel (CEDAW), 34.

23 Ibid., 17.

24 "National Report: Beijing +10" (Rabat: Secrétariat d'Etat auprès du Ministre de L'Emploi, des Affaires Sociales et de la Solidarité, Chargé de la Famille, de la Solidarité et de l'Action Sociale, April 2004).

25 The government makes grants to political parties to finance their election campaigns.

26 However, the number of candidates was larger.

27 *ENBTF.*

28 Rahma Bourqia, et al., "Moroccan student youth: Values and strategies" (Rabat: Rabat Faculty of Literature and Humanities, Essays and studies series, No. 14, 1995).

29 *ENBTF.*

30 Data taken from l'Enquête Nationale sur la Fécondité et la Planification Familiale (ENFPF) (1979–80); "2003 World Population Data Sheet" (Washington, D.C.: Population Reference Bureau, 2003).

31 Yakoubd Abdel-Ilah, "Gender and health in Morocco," Workshop on Men and Women in Morocco, 2003.

32 Portion of population 15–49 with HIV/AIDS by the end of 2003 was 0.1 percent. "2004 World Population Data Sheet" (Washington, D.C.: Population Reference Bureau, 2004).

33 In 1998–1999, the poverty line was set at 3,922 dh per year in urban areas and 3,037 dh per year in rural areas. This represents an average daily expenditure of US$1 for city dwellers and US$0.8 for people living in the country.

34 *ENNVM* (1998–1999).

35 Widows and divorcees make up 13.6 percent of the total female population.

Oman

by Mary-Jane Deeb

Oman

Population: 2,600,000
GDP Per Capita (PPP): $13,340
Economy: Capitalist-statist
Ranking on UN HDI: 74 out of 177
Polity: Traditional monarchy
Literacy: Male 82.0% / Female 65.4%
Percent Women Economically Active: 20.0%
Date of Women's Suffrage: 2003
Women's Fertility Rate: 4.1
Percent Urban/Rural: Urban 72% / Rural 28%

Country Ratings for Oman
Nondiscrimination and Access to Justice: 2.0
Autonomy, Security, and Freedom of the Person: 2.1
Economic Rights and Equal Opportunity: 2.7
Political Rights and Civic Voice: 1.2
Social and Cultural Rights: 2.1
(Scale of 1 to 5: 1 represents the lowest and 5 the highest level of freedom women have to exercise their rights)

Introduction

Oman is a monarchy that has been independent since the expulsion of the Portuguese in 1650. Sultan Qaboos bin Said Al Said, who overthrew his father in a coup, has ruled the country by royal decree since 1970. He serves as both chief of state and head of government, as well as supreme commander of the armed forces, prime minister, and minister of defense, foreign affairs, and finance. Sultan Qaboos also appoints and presides over the council of ministers.

Limited political reform occurred in the 1990s with the establishment in 1991 of the *Majlis al-Shura* (Consultative Council), which was later expanded under the 1996 promulgation of "The White Book: the Basic Law of Oman." The Basic Law, which serves as Oman's constitution, provides for a bicameral parliament, the Council of Oman, which comprises a 57-seat appointed upper chamber, the *Majlis al-Dawla* (State Council), and the expanded *Majlis al-Shura* (Consultative Council) as the lower chamber. The Consultative

Council serves as an advisory body, which has no binding legislative powers and may only recommend changes to new laws. The 83 members of this body are elected by limited suffrage for four-year terms. It was only in 2003 that suffrage became universal for adult Omani citizens, both men and women.

Sultan Qaboos began to liberalize Oman's economy in the 1970s, transforming it from a poor country with no infrastructure to a highly developed, rich country. Oman now has an annual per capita GDP of $13,340. While the country has significant oil reserves, these reserves are likely to run out within the next 20 years. Today, the petroleum sector contributes about 40 percent of Oman's gross domestic product, down from 70 percent in the 1980s. The sultan has pursued policies to liberalize the economy for long-term economic growth by investing extensively in the environment, education, and tourism industries. Oman gained full membership in the World Trade Organization in 2000.

Oman has a population of 2.6 million, less than 2 million of whom are Omani citizens. The majority of noncitizens are foreign guest workers, chiefly from South Asia, Egypt, Jordan, and the Philippines, who are not afforded the same legal protections as citizens. Islam is the state religion, and the Basic Law establishes *Shari'a* (Islamic law) as the source of all legislation. While 75 percent of Omanis are Ibadi Muslims, there are sizable minorities of Sunni and Shi'a Muslims, as well as small Christian and Hindu communities.

Rights of assembly and association are extremely limited in Oman, and no meaningful organized political opposition exists. Public gatherings require government permission, and political parties are banned by law. While the government permits the formation of nongovernmental organizations (NGOs), there are no human rights or women's rights NGOs and no labor or trade unions. Freedom of expression and democratic debate are also extremely limited.

Women in Oman have made steady progress over the past decade. There are currently more women than men enrolled in higher education at the university level despite gender-discriminatory practices in the enrollment process. Women's rate of participation in the labor force is on the rise, and an estimated one-third of all civil servants are women. In 2000, the sultan appointed five women to the State Council, and this number was raised to eight in 2003. In March of 2004, Sultan Qaboos appointed Oman's first woman minister with a cabinet portfolio to head the ministry of higher education. Nevertheless, women's participation in the political process remains low, and they hold only two of the 83 seats in Oman's Consultative Council.

One of the major challenges to women's rights advocacy and women's status in Oman is the overall denial of basic civil liberties such as freedom of association and expression. Women also face legal discrimination and are afforded unequal rights under Oman's personal status law. The personal status law, interpreted from Shari'a, governs matters of the Muslim family such as inheritance, marriage, divorce, and child custody. Oman is one of the few remaining members of the United Nations that has not yet ratified the UN Convention on the Elimination of All Forms of Discrimination Against Women (CEDAW).

Nondiscrimination and Access to Justice

Oman's legal system is founded upon the Islamic Shari'a traditions of the Ibadi school. Civil, criminal, and commercial cases are handled by the courts of first instance; matters of personal status and family law fall under the jurisdiction of Shari'a courts. Although the Basic Law states that the judiciary is independent, it remains subordinate to the sultan and the ministry of justice.

The 1996 Basic Law granted citizens certain civil liberties, banned discrimination, and clarified the process for royal succession. According to Article 17 of the Basic Law, "All citizens are equal before the Law, and they are equal in public rights and duties. There shall be no discrimination between them on the grounds of gender, origin, colour, language, religion, sect, domicile or social status."[1]

The Basic Law, however, does not apply to or protect noncitizens from discrimination. Considering that foreign guest workers, many of whom are women, constitute over a quarter of Oman's population, many Omani residents are left without legal protections. In March 2003, Human Rights Watch sent an open letter to Sultan Qaboos requesting the government to endorse the International Convention on the Protection of the Rights of all Migrant Workers and Members of their Families.[2]

Although the Basic Law prohibits discrimination on the basis of gender, women may still undergo legal and social discrimination. Oman's Shari'a courts favor men in matters of personal status, and women are legally restricted from traveling abroad without the permission of a male relative.

According to Article 12 of the Basic Law, "Justice, equality, and equality of opportunity between Omanis are the pillars of society, guaranteed by the State." Both men and women are free to appear before the courts and gain access to legal defense; however, it was only recently that a royal decree established criminal rules of procedure for criminal cases before the court, providing rules of evidence, procedures for entering cases into the criminal system, and detailing provisions for a public trial.[3] Most Omanis remain uninformed about the new procedures. Rural women in particular do not have access to such information or legal literacy.

Oman's penal code was established in 1974 by royal decree No. 7. While women are treated equally with men in most areas of the penal code, some articles are discriminatory against women due to their gender. For example, men receive reduced sentences based on a crime's circumstances as defined in Article 252, which stipulates that a man who surprises his wife or a female relative committing adultery (*in flagrante delicto*) and immediately kills or injures her and/or her partner may be exempted from liability or be liable to a reduced penalty in accordance with Article 109 of this law.[4] Article 109 of the penal code specifies that the penalty for such a crime should be applied as follows: "if the action is a felony giving rise to the capital punishment or life imprisonment it shall be reduced to prison for at least one year."[5] Furthermore, while Omani law prohibits rape, spousal rape is not considered to be a crime.

Protections against arbitrary arrest, detention, and exile are not defined in gender-related terms within the Basic Law but rather in terms of citizenship. Article 16 of the Basic Law forbids the state to deport or exile an Omani citizen or prevent them from returning to the country. While no human rights monitoring groups are able to operate in Oman, arbitrary arrests and detentions are believed to be rare for both men and women.

Overall, few NGOs are active in Oman, and the government prohibits the establishment of human rights and women's rights NGOs. Work on women's issues is controlled by the government ministry of social development, which supports and funds the activities of the Oman Women's Association (OWA). The OWA, established in 1970, is considered the first women's organization in Oman. It now has 38 chapters and an estimated membership of more than 3,000 women. The activities of these chapters include informational lectures on health practices, kindergarten services, handicrafts training, informal advice, and support for women seeking legal actions such as divorce or suffering from domestic abuse or marriage against their will.[6] The OWA also promotes traditional Omani customs and values.[7]

There are also a number of government-approved women's associations, some of which are self-funded, others that receive government financial or in-kind assistance, while still others operate with membership fees, donations, and product sales. By the end of 2003, 40 nongovernmental women's associations were in operation; their goals are reportedly "to develop women's perceptions and raise their awareness in various spheres, organize charity fairs and markets, hold seminars, lectures and workshops, and set up productive projects."[8] No international women's rights NGOs operate in Oman.

One major obstacle to the improvement of women's status in Oman is the fact that many women are not aware of their rights under the laws and are thus unable to exercise them effectively. There is an urgent need to start legal literacy programs for women, especially women in rural areas and women with low literacy so that more women can become aware of their rights and the means by which to exercise them. The small number of women lawyers is also an obstacle to women's access to justice, and the government does not facilitate the employment of women law school graduates in legal aid jobs or social justice assistance positions in rural areas.

RECOMMENDATIONS

1. The government should ratify CEDAW, without reservations, take steps to implement it locally, and bring national laws into conformity.
2. The government should work with NGOs to design national programs to create awareness about women's human rights protections currently available in Omani laws.
3. The government should bring its national laws into conformity with the equality clause in the Basic Law to ensure that laws do not discriminate against women.

Autonomy, Security, and Freedom of the Person

While Islam is the state religion of Oman, Article 28 of the Basic Law guarantees freedom of religion, stating, "The freedom to practice religious rites in accordance with recognized customs is guaranteed provided that it does not disrupt public order or conflict with accepted standards of behavior." The government generally respects this right in practice, and Oman is, overall, a religiously tolerant society. While non-Muslim residents are able to practice their religious rites freely, they are required to register with the government and may not proselytize or publish religious materials.[9] Muslim women do face some restrictions under Oman's interpretation of Islamic law, however. For example, an Omani Muslim woman is forbidden to marry a non-Muslim man, but Omani Muslim men are free to marry outside the religion.

Omani laws do not prohibit women from traveling abroad; however, women's freedom of movement is restricted in that the law requires them to have the permission of a male family member, such as a husband or father, in order to travel outside the country.[10]

Oman's personal status law tends to favor the rights of men over the rights of women in marriage, divorce, inheritance, and child custody. However, the interpretation of the family law by Oman's individual judges may vary. Both Omani men and Omani women are required to seek the permission of the state in order to marry noncitizens. This process may include long delays and in some cases permission may be denied. Secret marriages that are not recognized by the state are occasionally performed; yet, marriages without government permission may result in the spouse being prevented from entering the country or a child from that marriage being refused citizenship. However, in general, Omani women have the right to choose their husbands and are free to accept or refuse a marriage partner suggested by their family.

Protection from slavery and slavery-like practices is guaranteed under Article 12 of the Basic Law, which states, "Every citizen has the right to engage in the work of his choice within the limits of the Law. It is not permitted to impose any compulsory work on anyone except in accordance with the Law and for the performance of public service, and for a fair wage." Although it is clear that this law is intended to apply to both citizens and noncitizens of Oman, as it refers to the illegality of imposing compulsory work on "anyone" rather than just "any citizen," in practice, this law is not always respected or fully implemented.

Employers sometimes withhold the wages or the official papers or passports of foreign workers, thus forcing them to work under slave-like conditions. Women foreign domestic workers have been known to be victims of this practice. Although foreign workers have the right to file complaints with the Labor Welfare Board against their employers for illegal practices, most workers are either unaware of their rights and protections or are fearful of losing their jobs or being deported. Oman's recent 2003 labor law defines employment conditions for some citizens and foreign workers but does not cover domestic servants, temporary workers, or those with work contracts for less than three months.[11]

According to Article 20 of the Basic Law, "No person shall be subjected to physical or psychological torture, enticement or humiliating treatment, and the Law lays down the punishment for anyone who is guilty of such actions." There were no reports of torture or harsh and degrading punishments of either male or female Omanis during 2003. Prisons generally adhered to international standards for the treatment of prisoners.[12] Women prisoners were estimated to comprise 5 percent of the prison population in 2000.[13] However, it is difficult to get full information about the status of women in prisons in Oman, as no data are available and human rights monitoring groups are not permitted in the country.

Oman has no specific legislation that criminalizes domestic violence. While issues of domestic violence are not present in the media or in public reports, domestic violence does exist in Omani society at various levels. Information about domestic violence and gender-based violence outside the home is rare partly due to a complete lack of documentation processes or facilities for women to report violence in confidentiality. However, a number of cases have been filed by women victims of domestic violence in Omani courts in recent years.

Although it is widely believed in Omani society that a woman seeking legal help for domestic violence will receive support from government authorities, most women still do not report such cases. Doctors do not have a legal responsibility to report spousal abuse to the police, and battered women often prefer to seek assistance and protection from their families rather than from the police or the courts.[14]

The ability of women's groups to advocate for women's rights in Oman is unclear. While the Basic Law grants citizens freedom of association in Article 33, it stipulates that the associations must have "legitimate objectives" that do not conflict with the aims of the Basic Law. The ambiguity of this article seems to perpetuate state control over civil society and to effectively prevent the formation of any significant opposition groups that could pose a challenge to the regime in power. However, the government has been promoting gender awareness in conferences, workshops, and communication initiatives. Through its support and funding of the Omani Women's Association, the state provides informal counseling for women with divorce-related problems and for those who might be forced to marry against their will.[15]

RECOMMENDATIONS

1. The government should design programs to increase the number of women in courts as officials, judges, and lawyers.
2. The government should provide training and guidance to medical, police, and judicial officials who handle cases of violence against women, including family violence.
3. The government should gather statistics on violence against women and create educational campaigns aimed at raising public awareness about the problems of violence against women.
4. The government should allow the formation of independent women's NGOs to address all women's issues freely and to work with international women's groups without government interference.

Economic Rights and Equal Opportunity

In 2000, Oman launched its sixth five-year plan for the economy, which emphasizes the "Omanization" of the labor force, job creation in the private sector, and more specific focus on Oman's interior regions, which continue to lag behind the coastal regions. Foreign workers constitute at least 50 percent of the work force and as much as 80 percent of the private sector work force.[16]

A woman's right to own and dispose of her property independently is included in Article 11 of Oman's Basic Law, which declares, "Private property is protected. No one shall be prevented from disposing of his property within the limits of the Law." Nevertheless, this law is not always successfully implemented, as authorities rarely intervene in these situations, which are socially considered domestic matters. The ways in which a woman can dispense her income and assets are usually decided by the head of the household, who is traditionally a man; however, women are gaining more decision-making power within the family due to their increasing participation in the labor force and their abilities to contribute financially to the family. While women have the legal right to enter into business contracts and activities at all levels, the decision to so is also traditionally made within the family and almost never individually.

Women are not afforded equal rights with men under Oman's laws of inheritance, which are in accordance with the country's interpretation of Shari'a, as specified in Article 11 of the Basic Law. While women have the option of approaching the courts should a conflict arise over inheritance, they are often afraid to initiate a case in court, out of fear of alienating their families.[17]

Women have made extensive gains in the field of education since the 1970s. Prior to the reign of Sultan Qaboos, girls were not able to receive an education. Equal access to education without gender discrimination is now guaranteed by law and is free of charge for all students; however, education is still not compulsory. Article 13 of the Basic Law declares, "Education is a fundamental element for the progress of society which the State fosters and endeavors to make available to all." At the elementary school level, as many girls are enrolled as boys, and at the tertiary level, there are more women than men.

Despite early efforts in the 1970s toward the education of girls and women, only 16 percent of adult women were literate in 1984.[18] However, women's literacy rate (age 15 and above) today is 65.4 percent, an impressive gain.[19] Women's literacy rate still falls behind that of men, however, which is 82 percent.

Women constituted 54 percent of the students entering Sultan Qaboos University in 2002. Of Omanis studying abroad, 24 percent are women. Nevertheless, while women's gains in education are impressive, they are restricted by a gender quota system applied in the higher education institutions that aims to enroll more men than women in certain disciplines such as medicine and engineering. The number of male and female students graduating from high school is about equal, but only a limited number of seats are allotted for women at professional and technical colleges. Every year, thousands of women are not able to continue their studies after high school due to these limitations. In 2000, the majority of women at the tertiary level were enrolled in the fields of arts, education, and humanities (83.1 percent of women versus 45 percent of men).[20] No women graduated from Sultan Qaboos University with a degree in engineering in 2002. Furthermore, requirements for the admission of female students in some academic fields are more rigorous than those for male students.

Women are legally entitled to pursue the career of their choice in Oman. Article 12 of the Basic Law states, "Every citizen has the right to engage in the work of his choice within the limits of the Law." However, a woman's profession is usually decided in consultation and negotiation with her family members, such as her father, brothers, and/or husband. Women may face social obstacles if their choices are not supported by their male family members. The government does not interfere in family disputes concerning a woman's career choice, and women often must agree with the decisions of the patriarch of the family on these matters. Nevertheless, women's participation in the labor force is on the rise; the 2004 UNDP Human Development report estimated that 20 percent of Omani women are economically active.[21]

Protections against gender-based discrimination in the labor sector are specified in Article 12 of the Basic Law, which claims that "Justice, equality, and equality of opportunity between Omanis are the pillar of society, guaranteed by the State." By law, men and women should receive equal wages for the same work, although women may not be provided with the same benefits as men, such as pensions. Men tend to collect more employment-related benefits and concessions, as they are considered to be "head of household."

The government has taken some steps to implement the law and the policy of nondiscrimination with the hiring of public sector employees. Currently, one-third of government employees in Oman are women, although few women have been appointed to high-level decision-making posts. Women are present in many private-sector companies as well, and educated women have attained positions of power and responsibility in many parts of the economy. However, many women complain of a glass ceiling with respect to promotions in employment. Omani women also face discrimination in the hiring process due to employers' fear that women employees will marry or have children and leave their jobs.

Women have some gender-specific protections in the private and public sectors such as the right to maternity leave, but they often face discrimination based on their gender within employment contracts and labor benefits. While most employers provide insurance to their workers and benefits to families of deceased male workers, equal benefits are not provided to women workers or their families. This is partly because women are not considered heads of households in Oman. Discrimination in benefits affects both citizen and noncitizen women workers who do not receive job benefits, family benefits, or insurance packages equal to those of male workers. The government of Oman has not taken any steps to eliminate this form of gender-based discrimination in the law.

In April 2003, a Labor Law went into effect that abolished a 1973 prohibition on strikes, and details the processes for dispute resolution. Under the 2003 decree, neither men nor women workers have the right to collective bargaining or to unionize, but they can select a representational committee to voice their demands and represent their interests. However, these committees are still not allowed to discuss wages, hours of work, or conditions of employment.[22]

Oman does not have a law against sexual harassment in the workplace. Reports of the sexual and physical abuse of female domestic workers and nurses by employers and co-workers continued to emerge during 2002 and 2003, with no reported actions taken against the perpetrators of these crimes. Social pressures in Oman that place greater responsibility on women than men to uphold "proper moral behavior" often hinder women's efforts to report cases of sexual harassment in the workplace. Many women also fail to report abuse or harassment in the workplace out of fear of losing their jobs.

RECOMMENDATIONS

1. The government should enact laws criminalizing sexual harassment in the workplace and should establish programs to provide information and support to female victims of sexual harassment.
2. The government should allow female workers to form unions that promote and protect their rights.
3. The government should eliminate gender-discriminatory policies in the education sector and provide equal access, funding, and resources to higher and technical education facilities for women and men.
4. The government should ensure that all government jobs, including the posts of judges, are open to women, and it should encourage women to enter the workforce.

Political Rights and Civic Voice

Omani men and women do not have the right to change their government democratically. They have limited rights to peaceful assembly and freedom of speech and do not fully participate in the political life of their country. Nevertheless, Oman is liberalizing gradually; women are beginning to play more important roles in the upper level of government, are registering to vote in large numbers, and are increasingly running as candidates in parliamentary elections. Women have also been appointed as cabinet ministers, undersecretaries of state, and ambassadors. Universal suffrage was offered for the first time to both men and women in the 2003 elections. In previous elections, only a limited number of citizens selected by tribal leaders were allowed to vote.

Women's rights to peaceful assembly and association exist within the limits of Omani law. All organized activities require prior government approval, which may or may not be given. Political parties are banned, and no activities deemed to be in opposition of the government are permitted to take place.

Article 29 of the Basic Law declares the rights of all Omanis to free speech, declaring, "Freedom of opinion and expression whether spoken, written, or in other forms, is guaranteed within the limits of the law"; however, restrictions exist in practice. Freedom of the press is restricted, and it is illegal to criticize the sultan in any form. Journalists, therefore, are known to practice self-censorship. Restrictions on freedom of expression and the press are applied equally to both men and women journalists and to activists in Oman.

Elections are held in Oman for the Majlis al-Shura, in which men and women are allowed to vote and to compete as candidates for office. The minimum voting age was lowered from 30 to 21 in the 2000 elections, and the number of women eligible to vote rose from 5,000 to 52,000 as a result.[23] The most recent legislative elections occurred in October 2003, in which 95,000 women registered to vote.[24] Three women served on the 12-member Main Election Committee, a committee of the Consultative Council.[25] Out of a total of 506 contenders for the 83 seats of the Consultative Council, 15 women ran as candidates, but only 2 were elected, and both were incumbents.

Much change is still needed in social attitudes toward the role of women in positions of power. A number of Omani publications in recent years have addressed the role of women in politics and have concluded that while Muslim women can participate fully in the political affairs of the state, they should not rule.[26]

Despite Oman's legal guarantees for equal opportunity in employment, women are not allowed to serve as judges in the country's courts. Women are represented in the civil service, however, and while still in limited numbers, also fill positions within the upper level of the government. The government is the largest employer of women; in 2002, women constituted 33 percent of civil servants. In 2003, 8 women were serving in the 57-member State Council. That same year, a woman was appointed for the first time at the ministerial rank (without portfolio) as president of the newly established Public Authority for Craft Industries.[27] Four women were also appointed in 2003 as undersecretaries and two women as ambassadors. In addition, an Omani woman was appointed as head of the United Nations Information Centre based in Geneva in July 2003.[28] On March 8, 2004, International Women's Day, Sultan Qaboos announced that Oman's first woman minister with a cabinet portfolio had been appointed as minister of higher education.[29]

With regard to the right to participate in civic life issues and influence decision making, Article 34 on "Petitions, Public Affairs" does not differentiate between the rights of men and women. The article simply states, "Citizens have the right to address the public authorities on personal matters or on matters related to public affairs, in the manner and on the conditions laid down by the Law." In reality, men constitute the vast majority of policy makers in the executive, legislative, and judiciary branches of government. Women have just begun to play a role as decision makers on the national scene.

A member of the State Council of Oman recently proposed at a conference in the UAE on "The Parliamentary Performance of Arab Women" that a certain number of seats be reserved for women in Arab parliaments. She argued that a quota system would help Arabs view women as decision makers and help women acquire more political rights in their society.[30] Presumably, the traditional image of women's role in Omani society would change if women were seen as leaders and decision makers. Women, therefore, could further serve as role models for the younger generations.[31]

Women have begun to make use of their right to access and use information to empower themselves in Oman as well as share knowledge regionally. In 2003, an Organization of Arab Women was established as a specialized government agency in the League of Arab States to defend and promote the rights of Arab women. Oman was one of 11 signatories to the agreement to establish the organization.[32]

RECOMMENDATIONS

1. The government should allow independent political parties to operate freely and mandate the reservation of seats in political bodies for women.
2. The government should allow independent civil society organizations to operate freely in all parts of the country.
3. The government should establish mechanisms to ensure that women are not discriminated against in the hiring policies of government structures and to ensure that women are promoted to senior positions within all branches of the government.

Social and Cultural Rights

No laws or particular injunctions affect women's rights to make decisions about their health and reproductive rights. Women and men are legally entitled to equal access to health services, and health care is free in public hospitals. Article 12 of the Basic Law states that "The State cares for public health and for the prevention and treatment of diseases and epidemics. It endeavors to provide healthcare for every citizen."

Family planning is practiced in Oman, and a birth spacing program was initiated by the government in 1994 that aimed to educate married couples about the benefits of spacing births and its positive effects on the health of the mother, child, and family.[33] Birth control and counseling services are free in all institutions affiliated with the ministry of health; however, abortion is illegal in Oman. Government efforts toward women's health and family planning have had direct and positive results in lowering the number of unattended births and the maternal mortality rate. ESCWA reported in 2003 that all of the urban population and 90 percent of the rural population had access to health services, and 98 percent of deliveries were attended by trained personnel.[34] In 1993, women's fertility rate was reported at 6.9 children per mother;[35] this rate has now dropped to 4.1.[36]

With respect to protection from gender-based harmful traditional practices, Oman does not have any laws against female genital mutilation (FGM). While FGM is not common in Oman, some small communities, including those in the Dhofar region, still practice it.[37] However, FGM seems to be on the decline.[38] The government has not officially issued a ban on this practice or initiated any public education campaigns for Omani women on the dangers of FGM.

Women are not legally prevented from exercising their right to own and use housing, but social pressures and traditions often make it difficult for women to gain access to housing independently. While they are legally entitled to property and loans, government officials will often deny women housing loans or land grants due to their gender, preferring to deal with their male relatives.[39] Older women who are illiterate also find it difficult to own property or participate in economic activities in the modern sector of the economy.

Omani women are active participants in community life and social development policies. Women have increasingly been appointed to upper-level positions in the ministries that have an impact on the country's development policies such as the ministry of social affairs, labor and vocational training; the ministry of education, which addresses Oman's school system; and the ministry of higher education, which affects the affairs of Oman's colleges and universities.

Divorced and widowed women are among the most vulnerable to poverty in Omani society. While the ministry of social development supports 50 local community development centers (LCDC) that work to improve the quality of life for families, these centers need additional support and staff training in order to be more efficient in helping women in rural areas and women throughout the country. People suffering from poverty do receive small amounts of financial aid from the ministry of social development, but it is never enough to meet their basic needs. Oman's Social Security Act covers five categories of women: widows, divorcees, abandoned women, unmarried girls, and women with a family member in prison, as well as both men and women who may be orphaned, work-disabled, or aged. In 2002, the proportion of social insurance cases and payments to women from the five designated female categories was 30 percent of total cases.[40] Omani families tend to provide for family members who are not able to support themselves.

The Omani government prohibits the establishment of human rights NGOs and women's human rights NGOs in Oman, and there are no government-controlled or autonomous human rights organizations in the country.[41] Although women's organizations do exist and work to provide vocational training, health care, and literacy campaigns for women, these groups do not have the authority to defend women's human rights and lack proper training and knowledge of women's rights and advocacy methods.

RECOMMENDATIONS

1. The government should allow women's human rights groups to organize and advocate for women's rights.
2. The government should design a national program that provides supportive services and income-generating training programs for women facing poverty, especially widows and unemployed women.
3. The government should issue a law that bans female genital mutilation and initiate public education campaigns against this harmful practice.
4. The government should set up adult literacy programs for women, especially in rural areas, that also help women to understand their rights under the law.

AUTHOR: Mary-Jane Deeb is the Head of the Near East Section at the Library of Congress and is on the faculty of the School of International Service at American University in Washington, D.C. Dr. Deeb previously served as the Editor of The Middle East Journal *and Director of the Omani Program at The American University in Washington, D.C. She holds a Ph.D. in International Relations from the School of Advanced International Studies at Johns Hopkins University.*

Notes

[1] "The White Book: The Basic Law of the Sultanate of Oman" (Muscat: Sultanate of Oman, Ministry of Information, 1996), http://www.omanet.om/english/government/basiclaw/overview.asp?cat=gov&subcat=blaw.

[2] "Letter to His Majesty Qaboos bin Said Al Said, Sultan of Oman," *Human Rights News*, March 2003, http://www.hrw.org/press/2003/04/gccoman.htm.

[3] *Country Reports on Human Rights Practices – 2003: Oman* (Washington, D.C.: U.S. Dept. of State, Bureau of Democracy, Human Rights, and Labor, 2004), http://www.state.gov/g/drl/rls/hrrpt/2003/27935.htm.

[4] Lynn Welchman, "Extracted provisions from the penal codes of Arab states relevant to 'crimes of honour'" (London: Centre of Islamic and Middle Eastern Laws [CIMEL]and International Centre for the Legal Protection of Human Rights [INTERIGHTS], "Honour" Crimes Project: Arab Laws, http://www.soas.ac.uk/honour-crimes/Mat_ArabLaws.htm.

[5] Ibid.

[6] *Country Reports* (U.S. Dept. of State, 2003).

[7] "OWA Promises All Support to Women to Fulfill Dreams," *Aman Daily News*, 13 August 2002, http://www.amanjordan.org/english/daily_news/wmprint.php?ArtID=388.

[8] Oman's response to the "Questionnaire on Implementation of the Beijing Platform for Action (1995) and the Outcome of the Twenty-Third Special Session of the General

Assembly (2000)" (Muscat: 2004), http://www.un.org/womenwatch/daw/Review/responses/OMAN-English.pdf.

9 *International Religious Freedom Report – 2003: Oman* (Washington, D.C.: U.S. Dept. of State, 18 December 2003).

10 "Gender-Oman" (Beirut: UNDP Programme on Governance in the Arab Region [POGAR]), http://www.pogar.org/countries/gender.asp?cid=13.

11 *Country Reports* (U.S. Dept. of State, 2003).

12 Ibid.

13 "Prison Brief for Oman" (London: King's College London, International Centre for Prison Studies), http://www.kcl.ac.uk/depsta/rel/icps/worldbrief/middle_east_records.php.

14 Ibid.

15 Radhika Coomaraswamy, "Integration of the Human Rights of Women and the Gender Perspective: Violence Against Women" (Geneva: UN High Commissioner for Human Rights [UNHCHR], E/CN.4/2003/75, 27 February 2003), http://www.unhchr.ch/huridocda/huridoca.nsf/(Symbol)/E.CN.4.2003.75.Add.1.En?Opendocument.

16 *Country Reports* (U.S. Dept. of State, 2003).

17 Ibid.

18 "Gender-Oman" (UNDP POGAR), http://www.pogar.org/countries/gender.asp?cid=13.

19 *Human Development Report 2004* (New York: United Nations Development Programme [UNDP], 2004).

20 "Country Profiles – 2003: Oman" (Beirut: United Nations Economic and Social Commission for Western Asia [ESCWA]), http://www.escwa.org.lb/ecw/index.asp.

21 *Human Development Report 2004* (UNDP, 2004).

22 *Country Reports* (U.S. Dept of State, 2003).

23 Ibid.

24 "Elections: Oman" (POGAR), http://www.pogar.org/countries/elections.asp?cid=13.

25 *Country Reports* (U.S. Dept. of State, 2003).

26 See, for example, the discussion in "Al-mar'at wa al-`amal al-siyasi," in Dawr al-mar'at fi bina' al-mujtama`, quoted in http://www.al-Balagh.com (in Arabic).

27 "Developments in the Situation of Arab Women" (UN ESCWA, Center for Women, April–June 2003), http://www.escwa.org.lb/ecw/index.asp.

28 "Developments in the Situation of Arab Women" (UN ESCWA, July–September 2003), http://www.escwa.org.lb/ecw/index.asp.

29 Sunil Vaidya, "Letter from Oman: Women Making Inroads into Male Domain," *Gulf News,* 11 March 2004.

30 "Arab Parliaments Urged to Reserve Seats for Women" (London: Women Living Under Muslim Laws [WLUML], 27 May 2004), http://wluml.org/english/newsfulltxt.shtml?cmd[157]=x-157-51393.

31 "Getting the Balance Right in National Parliaments" (New York: Women's Environment and Development Organization [WEDO]), http://www.wedo.org/5050/5050factsheet4.pdf.

[32] "Developments in the Situation of Arab Women," (UN ESCWA).

[33] Oman's response to the "Questionnaire to Governments . . ." (Muscat, 2004).

[34] "Country Profiles – 2003: Oman" (ESCWA), http://www.escwa.org.lb/ecw/index. asp.

[35] Oman's response to the "Questionnaire to Governments . . ." (Muscat, 2004).

[36] "2003 World Population Data Sheet" (Washington, D.C.: Population Reference Bureau, 2003).

[37] "Integration of the Human Rights of Women . . . " (UNHCHR), http:// www.unhchr.ch/huridocda/huridoca.nsf/(Symbol)/E.CN.4.2003.75. Add.1.En?Opendocument.

[38] *Country Reports* (U.S. Dept of State).

[39] Ibid.

[40] Oman's response to the "Questionnaire to Governments . . ." (Muscat, 2004).

[41] *Country Reports* (U.S. Dept of State).

Palestine*

by Suheir Azzouni

Palestinian Authority and Israeli-Occupied Territories

Palestine
(Palestinian Authority and Israeli-Occupied Territories)

*Palestinian Authority and Israeli-Occupied Territories

Population: 3,390,000
GDP Per Capita (PPP): $921
Economy: Capitalist
Ranking on UN HDI: 102 out of 177
Polity: Parliamentary (military and partly foreign-occupied)
Literacy: Male 96.3% / Female 87.4%
Percent Women Economically Active: 9.5%
Date of Women's Suffrage: N/A
Women's Fertility Rate: 5.7
Percent Urban/Rural: Urban 57% / Rural 43%

Country Ratings for Palestine
Nondiscrimination and Access to Justice: 2.6
Autonomy, Security, and Freedom of the Person: 2.7
Economic Rights and Equal Opportunity: 2.8
Political Rights and Civic Voice: 2.6
Social and Cultural Rights: 2.9

(Scale of 1 to 5: 1 represents the lowest and 5 the highest level of freedom women have to exercise their rights)

Introduction

The Palestinian Authority (PA) was established in 1994 with limited authority over the Palestinian population living in the Israeli Occupied Territory, which includes the West Bank, East Jerusalem, and the Gaza Strip.[1] The areas under limited PA rule are not contiguous but are separated by 102 Israeli checkpoints in the West Bank and 21 in Gaza.[2] Checkpoints, curtailing Palestinian freedom of movement, and lack of security in a situation close to war, have devastated the Palestinian economy. According to the Palestinian Central Bureau of Statistics (PCBS), at the beginning of 2002, 66.5 percent of Palestinian households were living below the poverty line.[3] The situation now is graver still.[4] Palestinians are generally prevented from traveling between towns, and restrictions on movement have had a serious effect on Palestinian women's access to health care facilities, employment locations, and educational institutions.

219

Continued political unrest and ongoing armed conflict, combined with restrictions on freedom of movement, the inability of most PA courts to enforce decisions, and a slow process of new legislation, make it extremely difficult for Palestinian women to advocate for women's rights in the face of continuing violence and poverty. As a result, Palestinian women suffer from insufficient legal protections and inconsistent enforcement of laws.

Of the 3.39 million Palestinians[5] in the West Bank and Gaza, almost 1.5 million have been refugees since the 1948 war and more than 800,000 live in refugee camps scattered through the Territory. The vast majority of Palestinians, refugees and non-refugees, are stateless.[6] Most Palestinian residents of the occupied territories are Sunni Muslims. However, significant populations of Palestinian Christians, a majority of whom are Greek Orthodox, live in the territories, as well as Roman Catholics and Greek Catholics, Protestants, Syriacs, Armenians, Copts, Maronites, and Ethiopian Orthodox. In general, Christians are concentrated in the areas of Jerusalem, Ramallah, and Bethlehem. Jewish Israeli settlers also live in the West Bank, Gaza, and Jerusalem, but not under Palestinian jurisdiction.[7]

All discussions about Palestine's constitution, its laws, and their impact on women must be viewed through the limitations imposed by the Israeli occupation. The occupation dictates the ways in which the Palestinian Authority conducts its affairs and how Palestinians go about their daily lives. It also greatly impacts Palestinians' personal security. From the beginning of the second Intifada—the uprising started in September 2000—until May 2003, 2,484 Palestinians were killed—among them 152 women.[8]

The status of women inside the family and in Palestinian society is determined in part by recent Palestinian legislation and in part by laws inherited from the Jordanian and Egyptian laws in effect in the West Bank and Gaza before the 1967 Israeli occupation. While there have been many positive changes for women under laws adopted by the Palestinian Authority, gender-based discriminatory practices enshrined in the Jordanian and Egyptian laws still apply to situations not covered by new legislation. Personal status law for Palestinians is based on religious law. For Muslim Palestinians, personal status law is derived from Shari'a, while the varied ecclesiastical courts rule on personal status issues for Christians. Civil courts do not adjudicate on such matters.

Nondiscrimination and Access to Justice

The third draft constitution[9] (The Basic Law) of Palestine, which appeared in the Official Gazette in March 2003, views Palestinians as equal before the law. Article 9 of the constitution states that Palestinians will not be subject to "any discrimination on the basis of race, sex, color, religion, political convictions or disability."[10] The draft also states that the principles of Islamic Shari'a are a major source of legislation.

Article 32 of the draft constitution states that any violation of personal liberties or the privacy of the person or other general civil rights that are protected by the constitution or the law will be considered a crime. A presidential decree in 1993 established the Palestinian Independent Commission for Citizens Rights (PICCR), with a mandate to ensure respect for citizens' rights in Palestine.[11]

Although the draft constitution states that the rights and liberties of all citizens shall be protected and that citizens—men and women—will be treated equally without discrimination, many laws do not make gender discrimination punishable. A few of the newly drafted laws are more gender-sensitive, however; they refer to citizen, employee, or person, refer to both males and females, and some even contain provisions that clearly render discrimination illegal.[12]

The Palestinian women's movement has actively engaged in dialogues with the Palestinian Legislative Council to secure a woman's right to extend citizenship to her husband and their children.[13] However, citizenship rights remain covered by the laws and regulations valid before 1967 in the Palestinian territories; the Jordanian nationality code no. 6 of 1945 and its amendments are applied in the West Bank,[14] and the Egyptian code is applied in Gaza. Both codes deny the right of women to pass their nationality to their husbands or children. Additionally, a woman is not entitled to maintain her nationality if she marries a non-Palestinian unless she submits a written application to the Minister of Interior within one year following her marriage. In practice, however, women married to non-Palestinians are not always asked by the Ministry of Interior to give up their Palestinian nationality.

Palestinians living in Jerusalem under Israeli rule hold Jerusalem identity cards. These cards serve as residence permits and enable Palestinians to live, travel, work, and attend school. Many of the women—and some men—holding Jerusalem identity cards and married to Palestinians from the West Bank and Gaza cannot obtain Jerusalem identity cards for their spouses, and their spouses are not allowed to live in Jerusalem.[15] Children also find it difficult to live or attend school in Jerusalem if only their mother and not their father holds a Jerusalem identity card.[16]

Under Islamic law (the Jordanian and Egyptian Laws that were in effect before the 1967 occupation), a Muslim woman has the right to keep her maiden name after marrying if she wishes. In the PA and Israeli Occupied Territories, however, there are neither legal stipulations that entitle a woman to maintain her maiden name after marriage nor stipulations that oblige her to adopt her husband's name. In practice, Palestinian women's family names are automatically changed at marriage because the Palestinian passport, like the Israeli identity card, automatically changes women's family names to those of their husbands.[17] The names of Palestinian women holding Jerusalem identity cards are also automatically changed to their husbands' family names.

Women are discriminated against in laws governing marriage, divorce, custody of children, inheritance, and violence against women. Palestinian men and women do not have equal access to justice, and women are particularly discriminated against in the penal code, which is derived from Jordanian and Egyptian law.[18] The law enforcement structure is male dominated and sometimes biased against women. Women are marginally represented among judges and police, which may make women hesitant to turn to the courts or law enforcement for help. Access to justice has proved a challenge for both men and women throughout the second Intifada (2000 to present). The existing political situation, in addition to Israeli incursions and the inability of the Palestinian Authority to enforce the law properly, has rendered the judiciary and law-enforcement mechanisms weaker than ever. It has also strengthened the use of tribal and customary law.

The judiciary system in Palestine is composed of a hierarchy of courts.[19] Women are not recognized as full persons before the courts as witnesses or in matters related to marriage, divorce, and custody of children. The Women's Center for Legal Advice and Counseling (WCLAC) report for 2000 states that the Palestinian judiciary exhibits views of women as "inferior"[20] and that women generally are "looked down upon and treated with scorn." It also reports that "a divorced woman is treated as though she has been 'indicted' for failing to try to sustain the marriage."

Women suffer disproportionately from law enforcement that is weakened by the fact that Palestinians fall under four different legal systems—Israeli, Jordanian, Egyptian, and Palestinian—and there are no legal agreements between the various authorities. For example, a father with an Israeli passport or a Jerusalem identity card can kidnap his child and go to the Israeli area, where the Palestinian Authority cannot enforce child custody laws. The same holds true for alimony cases in which husbands living inside Israel can escape their legal obligations to their former wives.

A number of Palestinian women have been murdered by family members for "tarnishing the name and the honor of the family," although statistics are difficult to obtain because police often report these crimes, or "honor killings," as suicides or other causes of death. It is estimated that there are about 20 documented cases of honor crimes in Palestine annually. The WCLAC in Jerusalem states in its report on the situation of Palestinian women in 2001 that 38 cases of femicide were documented between 1996 and 1999, 12 of which occurred in the West Bank and 26 in Gaza; the murders were all committed by close male relatives such as fathers, brothers, and uncles.

Article 340 of the Jordanian penal code, still in effect in the West Bank, enables male relatives to benefit from a lessened sentence should they commit a "crime of honor"[21] and murder a female relative for a perceived misuse of her sexuality. At the same time, there are many stories of Palestinian police providing shelter for women after they have received a death threat. Despite the fact that the Jordanian penal code was amended in Jordan in 2001 to give equal treatment to men and women, the older version still applies in the West Bank. For adultery cases in the West Bank, the code states that: "He who surprises his wife, or one of his [female] Mahrams committing adultery with somebody [*in flagrante delicto*], and kills, wounds, or injures one or both of them, shall be exempt from liability." It also stipulates that: "He who surprises his wife, or one of his female ascendants or descendants or sisters with another in an unlawful bed, and he kills or wounds or injures one or both of them, shall be liable to a lesser penalty."[22]

In the Gaza Strip, the Egyptian penal code on adultery applies. It states that "he who surprises his wife committing adultery [*in flagrante delicto*] and immediately kills her and the person committing adultery with her, shall be liable to a prison sentence instead of the penalties provided for in Articles 234, 236." The same lesser penalties do not apply to women surprising their husbands, however. The draft criminal code that was prepared on April 14, 2003 and was circulating in 2003, but is not yet in force, would treat men and women equally in all civil matters, should it become law in Palestine.[23]

Palestinian men and women are subjected to arbitrary arrest, detention, and exile by the Israeli Occupying Authorities. There have been numerous cases of "administrative detention,"[24] in which the Israeli Authorities keep Palestinians in jail for periods of six months, subject to multiple six-month renewals without trial.[25] PICCR reports that as of December 31, 2003, the Israelis held 6,206 Palestinians in their prisons and detention centers. Among the detainees were 275 children and 77 women.[26] Palestinian women prisoners held in Israeli jails are vulnerable to harsh and humiliating treatment, and their treatment does not meet all international standards for prisoners' rights. In some cases, female prisoners are denied contact with their families.

The Palestinian government has not ratified the UN Convention on the Elimination of All Forms of Discrimination Aganist Women (CEDAW), because Palestine is not an independent country and as such cannot be signatory to international treaties and conventions.

Palestinian women's organizations and official bodies, such as the prominent women's coalition, Palestinian Women's Affairs Technical Committee, have been very active in ensuring that women's issues are addressed in the new Palestinian entity. They have worked together to win the reversal of a few regulations and to ensure that newly drafted laws discussed by the Palestinian Legislative Council do not discriminate against women. Because of their collective work, the Palestinian Labor Law and Social Status Law are now mostly gender-sensitive. However, while women's organizations were more visible and outspoken in the relatively peaceful period that followed the Oslo Accord, they have been less visible and vocal during the second Intifada for a number of reasons, including the need to focus on day-to-day issues involved in life under occupation.

The freedom that Palestinian women's organizations enjoy depends heavily on the political situation in the area. When the situation is more stable, women's groups have more freedom to address the concerns and issues of women. Another factor that influences the level of freedom women's organizations enjoy is the nature of the issue they address. While women feel more empowered and able to address issues dealing with discrimination related to passports, citizenship rights, and raising the minimum age of marriage,[27] they are more severely attacked by extremist Islamic groups when they try to tackle issues dealing with family and inheritance. For example, during the Model Parliament project in 1998, Islamic groups verbally attacked women's organizations and a few activists, claiming that they were sabotaging culture and tradition and introducing concepts contradictory to Islamic Shari'a.

RECOMMENDATIONS

1. The future Palestinian nationality law should grant women the right to pass their nationality to their husbands and children without any discrimination and allow women the option of maintaining their maiden names on their passports.
2. The Palestinian Authority should ensure that divorced women receive alimony.
3. The Palestinian Authority should punish all perpetrators of "honor crimes."
4. The Palestinian Authority should appoint more women in the judiciary and provide court and police officials with compulsory training in women's rights.

Autonomy, Security, and Freedom of the Person

The third draft constitution (The Basic Law) guarantees freedom of religion and religious practice as well as freedom of thought. Christians and Muslims live peacefully together in Palestine, with few problems of discrimination on the basis of religion. There are examples of Christian-Muslim marriages, although such marriages are easier when they take place between Christian women and Muslim men, as these women are able to remain Christians.[28] Muslim women cannot marry Christian men unless the men convert to Islam.

Women in Palestine do not enjoy complete freedom of movement. The Jordanian passport regulations that applied in the West Bank following the Oslo Accord of 1993 required women to secure the written permission of their "guardians" in order to obtain passports. This regulation was reversed when the Women's Affairs Technical Committee held a five-month advocacy campaign in 1996. The campaign resulted in women gaining the right to obtain passports without the consent of their guardians after the age of 18.[29] However, while women who are aware of the change in this regulation can demand that this right be respected, officers at the Ministry of Interior continue routinely to require women to obtain written consent.

Changing political, economic, and social conditions also affect the mobility of women. The newly erected separation wall and the 123 checkpoints in the West Bank and Gaza prevent free mobility of all Palestinians. Israeli checkpoints have prevented women from reaching hospitals and health care centers in time to give birth and also hinder free access to education and employment, especially in areas where secondary schools are scarce and where jobs require moving from one village or city to another. Existing family law provisions also restrict women's freedom of movement. Though rarely invoked, a provision of Egyptian and Jordanian family laws termed the "house of obedience" forces women to return to their husband's house and prevents them from leaving the country if their husband obtains a court order.

The Jordanian Personal Status Law of 1976 remains in effect in the West Bank, as does the Egyptian Law[30] on Family Rights of 1954 in Gaza.[31] The laws are discriminatory in all matters relating to marriage, divorce, and custody of children.[32]

In accordance with the local interpretation of Islamic Shari'a, women can have many rights within a marriage if they are specified in their marriage contract. Prevailing customs however, discourage many women from spelling out these rights.[33] Men are reluctant to marry a woman who has the right to divorce, and families discourage women from adding conditions that may drive the bridegrooms away. It is noteworthy, however, that a 1999 survey by PCBS[34] showed that over half of married women—55.5 percent—were responsible for their decision to marry (43.5 percent in the West Bank and 78.7 percent in Gaza). A woman's parents made the decision for her to marry 39.8 percent of the time, and 2.6 percent of women surveyed said that a brother or a sister made the decision for them. The survey shows that among those who made the decisions by themselves to marry, 63.7 percent were from urban areas and 36.0 percent were from rural areas.

There is no known practice of slavery of women in Palestine, and there are no laws that address slavery. Additionally, no laws or provisions specifically protect women against torture and cruel, inhuman, or degrading punishment.

Violence against women is extensively reported by local women's institutions and seems to increase during times of political and economic turmoil in the Territory. Currently no laws or provisions in the Territory specifically protect women against domestic violence; however, violence is punishable, whether it is perpetrated against males or females, and women can use such provisions to access the judicial system and law enforcement. Although women can use existing gender-neutral laws like the criminal law to achieve justice, several factors explain why many battered, abused, raped, and threatened women do not invoke these laws against their abusers, such as: social norms that shame a woman who reports her abuse to the police; the feeling that women should remain silent because of their children or because they have no alternative place of residence; and the lack of shelters. There is currently only one shelter in Nablus and a second under construction in the Bethlehem area.[35]

A proposed criminal law[36] would punish those who commit acts of physical violence but does not specify the gender of the violator or his relation to the victim. The Jordanian and Egyptian laws in effect also punish violators without regard to the gender of the victim or perpetrator.[37] Data provided by women's organizations dealing with issues of violence in the West Bank and Gaza indicate that they receive hundreds of cases in which women were victims of sexual, physical, and psychological violence. About 30 percent of the cases involve single women or girls who live with their parents. According to data available from the Working Women's Society in Ramallah, 75 percent of sexual assault cases against women involve men closely related to them. A number of women's organizations freely express their views about violence and the difficulties women face because of Palestine's discriminatory laws and enforcement policies.[38] Women's organizations in Palestine offer a wide array of services, ranging from lobbying and advocacy work to training and psychological counseling.

RECOMMENDATIONS

1. The Palestinian Legislative Council (PLC) should draft a family law that grants women full and equal rights in all areas, especially in matters of marriage, divorce, and custody of children.
2. The minimum age of marriage should be raised to 18 years for both men and women.
3. The Palestinian Authority and PLC should abolish laws and policies that reinforce women's inferior status, including the "house of obedience" law and the "honor crime" plea which allows for reduced sentences for crimes committed in the name of honor.
4. The Palestinian Authority and PLC should introduce new laws to protect women from all forms of violence at home and in all public places, and create special units inside police stations to handle cases of family violence.

Economic Rights and Equal Opportunity

Palestinian women have the legal right to own land and property and to exercise control over their property.[39] However, prevailing traditions and customs, such as those that encourage women to give up their share of inheritance to their brothers, or those encouraging men to keep property in their names rather than jointly with their wives, render the percentage of women owning property marginal. PCBS showed in its 1999 survey that only 7.7 percent of women in the Palestinian Territory own or share a house/real estate (5.7 percent in the West Bank and 11.1 percent in Gaza). The survey also shows that 5 percent of women own or share a piece of land (5.4 percent in the West Bank and 4.3 percent in the Gaza strip) and only 1 percent own a private car (1.3 percent in the West Bank and 0.4 percent in Gaza).

Despite the de jure independent financial status of men and women under Islamic Shari'a and the property laws in effect in Palestinian areas, there are still women who do not have control over their income and assets. This is mainly due to customs and traditions that continue to view men as the breadwinners and thus assume that financial decision making is the right of the man. However, a large percentage of women in Palestine do claim that they are participants in the main decision making that takes place inside the household. A PCBS survey in 1999 concluded that the "main decision-making concerning the household is done in consensus with the participation of all household members as stated by 88 percent and 92 percent of men and women respectively."

The Jordanian law governing inheritance still applies in the Territory and gives women the right to half the share entitled to a man. Many Palestinian women—especially in rural areas—do not enjoy this right, as they are shamed by society if they claim their legal share of inheritance. Palestinian families in general prefer that their sons inherit so that the family possessions stay in the family and do not go to the family of the daughter's husband. There have been a few campaigns by women's institutions encouraging women to claim their share of inheritance. The 1999 PCBS survey concluded that 20 percent of women entitled to inheritance claimed their share.[40]

No legal barriers prevent women from entering into businesses or economic-related contracts and activities. However, discriminatory family upbringing and social norms—especially in the rural areas—may hinder women from engaging in economic contracts. The new Palestinian Labor Law of 2000, although much advanced from previous law, still contains discriminatory provisions whereby women are not granted the same benefits and allowances as men.

Since its establishment in 1994, the Ministry of Education in the Territories has made impressive efforts to make education accessible for boys and girls. Fewer schools were built for girls than boys during the occupation, and the ministry has since concentrated on the establishment of schools for girls, especially in rural areas. The ministry has further enabled schoolgirls who are engaged or married to return to the classroom to complete their compulsory school education. Prior to that, girls who were married were dismissed from school.[41]

The Labor Force Survey 2003 conducted by PCBS showed that the literacy rate is 91.9 percent among individuals aged 15 years and over in the Palestinian Territory. This rate is 96.3 percent for males and 87.4 percent for females.[42] Despite the high initial enrollment rate at schools, however, there remains a drop-out problem for children at the secondary school level. The female drop-out rate is a result of early marriage and the scarcity of girls' schools at the higher levels in rural areas and refugee camps.[43]

The syllabi, especially in secondary schools,[44] remain traditional and promote stereotypical roles for women and men. Girls are also encouraged by their parents to pursue education that leads to jobs that are an extension of their perceived future roles as mothers and caregivers.

Women's access to education has also been restricted by the ongoing armed conflict in the area and by the construction of the "separation wall" between Israeli and Palestinian areas. Palestinian women living close to the wall now must walk longer distances in order to get to their schools and universities. The wall has also placed new economic burdens on Palestinian families who must arrange transportation services for girls and women in the family to attend schools.[45]

A large percentage of women remain outside the labor force in the Palestinian Territory. Another large percentage work as unpaid family members or in the informal sector, where they do not enjoy the benefits and protections provided by the Labor Law. According to the UNDP, 90.5 percent of women in the Palestinian Territory are outside the labor force.[46] Of the women who received 13 or more years of education, 55.7 percent are outside the formal labor force, and less than 1 percent own their own business.

One of the main obstacles keeping women out of the labor force—apart from the declining economic situation—is the lack of adequate services to help women balance work with their reproductive roles, according to PCBS. Very few establishments in the Palestinian Territory include child-care services. Both the Labor Law and the Civil Administration Law grant women a maternity leave of 10 weeks and a paid nursing hour for the first year after delivery. Many businesses continue to discriminate against married women, however.[47] In the banking sector, especially at Arab Bank and the Cairo Arab Bank, women are asked to submit their resignation when they wed. The government has done nothing to require these banks to change their regulations, despite the law that prohibits such discrimination. The law itself prohibits women from working in jobs that are deemed "dangerous or hard," or that involve night hours, with few exceptions.

Women reportedly earn only 65 percent of men's wages in the West Bank and 77 percent in the Gaza Strip; many women earn less than minimum wage. Many women also work under discriminatory conditions and are denied their rights to maternity leave and weekly and annual holidays and vacations.[48] Finally, time spent crossing Israeli checkpoints to reach job opportunities further extends women's working hours outside the home, leaving them less time to handle their domestic burdens.

Women's organizations have regularly called for an act to protect women from sexual harassment in the workplace, but no such law yet exists. Women find it difficult to make sexual harassment public because they may be shamed or held responsible for the harassment, as social norms tend to further stigmatize the victim.

Women's advocacy groups in general have been more successful in seeking changes in formal legislation than in winning changes in law enforcement practices and cultural attitudes that inform law enforcement. Convincing society to change its perception of a woman's role remains a daunting task.

RECOMMENDATIONS

1. The Palestinian Legislative Council (PLC) and the Palestinian Authority (PA) should create mechanisms to ensure that all women have access to their full and equal inheritance rights.
2. The PLC should enact and enforce laws that ensure gender equality in labor and insurance rights.
3. The Ministry of Education should open up more vocational education training for girls in the Palestinian Territories.
4. The PLC should draft and ensure the enforcement of laws that protect women against all forms of discrimination and harassment in the workplace.

Political Rights and Civic Voice

The civil and political rights of all Palestinians are adversely affected by the continued occupation by Israel and the resulting restrictions on their freedom of movement. Women's access to, and full enjoyment of civil liberties and political rights are also affected by the economic, social, and cultural restraints placed on their lives within Palestinian society.

In general, women do not face many barriers to peaceful assembly inside the PA-controlled area and away from Israeli checkpoints. In order to march or demonstrate, women and other groups require permission from the governor, and such permission is usually granted without problem. In some cases, protests against Palestinian government officials are not permitted due to a fear of violence. Palestinian women who assemble in Jerusalem or near Israeli checkpoints to protest the human rights violations of Palestinians may at times be attacked, beaten, imprisoned, or shot at by Israeli army and police.

While women enjoy freedom of expression, they also find it difficult to advocate for their social rights when all of Palestinian society suffers under Israeli occupation. The community may also expect women to prioritize the nationalist movement over their own gender-sensitive issues and problems within Palestinian society. This is an additional pressure on women's rights advocates working locally in areas under armed conflict.

There is a modest degree of freedom of the press in Palestine. Women have their own media outlets and express their views freely. However, women seldom touch upon the issue of sexuality or political violence, as these issues represent social taboos. Women have free access to information via the Internet, mostly at home; young men tend to dominate the majority of public Internet cafes.

Women are guaranteed equal voting rights, though only one legislative election has taken place in Palestine since the establishment of the Palestinian Authority. No municipal elections[49] have been held, though preparations are ongoing for a second legislative council election. Palestinian men and women over 18 can vote and stand for elections. However, prevailing cultural attitudes and stereotypes about women and their abilities, as well as women's limited financial resources, present barriers to women running for office.

Of the 46 judges working in the West Bank 4 are female, as is the case also in Gaza.[50] Out of the 1,332 lawyers in the Palestinian territories, 141 are female. Reasons for the low representation of women in the judiciary include the high costs of legal education and society's expectations concerning the roles of women. Also, women are not often promoted in the judicial hierarchy, and female lawyers are not afforded equal opportunity to train, qualify, and develop skills to be able to compete for high posts.[51]

Available statistics indicate a very low level of representation for women in the upper echelons of public office. Although women represent 13 percent of the staff in administrative positions, they hold only 3 percent of top decision-making posts—such as legislators and upper-level public servants—according to PCBS.[52] There are also only one female ambassador and two women holding the post of minister. As for the 88-seat Palestinian Legislative Council, 5 women were elected, representing slightly less than 6 percent.

No more than 30 women are represented in local governments out of a total of 3,081 officials, and this is only after extensive lobbying by a leading women's organization for a quota system. As no elections have been held for municipalities and local government, these numbers are all the result of appointments by the ministry.

Political parties in the Territory are male dominated, with reportedly 8 women in decision-making posts in the largest party in Palestine (Fatah), versus 188 men.[53] After women demanded a quota of 30 percent in all decision-making bodies in 1996,[54] some parties like the People's Party agreed to grant women 20 percent of seats in their decision-making ranks.

The women's movement enabled Palestinian women to establish the Ministry of Women's Affairs in 2003, in addition to gender desks inside various ministries, and the Women's Affairs Technical Committee. They reversed the regulation requiring women to secure permission of "guardians" to obtain passports and included many provisions to make the Civil Status Law, the Civil Administration Law, the Labor Law, and the Elections Law less discriminatory against women.

A number of women's organizations exist throughout Jerusalem, the West Bank, and Gaza. Since 1991, women have been freely advocating for the rights and concerns of women on economic and social issues, as well as the representation of women in decision-making posts. Hundreds of workshops are held annually to train women and men on gender issues, democracy, and human rights. Women also have their own publications and radio and televised programs through which they are able to express their concerns freely. While 92.8 percent of households in Palestine own a television[55] and 55.9 percent own cable dishes, less than 5 percent of the population tends to watch cultural or educational programs.[56] The publications and newsletters that women's organizations publish are distributed on the Internet or for free through grassroots organizations, which is difficult when freedom of mobility is restricted by Israeli checkpoints. Information dissemination through the Internet has not been very popular in Palestine because only 19.1 percent of Palestinian households own computers and only about 4 percent have an Internet connection.

RECOMMENDATIONS

1. The international community should work with Israel and the Palestinian Authority (PA) to resolve existing political disputes in order to end the occupation, ensure peace in the region, and provide a state for Palestinians where all men and women can choose their leaders through free, competitive, and fair elections.

2. The PA should accept the demands of the Palestinian women's movement to increase the representation of women to at least 30 percent in the PLC and in all branches of government, especially in positions as ministers, deputy ministers, general directors, and heads of units in ministries and offices and in diplomatic missions.

3. The PA should support political rights training programs for women in government offices to upgrade their leadership skills and capacities.

Social and Cultural Rights

Palestinian women have one of the highest fertility rates in the region: 5.7 children per woman.[57] Socio-political, cultural, and economic factors influence these high fertility rates, including pressures placed on women to bear more children to compensate for deaths related to armed conflict. The early median age of marriage (18 years), in addition to the low percentage of women in the labor force, are additional contributors to the high fertility rates. Families tend to marry a daughter early when the family is economically unable to provide for her education; high transportation costs are involved in commuting to the nearest secondary school.

Palestinian women do not appear to have much control over decisions concerning their reproductive rights. A survey conducted in 2000 by PCBS shows that only 6.9 percent of women reported being the one to decide how many children to have.[58] Although 99 percent of women say that they are aware of birth control methods, only 51.4 percent of women said that they used contraceptives.[59] Research from Birzeit University shows that there is a link between education and fertility, namely that when women are given an education that leads to income generation, they tend to have lower fertility rates. PCBS reports that the fertility rate of women with less than a secondary education is 6.32 children per woman; for those with a secondary education, 5.57; and for those with more than a secondary education, the rate is 4.52.

Since 1994, the Ministry of Health in Palestine has accorded special importance to the health of women. A strategic national health plan that includes awareness campaigns was initiated to develop health facilities and counseling programs.[60] However, a survey by PCBS in 2001 reported that 88.4 percent of married women surveyed had never heard of the term "reproductive health" and that while 94 percent of women gave birth in hospitals, 73.7 percent did not get post-natal care.

Abortion is not allowed in the Palestinian Territory and is considered a crime unless the physical health of the mother is threatened. Women can obtain abortions in some hospitals inside Israel if they are able to pass the checkpoints and afford the cost. In some cases, women's organizations have helped victims of rape or incest with such expenses and access to hospitals inside Israel.

Women in Palestine seem to be at even more of a disadvantage when it comes to the availability and quality of health services. A 2001 WCLAC report noted a "marked discrimination in favour of men, who receive qualitatively better health services."[61] The report states that 40 percent of adolescent girls reportedly suffer from some form of malnutrition or anemia, coupled with immense social and psychological stress. Women in the reproductive age face malnutrition and anemia that are mainly caused by early marriage and recurrent and successive pregnancies. Many women in the menopause stage of their lives suffer from osteoporosis, which results from malnutrition and poor health habits. No special programs target elderly women who, according to the report, are the most marginalized in society.

Women's access to health care services is additionally challenged by the travel restrictions related to the armed conflict and the Israeli checkpoints. Women sometimes have to wait for long periods of time in order to reach hospitals or medical care inside the PA or Israel that was not available to them in their area. Delays at checkpoints have resulted in numerous unattended births and unnecessary deaths.

Laws do not protect women against such traditional practices as female genital mutilation (FGM). Research by the Culture and Free Thought Association in 1999 to 2000 shows that female genital mutilation is still being practiced in Gaza—especially in areas close to Egypt—although the study does not mention the extent of the practice. Of the 176 individuals interviewed for the study, 64.8 percent believed that there were advantages to having the circumcision performed. Of those mutilated, 88.6 percent reported that the operation was conducted without anesthesia and 86.4 percent said that the tools were not sterilized. Finally, early marriage continues to be a harmful tradition for women in Palestine.

Women are free to participate in and influence a number of media outlets. They have had their own radio and televised programs, which include "No to Silence," a radio program run by the Women's Affairs Technical Committee in Palestine on The National Palestinian Radio. "Bisaraha," a women's television program that focused on women's social problems, was suspended at the beginning of the Intifada because PA government officials deemed the timing inappropriate for such programs, considering the many casualties among Palestinians.

The Palestinian non-government coalition, the Women's Affairs Technical Committee also has a bi-weekly newspaper supplement called Sawt-An-Nissa (the voice of women), which is freely distributed inside one of the widely circulated daily newspapers. In addition to the paper's 20,000 daily circulation, the Women's Affairs Technical Committee prints some 500 more copies of its supplement that are distributed in various geographical areas where the organization holds awareness activities.

Many media outlets discriminate against women and project stereotyped roles of men and women. The *Al-Quds* newspaper, for example, seldom publishes articles that encourage a more active role for women. Most of its articles encourage the traditional division of labor and are conservative in outlook. However, *Al-Ayyam* newspapers portray more progressive views.

Female-headed households are among the poorest in Palestine. Research shows that such households represent 9.5 percent of all households and that

73 percent of them live in extreme poverty, struggling to meet the basic needs of nutrition, housing, and clothing. The newly created Ministry of Women's Affairs aims to provide assistance to female heads of households and to the poor in society. It also encourages other government ministries to attend to the needs of poverty-affected populations by offering training, assistance, and employment. A number of international aid organizations also provide assistance to the poor in Palestine in the form of emergency aid programs.

Women and their organizations are free to advocate openly about the promotion and the protection of women's human rights. Women and their organizations, however, find addressing issues such as equal rights in marriage, divorce, and inheritance extremely challenging. They tackle these issues through large coalitions and by working with other civil society institutions to press for change.

RECOMMENDATIONS

1. The Palestinian Authority (PA) should increase its budget allocations and services for women's health programs, with a special focus on rural women.
2. The international donor community should assist the Palestinian Ministry of Health to provide modern and adequate health services for women, especially for illnesses that are currently not treatable inside the PA, such as osteoporosis and breast and cervical cancer.
3. The Ministry of Health, in cooperation with Palestinian NGOs, should ensure that mothers are provided with adequate prenatal and postnatal care and that women are provided with public education on family planning and knowledge of the impact of early marriage on the health of women and girls.
4. The government of Israel should ensure that Palestinian women's access to hospitals is not impeded at checkpoints.

AUTHOR: Suheir Azzouni is a Palestinian women's rights leader and an expert on gender and human rights. She established the Women's Affairs Technical Committee (WATC) in the Palestinian Territory, serving as General Director from 1994 to 2001. Ms. Azzouni has worked on gender mainstreaming projects in Bangladesh, Brazil, Egypt, Jordan, Lebanon, Mauritania, Palestine, Sudan, Tanzania, Tunis, and the United States. She holds an MA degree in Gender, Law, and Development from Birzeit University.

Notes

[1] In 1993, the Oslo Accords (representatives from the Palestinian Liberation Organization and Israel) divided the Palestinian Territory into three areas: Area A would be under Palestinian authority; B under joint authority; and C under Israeli authority until the final negotiations were concluded. Negotiations have broken off, however, and most of the land remains under Israeli control.

[2] "Israeli Miltary Checkpoints in the West Bank" (Palestinian Economic Council for Development and Reconstruction [PECDAR]), http://www.palestinemonitor.org/maps/westbank_checkpoints.htm.

[3] According to UNRWA, 12,737 Palestinians were made homeless by Israel's military campaign of house demolitions between September 2000 and 30 April 2003.

[4] "Impact of the Israeli Measures on the Economic Conditions of Palestinian Households; 9th Round (April–June 2004)" (Ramallah, Palestine: Palestinian Central Bureau of Statistics [PCBS], 2004).

[5] It is estimated that more than 3 million Palestinians live outside Palestine, in Lebanon, Syria, Jordan, North America, and Europe.

[6] Dr. Bernard Sabella, lecture, 26 January 2004 (Bethlehem University, Holy Land Christian Ecunemical Foundation, HCEF, 2004). The proportion of Christians was estimated at around 7 percent by the Palestinian Central Bureau of Statistics in 1997. Sabella says that the number has dropped to less than 2 percent of the population due to emigration after the second Intifada.

[7] "International Religious Freedom Report, 2003" (Washington, D.C.: U.S. Dept. of State, Bureau of Democracy, Human Rights, and Labor, 18 December 2003).

[8] "Men and Women in Palestine" (PCBS), 13, http://www.pcbs.org.

[9] The draft constitution views the Palestinian people as part of the Arab and Islamic nations with Arab unity as a goal (Article 1). It considers Islam the official religion of the country and Arabic as the official language while equally revering and respecting Christianity and other religions. Article 2 of the constitution clearly states that the "principles of Islamic Shari'a are a major source of legislation."

[10] While Article 10-1 considers human rights and liberties as "binding and must be respected," part 2 of the article states that the state "will strive to join international declarations and conventions that guarantee human rights." Article 11 states that "personal freedom is a guaranteed right." "Appropriate housing" is named as a right of every citizen, and according to Article 23 the state will work to guarantee shelter to those who do not have it.

Education is viewed by the third draft of the constitution as a right and is compulsory until the end of the elementary level and free of charge in all public schools and training institutions. As to the human right to labor, the draft constitution asserts that it views employment as a right, an honor, and a duty and that the state will seek to provide work opportunities to all those able to work.

The draft constitution recognizes the political rights of Palestinians. It states that citizens shall have the right to assume public office, on the basis of competence, merit, and equal opportunity in accordance with the requirements of the law. Furthermore, every citizen has the right to participate in political activity, run for office, or nominate a person who meets the electoral requirements. Additionally, every individual has the right to organize private meetings in accordance with the law and without the presence of the police. Citizens have the right to assemble and organize public meetings and to demonstrate peacefully (Article 26).

[11] The Palestinian Independent Commission for Citizens' Rights [PICCR] (Ramallah, Palestine), http://www.piccr.org/about/about.html.

[12] One example is Labor Law No. 7 for 2000.

[13] "Governmental Report on the Status of Palestinian Women—Five Years After Beijing" (Ramallah: Palestinian National Authority [PNA], Inter-ministerial Commiteee for the Advancement of Women, 2002), 61.

[14] "A Report on the Situation of Women's Human Rights during the Second Intifada: Report presented to the UN Human Rights Commission Fact-finding Mission" (Jerusalem: The Women's Center for Legal Advice and Counseling [WCLAC], 16 February 2001), 21.

[15] On 31 July 2003, Israel complicated the process further when it passed a law barring family unification for married couples in which one partner holds an Israeli passport and the other is a resident of the Occupied Territories. This new law is retroactive, meaning that thousands of couples who have been living in Israel awaiting a decision on their status will be required to separate or leave Israel. A January 2004 report by B'Tselem and HaMoked examines the issue further.

[16] An Israeli identity card is the document that was given to all Palestinians who were in the West Bank and Gaza when Israel occupied the Palestinian territories in 1967. As Israel wanted to annex Jerusalem to Israel, it gave Palestinians in Jerusalem different identity cards classifying them as mere residents of the city and not citizens. West Bankers now hold different kinds of identity cards that do not entitle them even to enter Jerusalem or Israel.

[17] The Women's Affairs Technical Committee in Palestine lobbied in 1998 to reverse this discrimination, and a few women were able to change back to their maiden names. However, to maintain one's name in one's passport after marriage has proved to be a lengthy bureaucratic procedure because it also involves the acceptance of the Israelis. Thus, while the Palestinian Ministry of Interior has recognized this as a right for women, few women are willing to go through the strenuous process to maintain their names.

[18] Laws based on Jordanian and Egyptian law, however, are not always amended or updated to correspond to the progressive changes that have been made in the laws of Jordan and Egypt today.

[19] Article 99 of the Draft Law provides for a Supreme Court composed of a High Constitutional Court; a Court of Cassation to hear civil, criminal, and commercial matters; and a High Court of Justice to hear administrative disputes. The High Constitutional Court has the authority to review laws and rules to ascertain their constitutionality. The Court of Cassation and the High Court of Justice are at the apex of the ordinary judicial structure and serve as the final courts of appeal for issues in their respective departments.

[20] "A Report on the Situation . . ." (WCLAC), 37.

[21] A "crime of honor" is a crime in which a woman is killed due to an allegation that she had sex outside the institution of marriage; it is usually punishable by six months of imprisonment or less.

[22] Lynn Welchman, "Extracted Provisions from the Penal Codes of Arab States relevant to 'crimes of honour'" (London: School of Oriental and Asian Studies), http://www.soas.ac.uk/honourcrimes/Mat_ArabLaws.htm.

[23] Chapter 7 of the proposed law punishes crimes of rape with imprisonment for a period of time; if the perpetrator is a supervisor or a close relative or a guardian, his punishment would be imprisonment for life. However, engaging in a sexual relation with a girl aged over 18 years is also considered a crime for both the male and the female even if the sexual relation takes place with the consent of the female (Article 258). If the perpetrator is a guardian, supervisor or close relative, he will be imprisoned for no less than five years. Homosexuality is also a crime punishable by law. Sexual harassment, includ-

ing that which causes psychological harassment, is punishable by law according to the proposed law (Article 264 – 1). Prostitution and adultery are also punishable, and men and women are both equally liable to prosecution.

[24] Administrative detention is detention without charge or trial authorized by an administrative order rather than by judicial decree. Since the beginning of March 2003, Israel has held more than 1,000 Palestinians in administrative detention according to B'tselem, an Israeli Information Center for Human Rights in the Occupied Territories (http/www.btselem.org/English/Administrative_Detention/Index.asp).

[25] According to figures provided by the Israeli Defense Forces (IDF) spokesperson, the IDF was holding, as of 7 July 2004, 737 Palestinian administrative detainees.

[26] Ninth Annual Report (Ramallah, Palestine: The Palestinian Independent Commission for Citizens' Rights [PICCR] 2003), http://www.piccr.org/report/annual03jan/summary.pdf.

[27] In 1995 women's organizations were able to reverse a discriminatory regulation that required women to have the consent of their guardians to obtain passports.

[28] There have been some cases in which couples secretly married each other twice, once the Muslim way and the other the Christian way. Such alliances are more frequent in cities, especially in Ramallah. However, in the case of divorce, the Muslim divorce laws prevail. There have been no documented cases of Muslims converting to Christianity.

[29] "Letters from the Ministry of Interior to the Center" (WATC, Archives, Letter no. 528, 2 February 1996).

[30] See http://www.law.emory.edu/IFL/legal/palestine.htm. Gaza: Marriage age: 15 for females and 16 for males. Guardianship: Guardian gives consent, and if there is no guardian, the Qadi assumes this role. Polygamy: Laws specifically permit a woman to stipulate in a marriage contract that her husband will not take another wife while married to her and to petition for divorce on the basis of this stipulation if he proceeds to break the terms of the stipulation. Divorce: Women may petition for divorce on the grounds of injury. Post-divorce maintenance: No compensation for arbitrary *talaq* and no arrears predating submission of the maintenance claim. Custody of children: Hanafi rules, allowing limited extension of mother's custody of girls up to eleven years and boys up to nine.

[31] See http://www.law.emory.edu/IFL/legal/palestine.htm. Also in effect in Gaza are the Law of Shari'a Court Procedure No.12/1965 (Gaza Strip), Law No.13/1962 on the Obligatory Bequest (Gaza Strip), and Administrative Decision No. 78/1995 of the Qadi al-Quda (on the age of marriage—Gaza Strip).

[32] See http://www.law.emory.edu/IFL/legal/palestine.htm. West Bank: Legal age for marriage: The Personal Status Jordanian Law currently in effect in the West Bank allows the marriage of girls at the age of 14 years and 7 months and boys at the age of 16. Married women's rights: Under the Jordanian laws still in effect in the Occupied Territory, a woman has the right to prompt and deferred dower, in addition to keeping all income from her own labor and inheritance, while the duty of the husband is to provide for his wife and children. In reality, most working women provide for their families, yet few continue to benefit from substantive dowers or compensation for their financial contributions that will sustain them if they find themselves divorced. Some commentators have noted that enforcement of provisions regarding a husband's repayment to a wife may be weak, but there are no studies that document the extent of enforcement of legal provisions and protections to women. Polygamy is also permitted: A man can take up to four wives provided that he gives them equal treatment; however, no mechanisms ensure such equal treatment.

Divorce: Divorce is governed by both statutory and Shari'a law. Under the former, Article 108 of the Personal Status law of 1976 provides for a separation known as the

Mokhala'a provision, whereby the husband's consent is required for the marriage to be dissolved in this manner, and the wife is required to pay back any dowry she had received. Divorce in this way, however, is conditional upon the husband's consent. Under the latter, Shari'a, there are two types of divorce, a talaq or a khul'. Most marriages are terminated through the pronouncement by a husband of a talaq, which under the current law can take place outside a court. Talaq is the repudiation of the wife by the husband—the wife has no say in it. Although the Jordanian Personal Status Provisional Law of 2001 granted women the right to divorce their husband under a provision known as khul', this law is not in effect in the West Bank. Upon divorce, although women are entitled to maintenance for one year, they are not entitled to the share of wealth accumulated during marriage. However, no clear mechanism ensures that women are receiving their due maintenance because of the weak enforcement of the law due to the current political situation.

[33] A woman can add a number of conditions in her marriage contract including the right to divorce, financial compensations in case of divorce, and access to labor and education. Women seldom take advantage of such rights provided by Islamic Shari'a due to prevailing social norms and traditions. Men are usually shamed if women enter such provisions in their marriage contract and thus women find themselves vulnerable after divorce.

[34] "Woman and Work in Palestine: A study in Paid and Unpaid Labor from the Time-Use Survey 1999–2000" (in Arabic) (Ramallah, Palestine: Palestinian Central Bureau of Statistics).

[35] The almost all-male structure of law enforcement in Palestine renders it difficult for women to turn to this structure for help, although there have been several cases in which women have been placed in prison so as to protect their lives against male relatives who wanted to harm them. Several women's organizations offer help-line services to victims of violence but they all fall short on protecting them because the organizations lack resources.

[36] Law No. 93/2001 (Articles 239, 240, 241, 242, and 243).

[37] There are yet no provisions in any approved Palestinian law that protect women against violence in the workplace. There is also no clear provision that deals with forms of sexual harassment in the streets and other public places, although if women report a violation, the police would place the harasser in prison for a period of time.

Articles 257, 258, 259, and 260 of the proposed Criminal Law speak about punishments of rape and incest. Battering is punishable if it leads to abortion. In that case, a violator is to be imprisoned for a period of 10 years according to Article 249 of this proposed law. A woman is punished by imprisonment if she aborts upon her own will, unless her health was endangered or if the pregnancy was a result of rape or incest.

[38] The Women's Affairs Technical Committee in Palestine issues a biweekly newspaper that voices the concerns of women, and the Working Women's Committees also host various publications about issues of violence against women.

[39] These include the Jordanian laws in effect in the West Bank and the Law No.1/1965 on the application of the Shari'a rules to property in effect in the Gaza Strip.

[40] http/www.pcbs.org/gender/own_main.aspx.

[41] However, there have been cases in which communities, including mothers of young girls, oppose the return of married girls to school, fearing that these girls will share with their age peers information about sexual matters.

[42] "Literacy Rate of Palestinian Population (15 Years and Over) by Age Groups, Sex and Region" (PCBS, 2003), http://www.pcbs.org/educatio/educ10.aspx.

[43] "A Report on the Situation . . ." (WCLAC), 21.

[44] The Ministry of Education worked on new syllabi that are not yet completed for all levels. The textbooks that were updated are much more gender sensitive than those that existed before.

[45] Interview of Palestinian women by Freedom House staff, June 2004.

[46] Table 27, "Gender inequality in economic activity," in *Human Development Report 2004: Cultural Liberty in Today's Diverse World* (New York: United Nations Development Programme [UNDP], 2004), 229-232. http://www.law.emory.edu/IFL/legal/palestine.htm.

[47] The Arab Bank and the Cairo-Amman Bank in the Palestinian Territory only employ single women and force women to resign upon marriage.

[48] "A Report on the Situation . . ." (WCLAC), 32.

[49] The first municipal elections under the PA took place on 23 December 2004 in selected towns in the West Bank. The rest of the municipalities will hold elections in the first part of 2005. The new Palestinian Local Election Law from 2004 demands that at least two women are elected to each council, which in most places will amount to 15%.

[50] (PCBS, 2004), http://www.pcbs.org/victmz/main.aspx.

[51] "A Report on the Situation . . ." (WCLAC), 19.

[52] Women's Affairs Technical Committee, "Women in political parties: Between discrimination and ambition," *Sawt An-Nissa'* 91, 10 Feb 2000, 4.

[53] Interview with WATC employee, June 2004.

[54] In 1996, the Women's Affairs Technical Committee, a coalition of women in six political parties and several specialized centers demanded a quota of 30 percent of seats of the legislative council and decision-making posts in political parties.

[55] http://www.pcbs.org/pcbs/house/tab15.aspx.

[56] http://www.pcbs.org/pcbs/culture/media00_tab_16.aspx.

[57] "2003 World Population Data Sheet" (Washington, D.C.: Population Reference Bureau, 2003).

[58] http://www.pcbs.org/pcbs/gender/health.pdf.

[59] http://www.pcbs.org/pcbs/gender/health.pdf.

[60] "A Report on the Situation . . ." (WCLAC), 46.

[61] Ibid., 44.

Qatar

by Jill Crystal

Population: 600,000
GDP Per Capita (PPP): $19,844
Economy: Mixed capitalist-statist
Ranking on UN HDI: 47 out of 177
Polity: Traditional monarchy
Literacy: Male 84.9% / Female 82.3%
Percent Women Economically Active: 42.1%
Date of Women's Suffrage: 1999
Women's Fertility Rate: 3.5
Percent Urban/Rural: Urban 91% / Rural 9%

Country Ratings for Qatar
Nondiscrimination and Access to Justice: 2.0
Autonomy, Security, and Freedom of the Person: 2.1
Economic Rights and Equal Opportunity: 2.8
Political Rights and Civic Voice: 1.7
Social and Cultural Rights: 2.5
(Scale of 1 to 5: 1 represents the lowest and 5 the highest level of freedom women have to exercise their rights)

Introduction

Qatar is a monarchy governed by an emir who exercises power with few restraints. After Qatar gained independence from Britain in 1971, Emir Khalifa bin Hamad al-Thani ruled the country until 1995, at which time his son Sheikh Hamad al-Thani deposed him in a bloodless coup. Since accession to power, Sheikh Hamad has taken gradual steps to introduce political, social, and economic reforms, some of which have benefited women. In 1999, women were granted equal suffrage, and the country held the first elections for its 29-member municipal council. Approximately 97 percent of voters approved a new constitution in a referendum on April 29, 2003. The new constitution formally grants women equality and also provides for a legislative advisory council comprising 30 elected and 15 appointed members. In April 2003, the first woman cabinet minister was elected in Qatar's second municipal council elections.

241

Qatar is a small, petroleum-rich Arabian Gulf state with vast natural gas reserves and a high per capita GDP of $19,844. The state religion is Islam, and the majority of Qatar's residents are Sunni Muslims. The country has a population of approximately 600,000, of whom an estimated 150,000 are citizens. Noncitizens, who comprise about 75 percent of the local population, are mostly foreign workers and their families who come from South Asia and other Arab countries. Foreign workers on short-term employment contracts represent about 85 percent of the workforce.[1] The rights and state benefits afforded to Qatari citizens such as free education and health care, are not extended to the country's noncitizen population.

Rights of assembly and association in Qatar are limited. Public protest and political demonstrations are rare. All nongovernmental organizations (NGOs) require permission from the state to operate. Political parties, trade groups, women's groups, and human rights groups have been refused licenses. However, the state did establish the Supreme Council for Family Affairs, with its subsidiary body, the Women's Affairs Committee, in December 1998.[2] In 2002, the emir decreed the establishment of the National Committee for Human Rights, which aims to implement the goals of international human rights charters and to report and investigate human rights violations.[3]

Oil wealth has provided the Qatari government with the resources to build and staff high-quality health and educational facilities and to establish an extensive welfare system for its citizens. The female literacy rate and life expectancy have increased over the past few generations, and women are well represented in the education sector. Oil revenues have also provided Qatari women with a growth in professional employment opportunities and a lessening of household responsibilities, as a result of the increased economic ability to hire domestic staff. Nevertheless, with increasing numbers of Qatari households employing domestic workers, a new class of exploited foreign domestic, predominantly female, workers has developed.

While some women have benefited from the recent reforms in Qatar, women in general continue to face legal and societal problems in a number of areas. Women's rights and freedoms in the public sphere, whether economic, political, or social, remain limited. The lack of protections against discrimination, increases in polygamy, restrictions on the freedom of movement, mistreatment of foreign domestic workers, and limits on the freedom to organize and advocate for their rights still pose obstacles for women. There are no laws against domestic violence and no shelters or women's groups offering assistance to victims.

Gender-disaggregated statistics and studies on women's issues, particularly with respect to health, the economy, and the environment, are scarce in Qatar. The lack of information serves as an obstacle to many, including planners, policy makers, and women's rights advocates.[4]

Nondiscrimination and Access to Justice

Qatar's constitution guarantees women equal rights as citizens: Article 35 explicitly stipulates, "[A]ll people are equal before the law. There shall be no discrimination on account of sex, origin, language or religion." While Qatar's constitution provides general protection to Qatari women from gender-based discrimination, no formal mechanisms exist whereby women can file complaints about discrimination. The government has not acted to ensure that women are not in fact discriminated against and has not taken measures to inform women of their legal rights and protections. In addition, most rights in the constitution (among them, rights related to employment and property ownership) apply only to Qatari citizens, a fact of great importance in Qatar, where the vast majority of residents are noncitizens.

The law treats women as full and equal persons. However, in practice, most women living in Qatar are not always treated as equals. The implementation of Islamic laws in Qatar is often discriminatory against women, particularly the laws that govern inheritance and child custody.

Qatari citizenship is difficult to acquire. A 1961 law grants citizenship only to descendants of those who resided in Qatar before 1930. While some non-nationals have received citizenship, such exceptions are very rare and usually occur as a result of specific circumstances (e.g., soccer players admitted to make the country eligible for international competitions). Discrimination in favor of Qataris, especially citizens with power and influence, such as members of the large ruling family, occurs in all spheres of economic and social life.[5]

Qatar's judicial system is composed of two sets of courts (unified in 1997 under the umbrella of a Higher Judicial Council): Islamic (*Shari'a*) courts that implement Islamic law, and non-Islamic courts. The Islamic courts in Qatar have jurisdiction over only a narrow range of issues—primarily personal status law (roughly, family law and probate). While Shari'a law may grant overt preference to men in matters of the family, case outcomes are occasionally tempered by the fact that *Hanbali* (Qatar's dominant sect) practice allows for a high level of judicial discretion.[6]

Qatar's interpretations of Islamic law deem the testimony of two women to be equal to that of one man. However, judicial discretion works to make the courts flexible in applying this rule, and the judge ultimately decides the credibility of witnesses.[7] Women usually attend court proceedings in legal cases but are typically represented by a male relative or, increasingly, a (male) attorney, although women may represent themselves if they choose. Half of Qatar's judges are non-Qataris who are at-will employees who can be fired and consequently deported at any time, a circumstance that limits their independence.[8] There are no women judges in Qatar. Only in the year 2000 did

Qatari authorities grant the first woman, Haifa Al-Bakr, a license to practice law.[9] While the number of women lawyers in Qatar is growing, their proportion within the legal profession and their work remain very limited.

Most foreign women laborers work as domestic workers in Qatar and have only moderate access to justice. These women are often isolated within households, where their employers may restrict their freedom of movement. While they do have some legal rights and appear before the same court system as Qatari citizens, fear of expulsion and job loss often prevents these workers from exercising what rights they technically possess. The state does very little to protect foreign women, especially domestic workers.

The Shari'a prohibits all forms of physical violence. However, the legal system often treats leniently those men who commit acts of violence against women who, in their view, behave immodestly or defy the man's authority.[10] While "crimes of honor" are rare, the legal system treats convicted perpetrators lightly. In September 1999, Ali Said Al-Khayareen, a former government minister, murdered his two half-sisters for alleged sexual misconduct. He was released later that year.[11] The maximum penalty for rape in Qatar is death, yet the Shari'a law in Qatar does not consider spousal rape a crime.

Article 36 of the constitution states that no one shall be arrested except under provision of the law. In practice, unjustified gender-based imprisonment and detention are rare. Prisons meet international standards, and women are held separately from men. The proportion of women in the prison population for the year 2000 was 11.8 percent.[12]

At the end of 2003, Qatar remained one of only three Arab countries (with Oman and the UAE) that had not signed the Convention on the Elimination of All Forms of Discrimination against Women (CEDAW). Qatar has signed very few international human rights conventions.[13]

The government prohibits nongovernmental women's rights groups, in addition to most other types of associations, from forming or working freely to promote the status of women.[14] Although the new constitution provides for freedom of association, in practice, the government has limited this right. All nongovernmental groups must apply for registration with the Ministry of Interior, which monitors their activities.[15] It remains to be seen whether groups will be allowed to form once the constitution goes into effect fully, a change slated for 2005.

The only active women's group is governmental, the Supreme Council for Family Affairs, which is independent of other governmental structures and is under the directorship of the emir's wife, Shaikha Muza bint Nasir al-Misnad. Much of its work centers on advocacy for women and children.[16] The council's Women's Affairs Committee has called for reform of the Personal Status Law, increased public awareness of women's issues, promoted women's sports, and generally advocated for a range of women's issues. As a result of the council's work, the age of marriage was raised from 14 to 16, women gained the right to divorce their husband without losing custody of their children, and divorced women became eligible to receive three years of alimony. The Supreme Council has further advocated hiring more women in top governmental decision-making positions. The Qatar Red Crescent Society also carries out gender-related work and particularly focuses on issues of welfare.[17]

RECOMMENDATIONS

1. The government should ratify CEDAW, without reservations, and take steps to implement it locally by bringing national laws in conformity with CEDAW.
2. The government should ensure that new laws are consistent with constitutional guarantees of gender equality.
3. The government should clarify regulations and guidelines for establishing NGOs so that women activists can organize their efforts.
4. The government should appoint more women as judges.

Autonomy, Security, and Freedom of the Person

The state religion of Qatar is Islam, as interpreted by the conservative *Wahhabi* tradition of the Hanbali school of Islam.[18] Women are largely free to practice their religion and beliefs. Article 50 of the constitution formally guarantees freedom of worship to all, and in practice this freedom has seen expansion in recent years. Although the national population is overwhelmingly Sunni, specifically Hanbali, the expatriate population includes a significant number of other religions. The current emir recently allowed for Christian worship, which had been banned in the past. In 1999, permission for the construction of Qatar's first church was granted. The government has since granted formal legal status to a number of Christian denominations (Catholic, Anglican, Orthodox, Coptic, and several Asian Christian denominations), in effect giving them permission to hold public services and providing them with registration numbers that allow them to open bank accounts and sponsor clergy for visas. The small number of predominantly Indian Hindus, Asian Buddhists, Iranian Baha'is, and Jews do not practice openly, but they do not face government harassment.[19] Shi'a Muslims are allowed to practice their religion, but some public Shi'a ceremonies (such as self-flagellation) are banned.[20]

Women have restricted freedom of movement. While foreign women may obtain a driver's license, Qatari women are required to have the permission of their male guardian (husband, father) to get a license and must prove that their daily life necessitates movement.[21] Social norms restrict interactions between unrelated men and women, and areas of the public sphere such as workplaces and schools are largely segregated. Restaurants have family rooms for women and families, health clubs have ladies' hours, and banks have women's sections. These practices are enforced by social norms and tradition; Qatar has no religious police. Women are not legally required to have a male guardian's permission to travel abroad, but few women travel alone. Men can prevent female relatives from leaving the country by giving their names to immigration officers at departure ports.[22] Employers often restrict the freedom of movement of non-Qatari women, particularly domestic workers, and their ability to travel abroad. It is not illegal for employers to withhold the passports of their workers. Employers must give consent before exit permits are issued to foreign workers wishing to leave the country.[23]

The Supreme Council's Women's Affairs Committee recently reviewed Qatar's Personal Status Law and proposed amendments, some of which were accepted. In 2003, the Shari'a courts applied the principles of the draft Family Status Law, yet a revised law is expected to be adopted in the near future.[24] Law in matters of personal status tends to discriminate against women, notably in cases of inheritance and child custody. In matters of divorce, women are typically granted custody of younger children, while fathers will gain custody of older children. In practice, once a boy reaches the age of seven and a girl reaches puberty, the father will usually be granted full custody if he so desires.[25]

Qatari law allows a woman to seek a divorce by petitioning the court. The court will grant a woman a divorce only if she is able to prove that she can no longer continue to live with her husband. According to reports, women do not often employ this procedure.[26] Women have the legal right to negotiate a marriage contract that may grant them greater rights than those guaranteed by law. Nonetheless, they do not have full and equal freedom to choose their marriage partner. Polygamy is quite widespread and accepted as a Qatar tradition.

The law prohibits forced or bonded labor, and Qatari women are protected from slavery and gender-based slavery-like practices to some degree. Yet, despite measures taken by the government, Qatar is a destination country for women who are trafficked and placed in situations of coerced labor.[27] Domestic workers, particularly from Asia, often labor under conditions approaching involuntary servitude (long hours, withheld pay, restricted movement), and some are sexually exploited.

Article 36 of the constitution asserts that no one shall be subject "to torture or humiliating treatment. Torture is considered a crime and shall be punished by the law." Qatari women are generally free from torture and cruel, inhuman, and degrading punishment; there were no reported incidents in 2003.[28] However, no specific law protects women from domestic violence or abusive employers, and victims of such violence have little recourse. Foreign embassies occasionally provide shelter for domestic workers who have left employers due to abuse or for other reasons.[29] Runaway domestics are also provided shelter in deportation centers by the Qatari government.[30]

Protection from domestic violence is provided more by social networks, notably the tendency toward family endogamy (a cultural preference for cousin marriage) than by law. Thus an abuser married to his cousin would have to answer to his wife's parents: his own uncle and clan, who would probably come to her defense. As family standing is critical to economic and social access and success, this pressure can be formidable. Nonetheless, the topic of domestic abuse remains largely taboo, the extent of the problem is unknown, and women who lack such family support are at high risk.

Qatar is a rather safe society with low crime rates. Violence against women outside the home is rarely reported.

There are no independent women's rights groups working on domestic violence or immigrant women's rights issues in Qatar, and no organizations of women lawyers or independent legal aid groups operate in the country. In 2003, the wife of the emir helped to establish the Qatari Institution for the Protection of Women and Children. According to the government, the objectives of this institution are to "protect women and children from deviant practices in the home, in society, and in the workplace."[31]

RECOMMENDATIONS

1. The government should rescind the law requiring a male guardian's permission for a woman to obtain a driver's license and abolish rules that may prohibit women from traveling freely.
2. The government should increase the number of Qatari women employed in the police force and expand their role to include cases of domestic violence.
3. The government should work with women's rights advocates to develop services to support female victims of violence.
4. The government should work with women lawyers, universities, and the media to inform women about their legal rights, including rights in marriage.

Economic Rights and Equal Opportunity

Qatari women have the formal right to own land and property, and they enjoy full and independent use of their income and assets. Noncitizens, on the other hand, are not permitted to own property.[32] Women do not enjoy equal rights to inheritance under the Shari'a. Qatar's inheritance laws grant wives half the amount of inheritance of male relatives. Non-Muslim wives will not inherit unless previous formal arrangements have been made to provide them with up to one-third of the total inheritance.

Women are legally allowed to enter into business and economic contracts and activities. However, a woman's participation in business activity that requires close contact with unrelated men will typically face family opposition. Women rarely engage in investment activities, although they are beginning to enter the business and investment market. A number of mechanisms have been established in recent years to support the participation of women in this sector, including the Women's Investment Company of Qatar and the Businesswomen's Club, which is a branch of the Qatar Chamber of Commerce and Industry.[33]

Qatari women have access to education at all levels and take full advantage of Qatar's free education system. Article 49 of the constitution states, "Education is the right of every citizen. The State shall endeavor to provide free and compulsory public education in accordance with the laws in force."[34] Education is compulsory for all children up to the age of 18 or until the end of the intermediate level of schooling. Free education is not offered to Qatar's noncitizens, however. In 2003, women's literacy rates were 82.3 percent, a little lower than men's rate of 84.9 percent.[35]

The country's educational system is segregated by gender; the University of Qatar has separate campuses for women and men. In 2002, women comprised 73 percent of the student population at the University of Qatar.[36] The government has recently permitted branches of foreign universities to open in Qatar to provide modern education for both men and women.

Opportunities for women within the education system are still limited, however. Due to cultural and societal limits on a woman's ability to travel, females account for only 37 percent of the students who study abroad.[37] Most specialized schools are limited to men; women are not allowed in specialized secondary schools or in the fields of engineering or law at the University of Qatar. Women generally enroll in the theoretical sciences and tend to graduate with similar skills. Consequently, one factor that contributes to women's high unemployment is that there is an oversupply of qualified women competing for positions in fields with little demand.[38]

Women make up 14 percent of the total workforce and 26 percent of the Qatari national workforce; however, women's contributions to the economy are still predominantly under-reported because much of women's labor remains unpaid.[39] While women have few legal restrictions on their right to choose a profession, in practice, cultural and family pressures have led the majority of employed women to work in the fields of education and health care. Nearly 100 percent of employed women are concentrated in the service sector. The diversity of career opportunities is expanding nonetheless. In 2003, Qatar graduated some 100 female police cadets and began to move toward creating the country's first female soccer team. Whether a woman can become a judge or an ambassador, however, is up to the emir, who makes appointments to such posts. Women filled only 4.7 percent of administration and senior management positions in 2001.[40]

Qatar's newest labor law (Law No. 14 of 2004) is intended to provide for equality between men and women in rights arising from work relations. However, the law is ambiguous. Article 93 grants women the same wages as men for similar work, as well as the same training and promotion opportunities. Article 94, on the other hand, bans women from work that is "hard, hazardous, unsafe or morally harmful, or of other nature to be defined by Ministerial decision."[41] It is still too early to predict how this new law will be implemented.

There are no laws to protect women from sexual harassment in the workplace and no complaint mechanisms for women to report such cases. Workers are not permitted to unionize or engage in collective bargaining, and the standards of work and protections provided for Qatari citizens are vastly different for noncitizens. Beginning in 1962, a series of restrictive labor laws granted many privileges to citizens, such as preference in hiring.[42]

Qatari women do not always receive equal employment benefits to cover transportation and housing, but gender-specific protections in the workplace are generous. Employers are required to provide at least 50 paid days of maternity leave.[43] In the public sector, female employees receive two hours of breaks a day for one year to breast-feed. State-employed Qatari women who have worked for more than four years can receive two-year leaves (the first paid, the second at half pay) on two occasions in their working lives to care for young children. The government (which employs the majority of women in the workforce) provides working hours that allow most mothers to be home after school if they desire. Most Qatari households employ a domestic worker who provides childcare along with many other household services. However, preschools are rare, and high-quality childcare is difficult to find. The Supreme Council is currently working on developing a kindergarten program. In practice, none of these benefits applies to non-Qatari domestic workers.

RECOMMENDATIONS

1. The government should increase the recruitment of women into more diverse and upper-level governmental positions, including all ministries.
2. The government should establish a mechanism for enabling women workers to report cases of discrimination and harassment.
3. The government should enact a clear law that protects all women in Qatar, citizens and non-citizens, from harassment in the workplace in both public and private sectors.
4. The government should ensure the right of all workers to accept and leave jobs at will, and it should publish and disseminate information in relevant languages to female foreign workers on their labor rights and basic human rights.

Political Rights and Civic Voice

The right to peaceful assembly, for both men and women, is severely restricted in Qatar. Public demonstrations and political parties are banned. The government typically asserts that parties and demonstrations are not needed, as there is no political opposition.[44] Political groups in civil society are not permitted to function openly; the government is selective in granting authorization and often disqualifies civil society groups that it deems overly political.

While formal censorship was lifted in 1995 and the Information Ministry abolished, considerable self-censorship is still exercised by reporters and editors. Local media, while critical of events outside the country, rarely tackle political, domestic, or women's issues. Most broadcast media are government-owned and reflect the official position. Foreign print media are monitored and censored for sexual content. *Al-Jazeera* satellite television, a private station heavily reliant on Qatari government subsidies, is vocal and critical in its coverage of the United States and other Arab states but practices considerable self-censorship when covering Qatari news. Al-Jazeera airs a number of programs on women's rights and women's global equality issues, in addition to covering the issues of displaced and refugee women, but the station does not highlight the domestic problems of Qatar's women migrant workers. Domestic politics and policy are usually avoided or presented in a positive light.[45]

The constitution grants women the right to participate in competitive and democratic elections with full and equal suffrage. However, Qataris are at present restricted to electing municipal council members who can act only on a very narrow range of concerns. In 1999, the emir granted women suffrage by decree. Six women competed as independent candidates in the municipal elections of 1999, but none was elected. One female candidate, Muza al-Malki, speculated that female candidates had lost because they didn't win the women's vote, claiming that 80 percent of their votes came from men.[46] In April 2003, the first woman was elected to public office as a member of the 29-member municipal council. No other elections have been held.

Women are not represented in the judiciary; no woman was granted a license to practice law until the year 2000. Most of Qatar's lawyers have been educated abroad; students seeking a degree in Western law must attend a university in another state. However, the Faculty of Shari'a Law and Islamic Studies at the University of Qatar now offers an undergraduate degree in Islamic law.

Women are increasingly gaining representation in the national government. In 2003, Shaikha bint Ahmad al-Mahmud was appointed Qatar's first woman minister of education, having served as under-secretary since 1996. The president of the University of Qatar and the dean of the Faculty of Shari'a Law and Islamic Studies are also women. Nevertheless, the representation of Qatari women in government remains thin, with nearly all important decision-making positions restricted to men.[47] Only four Qatari women fill high-ranking posts, although substantially larger numbers of women have mid-level positions. Women's influence in governmental decision-making is largely limited to the fields of education and social affairs.

Women have the right to participate in local politics, and a number have run for local office. While there is no national parliament, the new constitution calls for a consultative Shura Council, with two-thirds of the membership to be elected. The emir has not yet announced a date for these elections.[48] Women's political participation would be more meaningful were they allowed to run for genuinely legislative bodies (such as a national parliament). Nevertheless, women would then be likely to face increased and organized opposition to the expansion of women's rights from extremist Islamist groups. A more democratic and open political system is ultimately vital to the preservation and expansion of women's rights.

Access to the Internet has provided women with a new and broad source of information. The Ministry of Foreign Affairs has set up a technology information center, which includes a women's unit, and in Doha, Internet cafes exist exclusively for women. At one time, Q-Tel, an Internet provider, had 10,000 subscribers, 30 percent of whom were believed to be female.[49] Unfortunately, the restrictions on women's right to associate greatly hinder their ability to use information to empower themselves in their civic or political lives.

RECOMMENDATIONS

1. The government should continue to expand its policies and programs on women's political rights and facilitate women's equal access to all stages of the political process.
2. The government should allow the establishment of independent political parties to enhance a free and democratic political process in which women and men can benefit.
3. The government should establish an affirmative action plan to increase women's role in parliament, political parties, and government ministries.
4. The government should allow women to organize women's groups to work on political issues.

Social and Cultural Rights

Qatar remains an insular society in which family life is central. For both men and women, little meaningful social, economic, or political life takes place outside the family. In the home, women retain important roles. They organize the daily routine and holiday family gatherings, and they play a central role in arranging marriages. Public life is customarily segregated by gender, with most public entities having separate times or space for men or for "families" (women and children). Although it is not compulsory, most women wear the hair-covering *hijab* and the black cloak-like *abaya* in public.

Qatar nationals have free access to a government-supported health-care system; noncitizens, on the other hand, are required to pay for services. Qatar's health-care system covers a range of health issues, including mental and dental care and a complete maternity care program. Women have significant freedom to make independent decisions about their health. The vast majority of women receive professional pre- and postnatal care.[50] Employers of non-Qatari women, particularly domestic workers, sometimes infringe upon women's right to health care by restricting their freedom of movement.

With the permission of both parents, abortion is permitted in the first trimester if a physician determines that the pregnancy would cause harm to the mother's health or if the fetus has a serious, incurable physical or mental defect. Qatari society is pro-natalist, and women are typically pressured by their families to have children. Women's reproductive rights are rarely discussed in public; issues such as rape and even non-marital sex are seldom addressed; there is little information available on how resulting pregnancies are handled.

While it is not legally prohibited, few Qatari women or men live alone. Young women would be likely to face familial opposition and possibly male harassment if they tried to live on their own. Older widows, on the other hand, have greater freedom to live by themselves. Housing allowances available to male Qatari government employees are not generally available to women. The man is considered the head of household in Qatar and is therefore responsible for providing housing for his wife and the family.

Community life centers on the family. While women are able to participate in all matters related to the family (marriage, children's education, health care, housing), their ability to influence key decisions in the family remains unclear. The government does not interfere in family and community relations, and women may consequently face obstacles in seeking governmental assistance or support in cases of domestic violence or marital rape, neither of which is considered a crime.

Women work in both print and broadcast media in Qatar, employed as journalists, reporters, broadcasters, and producers. However, women have only recently gained access to jobs in the media, and their numbers in the field are modest. In 2002, the sector employed 279 Qatari women.[51] Qatar University has established the Project for the Development of Media Training for Women in conjunction with UNESCO. Among the obstacles to women's participation in the media are the social customs that restrict women's work to a narrow field of careers. The media tend to portray women in stereotypical roles. There is also little coverage, particularly on international networks such as Al-Jazeera, of the problems of and restrictions on women's lives.

Little research has been conducted on the problem of poverty in Qatar. Information on the economic, social, and cultural problems of non-Qatari women is also not available, partly due to the lack of independent groups to investigate these issues.

Qatar's new constitution does not come into full effect until 2005. While many recent reforms have affected women positively, they remain unfamiliar and untested. Many reforms are closely associated with the activism of the emir's wife, Shaikha Muza, and may not survive in the absence of so high-placed and active an advocate. The very reforms that have provided women with important rights have come about not through democratic mechanisms but through decrees from the top. If the reforms are to endure, they must be institutionalized through democratic means, such as an elected national parliament that will outlive the current emir. Such a body, however, is more likely to favor restrictions on women's rights than the emir. In a society where social norms, not laws, are the source of most restrictions on women's lives, and where laws are often unknown, inconsistently enforced, and not subjected to any form of constitutional review, legal reforms alone will be of limited consequence.

RECOMMENDATIONS

1. The government should abolish laws that discriminate against women in housing and job-related benefits.
2. The government should expand the work of the Supreme Council for Family Affairs, and the government should allow independent women's groups to function, both to advocate for women's rights and to provide more protection for non-Qatari women.
3. The media in Qatar should focus on women's problems and their lack of equal rights.

AUTHOR: Jill Crystal is a professor in the Department of Political Science at Auburn University. She is the author of two books, Oil and Politics in the Gulf: Rulers and Merchants in Kuwait and Qatar *(Cambridge University Press, 1995) and* Kuwait: the Transformation of an Oil State *(Westview, 1992), as well as several articles and book chapters.*

Notes

1 "Background Note: Qatar" (Washington, D.C.: U.S. Dept. of State, 2003); *Country Reports on Human Rights Practices–2003:* Qatar (Washington, D.C.: U.S. Dept. of State, Bureau of Democracy, Human Rights, and Labor, 25 February 2004).

[2] "Reply by the State of Qatar to the Questionnaire to Governments on Implementation of the Beijing Platform for Action (1995) and the Outcome of the Twenty-third Special Session of the General Assembly (2000)" (Doha: Supreme Council for Family Affairs, 2004).

[3] *AI Report 2003*: Qatar (London and New York: Amnesty International [AI], 2003); *Aman Daily News*, 17 November 2002.

[4] "Reply . . . to the Questionnaire to Governments . . ." (Supreme Council for Family Affairs, 2004).

[5] See Nathan Brown, *The Rule of Law in the Arab World: Courts in Egypt and the Gulf* (Cambridge: Cambridge University Press, 1997), ch. 6.

[6] "Qatar: Women in Public Life" (United Nations Development Programme, Programme on Governance in the Arab Region), www.pogar.org/countries/Qatar/gender.html.

[7] *Country Reports* . . . (U.S. Dept. of State, 25 February 2004).

[8] See "Qatar," *Freedom in the World 2003* (New York and Washington, D.C.: Freedom House, 2004); *Country Reports* . . . (U.S. Dept. of State, 25 February 2004).

[9] "Woman in Qatar gets the right to be lawyer for the first time," ArabicNews.com, 17 February 2000.

[10] *Country Reports* . . . (U.S. Dept. of State, 25 February 2004).

[11] *Country Profiles* "Qatar" (Beirut: United Nations Economic and Social Commission for Western Asia [ESCWA], 2002), http://www.escwa.org.lb/ecw/index.asp.

[12] "Prison Brief for Qatar" (London: International Centre for Prison Studies, 2004), http://www.kcl.ac.uk/depsta/rel/icps/worldbrief/middle_east_records.php?code=182.

[13] For a list of the human rights conventions Qatar is and is not signatory to, see "Ratification of International Human Rights Treaties – Qatar" (University of Minnesota, Human Rights Library, 2004), http://wwwl.umn.edu/humanrts/research/ratification-qatar.html.

[14] *Country Reports* . . . (U.S. Dept. of State, 25 February 2004).

[15] Ibid.

[16] "Report containing additional information about the initial report submitted by the State of Qatar to the Committee on the Rights of the Child" (Doha: Supreme Council for Family Affairs, July 2001).

[17] *Country Profiles* "Qatar" (Beirut: United Nations Economic and Social Commission for Western Asia [ESCWA], 2002), http://www.escwa.org.lb/ecw/index.asp.

[18] "Qatar: International Religious Freedom Report 2003" (Washington, D.C.: U.S. Dept. of State, Bureau of Democracy, Human Rights, and Labor, 18 December 2003), http://www.state.gov/g/drl/rls/irf/2003/24460pf.htm.

[19] Ibid.

[20] Ibid.

[21] *Country Profiles* "Qatar" (Beirut: United Nations Economic and Social Commission for Western Asia [ESCWA], 2002), http://www.escwa.org.lb/ecw/index.asp.

[22] *Country Reports* . . . (U.S. Dept. of State, 25 February 2004).

[23] Ibid.

[24] "Reply . . . to the Questionnaire to Governments . . ." (Supreme Council for Family Affairs, 2004).

[25] "International Parental Child Abduction – Qatar" (U.S. Dept. of State, 29 June 2004), http://travel.state.gov/family/abduction_qatar.html.

26 "Reply . . . to the Questionnaire to Governments . . ." (Supreme Council for Family Affairs, 2004).

27 "Trafficking in Persons Report" (Washington, D.C.: U.S. Dept. of State, 11 June 2003).

28 *Country Reports.* . . (U.S. Dept. of State, 25 February 2004).

29 Ibid.

30 "Trafficking in Persons Report" (U.S. Dept. of State, 11 June 2003).

31 "Reply . . . to the Questionnaire to Governments . . ." (Supreme Council for Family Affairs, 2004).

32 *Country Report* . . . (U.S. Dept. of State, 25 February 2004).

33 "Reply . . . to the Questionnaire to Governments . . ." (Supreme Council for Family Affairs, 2004).

34 Ibid.

35 Table 24, "Gender-related development index," in *Human Development Report 2004: Cultural Liberty in Today's Diverse World* (New York: United Nations Development Programme [UNDP], 2004), 217-220. http://hdr.undp.org/reports/global/2004/.

36 "University of Qatar Students" (University of Qatar web page), http://www.qu.edu. qa/home/aboutqu/students.htm.

37 "Reply . . . to the Questionnaire to Governments . . ." (Supreme Council for Family Affairs, 2004).

38 Ibid.

39 *Country Report* . . . (U.S. Dept. of State, 25 February 2004).

40 "Reply . . . to the Questionnaire to Governments . . ." (Supreme Council for Family Affairs, 2004).

41 The entire law is published in *The Peninsula*, 20 May 2004.

42 Jill Crystal, *Oil and Politics in the Gulf, Rulers and Merchants in Kuwait and Qatar* (Cambridge: Cambridge University Press, 1995), 248.

43 "Emir Issues New Labour Law," *The Peninsula*, 20 May 2004.

44 See, for example, the not atypical interview with Qatar's powerful foreign minister, Hamad Bin Jasim al-Thani, who says, "First of all, there is no Qatari opposition. What is called a Qatari opposition is a lie," in "Qatari foreign minister discusses relationship with Al-Jazeera," Africa Intelligence Wire, 2 October 2003.

45 Mohammed El-Nawawy and Adel Iskandar, *Al-Jazeera* (Cambridge: Westview, 2002), 75–79.

46 Ibid., 75.

47 "Reply . . . to the Questionnaire to Governments . . ." (Supreme Council for Family Affairs, 2004).

48 "Qatari emir proclaims his country's 1st written constitution," AFP, 9 June 2004.

49 *Country Profiles* "Qatar" (Beirut: United Nations Economic and Social Commission for Western Asia [ESCWA], 2002), http://www.escwa.org.lb/ecw/index.asp.

50 "Reply . . . to the Questionnaire to Governments . . ." (Supreme Council for Family Affairs, 2004).

51 Ibid.

Saudi Arabia

by Eleanor Abdella Doumato

Population: 24,100,000
GDP Per Capita (PPP): $12,650
Economy: Mixed capitalist-statist
Ranking on UN HDI: 77 out of 177
Polity: Traditional monarchy
Literacy: Male 84.1% / Female 69.5%
Percent Women Economically Active: 22%
Date of Women's Suffrage: No suffrage
Women's Fertility Rate: 5.7
Percent Urban/Rural: Urban 83% / Rural 17%

Country Ratings for Saudi Arabia
Nondiscrimination and Access to Justice: 1.2
Autonomy, Security, and Freedom of the Person: 1.1
Economic Rights and Equal Opportunity: 1.4
Political Rights and Civic Voice: 1.0
Social and Cultural Rights: 1.6

(Scale of 1 to 5: 1 represents the lowest and 5 the highest level of freedom women have to exercise their rights)

Introduction

The Kingdom of Saudi Arabia is an absolute monarchy that has been ruled by the Al Saud family since the country's unification in 1932. Saudi Arabia's 1992 Basic Law declares that the *Quran* and the *Sunna*[1] are the country's constitution. Succession is limited to descendants of Abd al-Aziz Ibn Saud, the founder of the kingdom. Crown Prince Abdullah has for the most part governed the country's affairs since 1997 because the current king, Fahd, suffered a stroke in 1995. The monarch appoints both the Council of Ministers, which is responsible for government administration, and the 120-member *Majlis al-Shura* (Consultative Council), which studies legislation and offers advice to the ruling family. The king also appoints emirs, all currently members of the Al Saud family, to administer the kingdom's regional sectors. Women are legally prohibited from participating in any public decision-making bodies. Neither men nor women have the right to vote in Saudi Arabia, and political

257

parties are forbidden. In October 2003, the government announced plans to hold elections for half of the members of municipal councils in 2004.

Saudi Arabia, which occupies most of the Arabian Peninsula, is the world's leading oil producer and exporter. The GDP per capita is $12,650. The kingdom holds a special place of importance for Muslims all over the world, in that it houses two of the holiest cities of Islam, Mecca and Medina. Mecca becomes a destination for some 2 million pilgrims who travel there for the annual *Hajj* (pilgrimage). The country's total population is about 24.1 million, with foreign residents on temporary work assignments comprising about 67 percent of the workforce.[2] About 10 percent of the population are Shi'a, who are discriminated against in hiring, education, and government services. The unemployment rate for Saudi nationals is between 25 percent and 30 percent.

In recent years, Saudi Arabia has made some progress in women's education and employment. However, gender discrimination is built into Saudi Arabia's governmental and social structures and is integral in the country's practice and interpretation of their particular version of religious teachings. Women's access to employment opportunities is limited, and they do not enjoy the full benefits of citizenship or legal adulthood. Reformers within Saudi Arabia who are willing to take risks for the sake of democratization have recognized the need for change. This represents an unprecedented opening for the international community to support efforts toward reform.

Nondiscrimination and Access to Justice

Saudi Arabia follows its own state-sponsored version of Sunni Islam, known as *Wahhabism*,[3] which is considered one of the most conservative interpretations of the faith. The government and judicial system are based on the Saudi construction of Islamic law, which does not accept the premise that men and women should be treated equally. The Saudi justice system lacks procedures to insure due process, legal representation for defendants, or protection from torture. Women are subject to tighter legal restrictions on personal behavior than are men, and laws in general are applied arbitrarily, with more latitude afforded to well-connected Saudi citizens than to foreigners.

Article 8 of the country's Basic Law declares equality for all: "Government in the Kingdom of Saudi Arabia is based on the premise of justice, consultation, and equality in accordance with the Islamic Shari'ah."[4] Islamic law in Saudi Arabia, however, does not offer equality to women. The text of the Quran and *Hadith*[5] are often subject to individual interpretations that favor the position of men over women. At the same time, Saudi Arabia is a hierarchical society that privileges notables and the well connected over ordinary citizens and outsiders. It also favors a hierarchical family model that values obedience, with the younger deferring to the older and women deferring to men.[6] Consequently, the biases built into the laws of the kingdom and into their application reflect the biases in both society and scripture. This is quite visible in the varying treatment of foreigners in Saudi Arabia, where workers are treated differently depending on their country of origin.

While Saudi Islamic law does not ensure equal rights for men and women, the law is viewed as aiming to assure gender equivalence. This means that rights in law should be balanced according to the prescribed rights and duties of men and women in relation to each other. While most laws discriminate against women, the principle of equivalence is believed to sometimes work in women's favor. For example, while daughters inherit half of what sons inherit, by law women retain ownership of their own property after marriage and have no obligation to spend their wealth on behalf of their husbands or children. Married men, on the other hand, are obligated to provide the full maintenance of their families. Similarly, the principle that men are responsible for the protection of women means that in practice, men may be obligated to stand in for women when it comes to dealing with government bureaucracies or the courts. For instance, in Saudi Arabia, the head-to-toe dress code (*niqab* and *abaya*) is imposed on all women with the idea that it is a woman's obligation to ensure the moral behavior of men and protect the "honor" of her family. Should a woman be admonished by the *mutawwaʿin* (foot-soldiers of the Saudi government's Society for the Promotion of Virtue and Prevention of Vice) for not appearing sufficiently modest, or apprehended for immoral behavior such as eating in a restaurant with an unrelated male, it is usually the woman's male guardian or her *mahram* (her husband or closest male family relative) and not the woman herself, who is likely to be punished by the court with either fines or imprisonment.

As holders of Saudi nationality, women are at a disadvantage when it comes to gaining access to the benefits of the state. Saudi women who marry a non-Saudi are not permitted to pass their nationality on to their children, nor can their husband receive Saudi nationality. A man with Saudi nationality who marries a non-Saudi, however, is entitled to apply for, and receive, Saudi nationality for his wife and children. Only Muslims can obtain Saudi citizenship. In 2002, women were allowed to apply for their own individual identity cards, although they must still obtain the permission of their mahram in order to do so. Before this, women appeared as nationals in state records only by virtue of being included as members of their father's family, making it difficult or impossible for widowed, abandoned, or single women to receive state subsidies or other benefits on their own.

Women do not have equal access to the courts or an equal opportunity to obtain justice. Saudi women are not allowed to act as lawyers, and a woman seeking access to the courts must either work through a male lawyer, have a male relative represent her, or represent herself before a court of all-male judges. Consequently, a Saudi woman may be forced to provide intimate details of her legal, financial, or family affairs to male judges and lawyers. In cases involving divorce or child custody, women sometimes have to rely on their husbands, who are also their legal adversaries, to represent them. This, in effect, discourages Saudi women from pursuing access to justice at most levels. A woman is not considered a full person before the court. In accordance with the Saudi interpretation of Shari'a, the testimony of one man is equivalent to that of two women.

In the penal code, men and women are assigned punishments for crimes according to the Saudis' version of Shari'a. In some cases, the penal code prescribes equal punishment, and in others, the punishment is gender-specific. For example, for purposes of compensation in cases of accidental death or injury, a woman's worth is always figured at half that of a man's, as determined on analogy with the law of inheritance.

Article 36 of the Basic Law[7] prohibits arbitrary arrest and detention by any of the arresting authorities in the Saudi kingdom, including agents of regional governors, public security agencies, police departments, and drug, traffic, and passport agencies, in addition to the mutawwa'in. Nevertheless, laws and regulations are applied arbitrarily with reference to the status of individual litigants and defendants. Foreigners, Shi'a, and less-privileged citizens are subject to arbitrary arrest.

During 2003, there were cases in which the mutawwa'in harassed, abused, and detained citizens and foreigners of both genders.[8] Women of many nationalities were detained for what is considered inappropriate behavior, such as dining in restaurants with unrelated males, riding in a taxi with a male who is not their relative, or appearing in public with their heads uncovered.[9] Offenses such as being alone in the company of an unrelated person of the opposite gender may be punished by caning. Global attention focused on the actions of the mutawwa'in in March of 2002, when they were accused of interfering in rescue efforts during a fire in a girls' public intermediate school in Mecca in order to enforce Saudi Arabia's obligatory Islamic dress code. Some of the fleeing girls were reportedly not wearing the required head coverings and *abayas* (long black cloaks). A report prepared by Mecca's Civil Defense Department noted that mutawwa'in were at the school's main gate and "intentionally obstructed the efforts to evacuate the girls. This resulted in the increased number of casualties." The fire claimed the lives of at least 14 girl students.[10]

Especially vulnerable to rights abuse are women from the Philippines, Sri Lanka, Indonesia, and other countries who work in Saudi Arabia as domestic helpers. Being unmarried, or living without their husbands, migrant women are subject to accusations of wrongdoing that don't apply to men, such as "illegal pregnancy,"[11] witchcraft, or being in any public place, especially at night, where they may be assumed to be soliciting for prostitution. At the same time, domestic workers are always vulnerable to sexual exploitation and other abuse by their Saudi employers. They cannot complain to police because reporting an employer's misconduct may be considered a false allegation and hence criminal behavior on the part of the woman worker. Women interviewed by Human Rights Watch in Malaz prison in Riyadh in 2003 indicated that they had no access to lawyers and were unsure of the charges against them, even though the code of criminal procedures that came into effect in 2002 recognizes the right to legal counsel for criminal suspects.[12]

Saudi Arabia ratified the UN Convention on the Elimination of All Forms of Discrimination Against Women (CEDAW) in 2000, with reservations, stating, "In case of contradiction between any term of the Convention and the norms of Islamic law, the Kingdom is not under obligation to observe the contradictory terms of the Convention."[13] Based on Saudi Arabia's interpretation and implementation of Islamic law, this reservation acts to nullify some of CEDAW's articles. To date, the Saudi government has not filed any follow-up reports to CEDAW, nor has it taken any steps to bring its national laws into conformity with the universal standards on women's human rights.

RECOMMENDATIONS

1. The government should review all laws and policies and amend the Basic Law to ensure gender equality and to prohibit the discrimination of women and foreign nationals.
2. The government should remove all reservations to CEDAW and take steps to implement it locally by bringing national laws in conformity with CEDAW.

Autonomy, Security, and Freedom of the Person

Freedom of religion is highly restricted in Saudi Arabia. Muslims in Saudi Arabia are required to accept the state-sponsored version of the Wahhabi school of Sunni Islam as interpreted by the official clergy; all other Muslim schools of thought or jurisprudence and other forms of Islamic ritual are illicit, including Shi'ism in all its variant forms, as well as Sufism. Public practice or preaching of religions other than Islam are forbidden and punished. Saudi women, who may not agree with the more conservative and patriarchal interpretations of Islam in Saudi Arabia, do not have open or safe ways to express their dissent or to present alternative interpretations of Islam. Despite the historical role played by women in early Islam in what is now Saudi Arabia, women are not allowed to fill any leadership positions in the country's religious institutions. Women are encouraged to pray at home, where they are considered "safer," although solitary prayer at home deprives women of the benefit of communal worship, which is preferred in Islam.

Women's freedom of movement in Saudi Arabia is limited through a combination of legal and social controls and religiously sanctioned local practices. While some Saudis perceive the laws and practices that govern women's movement as necessities to insure the protection of women, others view them as insuring the perpetuation of male dominance. Modern restrictions on women's movement are basically derived from two practices in Saudi society. First, a woman is not to be outside her own neighborhood except in the company of her mahram; and second, an unrelated man and woman are not to be in physical contact with one another. A woman may not drive cars, check into a hotel alone, rent an apartment for herself, or get on an airplane without her mahram's permission. She is not supposed to ride in a car unless the driver is her mahram, though women do so out of necessity.

Visible and invisible spatial boundaries also limit women's movement. Mosques, most ministries, public streets, and food stalls (supermarkets not included) are male territory. Furthermore, accommodations that are available for men are always superior to those accessible to women, and public space, such as parks, zoos, museums, libraries, or the national Jinadriyah Festival of Folklore and Culture, is created for men, with only limited times allotted for women's visits.

Restrictions on women's movement have a negatively disproportionate effect on foreign women, especially women from developing countries. Saudi employers routinely take workers' passports on arrival and will hold them until the employee departs the kingdom. A foreign woman worker is therefore restricted from traveling outside her town of residence and prohibited from leaving the country of her own volition. Furthermore, some employers use the mahram rule to justify locking women employees in at night.[14] Prohibited from driving themselves, unable to afford private transportation, and a lack of public transportation, restricts the options of working women to walking on the streets, precisely where they can be apprehended by the religious police on an accusation of solicitation.

Laws of personal status follow the Shari'a, as interpreted and applied in Saudi Arabia, which favors males in matters of marriage, divorce, child custody, and inheritance. Marriage is recognized by a contract between the husband-to-be and the mahram of the intended bride. The marriage contract provides room for the amount of the *mahr* (money or other valuables gifted to the bride-to-be by the prospective husband, which she is legally entitled to retain) and allows for the insertion of marriage stipulations. An example of these stipulations could involve the husband-to-be's pledge that should he choose to take a second wife, the bride would be entitled to an automatic divorce. Stipulations that run counter to the Saudis' version of Shari'a, however, may be disallowed in a Saudi court. The marriage contract requires the bride to specify whether she is a virgin, widow, or divorcee, but does not require the husband to do the same. While the formal contract seems rigid and excludes the bride, the contract itself is merely the legal confirmation of decisions taken jointly by two families, and most often today, jointly by the husband-to-be and his prospective bride. The degree to which a woman participates in decisions surrounding her own marriage depends entirely on her family and her own personal situation.

The husband is entitled to a divorce without explanation simply by registering a statement of his intention with a court and repeating it three times. By law, a man is obligated to provide maintenance for his wife for a period after divorce, but there are no enforcement mechanisms. The wife, by contrast, may obtain a divorce only if her husband granted her the right of divorce at the time of the signing of their marriage contract. The majority of women in Saudi Arabia lack this right, in which case, a Muslim wife can only obtain a legal divorce by proving in court desertion or impotence on the part of the husband, which is humiliating and logistically burdensome. She may also buy her way out of the marriage through a method known as *khul,* in which a wife usually must forgo all her maintenance rights and mahr.

A woman is constrained in seeking a divorce, or in leaving a husband who has taken a second wife, because her children legally belong to the children's father, and so to leave him means to give up her children. For Saudi women nationals, there are some mitigating factors such as family influence in negotiating with, or in some cases, buying off either the court officials or the husband. In addition, some judges may decide to consider the fitness of the parents in awarding custody. Nevertheless, even in cases in which the father is patently unable to parent properly, paternal grandparents may have a prior claim to the children over the mother. Non-nationals, mostly foreign women because Saudi women rarely marry foreign men, have few options, and once the father has physical custody of the children inside the kingdom, there are no legal avenues within the Saudi justice system to pursue custody.

The government of Saudi Arabia outlawed slavery in 1962, but the country is a destination for trafficked persons.[15] Human Rights Watch has documented cases of workers forced into situations of coerced labor or slave-like conditions. Some female foreign workers are trapped in places of employment, especially private homes, and are unable to leave the premises, forced to work very long hours for payment that may never be delivered, deprived of food and sleep, and subjected to sexual abuse.[16] There is no reported information on Saudi women nationals living in conditions of servitude, but women can be trapped in slave-like conditions as a result of poverty, illiteracy, physical isolation, or dependence on the mahram. This problem is exacerbated by the Saudi concept of "obedience due the husband," which is also incorporated in the schoolbooks of the national curriculum.

In 2001, the Council of Ministers approved a 225-article penal code, under which the use of torture is forbidden.[17] Nevertheless, torture is a known practice in Saudi prisons.[18] Once apprehended, a person may be held incommunicado and subjected to torture, commonly used to extract confessions that are presented in court as conclusive evidence of the detained person's guilt.[19] In addition to prison torture, Saudi authorities regularly implement their version of Shari'a punishments: flogging, amputation, and beheading are inflicted on both men and women.[20] In almost all such cases, the accused do not get due process of law, and foreigners in particular are at the mercy of Saudi police. There is no evidence, however, to suggest that women fare worse in regard to torture or mutilation than men.

Domestic violence and marital rape are problems that are well known in Saudi Arabia but never discussed publicly. Saudi political culture promotes a mythology of the Muslim family, "the fundamental building block of society," in which each person is allocated rights and duties and derives justice through membership. At the same time, the privacy of women is fused with ideals of family "honor." Consequently, society and media in general cannot talk about the reality of domestic violence without challenging public myths about themselves, and women in particular find it extremely difficult to talk about their personal situation without the fear of damaging their family's "honor" and their own reputation.

In April 2004, television host Rania al-Baz broke the wall of silence when she allowed photographs to be made public of her battered face after she had been beaten and choked by her husband. Despite the outpouring of interest and sympathy that the disclosure evoked, the al-Baz incident may not have established a precedent for other women to come forward, or have changed social attitudes toward domestic violence. The outcome of the al-Baz case illustrates how powerful these social constraints continue to be for women and how domestic violence continues to be viewed as a family matter. Al-Baz's husband was sentenced to only six months and 300 lashes and was then released after serving only half that sentence once he worked out an arrangement with al-Baz, who wanted a divorce and custody of her sons.

There are no laws in Saudi Arabia that protect women from gender-based violence, domestic violence, or marital rape. These acts are not accepted grounds for divorce, and one woman's testimony of violence is often not accepted as evidence against her husband. Women who report sexual abuse or rape, whether perpetrated by an employer or otherwise, are unlikely to find a sympathetic hearing with judicial authorities. Instead of protection from the perpetrator, women may find themselves accused of illicit sex. Usually the burden to prove rape charges is on the woman victim, who must produce all required witnesses. The only basis for a rape conviction is a confession or the evidence of four witnesses.[21] Lack of government support services and shelters for women victims of domestic violence and the absence of proper laws discourage women from coming forward with such cases. No government policies or procedures exist for training police or hospital officials to identify and support women victims of violence, nor are there any legal guidelines to ensure that perpetrators of violence receive punishment and do not harass their victims.

RECOMMENDATIONS

1. The government should allow Saudi women to study and practice law in the country.
2. The government should enact laws against domestic violence and assess the scope of this problem in order to formulate appropriate responses to protect women, including confidential hotlines and shelter and counseling services.
3. The government should hire women police officers to handle cases involving women.

Economic Rights and Equal Opportunity

Both Saudi Arabian law and the country's interpretation of Shari'a provide women with the right to own and manage their property and other assets, including real estate, the mahr given at marriage, and earned income. However, by tradition, women who live among the less than 20 percent of the country's population that is rural do not receive the inheritance to which they are legally entitled, as they are considered to be supported by their fathers or husbands.

In general, women's use of their personal wealth and property is restricted by a combination of social customs, traditions, and religious values that have been incorporated into the kingdom's commercial regulations and bureaucratic rules. The requirement for unrelated men and women to be separated in all public places, including the work place, government ministries and offices, retail establishments, hotels, restaurants, recreational facilities, and banks, greatly affects women's ability to independently own and use their assets, income, and property. Based on gender-segregation rules and the mahram rule placing women under the legal guardianship of men, there is an additional requirement that a woman who wants to go into business must hire a male manager before receiving a commercial license. It is apparent that in practice, the Saudi government has not taken concrete steps to facilitate the right of women citizens to have full access to their economic opportunities.

Saudi families have creatively found ways in which to increase women's economic opportunities, despite the constraints imposed on women's economic rights. They have successfully advocated for the establishment of separate women's bank branches and women-only shopping malls, while private businesses and some ministries have set aside women-only offices. Most employed women work in the gender-segregated schools, colleges, and universities, but women entrepreneurs also invest in manufacturing and the service industries, real estate, and education, most notably in private training institutes that teach young women marketable skills. Women with professional skills such as architecture, journalism, and translation also establish businesses in their own homes.

Saudi customs involving gender-segregation have softened in some circles over recent years. Saudi women have reappeared on local television, and women health-care professionals, including doctors and nurses, administrators, lab technicians, and social workers, work in a completely mixed-gender environment in government hospitals. The government is actively searching for ways to increase women's participation in the work force and has established industrial projects to employ women.[22]

Despite a growth in the number of employed Saudi women, the state estimates that nearly six times more Saudi men were employed in the kingdom than Saudi women in 2002.[23] The state also estimates that despite the vast diversification of educational opportunities, less than 10 percent of Saudi women over the age of 15 are in the work force.[24] The lack of Saudi government–approved "legitimate" (i.e. gender-segregated) places of work is a major obstacle to women's employment. The Saudi government has not taken concrete steps to provide convenient, affordable, or safe transportation or working space facilities for Saudi or foreign women workers in the country.

In regard to women and government employment, a limited number of positions are available in education, and jobs in the ministries are largely the bailiwick of men. Potential employers are hindered by the intricacies of the burdensome mahram system required for women working in business, as well as the additional costs incurred to employ and work through male intermediaries. Employers' reluctance to set up a complex gender-segregated work facility for women is another obstacle. Hundreds of thousands of administrative and secretarial jobs in the private sector that could go to women are filled by foreign men as a result of gender segregation. Finally, the labor law, while beneficial to women workers with its generous maternity leave and time off during the work day for nursing, is at the same time a deterrent to hiring women in the private sector due to the financial burdens these benefits place on prospective employers.

Education in Saudi Arabia is free at all levels. Female students at the pre-college level have access to the same courses as male students, except that, until 2003, girls were not allowed to take gym or a course entitled "Civics." While a high rate of illiteracy characterizes the population above age 15 (30.5 percent for women and 15.9 percent for men), the figures drop considerably for the younger population aged 15 to 24 (9.7 percent for women and 5.1 percent for men), although the gender disparity remains.[25] At the elementary level, only 56 percent of school-aged girls are enrolled, which would suggest a possible parental gender bias when it comes to sending daughters to school, except that, by comparison, only 60 percent of elementary school–aged boys are in school.[26]

Women comprise an estimated 56 percent of the nearly 32,000 students in higher education institutions.[27] However, women are not allowed to study engineering and are not admitted to the King Fahd University for Oil and Minerals in Dhahran, on the grounds that they would not be allowed to work in the profession for which they would be trained. All Saudi universities that admit women have separate and inferior facilities for their female students. When King Saud University, the largest university in the kingdom, was built as a state-of-the-art institution in the early 1980s to accommodate 25,000 male students, women were moved to the old male campus of Riyadh University, which had no useful library. Nevertheless, gender discrimination in higher education is changing. A new campus for women is under construction in Riyadh, and there is a private college for girls in Jeddah, the first in Saudi Arabia designed to follow an American curriculum.

RECOMMENDATIONS

1. The government should guarantee Saudi women equal facilities and equal access to all fields of education.
2. The government should continue its ongoing reforms in the educational sector and should seek technical assistance from the international educational community to incorporate a broader perspective of world events into the Saudi school curriculum.
3. The government should establish women's studies centers and departments in Saudi colleges and schools to help students, teachers, and the broader society obtain a better understanding of women's human rights issues.
4. The government should provide all women with efficient, safe, and affordable transportation and remove all restrictions on women's driving, travel, and employment.

Political Rights and Civic Voice

There are no elections or political parties in Saudi Arabia, and there are no constitutionally guaranteed rights to free speech, press, or assembly. Neither Saudi nationals nor non-nationals have the right to vote or participate in any political activity. Forming trade unions, striking, and engaging in collective bargaining are forbidden. While women are becoming more active and visible in the current movement of reform, they are still marginalized, and women's status remains a muted issue.

The Majlis al-Shura (Consultative Council) is an all-male 120-member advisory body first appointed by the king in 1992 with a mandate to study the king's legislative initiatives. In 2004, at the same time as the prerogatives of the Council increased to include introducing new legislation and amending existing legislation, three women were appointed to serve on an advisory council to the Majlis but not to serve as members. The first-ever municipal elections, announced in 2003, are now slated to begin in 2005, but only males over the age of 21 who are not in military service will be allowed to vote and run for office. Saudi women are petitioning for the right to participate.

The weekly *majlis* (gathering) that is held by the king and provincial governors is the one institution that supposedly provides direct access to the government. This forum permits nationals to petition for redress of grievances or for personal favors. While the majlis is "open to all citizens and to anyone who has a complaint or a plea against an injustice,"[28] women are traditionally not allowed to attend; they must send a written petition on their own behalf. On majlis days, female petitioners wait in the streets outside the meeting and try to hand their petitions through the windows of limousines.

Despite women's need for legal representation in the courts and the availability of trained women lawyers, Saudi Arabia's conservative *ulama* (religious scholars) forbid women to participate in the judiciary, either as judges or as lawyers.

Saudi men and women submitted a series of reform petitions to the government in 2003. While the petitioners pledged their allegiance to the monarchy, they demanded changes in the system of governance, including, albeit indirectly, calls for women's rights. In January 2003, 104 citizens sent the crown prince a letter entitled "A Vision for the Nation and its Future" that called for social justice, the public election of the Majlis al-Shura, an end to corruption, an independent judiciary, and freedom of speech, assembly, and association. In April, a second petition signed by 450 Shi'a men and women, entitled "Partners in One Nation," expressed sympathy with the signatories of the January letter and asked for relief from discrimination and for greater Shi'a representation in government positions, education reform, and religious freedom. On September 24, 2003, 306 Sunni and Shiite men and women sent another petition, "In Defense of the Nation," calling for political reform, separation of powers, freedom of speech, right of assembly, and religious tolerance and cited as problems administrative corruption, fiscal irresponsibility, poverty, unemployment, and the second-class status of women. The petition also criticized the slow pace of reform and the absence of popular participation in decision-making, observing that the lack of freedom of expression fostered the growth of intolerance and extremism.

The crown prince, who has led efforts to respond to citizens' concerns, gave a friendly reception to the petitioners, but subsequent events suggest that the ruling family is ambivalent about how far to allow reforms to go forward. In October 2003, the government opened a conference on human rights sponsored by the Saudi Red Crescent Society but later arrested 271 persons during a demonstration that included women advocating for political reform and the release of political prisoners.[29]

The much-heralded National Dialogue Conference held in August 2003 included the subject of the "rights and duties of women," and the January 2004 Jeddah Economic Forum brought women's roles in the economy to national attention. Saudi women, notably businesswomen, also spoke on Saudi economic growth at the Economic Forum and participated in the same room with men—some without *hijab* (complete head cover).[30] However, the Grand Mufti, Shaikh Abd al-Aziz Al as-Shaikh criticized women's public presence in this mixed-gender gathering.

Saudi Arabia remains a country without the basic freedoms necessary for civil society to take root. Saudi nationals find it extremely difficult to start new organizations or women's groups, and any new NGO involved in journalism, human rights, or the "national dialogue" is quickly co-opted by the government. In August of 2003, King Fahd approved the establishment of an official human rights organization, the National Organization for Human Rights, and appointed 9 women out of 41 members; the chairman and executive committee are also members of the Consultative Council.

RECOMMENDATIONS

1. The Saudi government should allow for political parties and truly free and competitive elections in which both women and men participate.
2. The government should ensure freedom of expression by permitting independent press and radio programs to present alternative viewpoints without the fear of attacks or intimidation by non-state actors.
3. The government should allow women's human rights groups to work freely and openly and provide them with security to prevent attacks by non-state actors.

Social and Cultural Rights

Saudi Arabia has invested heavily in public health services; Article 27 of the Basic Law of the kingdom secures Saudi welfare rights and declares, "The State shall guarantee the right of its citizens and their families in an emergency or in case of disease, disability and old age." State-of-the-art, government-funded medical care is available free of charge for Saudi citizens, especially in populous urban centers, though foreigners usually must rely on private medical care. Quality health services are less available in rural areas than in urban centers, but still, 83 percent of all births take place in healthcare facilities in rural areas and 95 percent in cities.[31] Despite the availability of health services, women's access to health care may be restricted. For example, women are forbidden to have surgical procedures without the approval of a mahram.

According to a Population Reference Bureau study, modern contraceptive methods are used by 29 percent of Saudi women aged 15 to 49. These figures suggest a change in policy since the 1970s and 1980s when it was illegal to sell or purchase contraceptive devices.[32]

Abortion is not easily available in Saudi Arabia and is illegal in most circumstances, including rape and incest, except under specific medical conditions. Unmarried women who become pregnant, especially non-Saudis, are at risk of arrest, prosecution, or loss of employment, should their marital status become known while they are seeking medical care in a hospital. Human Rights Watch reports that the Ministry of Health issued a directive in 2003 that prohibited hospitals from admitting pregnant women who were not accompanied by men willing to acknowledge paternity. A pregnant woman in such a situation who needed emergency care would be put under watch to prevent her from leaving. The purpose of this directive, according to Human Rights Watch, was to deal with the problem of unmarried women abandoning their babies at hospitals.[33]

Female genital mutilation (FGM) is not a common practice in Saudi Arabia, although anecdotal evidence suggests that the practice exists in some Shi'a communities in the Eastern Province, and FGM was documented earlier in the 20th century among some Bedouin groups.

Women are allowed to own housing, but women who live alone are not considered "respectable" in Saudi Arabian society. By law, women are not permitted to rent housing without the presence of a mahram, even if they are moving to be closer to their place of work.

Community life for women in Saudi Arabia usually entails socializing within the family and neighborhood networks and possibly being active in a woman's charitable society. A woman's participation in a community depends entirely on her family, her family connections, her education, and her own abilities. The government does not interfere in women's social activities so long as the activity does not cause offense and does not draw attention. Saudi women influence policies and social development in their roles as teachers, doctors, social workers, journalists, university professors, investors, and even as religious scholars who write about the role of women.

Women are employed as journalists and as television presenters and producers. However, women in the media must observe the Saudi dress code and they face restrictions on the issues they can deal with as journalists.

Saudi women can be trapped in poverty due to gender if they are born poor, because it is difficult to earn a living as a woman; but women may also be rich due to gender, because of their right to inherit while being maintained by others. The Millennium Development Goals Report for Saudi Arabia states that the proportion of people living in poverty is believed to be minimal.[34] Public and privately run programs and government subsidies, as well as Saudi culture and social traditions (family support networks) are large contributors to maintaining poverty at a low level.

All organizations must be registered with the Saudi government, which can easily shut them down without judicial recourse.[35] There are no independent women's human rights organizations working freely to document or publicize human rights abuses against women. Women are free to advocate for women's human rights only to the extent that they do so with deference to Islam and with praise for the country's leaders, or until they are silenced by being jailed, fired from their jobs, or threatened.

However, some women's rights advocates participated in the National Dialogue Conferences of 2004. Women were also signatories to the reform petitions, which incorporated calls for women's rights, though only as part of a larger package of reform. Saudi women are not allowed to work freely with women's rights groups from other countries, and international women's groups must go through the government of Saudi Arabia in order to work with any non-government group in the country.

The causes of gender discrimination in Saudi Arabia are systemic. They are rooted in the attitudes and policies of the ruling Al Saud family. Indigenous social hierarchies and interest groups, tribal and family allegiances, and the country's interpretation of religion are also factors. A solid majority of Saudi citizens are committed to reform. In a poll of Saudi citizens conducted under the direction of Nawaf Obaid, nearly 85 percent thought that political reform would benefit the country, over 90 percent wanted to grant women more rights, and 63 percent thought women should be allowed to drive.[36] Saudi reformers recognize how vast the problems facing democratization are, and the reform petitions put forward during 2003 emphasize the need for total reform in order for any meaningful changes to take place.[37]

RECOMMENDATIONS

1. The government should take steps to remove restrictions on women's access to health care information and access to health services, including eliminating the laws which require women to produce written permission from a male guardian in order to have surgery or other medical procedures.

2. The government should guarantee women's groups the ability to work independently to promote women's rights and equality issues.

AUTHOR: Eleanor Abdella Doumato is a Visiting Fellow at the Watson In-stitute for International Studies at Brown University. She is a past president of the Association for Middle East Women's Studies and the editor of the Middle East Women's Studies Review.

Notes

[1] The Quran is the holy book of Muslims, and Sunna is the tradition of the Prophet Mohammad.

[2] According to a Human Rights Watch report, "There are 8.8 million foreign residents in Saudi Arabia, according to the Labour Ministry. This figure is significantly higher than any previously reported. Foreigners account for 67% of the workforce and hold 90 to 95 percent of private sector jobs." *Bad Dreams: Exploitation and Abuse of Migrant Workers in Saudi Arabia* (HRW, Vol. 16, No. 5[E], July 2004).

[3] Wahhabism (sometimes spelled Wahabbism or Wahabism) is a movement of Islam named after Muhammad ibn Abd al Wahhab (1703–1792).

[4] All citations of the Basic Law are from this source: http://www.mideastinfo.com/documents/Saudi_Arabia_Basic_Law.htm.

[5] The Hadith are the collected sayings of the Prophet Mohammad that constitute the Sunna.

[6] The family institution is a key pillar in the state's self-legitimation. Article 9 of the Basic Law says that "the family is the kernel of Saudi society, and its members shall be brought up on the basis of the Islamic faith, and loyalty and obedience to God, His Messenger, and to guardians; respect for and implementation of the law, and love of and pride in the homeland and its glorious history as the Islamic faith stipulates." Article 10 says that the "state will aspire to strengthen family ties, maintain its Arab and Islamic values and care for all its members, and to provide the right conditions for the growth of their resources and capabilities."

[7] Basic Law, Article 36 (Arrest): "The state provides security for all its citizens and all residents within its territory and no one shall be arrested, imprisoned, or have their actions restricted except in cases specified by statutes."

[8] *Country Reports on Human Rights Practices*–Saudi Arabia (Washington, D.C.: U.S. Dept. of State, Bureau of Democracy, Human Rights, and Labor, 18 December 2003).

[9] Ibid.

[10] "Saudi Arabia: Religious Police Role in School Fire Criticized" (New York: Human Rights Watch [HRW], 15 March 2002), http://hrw.org/press/2002/03/saudischool.htm.

[11] "Women Workers: Forced Confinement, Labor Exploitation, and Sexual Abuse," in *Bad Dreams: Exploitation and Abuse of Migrant Workers in Saudi Arabia* (HRW, Vol. 16, No. 5[E], July 2004), http//hrw.org/reports/2004/saudi0704/7.htm#_Toc75678073. See also in *Bad Dreams*, "Migrant Workers in the Criminal Justice System: Rights Denied," in which HRW asserts, "Saudi Arabia is obligated under its own laws and international human rights law to protect everyone on its territory from torture and ill treatment, and to afford fair trials to individuals arrested for criminal offenses. The kingdom's law of criminal procedure specifically prohibits torture and degrading treatment of persons under arrest and in detention. Saudi Arabia is also a

state party to the Convention against Torture and Other Cruel, Inhuman or Degrading Treatment or Punishment (CAT), but government authorities continue to violate its provisions with impunity."

[12] Ibid.

[13] "Women Workers . . . ," in *Bad Dreams* (HRW, July 2004), http://hrw.org/reports/2004/saudi0704/7.htm#_Toc75678071.

[14] Ibid. "The forced confinement of women workers violates provisions of the Convention on the Elimination of All Forms of Discrimination against Women (CEDAW), which Saudi Arabia has ratified. This treaty requires state parties to 'accord to men and women the same rights with regard to the law relating to the movement of persons and the freedom to choose their residence and domicile.' The government's tolerance of the forced confinement of women workers perpetuates discrimination against women, which it is legally committed to eliminate. CEDAW obligates the government to legally protect the rights of women on an equal basis with men, and to 'ensure through competent national tribunals and other public institutions the effective protection of women against any act of discrimination.' The treaty also requires states parties to 'take all appropriate measures to eliminate discrimination against women by any person, organization or enterprise,' and 'to take all appropriate measures, including legislation, to modify or abolish existing laws, regulations, customs and practices which constitute discrimination against women.'"

[15] "Trafficking in Persons Report" (Washington, D.C.: U.S. Dept. of State, Office to Monitor and Combat Trafficking in Persons, 11 June 2003), http://www.state.gov/g/tip/rls/tiprpt/2003/21275.htm.

[16] Ibid.

[17] Ibid.

[18] "Migrant Workers . . . " in *Bad Dreams* (HRW, July 2004), http://hrw.org/reports/2004/saudi0704/10.htm.

[19] Ibid.

[20] "Saudi Arabia Remains a Fertile Ground for Torture with Impunity" (London: Amnesty International [AI] Secretariat. 1 May 2002), http://web.amnesty.org/library/index/ENGMDE230042002.

[21] "Saudi Arabia: Gross Human Rights Abuses Against Women" (Amnesty International, 27 September 2000), http://web.amnesty.org/library/Index/engMDE230572000?OpenDocument&of=COUNTRIES%5CSAUDI+ARABIA.

[22] Javid Hasan, "Saudi Women Make Debut in New Professions," *Arab News*, 28 August 2004.

[23] In 2002, there were 465,338 Saudi women employed in comparison to 2,683,381 Saudi men. "Labor Force (15 years and older) by administrative area, nationality, and sex, 2002," in *Social Statistics Labor Force Survey* (Riyadh: Kingdom of Saudi Arabia, Ministry of Economy and Planning, Central Department of Statistics), http://www.planning.gov.sa/statistic/sindexe.htm.

[24] "Saudi male population not in labor force (15 years and older), 2002, and Saudi population not in labor force (15 years and older), 2002," in *Social Statistics Labor Force Survey* (Riyadh: Kingdom of Saudi Arabia, Ministry of Economy and Planning, Central Department of Statistics).

[25] Table 24, "Gender-related development index," in *Human Development Report 2004: Cultural Liberty in Today's Diverse World* (New York: United Nations Development Programme [UNDP], 2004), 217-220. http://hdr.undp.org/reports/global/2004/;

Table 2, "Adult and youth literacy," in *Gender and Education for All: The Leap to Equality* (Paris: United Nations Educational, Scientific and Cultural Organization [UNESCO], EFA Global Monitoring Report 2003/4), p. 304.

26 Table A-2, "Net enrollment ratios in primary education by gender, 1999/2000," in *Arab Human Development Report 2003* (New York: United Nations Development Programme [UNDP], Arab Fund for Economic and Social Development, 2003), 192.

27 Table A-8, "Percentage of females among tertiary education students by levels of higher education, 1999/2000," in *Arab Human Development Report 2003* (UNDP), 195.

28 Basic Law, Article 43 (Royal Courts): "The King's Court and that of the Crown Prince shall be open to all citizens and to anyone who has a complaint or a plea against an injustice. Every individual shall have a right to address the public authorities in all matters affecting him."

29 Khalid Al-Dakhil, "2003 was a defining year for Saudi reform," *Daily Star* (Beirut), 8 April 2004.

30 "A Recent Debate on Women's Rights in Saudi Arabia," *Al-Quds Al-Arabi* (London), 18 January 2004.

31 *Women's Reproductive Health in the Middle East and North Africa* (Washington, D.C.: Population Reference Bureau [PRB], 2003).

32 Table 1, "Selected Reproductive Health Indicators in the Middle East and North Africa," in *Women's Reproductive Health* (PRB), 4; *World Development Indicators* (op.cit.) gives the figure of 21 percent of women using contraception during the years 1990–99.

33 "Women Workers . . . " in *Bad Dreams* (HRW).

34 "Millennium Development Goals: Report on the Kingdom of Saudi Arabia" (United Nations, Riyadh, 2002), http://www.undp.org/mdg/saudi.pdf.

35 "Saudi Arabia: Gross Human Rights Abuses Against Women" (London: Amnesty International, 27 September 2000), http://web.amnesty.org/library/Index/engMDE 230572000?OpenDocument&of=COUNTRIES%5CSAUDI+ARABIA.

36 Nawaf Obaid, "Yes to bin Laden rhetoric; no to Al Qaeda violence," *International Herald Tribune*, 28 June 2004.

37 Eleanor Doumato, ed., *Tailor-Made Islam: Religion, Identity and the Nation in Middle Eastern School Books* (forthcoming).

Syria

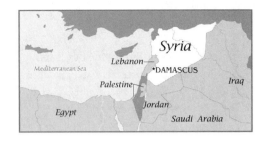

by Catherine Bellafronto

Population: 17,500,000
GDP Per Capita (PPP): $3,620
Economy: Mixed statist
Ranking on UN HDI: 106 out of 177
Polity: Dominant party (military-dominated)
Literacy: Male 91.0% / Female 74.2%
Percent Women Economically Active: 29.2%
Date of Women's Suffrage: 1949 (to vote), 1953 (restrictions lifted)
Women's Fertility Rate: 3.8
Percent Urban/Rural: Urban 50% / Rural 50%

Country Ratings for Syria
Nondiscrimination and Access to Justice: 2.7
Autonomy, Security, and Freedom of the Person: 2.2
Economic Rights and Equal Opportunity: 2.8
Political Rights and Civic Voice: 2.2
Social and Cultural Rights: 2.3
(Scale of 1 to 5: 1 represents the lowest and 5 the highest level of freedom women have to exercise their rights)

Introduction

Syria gained its independence from France in 1946 and today is a republic under a military regime. In 1963, the Ba'ath Party led a successful military coup and has since governed Syria with a pan-Arab, nationalist, secular, and socialist ideology that infiltrates all aspects of public life. Syrians do not have the right to change their government. The Syrian constitution, ratified in 1973, guarantees the Ba'ath Party's dominance in the People's Assembly—Syria's parliament—by reserving assembly seats for members of the Ba'ath Party and the National Progressive Front (NPF), the umbrella group of Syrian parties of which the Ba'ath Party is the legal head. The People's Assembly nominates the president, whose candidacy is then approved by a popular referendum. Current President Bashar Al-Asad and his father, Hafiz Al-Asad, who served as president for 30 years before his death in 2000, have run unopposed in all elections.

275

Syria is a middle-income developing country with a per capita GDP (PPP) of $3,620 and a Human Development Index rating of 0.710.[1] The centrally planned economy depends heavily on the agricultural sector and on oil-related products and services. The public sector is the primary source of jobs, employing 73 percent of the work force, but unemployment rates near 20 percent are pressuring the government to focus on private-sector growth.[2] President Al-Asad is slowly instituting market-oriented reforms, but members of the regime's "old guard" are largely opposed to them.

Half of Syria's estimated 17.5 million residents live in rural areas. The population is 90 percent Arab; there is also a sizable Kurdish population (approximately 1.5 million people), as well as other ethnic minority groups, including 409,662 Palestinian refugees.[3] While the Syrian constitution requires the president to be a Muslim, Syria has no official religion. A majority of Syrians (74 percent) are Sunni Muslim. The country is also home to other Muslim groups, and various sects of Christians (about 10 percent), as well as a small number of Jews. The Alawites, an offshoot sect of Islam, comprise about 12 percent of the population and dominate the Ba'ath Party, the executive, and the security branches of the government.

A state of emergency, imposed by the government the year the Ba'ath Party took power, remains in effect today.[4] Since its inception, the government and security agencies have used the state of emergency to curtail all civil society activity and suspend constitutional rights to expression, peaceful assembly, and privacy, resulting in a pervasive atmosphere of fear that has only recently begun to subside.

Syrian women balance growing opportunities in the public sphere with continuing social and legal restrictions in their private lives. Government policies over the past 10 years have encouraged women's education, participation in the work force, and use of family-planning services. Reflecting the government's efforts, women's literacy increased from 48 percent in 1990 to 74 percent in 2002; 29.2 percent of women are economically active; and 45.8 percent of married women now use contraception.[5]

Nevertheless, traditional values, discriminatory laws, and an authoritarian government deprive women of many basic legal and social rights. Syria's penal code, nationality code, and personal status code establish women's status as legal dependents of their fathers and husbands, while traditional ways of life reinforce patriarchal social structures. One of the primary sources of opposition to women's rights, however, lies in extremist Muslim groups in Syrian society who strongly influence government decisions to maintain women's unequal status under the laws and the personal status code. Syrian women's groups have limited abilities to combat this opposition or to effect social or legal change in women's lives due to the government's severe restrictions on freedom of association.

Nondiscrimination and Access to Justice

The Syrian constitution, ratified in 1973, delineates the same rights, freedoms, and responsibilities for women as it does for men. Article 45 of the constitution declares, "The state guarantees women all the opportunities that enable them to participate fully and effectively in political, social, cultural, and economic life. The state works to remove the restrictions that prevent women's development and their participation in building socialist Arab society." Yet, no laws protect women in the event of gender-based discrimination, and no formal mechanisms exist through which women may complain to the government if they do encounter discrimination.

The Syrian legal system derives from French civil law, Turkish law, and *Shari'a* (Islamic law). Although the constitution guarantees "full rights and opportunity" for all citizens, exceptions exist in the nationality code, the personal status code, and the penal code that do not afford women full and equal status as citizens. The personal status code, the body of laws regulating family relationships and inheritance, makes women legal dependents of their fathers or husbands and denies women status as full legal adults in matters of marriage, child custody, and divorce.

The nationality code of 1969 prevents a woman from passing Syrian citizenship to her non-Syrian husband or to her children, a right that is enjoyed by Syrian men.[6] Furthermore, in 1962, about 120,000 Kurds were stripped of their Syrian nationality. Along with their descendants, these Kurds remain stateless, a total of 275,000 to 290,000 people, unable to obtain a passport or, in many cases, any official identification documents.[7] This serves to disrupt numerous daily-life activities for both Kurdish men and Kurdish women, such as the ability to travel, own property, attend school, and obtain employment.

The Syrian judiciary is divided into secular and religious courts and is constitutionally independent from the executive branch. The secular courts are under the jurisdiction of the ministry of justice and hear both civil and criminal cases. Separate religious courts serve different religious groups concerning matters of personal status, family, and inheritance. While spiritual courts handle marriage, divorce, and custody cases for Druze and non-Muslims, the Shari'a court administers all other family law cases for Syrian citizens.

In addition to these courts, two additional court systems were created under emergency laws: the Supreme State Security Court, which hears cases involving threats to political and national security, and the Economic Security Court, which hears cases involving financial crimes. Neither male nor female citizens prosecuted within this system enjoy constitutionally guaranteed rights to a fair trial. Human rights organizations estimate that the Syrian government is currently holding between 800 and 4,000 political prisoners, many of whom were tried in the security courts.[8]

Women are treated as full persons in the civil and criminal court system. In the Shari'a court, however, a woman's testimony is considered to be worth only half that of a man. While there are no additional legal barriers to women's access to justice, social barriers prevent them from taking advantage of the judicial system to the same extent as men. For example, women are discouraged from presenting their claims in police stations, which are largely staffed by male police officers, for fear of experiencing shame, discomfort, or sexual harassment.[9] The state of emergency, imposed by the government in 1963, further deprives both women and men of their constitutionally guaranteed rights to justice.

The penal code of 1949 affords women special protections from verbal and physical harassment and violence perpetrated by men, yet a number of other laws deprive women of these protections, usually for the sake of family "honor." For example, Article 508 of the penal code states: "If there is a contracted marriage between the man who commits rape, sexual abuse, kidnapping, sexual harassment and the victim, then there is no charge or the punishment is stopped." Victims' families may favor this option in order to mitigate public scandal. Many women do not have the choice of refusing marriage in such cases either due to family pressure or due to fear of further harassment and social stigma.

The penal code condones violence against women. Marital rape is not a crime in Syrian law, and women have no legal recourse should their husband assault them.[10] Furthermore, a judge may legally reduce the sentence for a man convicted of a so-called "honor crime," —the murder or beating of or causing injury to his wife or female family member for alleged sexual misconduct.[11]

Adultery is a crime in Syrian law, but the conditions required for proving adultery in the court are different for men and women. In presenting a case against his wife, a man may produce any form of evidence—witnesses, physical proof, or written documents—before the judge. A woman, in contrast, may only present written evidence of her husband's infidelity. Additionally, the husband must have committed the crime of adultery inside the family home in order to be charged, while a woman may be prosecuted for committing adultery anywhere.[12] The punishment for adultery is more severe for a woman than it is for a man. If convicted of adultery, women may serve 3 months to 2 years in prison, while men serve only 1 month to 1 year.[13]

Under the state of emergency, all Syrian citizens are subject to arbitrary arrest, detention, or exile. However, women's lower rate of participation in politically sensitive opposition activities makes them less vulnerable to arbitrary detention or arrest. A woman threatened by family members or the community for supposed connection with an "honor crime" may be held by the authorities for her protection.

In 2003, the Syrian government ratified the UN Convention on the Elimination of All Forms of Discrimination Against Women (CEDAW), with reservations applied to Articles 2, 9(2), 15(4), 16(1)(2), and 29(1).[14] The government found these articles to be incompatible with national laws and the Shari'a. Syria's reservations predominantly concern a woman's right to pass her nationality to her children, freedom of movement and of residence and domicile, equal rights and responsibilities during the marriage and its dissolution, and the legal effect of the betrothal and the marriage of a child. Syria's reservations on Article 2 of the convention are most significant, as it is this article that establishes the purpose of the convention and commits the state to engage in efforts to eliminate discrimination against women. Syria has not yet ratified the Optional Protocol to CEDAW.

A small number of Syrian women's rights activists and other civil society actors are currently working to improve women's access to justice and are advocating for legal reform. However, all nongovernmental organizations (NGOs) are required to be registered with the government, and all meetings must be reported in advance to the ministry of interior.

The General Women's Union (GWU) is the only registered women's rights group approved by the government. The GWU follows the Ba'ath party mandate; its officials are appointed and promoted from within the party hierarchy. Formed in 1967, the GWU is a nationwide organization that works on women's welfare and political participation issues in Syria. It receives financial support from the government, which facilitates its development projects involving women in all parts of the country, especially in rural areas.

According to the Private Associations and Institutions Act No. 93 of 1958, and in line with Ba'ath Party philosophy, the GWU represents all Syrian women.[15] However, this assertion by the government is used to prohibit independent women's NGOs from registering. It advises all women's groups to work under the GWU. This presents serious problems for independent women's groups who may not agree with all government policies. A number of women's groups, such as the Syrian Women's League, operating since 1949, do work independently, but their members still face the threat of arrest and detention.

Independent women's groups in Syria face tremendous problems in raising and receiving funds to continue their work due to local laws that prohibit donor grants from abroad. As a result, unregistered groups find it difficult to attract members, funding, and participants for their activities. Many activists work informally and independently at the grassroots level raising awareness, publishing articles, giving interviews, and holding forums.

RECOMMENDATIONS

1. The government and People's Assembly should lift the state of emergency that prevents women from working openly and effectively to change discriminatory laws.

2. The Syrian government, in cooperation with NGOs, should lead a public campaign to inform women of their legal rights and encourage them to access the judicial system.
3. The Syrian president and People's Assembly should amend laws related to "honor crimes" and adultery that put women's lives in danger.
4. The government should remove all reservations to CEDAW and take steps to implement it locally by bringing national laws in conformity with CEDAW.

Autonomy, Security, and Freedom of the Person

While the civil liberties, security, and autonomy of all Syrian citizens are restricted, women suffer additional restrictions both legally and socially. The personal status code, contained in Legislative Decree No. 59 of 1983, regulates family relationships and inheritance and is the single greatest legal barrier to Syrian women's freedom. It codifies legal discrimination against women and reinforces the discriminatory traditions of a patriarchal society.

Syria does not have an official state religion. The Syrian constitution provides for freedom of religion, and the government generally respects this right in practice. Most religious activities are free from government involvement, although the government does monitor some religious sermons. Syrian Muslim women face some additional restrictions and are not allowed to marry non-Muslims, unlike Muslim men.[16]

Married women are subject to restrictions on their freedom of movement. Syrian law gives a husband the right to prevent his wife from leaving the country by submitting her name to the ministry of interior, although men rarely exercise this right. A woman no longer needs the permission of her husband to obtain a passport. Unmarried women over the age of 18 may travel domestically and abroad without the permission of male guardians. Yet social pressure restricts many women from traveling or living alone.

The Syrian marriage contract legally allows women to stipulate any provisions in the marriage contract. However, in practice, most Syrian women are unaware of this right and fail to exercise it. Marriage contracts are generally prepared according to existing patriarchal traditions in which the male family members negotiate the marriage contract for the bride and the groom. Less-educated families rely on the advice of the male religious leader who conducts the marriage ceremony. Women are rarely informed of all the rights they could claim in a Muslim marriage contract and often sign without reading it.

Women of all ages are required to have male guardians contract their marriages, while adult men are free to contract their own marriages.[17] If an adult woman marries without her guardian's consent, the guardian may invalidate her marriage.[18] The minimum age for marriage is 17 for females and 18 for males. However, minimum marriage-age laws are often not enforced, particularly in rural areas,[19] and a judge may authorize marriage for females as young as 13 and males at 15.[20] Because the guardian contracts the marriage, minors are not able to object to it. Early marriage remains a problem, although the average age of marriage for women has risen consistently to 25.2 in urban areas and 24.8 in rural areas.[21]

Syrian laws governing behavior within marriage discriminate against women. A woman must obey her husband or risk losing financial support.[22] While polygamy is legally permitted, it is restricted and relatively uncommon, though more prevalent in rural areas. According to Article 17 of the personal status code, a husband must seek permission from a judge to take a second wife and must prove he has both legitimate justification and the financial means to provide for a second wife. A husband may circumvent this restriction, however, if he obtains a civil marriage and later registers the marriage outside the court system by providing medical proof of his second wife's pregnancy.[23] Currently, a man's marriage to a second wife is not a legitimate reason for a woman to divorce him in the Syrian Shari'a courts.

Divorce continues to be much easier for men to initiate than for women and often leaves women unable to support themselves. Article 91 of the personal status code grants men the right to repudiation, the unilateral decision to end the marriage without naming a reason; the man simply registers the divorce with the government. In this case, a woman may receive alimony for up to three years if she can prove she is destitute. Women who are employed, however, often do not fall into this category and do not receive alimony.

For a woman to obtain a divorce, she must sue, stating a legitimate reason, specified as "dissension, prejudice, lack of affinity, absence or ailments," after which the court allows one month for reconciliation.[24] Alternatively, a woman can seek a consensual divorce, or *khol*, in which she agrees to return the dower (a sum of money given to a wife by her husband at the time of marriage) to her husband.[25] In practice, however, many women choose to forgo alimony from the spouse rather than repay him the dower.

Child custody laws allow a woman to be the legal guardian of her children only in the event that the father has died or is legally incapacitated, stateless, or unknown. A woman has the right to have and care for her children until the age of 13 for boys and 15 for girls. Yet, while the mother has the right to keep the children, she does not have the same rights as a guardian. For example, she cannot register her children for school or move with them. Furthermore, divorced mothers who remarry may lose custody of their children, but this possibility does not apply to a father who remarries.

Trafficking laws exist and are enforced.[26] Syria also legally prohibits torture in the penal code.[27] Nevertheless, Amnesty International has criticized the Syrian government for human rights abuses including torture. Syrian officials are legally protected from prosecution for any crimes committed while on the job, leaving victims of torture and their families with no avenue for redress.[28]

Syria has no laws to protect women from domestic violence. Patriarchal social customs tend to tolerate a man hitting his wife, and women are often discouraged from reporting violence against themselves or their children. Syrian police officials are not sympathetic to women victims of family violence and lack gender-sensitive training to deal with such cases. A woman's family may intervene on her behalf by speaking to her abusive husband, but families will rarely tolerate the public attention of a legal suit and will most often encourage the woman to remain in the marriage.

It is difficult to know the extent of violence against women as there are no reliable statistics on the problem. Social custom discourages families from reporting crimes, and crimes are often masked as accidents. While women receive special legal protection from verbal and physical violence outside the home,[29] they rarely, if ever, make use of these protections by reporting the crime. Many women remain silent about abuse, feeling shame and responsibility, because Syrian society places the burden of sexual morality on women.[30]

Syrian women activists speak openly in the press about the need to reform the personal status code, and women's rights groups have recently held conferences on combating domestic violence. Social discussion of domestic violence is still generally circumspect, however, despite its presence in the press and on television. No private or governmental organizations provide assistance to victims of domestic violence, and information is most often passed by word of mouth. Charitable religious organizations provide limited assistance such as shelter, counseling, legal aid, health care services, and rehabilitation.[31] Nevertheless, due to the lack of government attention to this issue, a large number of women victims of family violence do not have access to supportive services.

RECOMMENDATIONS

1. The government should review all laws and eliminate clauses that discriminate against women; it should bring its family law into conformity with constitutional guarantees of equality.
2. The government should pass laws to protect women from domestic violence and provide training to court and police officials on effectively dealing with these cases.
3. The government should work in close consultation with women's rights advocates to establish support centers for female victims of violence to receive legal aid, counseling, and related protective services.
4. Media and NGOs should reach out to families of victims of domestic violence in order to reduce the social stigma of this problem and provide the families with information on how to help the victim.

5. Syria's Central Bureau of Statistics should gather data on the prevalence, causes, types, and outcomes of violence against women.

Economic Rights and Equal Opportunity

The Syrian civil and commercial codes of 1949 ensure women's equality in owning property, managing businesses, and initiating legal cases.[32] Legally, women also enjoy full and independent use of their income and assets and are free to enter into business contracts. However, in practice, women who obtain property through inheritance or by their own financial means may be restricted from making use of it independently because many families discourage unmarried women from living alone. Families also expect women to contribute their personal income to the family expenses rather than put it aside for themselves.

In accordance with Syria's interpretation of Shari'a inheritance laws, daughters are entitled to half the inheritance of sons. Yet, many Syrian women are not aware of their inheritance rights and may turn over their lawfully inherited property to another relative. Furthermore, male descendants from a different line of the family may be able to compete with female descendants of the deceased if the deceased has no male heirs.[33] Non-Muslim women do not have the right to inherit from their Muslim husbands.[34]

Education is compulsory for all Syrian citizens up to the age of 11,[35] and all levels of education are free. Nevertheless, there is a huge drop in enrollment rates after the primary level, when students apparently leave school to enter the work force. Fewer girls than boys enter secondary school: the rate of enrollment for boys is a low 41 percent, while girls enroll at a rate of 37 percent.[36] Many girls who leave school, predominantly in rural areas, submit to family pressures to marry or work. UNICEF has criticized the Syrian government for not doing enough to combat the phenomenon of girl student drop-outs.[37] Kurdish children who are deprived of Syrian citizenship face further difficulties in trying to enroll in the Syrian school system.

While low participation rates are a problem, Syria has succeeded in considerably narrowing the gender gap in access to education and illiteracy since the 1970s. In 1970, 80 percent of women were illiterate compared to 40 percent of men, while women's illiteracy rate in 2002 was 25.8 percent, and men's was 9 percent.[38] Women are also receiving university degrees at a rate close to men. According to UNIFEM, the percentage of women graduates from Syrian universities was 40.6 and the percentage of women graduates from professional training institutes was 49.0 in 2000.

In line with the requirements of CEDAW, the government recently completed a project to rewrite the textbooks used in the school system to balance the presentation of men and women. Textbooks now show women in various professions and also emphasize that both Christianity and Islam view women and men as equals.

In 2002, 29.2 percent of women participated in the labor force, reflecting a moderate increase since the 1970s. Although women have made strides in education and labor force participation, very few have reached leadership positions in business. Women have only begun to infiltrate public leadership positions and are still excluded from the inner circle of Ba'ath Party leadership.

Syrian women are not totally free to choose their profession and are prohibited from working in jobs the government considers hazardous and/or immoral.[39] Many women who obtain university degrees in medicine, law, engineering, and the humanities find employment appropriate to their qualifications, but only 8.7 percent of women have university-level education.[40] Women and girls in rural areas often do not receive the same professional opportunities as women in urban areas and are under pressure from their families to perform unpaid domestic work rather than complete their education or seek work outside the home.

Women still tend to work predominantly in low-paid jobs performing manual labor. They dominate the agriculture sector, contributing 70 percent of agricultural activity, most often as unpaid farming laborers. By contrast, relatively few women work in administrative, service-oriented, technical, or industrial jobs, indicating that women are excluded from the sectors that contribute most to the modern development of the Syrian economy.[41] Women also make up a small percentage of the military and police force. Thirty percent of employed women work in the public sector,[42] where they comprise roughly one-fifth of all public sector employees. While women who work in the public sector tend to face less discrimination than in the private sector, they are still largely relegated to clerical and staff positions.[43]

Syria faces a serious unemployment problem as a result of low GDP growth and high population growth. But with increasing numbers of women entering the work force, women suffer disproportionately higher rates of unemployment as they try to break into the labor market.[44] Micro-enterprise loans through the Syrian government and UN Relief and Works Agency are provided for women at a far lower rate than for men. Furthermore, agency projects to reach potential borrowers generally target public places where men are working, and loan guarantee requirements tend to favor forms of wealth that are more accessible to the male population.[45]

While labor regulations insist upon women's equal access to job opportunities in the public and private sectors, as well as equal remuneration for labor, they do not provide any protections in the event of discrimination.[46] Nevertheless, gender-based discrimination in obtaining professional employment is reported to be low.[47] Women are at a disadvantage in the hiring process, however, because women's domestic obligations often require them to work fewer hours or prevent them from obtaining the additional professional training necessary for advancement in their career. The bulk of domestic responsibilities fall upon women, whether or not they work in or outside the home.

Labor regulations protect women from arbitrary dismissal during pregnancy, maternity leave, and sickness related to pregnancy and delivery.[48] Both private and public sector employers grant 120 days of maternity leave for the first child, 90 for the second, and 75 for the third. Women are permitted one hour during the workday for breast-feeding the child. Childcare is available in all public sector offices, although the quality of care needs improvement.

The government has not enacted any laws or policies to protect working women from harassment in the workplace, despite the demands of independent women's associations. Due to the lack of reporting mechanisms, it is difficult to measure the extent of the problem.

Nonprofit organizations such as Modernizing and Activating Women's Role in Economic Development (MAWRED) and Fund for the Integrated Rural Development of Syria (FIRDOS) were recently registered with the government and work openly to improve women's role in the Syrian economy. In addition, the ministry of agriculture (MOA) established the Rural Women Development Unit in 2000 to manage assistance projects for rural women who are most in need of information and access to paid employment.

RECOMMENDATIONS

1. Civil society groups should inform women about managing their personal finances in order to promote women's financial independence from their families.
2. The Syrian government and donors should support women to create and finance their own businesses through the provision of loans below market rate.
3. The ministry of agriculture (MOA) should involve rural woman in formulating and implementing MOA plans and programs to ensure that the needs of women are addressed in development projects.
4. The Syrian People's Assembly should enact laws that protect women from discrimination and harassment in the workplace.

Political Rights and Civic Voice

Syria has been ruled by a military regime since the Ba'ath Party led a coup in 1963 and imposed a state of emergency. Syrians have no ability to change their government and have little or no influence on government policies. The government continues to use the intelligence services and military to limit any potential opposition to the regime. Political opposition groups, religious activists, and independent human rights groups face severe restrictions on their activities, including the threat of torture and indefinite detention.

Restrictions on freedom of expression and assembly have loosened somewhat in the past couple of years, affording women's groups, both religious and secular, the opportunity to meet, discuss, and express their views publicly on issues of importance to them. However, public gatherings continue to be subject to government controls.

Syrian citizens do not have the right to peaceful assembly. The Private Associations and Institutions Act No. 93 of 1958 regulates the act of association.[49] Any meeting, with the exception of religious services, must be registered with the ministry of interior in advance. Permission is often denied and that denial is justified in the Institutions Act by a prohibition against any meeting for which the purpose is "to prejudice the integrity or form of the republican government."[50]

In practice, women's rights activists do meet and discreetly organize conferences and training sessions on women's issues. However, it is still extremely difficult and risky for human rights groups to meet and work openly. In recent years, the government has arrested a number of human rights activists for attempting to hold public pro-democracy demonstrations. The police usually disrupt public demonstrations that are not organized by the Ba'ath Party or government officials, and participants may be detained indefinitely.

Restrictions on freedom of expression have loosened under President Bashar al-Asad. The state media now have greater freedom to address previously taboo subjects—religion, gender, and the governing regime—although in circumspect terms and with limited criticism. The Syrian government runs all Syrian television and radio stations and most newspaper publishing houses, yet independent newspapers were permitted in 2001. Currently three weekly newspapers are printed by private organizations.[51]

Male and female journalists openly discuss the topic of domestic violence and the suggested reforms to the personal status code. While they are not widely distributed, both the pro-government General Women's Union and the independent Syrian Women's League do publish magazines. Although women write articles for government and private newspapers, many Syrians still practice self-censorship for fear of repercussions by the state. Most women do not have access to, or are not comfortable using the media, professional associations, or NGOs as forums for expressing their opinions.

Although elections in Syria are transparent, they are not democratic, free, or fair. The unicameral People's Assembly, Syria's parliament, is a 250-seat council whose members are elected by popular vote. However, elections are mostly orchestrated by the regime. The Syrian constitution guarantees the Ba'ath Party majority control of the People's Assembly by reserving assembly seats for members of the Ba'ath Party and the National Progressive Front. The government approves all candidates for election, thus preventing true opposition candidates from running.

Legally, women have the right to vote and be elected on equal footing with men, but women run for office in far smaller numbers than men do, largely because Syrian society discourages women from entering the public sphere.[52] Women first entered the People's Assembly in 1973 and now hold 10.4 percent of the seats, following the March 2003 election.

Women's representation in the judiciary has increased since 1970. Today there are 170 female judges (13.38 percent of the total), 33 state lawyers (14.47 percent of the total) and 250 assistant judges. A woman has held the highest judicial post, as Syria's general prosecutor, since 1998.[53]

The executive branch is the center of authority in Syria. Of the three branches of government, women are most underrepresented in the executive branch and tend to be assigned posts of secondary importance. The president, elected by a national referendum for seven-year terms, appoints two vice presidents, a prime minister, and a council of ministers. Women hold ministerial posts in the ministry of culture and the ministry of labor and social affairs and have previously been appointed to lead the ministries of education and expatriates. Four women serve as deputy ministers, and women also fill the positions of director-general (11), deputy director-general (27), branch director (47), and deputy branch director (23).[54]

While there is no legal restriction on women's participation in legislative activities, they tend to be underrepresented. Even though women are more active in local administration councils and organizations than ever before, their numbers still remain small. Women's participation in the governorate councils is 8.7 percent; district councils, 4.5 percent; and village councils, 1.3 percent.[55] In the parliamentary elections of March 2003, 30 women were elected through the National Progressive Front, but no independent women won seats.

Syrians do not have the right to form opposition parties. All political parties must join the National Progressive Front, headed by the Ba'ath Party, and support the principles of socialism and Arab nationalism. Nine parties comprise the National Progressive Front, which is guaranteed 167 seats in the People's Assembly through a constitutional clause. However, no women are represented in the highest levels of the Ba'ath Party. While there are no official religious parties, extremist Muslim groups have historically been the strongest opponents of the Ba'ath Party. The government monitors the activities of religious leaders and is cautious about implementing progressive reforms in women's rights for fear of agitating Muslim extremists in Syria.

Women's participation in civic life is unequal to men's. While some women provide community leadership through charities and NGOs focused on women's issues, they are poorly represented in political parties, professional associations, and religious leadership. The government prevents the organization of unions outside its control. However, women have the legal right to form unions, and they are members and employees of various unions, including the Union of Agronomists, the Union of Engineers, and the Union of Teachers.

Women do not have free access to information in Syria. The ministry of information, as well as the ministry of culture and national guidance, must approve all Syrian radio and television broadcasts on government-owned stations before airing. Nevertheless, television satellites are common, and the government does not interfere with satellite broadcasts. The ministries monitor all printed material and restrict information that deals with the government's human rights record, Islamic fundamentalism, the government's involvement in Lebanon, and any material that may be offensive to the country's various religious groups.[56] Internet access is generally unrestricted, however, with the exception of certain sites that criticize the government's human rights record. A wide variety of information is in theory available to women, but women often do not know where to find it and may be hesitant to seek it out.

RECOMMENDATIONS

1. The government and the People's Assembly should lift the state of emergency and allow political parties to work freely and participate openly in democratic and fair elections.
2. The government should reinstitute constitutional protections for freedom of expression and assembly and free all political prisoners.
3. The government should encourage and facilitate independent NGOs to initiate civic awareness campaigns through the media, the educational system, and religious institutions to encourage women to vote and run for public office.
4. The government should recruit more women into high-level decision-making posts, including the ministries of foreign affairs and the interior, which have traditionally been dominated by men.

Social and Cultural Rights

Syrian society traditionally grants men the public sphere and women the private sphere. Women throughout the country experience various restrictions on their social freedoms due to religious and social conservatism that limits their participation in public life. Generally women in rural areas and lower socioeconomic classes experience greater restrictions on their access to the public sphere, education, health care services, and marriage and family decisions.

Women's freedom to make independent decisions about their reproductive health has improved greatly as a result of the government's family planning campaign that began in the early 1980s. In 2003, the fertility rate was 3.8

children per woman.[57] Women can receive information and services, including contraceptives, from clinics operated by the ministry of health, the Syrian General Women's Union, the Syrian Family Planning Association (SFPA), and private operators. Although the distribution of such services remains illegal, this law is not enforced.[58] Nevertheless, family planning services for women in rural areas are limited. A culture of son preference prevails in Syria, and women, particularly in rural areas, are under family pressure to continue to bear children until they have sons.

Abortion is illegal under any circumstances and is criminalized under the penal code.[59] However, many doctors will perform clandestine operations for a large fee, a price too high for many women. Unsafe surgical conditions and self-induced abortions continue to endanger women's lives. The SFPA advocates openly for the protection of women from unsafe abortions, although they stop short of promoting the full legalization of abortion.

Primary health care is free and accessible through public health clinics, and approximately 70 percent of the population lives within a half-hour distance from a clinic.[60] Eighty-seven percent of women deliver children under the care of trained medical staff. Women in rural areas remain underserved however, but the proportion of rural women delivering children with medical supervision increased from 62.3 percent in 1993 to 81.2 in 1999.[61]

Although the official age of marriage in Syria is 16 years for girls, courts may permit girls as young as 13 to marry under Syrian law. According to Syrian women's rights leaders this practice of marrying girls at a young age is harmful to women's reproductive health, interrupts their education, and increases the likelihood that they will live in poverty.

Syrian women have the right to own and use housing, yet social custom discourages and often prohibits women from living alone. In the event of divorce, the law denies most women the use of the marital home for themselves and their children, and women are generally forced to return to the home of their parents.

Women's abilities to influence community life are limited by the fact that public life is largely the domain of men by social custom. Instead, women have an influence on community life through their family responsibilities. They shape attitudes toward social issues and influence the family's economic situation by controlling expenses. Within the community, women are free to speak out on neighborhood and quality of life issues. Women hold positions in the local government at a rate of about 4.2 percent, yet the ability of any group to influence policy is limited by the power of the Ba'ath Party.[62]

Women are underrepresented in Syria's media both in decision-making positions and as employees. While they contribute in a variety of capacities including as journalists, script writers, and talk show hosts, there are very few women in positions of leadership. Women enjoy somewhat greater freedom of expression in the press than on television, although television programming is increasingly presenting a positive image of women. Television dramas regularly draw attention to societal problems that women face, such as divorce and domestic violence. President Asad's wife Asma appears prominently in print and on television as a successful former businesswomen and a partner to the president.

Women in Syria are disproportionately affected by poverty. While the rate of women-headed households is low (5.3 percent in 1997), households headed by women are more likely to suffer from poverty than households headed by men. Forty percent of women-headed households have incomes below 6,000 SP, compared to only 16 percent of households headed by men.[63] Women also have higher rates of unemployment, and their work more often goes uncompensated. In addition, many women lack information on how to manage their finances and are therefore unprepared to support themselves and their children in the event of divorce or widowhood.

Government-sponsored and officially registered organizations such as the General Women's Union and the SFPA work openly to provide services to women and lobby the government for policy changes. However, independent organizations and activists critical of government policies, and women advocates belonging to opposition parties, must work more discreetly. Public discussions of gender-related topics are often limited to generalities.

RECOMMENDATIONS

1. The ministry of health should improve the quality of public sector health care and expand reproductive health services to cover underserved areas, such as rural regions.
2. Media organizations should promote more women to decision-making positions.
3. The Syrian government and NGOs should use the media, the educational system, and religious institutions to encourage women to seek the information they need to address financial and legal problems.
4. The government should lift all legal restrictions that prevent women from registering, attracting members, and collecting funds for independent organizations to work on women's rights issues.

AUTHOR: Catherine Bellafronto is a specialist in business development in the Middle East and North Africa. She is currently pursuing a master's degree in international affairs at Georgetown University's School of Foreign Service and has worked with small businesses in Morocco. Ms. Bellafronto conducted the fieldwork for this report in Syria during the summer of 2004.

Notes

[1] *Human Development Report* (New York: United Nations Development Programme [UNDP], 2003).

[2] *Syria: Country Strategy Paper 2002 - 2006* (Brussels: European Union).

[3] *Country Reports on Human Rights Practices – Syria* (Washington, DC: U.S. Dept. of State, Bureau of Democracy, Human Rights, and Labor (DRL), 25 February 2004), 8. As of June 2003, the United Nations Relief and Works Agency (UNRWA) for Palestine refugees in the Near East listed 409,662 registered Palestinian refugees residing in Syria.

[4] Military Order, Law No. 2, 8 March 1963.

[5] Men's literacy had increased from 82% in 1990 to 91% in 2002 (New York: United Nations Educational, Scientific, and Cultural Organization (UNESCO), Institute for Statistics, Work force information from Table 27, "Gender inequality in economic activity," in *Human Development Report 2004: Cultural Liberty in Today's Diverse World* (New York: UNDP, 2004), 229–32, http://hdr.undp.org/reports/global/2004/. Contraception information from *Evaluating the Status of Women* (Amman: United Nations Development Fund for Women [UNIFEM], 2003), 76.

[6] Nationality Code, Law No. 276, 1969.

[7] See *The Effect of Denial of Nationality on the Syrian Kurds* (Damascus: Human Rights Association in Syria, November 2003).

[8] *Country Reports* (U.S. Dept. of State, DRL).

[9] Author's interview with Syrian women lawyers, Damascus, July 2004. Also see *Evaluating* (UNIFEM), 10.

[10] Penal Code, Article 439, states: "Rape is considered to occur when a man forces a woman who is not his wife to have intercourse."

[11] Penal Code, Article 192, states: "Judge excuses or reduces the punishment if a person commits a crime under honor." Article 242 states: "For crimes committed in a state of passion, the judge may reduce the punishment." Article 548.1 states: "Anyone who catches his wife, one of his female ascendants or descendants, or his sister committing adultery or engaging in illegitimate sexual relations with another person and who, without intending to do so, murders, beats or injures his relative and her accomplice, is exempt from punishment." Article 548.2 states: "Punishment provided for by the law will be reduced for anyone who catches his wife, one of his female ascendants or descendants, or his sister in a suspicious situation with a man and commits murder or battery or inflicts injury."

[12] Author's interview with Syrian women lawyers, Damascus, July 2004.

[13] Rabea Naciri and Isis Nusair, *The Integration of Women's Rights into the Euro-Mediterranean Partnership: Women's Rights in Algeria, Egypt, Israel, Jordan, Lebanon, Morocco, Palestine, Syria, and Tunisia* (Copenhagen: Euro-Mediterranean Human Rights Network [EMHRN], May 2003), 19.

[14] See "Convention on the Elimination of All Forms of Discrimination Against Women" (New York: United Nations, 18 December 1979), http://untreaty.un.org/ENGLISH/bible/englishinternetbible/partI/chapterIV/treaty10.asp.

[15] Naciri and Nusair, *Integration of Women's Rights* (EMHRN), 41.

[16] Personal Status Code, Article 48.2, refers to the religion of the man and woman.

[17] Personal Status Code, Article 21.

[18] Article 27 states that "if a grown-up woman marries herself off without her curator's agreement, the marriage contract is kept valid if the husband is competent or made invalid if the curator demands separation of wedlock," *Evaluating* (UNIFEM), 14.

[19] "Convention on the Rights of the Child, Committee on the Rights of the Child, Consideration of Reports Submitted by States Parties under Article 44 of the Convention, Concluding Observations: Syrian Arab Republic" (New York: United Nations, 10 July 2003), http://www.unhchr.ch/tbs/doc.nsf/898586b1dc7b4043c1256a450044f331/4bd0895f88708624c1256da60053ad50/$FILE/G0342903.pdf.

[20] Personal Status Code, Article 16 and Article 18.

[21] The average age for marriage is 25.1 for women and 28.9 for men: *Evaluating* (UNIFEM, 24).

[22] Personal Status Code, Articles 73 and 74.

[23] According to Article 14, legitimate justification for marrying a second wife may be the first wife's illness, inability to conduct marital affairs, or sterility.

[24] Personal Status Code, Articles 105–12: *Evaluating* (UNIFEM), 15.

[25] Personal Status Code, Article 95.

[26] Author's interview with Syrian women lawyers, Damascus, 2004. Law 10 (1961), Articles 1, 2, 3, 4, 6, and 7 prohibit trade in women.

[27] Penal Code, Article 28.3, states: "No one may be tortured physically or mentally or be treated in a humiliating manner. The law defines the punishment of whoever commits such an act." Prisons Order, Article 30, states: "It is prohibited for any official or guard to use severity with prisoners, label them with degrading labels or make fun of them." *Torture in Syria*, (Damascus: Human Rights Association in Syria, January 2004).

[28] Law No. 14 (1969), Article 16, states: "It is prohibited to complain or file a case against any worker in the administration regarding crimes they commit whilst carrying out their work without a prior order from the director."

[29] Penal Law, Articles 476, 489, 491, 492, 493, 495, 496, 497, 502, 504, 505 and 506, prohibit violence and harassment against women.

[30] Author's interview with Syrian woman journalist, 14 July 2004.

[31] For instance, Nuns of the Good Shepherd Society in Syria provide limited services to women victims of family violence.

[32] Civil Code, Articles 40 and 46; Commercial Law, No. 149 of 1949, Article 15.

[33] Author's interview with Syrian women lawyers, Damascus, July 2004.

[34] Naciri and Nusair, *Integration of Women's Rights* (EMHRN), 19.

[35] UNESCO, Institute for Statistics, 2001.

[36] Ibid.

[37] UNICEF assessment of Syria. Can be accessed at http://www.unicef.org/infobycountry/syria.html.

[38] *Evaluating* (UNIFEM, 58); Table 24, "Gender-related development index," in *Human Development Report 2004* (New York: UNDP, 2004), 217–20, http://hdr.undp.org/reports/global/2004/.

[39] Syria's draft report submitted in 2004 in response to the UN "Questionnaire on Implementation of the Beijing Platform for Action (1995) and the Outcome of the Twenty-Third Special Session of the General Assembly (2000)," http://www.un.org/womenwatch/daw/Review/responses/SYRIAN-ARAB-REPUBLIC-English.pdf.

[40] *Evaluating* (UNIFEM), 57.

[41] UNESCO, Institute for Statistics, 2001.

[42] Syria's draft report on compliance with the Beijing Platform for Action, 2004.

[43] *Evaluating* (UNIFEM), 57.

[44] Syria report from the Programme on Governance in the Arab Region (UNDP), www.pogar.org/countries/gender.asp?cid=19.

[45] In 2000, rates of unemployment in urban areas: 7.5 for men; 28.1 for women. Rates of unemployment in rural areas: 7.0 for men; 13.4 for women. *Evaluating* (UNIFEM), 54.

[46] Author's interview with Lex Takkenberg, Deputy Director of UNRWA Affairs in Syria, 1 August 2004.

[47] Ibid.

[48] Author's interview with Syrian women lawyers, Damascus, July 2004, and National Team Leader, Syrian-European Business Centre, 18 July 2004.

[49] Ibid.

[50] Private Associations and Institutions Act No. 93 of 1958 states that "'Association' shall mean any grouping endowed with a permanent organization, established for a specified or indefinite period and consisting of individuals or bodies corporate, for a non-profit-making purpose."

[51] "The restrictions which this Act places on the establishment of such associations in order to protect public safety, national security, public order, public health and morals and the rights of others are the same as those placed on exercise of the right of peaceful assembly in order to protect the public interest. Under article 2 of the said Associations Act: 'Any association which is established for an illicit reason or purpose, or which contravenes the law or the moral code, or the purpose of which is to prejudice the integrity or form of the republican government shall be null and void.'" Syria Report to the Office of the UN High Commissioner for Human Rights (OHCHR) in 2000.

[52] *The People's Voice*, from the National Progressive Front's (NPF) Communist Party; *The Unionist*, from the NPF's Union Socialist Party; and *The Economist*, published by the editor-in-chief of a Paris-based magazine.

[53] Election Law, No. 26, 1973.

[54] Syria's draft report on compliance with the Beijing Platform for Action, 2004.

[55] Ibid.

[56] Ibid.

[57] Country Reports (U.S. Dept. of State, DRL).

[58] "2003 World Population Data Sheet" (Washington, D.C.: Population Reference Bureau, 2003).

[59] SFPA is a Syrian NGO established to promote awareness of family planning and provide reproductive health services. Penal Law, Articles 523 and 524, ban the advertising, promoting, selling, obtaining, or facilitation of contraceptive use.

[60] Under Syrian law, a fetus is recognized as a person before the law and is protected from harm by criminal penalties in Articles 58, 528, and 529 of the Penal Code. "Syria Report to the Office of the UN High Commissioner for Human Rights" (Geneva: UN Office of the High Commissioner for Human Rights [OHCHR], 2000).

[61] Reproductive Health Sub-Programme Document Between the Government of Syria and The United Nations Population Fund (Damascus: UNFPA, 2002).

[62] Evaluating (UNIFEM), 74.

[63] Ibid., 47.

[64] Ibid., 31.

Tunisia

by V. M. Moghadam

Population: 9,900,000
GDP Per Capita (PPP): $6,760
Economy: Mixed capitalist
Ranking on UN HDI: 92 out of 177
Polity: Presidential (dominant party)
Literacy: Male 83.1% / Female 63.1%
Percent Women Economically Active: 37.5%
Date of Women's Suffrage: 1959
Women's Fertility Rate: 2.1
Percent Urban/Rural: Urban 63% / Rural 37%

Country Ratings for Tunisia
Nondiscrimination and Access to Justice: 3.6
Autonomy, Security, and Freedom of the Person: 3.4
Economic Rights and Equal Opportunity: 3.1
Political Rights and Civic Voice: 2.8
Social and Cultural Rights: 3.3
(Scale of 1 to 5: 1 represents the lowest and 5 the highest level of freedom women have to exercise their rights)

Introduction

Tunisia is a republic dominated by a strong presidential system and a single political party, the Constitutional Democratic Rally (RCD). After the country gained independence from France in 1956, Tunisia's first president, Habib Bourguiba, implemented substantial social and economic reforms and invested heavily in education. Tunisia's 1956 personal status code, the *Code du Statut Personnel* (CSP), afforded women full and equal legal rights and remains one of the most progressive family laws in the Arab world today. In 1987, Bourguiba was deposed in a bloodless coup by current President Zine el-Abidine Ben Ali. While President Ben Ali maintained some of Bourguiba's positive initiatives, he also continued restrictions on political rights and civil liberties, falling short on his promises for greater political openness. A constitutional referendum was passed in 2003 to allow Ben Ali to seek an unprecedented fourth five-year term in the elections of 2004.

Tunisia's 1959 constitution provides authority to the president to appoint the prime minister and the executive Council of Ministers, as well as the country's 24 governors. The legislative Chamber of Deputies, a popularly elected unicameral body, is mostly dominated by the RCD, which holds 148 of the 182 seats; members of the seven legal opposition parties fill the remaining seats. Freedoms of the press, association, and expression are extremely restricted; the authorities often cite security concerns as a pretext for repression of political dissent and critical discourse across the political spectrum. Political prisoners and journalists are often subjected to arbitrary arrests, incommunicado detention, torture, unfair trials, and harsh prison conditions.

Tunisia has a per capita GDP of $6,760 and a diverse economy, with significant agricultural, energy, mining, tourism, and manufacturing sectors. The country's population of an estimated 9,900,000 is predominantly Muslim, with a small percentage of Christians and Jews who are free to practice their religions as long as they do not disturb public order. The urban population comprises 63 percent of Tunisian inhabitants.

While Tunisia's legal reforms and the 1956 CSP helped to expand women's rights in matters of marriage, divorce, custody, education, and employment, setbacks to women's progress occurred in the 1970s, when reduced public investment in education resulted in lower school enrollment for girls. The 1970s also witnessed a decline in women's political participation, as well as the Islamization (strengthening of Islamic content) of the educational curriculum. The growing influence of the Islamic revival movement was curbed in the late 1980s by a regime change that also worked to further improve women's legal status. Amendments to the CSP in 1993, as well as legal reforms to the nationality code, the penal code, and the labor law, helped to increase women's rights. However, general human rights were circumscribed in the 1990s as a result of a strengthened police state apparatus.

The Tunisian government ratified the Convention on the Elimination of All Forms of Discrimination against Women (CEDAW) in 1985, and the state has taken significant strides to implement the standards of CEDAW and to ensure that Tunisian laws are in compliance with international standards on women's rights. Nevertheless, the Tunisian government places restrictions on women's organizations and their ability to advocate for their rights, particularly groups that call for greater democratic freedoms and civil liberties. The work of most NGOs is closely monitored by state security agencies, and a 1959 law stipulates that all associations must apply for permission from the Ministry of Interior to hold meetings, conferences, or debates.

Women's progress is evident in their increased educational attainment at the tertiary level, access to paid employment, and diversity in professional career options. The government has stressed the education of girls, and today more than 50 percent of university students are women. However, women continue to face daunting unemployment rates, while inequalities persist between rural and urban women and between men and women in the political sphere.

Nondiscrimination and Access to Justice

Tunisia's legal system is based on the French civil law system and to a lesser degree Islamic law; the country has both civil and criminal courts. However, the judiciary is not completely independent from executive influence.

Tunisia's legal frameworks—including its constitution, the CSP, the labor law, social welfare policies, and the penal code—provide protections for women from gender-based discrimination. Following the amendments introduced pursuant to Constitutional Act No. 97-65 of October 27, 1997, the constitution strengthened the principle of the equality of citizens by explicitly decreeing, through amendments to Articles 8 and 21, the inadmissibility of discrimination between genders. The labor law was also amended in 1993 to refer explicitly to the principle of nondiscrimination.[1] Additionally, some gender-specific benefits exist for women in the labor force, particularly in the form of maternal protections.

While Tunisia's constitution provides for the equality of all citizens, women do not share the same rights as men under the nationality law (*Code de Nationalité*). A Tunisian woman is not permitted to transfer her nationality to her foreign-born husband, while a Tunisian man, on the other hand, can pass his nationality to both his foreign-born wife and the children of this union. However, the Code de Nationalité was amended in 1993 to allow mothers more rights to transfer their citizenship to their children. The law now allows a child born abroad to a Tunisian mother and a foreign father to become Tunisian if the child makes the request one year before reaching the age of majority, or with joint declaration by the father and mother.[2]

Most women have equal access to justice, due in large part to Tunisia's long history of women in the judiciary and the state's executive-level commitment to women's rights. The first woman judge was appointed in 1968, and by the 1990s an estimated 24 percent of magistrates were women.[3] An adult woman is recognized as a full person before the court, and a woman's testimony is considered equal to that of a man.

Following the 1993 amendments to the CSP, the penal code was also amended to criminalize domestic violence and remove gender-discriminatory language that had allowed for a reduction in sentencing for a man who committed acts of violence against his spouse. Article 207 of the penal code had permitted the reduction of a sentence to a simple misdemeanor for a man convicted of an "honor crime"—a crime in which a man murders or injures his wife and/or her partner who are caught *in flagrante delicto* in the act of adultery. The amended law now treats this crime as subject to the penalty applicable for manslaughter, namely life imprisonment.[4] Additional amendments to the penal code now treat domestic violence as more serious than typical assault and battery; one amendment provides that the person who commits the assault is actually liable for a heavier punishment if the victim is his spouse. The impact of this amendment, however, is often weakened by the proviso, "withdrawal of the complaint by a victim who is an ascendant or spouse shall terminate any proceedings, trial or enforcement of penalty."[5]

The penal code stipulates serious penalties for rape, which is subject to the heaviest penalty if accompanied by violence or armed threat or if the victim is under 10 years of age.[6] Yet the law does not recognize marital rape or consider it a crime, despite the existence of Tunisia's other laws and policies that emphasize women's rights to dignity and bodily integrity.

The Tunisian government ratified CEDAW in 1985, albeit with reservations to Article 9(2), which covers equal nationality rights, Article 16(c), (d), (f), (g), and (h), which deal with the granting of family names to children and the acquisition of property through inheritance, and Article 15(4) which addresses the right of women to choose their place of residence. The Tunisian government found these articles to contravene the CSP.[7] While the government seems committed to implementing CEDAW and prepares lengthy evaluative reports to the CEDAW committee, it has yet to sign the Optional Protocol to CEDAW. The Optional Protocol would allow a woman to file a complaint of gender discrimination directly with a CEDAW committee if she had exhausted all possible domestic remedies.

Women's governmental and nongovernmental organizations appear to be working freely and effectively to promote the status of women's rights within the family and the economic sphere. The 1990s witnessed increases both in the number of active women's organizations and in women's rights. However, women's NGOs, like most Tunisian NGOs, are seriously constrained by governmental restrictions on their associational rights and their freedom of expression. Women's rights activists and advocacy groups must tread carefully when approaching issues of political rights or governmental shortcomings.

The Tunisian national machinery for women—the *Ministère des Affaires de la Femme, de la Famille, et de l'Enfant* (MAFFE) (Ministry of Women, Family, and Children's Affairs), and *la Commission Nationale "Femme et Développement"* (CFD) (The National Commission on "Women and Development"), along with the research institute *Centre de Recherche, d' Etudes, de Documentation et d'Information sur la Femme* (CREDIF) (The Center for Research, Studies, Documentation, and Information on Women), and *l'Union Nationale de la Femme Tunisienne* (UNFT) (National Union of Tunisian Women)—continues to work in conjunction with independent Tunisian women's NGOs to implement the 1995 Beijing Platform for Action, a global agreement on women's rights.

RECOMMENDATIONS

1. The government should amend the Tunisian Nationality Law to ensure Tunisian women the right to transfer their nationality to their foreign-born husbands.
2. The government should revise its laws and practices to ensure that women feel free to report violations of their rights without fear of harassment by state agents.
3. The government should lift all restrictions on civil liberties to enable women's groups and civil society members to work freely and openly for women's rights.
4. The government should remove all reservations to CEDAW and take steps to implement it locally by bringing national laws in conformity with CEDAW.

Autonomy, Security, and Freedom of the Person

While Tunisia is a de facto secular state, Article 1 of the constitution declares Islam as the state religion, and Islam continues to play some part in Tunisian laws and the country's social life. Nevertheless, the constitution guarantees the free exercise of religions that do not disturb the public order, and Tunisia's non-Muslim populations are generally free to practice their religions. Socially, women are generally discouraged from marrying non-Muslims. The non-Muslim husband of a Tunisian woman can acquire citizenship through his wife only if he converts to Islam.[8]

Consistent with the nature of Tunisian family law, an adult Tunisian woman is not legally required to obtain the permission of her father or husband in order to travel. However, in Tunisia both men and women may be subject to severe state control on their freedom of movement and their abilities to travel in and out of the country, particularly if they are Islamists or are involved in opposition politics. Family members and spouses of dissidents may also face restrictions on their movement. In August 2003, a female citizen was reportedly refused permission to travel outside the country because she was the sister of a critic of the government who was living in France.[9]

Tunisia's 1956 code of personal status, also known as the *Majalla,* afforded women rights and legal protections that were significantly progressive in relation to the rest of the Arab/Muslim world at the time. The CSP abolished polygamy and repudiation, required that both parties to marriage be consenting, provided women with the right to divorce and child custody, and established a minimum marriage age for both girls (17) and boys (20). A 1981 amendment granted a woman lifelong alimony after divorce, instead of the previous rule that afforded a lump sum, and also provided a mother with automatic guardianship (legal control) over her child in the event of the father's death—in effect, ending patrilineal privilege.

The amended 1993 CSP dropped the clause requiring a wife to obey her husband, stipulated joint authority of parents, and established support for divorced mothers in need. Amendments to the CSP also created mechanisms to sanction the joint authority of the parents, the continued expenditure on children until the end of their education, and the compatibility of divorce proceedings with the children's interests. The amended CSP now allows a divorced mother to petition the court for guardianship if she feels the father was derelict or abusive.[10] The amendments also established a Fund for the Guarantee of Alimony in favor of women divorcees and their children in order to provide financial support to divorced custodial mothers not receiving adequate child support from the fathers of their children.[11] Two principles guided the reforms: the principle of symmetry and equality between the married couple and the principle of protection of the family and of the woman.[12]

Tunisian law prohibits slavery and bonded labor but does not specifically address trafficking of persons. There is no evidence of slavery or slavery-like practices, however, and available reports do not indicate that trafficking of women is a significant problem.

There is no evidence that women are subject to discriminatory arbitrary arrest, detention, and exile as a result of their gender, yet reports of the arbitrary arrest of family members of Islamist activists and human rights activists charged with "association with criminal elements" demonstrate that no one is immune from harassment.[13] State security forces have been accused of torture, which is prohibited by Tunisia's penal code, as well as cruel, inhuman, and degrading punishment of men and women alike. Women appear to have more often fallen victim to these practices during the early 1990s, when a number of women were interrogated concerning the political activities and whereabouts of their husbands and politically involved family members.[14] However, violence and harassment continue to be used to repress dissidents, Islamists, and activists today. Prison conditions do not meet international standards, yet prison conditions in women's jails are reportedly better than those of men.

Addressing the issue of domestic violence in Tunisia has been an important focus among women's rights activists, NGOs, and governmental women's affairs groups in Tunisia since the early 1990s, when it also became a matter of international concern. In 1991, for example, the UNFT conducted a study including lawyers, doctors, social workers, and a national representative sample of 1,000 people to analyze marital violence. The *Association Tunisienne des Femmes Democrates* (ATFD) (Tunisian Association of Democratic Women), an NGO also known as *les Femmes Democrates*, has operated the *Centre d'Écoute*, a support center for victims of violence located in their main office in Tunis since 1993. This group also disseminated the results of a study conducted in 1998 of reported cases of spousal abuse and family violence.[15]

The extent to which gender-based violence by non-state actors occurs outside the home is not fully known. Data on rapes and assaults on women are not available, but anecdotal evidence suggests that the Tunisian police are vigilant, an atmosphere of law and order prevails, and streets are relatively safe.

Tunisian women's groups, as well as human rights organizations, are generally able to work freely to expand women's rights within the family and eradicate violence against women. A significant amount of credit is attributed to these groups for instigating changes in Tunisian law and society. One Tunisian scholar-activist writes that the criminalization of "honor crimes" and domestic violence was in large measure the result of the research and advocacy of the Femmes Democrates.[16] The 1993 reforms of the CSP were also in large measure a response to the advocacy efforts of Tunisia's women's movement, including the roughly 12 member-groups of the Rihana Network. However, the ability of women's rights groups to work freely is often hindered by the possibilities of restrictions, monitoring, and harassment that Tunisian NGOs may face if they criticize state policies or the state's failure to ensure the rights of its citizens.

RECOMMENDATIONS

1. The government and women's NGOs should initiate a national public awareness campaign to inform the public of women's rights under amended domestic violence laws, as well as new protections against all forms of violence under the country's penal code.
2. The government should criminalize all forms of violence against women, including marital rape, and provide gender-sensitive training to its police and court officers to ensure that victims receive state services.
3. The government should facilitate the efforts of women's rights groups to establish documentation centers in police stations to record incidences of gender-based violence.

Economic Rights and Equal Opportunity

The Tunisian constitution, family law, and labor law provide for women's rights to own and control land, property, and income. Adult women do not need the permission of their fathers, husbands, or any male guardian to pursue education, seek employment, take out a loan, or set up a business.

Inheritance of family wealth is governed by Tunisia's interpretation of Shari'a law, which grants a larger share of inheritance to sons than to daughters. Muslim men and non-Muslim women who are married may not inherit from each other. Given women's advancements in the labor field and state efforts to enhance women's economic participation, such a policy seems anachronistic. As a fairly large proportion of Tunisian women draw on personal savings to start a business, the reform of inheritance laws could help to spur women's entrepreneurship.

In 1993, schooling was made compulsory for all children until the age of 16, and since then, illiteracy rates have declined, school enrollment has increased, and social statistics suggest that gender-based gaps in secondary schooling and at the tertiary level are rapidly disappearing. In 2002, the female literacy rate was 63.1 percent, compared with 83.1 percent for men. Figures were better for the age group of 15 to 24 year olds, with 90.6 percent female literacy, and school enrollments of males and females were almost equal.[17] However, older women and those in rural communities remain at a disadvantage in literacy and educational attainment, mainly due to the deployment of their labor in household economic activities.[18] In the higher education sector, the country has had more women than men students since 2000. Women, at present, account for 56.4 percent of all students.[19] Women are free to choose their field of study, although they tend to be concentrated in the humanities and social sciences.[20]

The right of women to work is guaranteed by Tunisia's labor law, by all texts regulating the civil service, and by the Collective Labor Agreement. Following the 1993 amendments to the CSP, a new article was added to the labor code that expressly proscribes discrimination between men and women. Furthermore, the principle of "equal skills, equal pay" is in force in the civil service.[21]

The proportion of economically active women is currently 37.5 percent.[22] Tunisian women have significant representation in the professions of dentistry and pharmacology and have made impressive inroads into the civil service, the banking sector, and the field of law. Nevertheless, women's unemployment rates remain high—about 15.3 percent in 2001.[23] In large measure, high unemployment has caused many women to move toward the informal sector and micro-enterprises; it is estimated that about one-fifth of jobs in the informal sector are held by women.[24] About 15 percent of the Tunisian female labor force is self-employed.

Indeed, the private sector has become increasingly important to Tunisian development and as a source of employment for women. In 2002, 5,000 heads of business in Tunisia were women, mainly in the sectors of textiles and garments, services, and information technology. The nongovernmental Association of Women Business Presidents promotes women's leadership in business by providing scholarships for female students at the Advanced Institute of Management (ISG) and the Institute of Advanced Business Studies (IHEC). However, women remain underrepresented in supervisory and management posts in the educational system, and Tunisian men continue to hold most executive and senior-level decision-making posts in the labor field.[25]

A recent study sponsored by CREDIF and the UNDP on women's entrepreneurship showed that in Tunisia, women have difficulty obtaining financing and loans for new enterprises. Women are also less likely than men to request bank financing and are less willing to carry debt. Of the women questioned in the study, 70 percent said they drew on personal savings to begin their business, although those at the level of micro-enterprise had frequently received credit from an NGO. Despite the obstacles, however, women-owned businesses appear to thrive; the survival rate after five years for women-owned businesses was almost twice as high as for businesses started and owned by men.[26] An estimated 54 percent of women entrepreneurs have secondary or higher education, as opposed to 40 percent of men.[27]

Tunisia has instituted forward-looking labor policies to enable working mothers to balance employment and family life. Article 66 of the labor law conforms to ILO conventions 41 and 49 regulating night work, underground work, and other hazardous work for women, especially those who are pregnant or lactating. But maternity leaves are not very generous. In the public sector, women receive two months at full pay, which may be taken along with annual leave. In the private sector, only 30 days at 2/3 pay are provided, with a medical extension for an additional 15 days, but no longer than 12 weeks (the ILO-recommended minimum).

Additional labor policies allow new mothers the option to take time off to nurse their babies for up to six months and require enterprises with at least 50 women to provide a special nursing room.[28] Since 1983, state employees can request four months of leave at half-pay to raise minors, with no loss of seniority; however, in 1988, this benefit was limited to the first three children only.[29] Mothers may also take up to two years of leave to raise children younger than six years or a disabled child; they also have the right to work part-time at their request—a measure that has no effect on periods of leave, promotion, allowances, and retirement schemes.[30] As CREDIF argues, the law tends to favor the gender division of labor in the household at the risk of compromising the equal opportunities of men and women in the labor market.[31]

As yet, Tunisia has no law or policy to protect women from sexual harassment in the public or private workplace. However, in 2002, at the initiative of the Femmes Democrates, a group of NGOs met with the Chamber of Deputies to submit a proposal for such a law.[32]

Tunisia has a strong welfare system and programs to promote women's employment, welfare, and citizenship rights.[33] Reforms to the social security system in the 1990s further improved funding and coverage. Among policies to encourage women's labor-force participation is the social security law, which provides for a full pension to a working mother of three children at 50 years of age after 180 months (15 years) of contribution. Other public sector employees may retire at age 55 with 35 years of service.[34] Moreover, Tunisia has enacted policies to help working mothers. National social security funds help to finance child-care centers for children whose mothers work outside the home.

Tunisian women's participation in the country's main trade union is not commensurate with their labor force participation, although more than half of women in the textiles and garments industry, and 23 percent in the field of education, are unionized.[35] Women make up 25 percent of the labor force, but just 12 percent of the membership of the *Union Générale des Travailleurs Tunisiens* (UGTT) (General Union of Tunisian Workers) and constitute only 1.1 percent of its management.[36] Women have also made some inroads, though still limited, in unions such as *l'Union Tunisienne de l'Industrie, du Commerce, et de l'Artisanat* (UTICA) (Tunisian Union of Industry, Commerce, and Artisans), and *l'Union Tunisienne pour l'Agriculture et la Peche* (UTAP) (Tunisian Union for Agriculture and Fisheries). The *Chambre Nationale des Femmes Chefs d'Entreprise* (CNFCE) (National Chamber of Women Heads of Businesses) was formed in 1990 and in 2001 had about 1,200 members.[37]

RECOMMENDATIONS

1. The government should apply its new principle of "the inadmissibility of discrimination" to the revision of inheritance and property laws to ensure that Tunisian women have equal rights.
2. The government should enact a law to protect women from sexual harassment in the workplace and ensure its implementation in both the public and private sector.
3. The government should ensure that women are well represented in high-level decision-making posts in the public and private sector.
4. The government should target the urban-rural gaps in girls' schooling and women's educational attainment so that the adult illiteracy rate, a largely rural phenomenon, is finally eliminated.

Political Rights and Civic Voice

Tunisians cannot change their government democratically. The country has been ruled since 1987 by one president, and one party, the RCD. Since the 1990s, women's political rights and participation in Tunisia's formal political sphere have expanded, along with a growth in women's rights organizations. Nevertheless, the authoritarian Tunisian state circumscribes the political rights of all Tunisians, thus reducing the overall impact of women's advancement and their freedom to exercise their rights. Global human rights monitors have released numerous reports on Tunisia over the past 15 years, criticizing the state's record of violations of freedom of speech, due process, and civil liberties. Human rights activists, journalists, lawyers, and independent women activists face great difficulties in their efforts to work openly for democratic freedoms in Tunisia.

Freedoms of speech and of the press are severely restricted. Both male and female members of opposition political parties and critics of government policy, including human rights defenders, lawyers, and journalists, may be subjected to arbitrary arrest, incommunicado detention, torture, and imprisonment. Dissidents are frequently subjected to heavy police surveillance, travel bans, dismissals from work, interruptions in phone service, and harassment of family members.[38] Although the constitution provides for press freedom, Tunisia's press freedoms are among the most restricted in the Arab world. The government controls domestic broadcasting as well as the circulation of both domestic and foreign publications. Internet access is tightly monitored, and the regime occasionally censors and blocks access to opposition Web sites.

The rights of Tunisians to associate and assemble freely are also sharply curtailed. Under the country's strict laws of association, persons wishing to form an association must submit an application to the Ministry of Interior that includes: a declaration mentioning the name, objectives, and the physical location of the association; a list of founding members and any directors or administrative staff, along with an address, date of birth, and profession for each; and the statutes of the association. Some types of organizations repeatedly face obstructions in trying to become legally established; the government refuses to legalize most independent human rights organizations. Even when an association is approved, such as the National Council for Liberties in Tunisia (CNLT), members may face harassment and surveillance. The government claims that there were more than 7,000 NGOs in the country in 2003; however, the number of human rights NGOs is closer to 10, of which five were authorized and five were unauthorized.[39]

Tunisian women gained the right to vote and to stand for elections in 1959, in the same year that the first woman was elected to parliament. However, Tunisian women, like men, have not been fully able to exercise their rights to free and democratic political processes due to repressive electoral practices in the country.

In 1999, 11.5 percent of the parliament was female, 21 out of 182 members, representing significant progress since the 1970s.[40] In 2001, two of 29 cabinet ministers were female. Nonetheless, the relatively limited participation of women in government bodies, particularly in executive roles (9.25 percent were female in 2001) remains an area of concern for Tunisian women's rights advocates.

The state has established mechanisms to increase women's participation and representation in decision making. The formation of the Ministry of Women and Family Affairs in 1992 was one measure taken by the government to bring women into senior level politics. In addition, at the instigation of President Ben Ali, a resolution was adopted by the ruling party, the RCD, to guarantee a 20 percent minimum of women's representation in their committees.[41] However, women's participation in decision making is generally limited to state agencies that work on women's issues and to the ministries that deal with social affairs, such as health, environment, and labor, albeit in sub-ministerial positions.

Tunisian women have made more notable progress in other areas of the political sphere, such as local elections and municipal bodies. In 2000, more than 20 percent of municipal councilors were women—compared to just 1.7 percent in 1975. The proportion of women who currently fill executive positions within the civil service staff is 22 percent, compared to 14 percent in 1999.[42]

The state has taken additional measures to increase women's participation in the judiciary, with the appointment of more women magistrates to various courts, and the appointment of women to the positions of chief justice of the Tunis Court of Appeals, director-general of the Center for Legal Studies, and director of civil affairs and director of criminal affairs in the Ministry of Justice.[43] Women fill about 25 percent of Tunisia's judicial magistrate positions.[44] The family magistrate and the children's magistrate are judicial offices created in 1993 and 1996, respectively, with the aim of instilling greater respect for the rights of women and children. Tunisian women lawyers also play an active part in all aspects of the political process and have been at the forefront of the democracy struggle.[45] However, lawyers who are critical of government policies or those who call for greater government accountability for women's rights, whether they are women or men, face equally severe restrictions on their work.

After one opposition party, the Democratic Forum for Labor and Freedom, was legalized last year—eight years after its formation—the number of political parties in the country grew to seven. However, several parties continue to be denied authorization. Increasing numbers of women are joining and starting political parties and civil society groups to advocate for civil liberties issues. Women members of the ruling party are allowed to take part in politics at all levels; women currently account for 26 percent of the Central Committee of the RCD.[46] While the Tunisian government often emphasizes women's participation in political life as symbolic of its commitment to women's rights, women members of opposition parties are not freely able to represent themselves in national platforms, state-controlled media, or international conferences and events.[47]

In the late 1980s and early 1990s, the Tunisian state was fighting the "Islamist wave" (or the *tendance Islamique*), a term commonly used to denote Islamic extremist groups seeking changes in laws, particularly family laws, and seeking political power for themselves. The Islamist wave in Tunisia, called the *an-Nahda* movement, emerged in the 1980s, challenged the government in the late 1980s, and was suppressed and banned by the Ben Ali government. The state encouraged the formation of women's organizations during this time, partly because such organizations were invariably anti-extremists. However, women's groups and the state authorities diverged sharply on the issue of political rights and civil liberties. The government used the issue of Islamist extremism to conveniently curtail overall political freedoms and civil liberties throughout the country.

Despite state constraints, women's groups and Tunisian feminists continue to press for greater civil and political rights. The number of women's organizations increased from 1 in 1956 to 21 in 2001, with many groups exerting influence at the national level; the studies of CREDIF and the CFD have been commissioned as background research for national development plans.[48] On March 8, 2002, the Femmes Democrates issued a paper declaring gender equality, secularism, and full and complete citizenship for women to be fundamental to a just legal system and a democratic society.[49]

RECOMMENDATIONS

1. The government should commit to a democratic system that allows for free, fair, and competitive elections, including those for the head of state, and guarantees Tunisian men and women full and equal political rights and civil liberties.
2. The government should abolish all restrictive laws and procedures that hinder the work of women's groups and civil society organizations.
3. The government should lift all restrictive laws and practices against the media.
4. The government should ensure adequate representation of women in political parties and high-level government posts.

Social and Cultural Rights

Tunisian women have legally had the freedom to make independent decisions about their health and reproductive rights since the country's independence; yet the realization of these rights has been limited among poor, illiterate, under-educated, and rural women. In addition to inequalities between women and men, inequalities between social classes and between rural and urban women persist. Nevertheless, the combination of proactive government policies and increasing literacy and schooling rates over the past 20 years has worked to lower fertility rates and to encourage better health outcomes for Tunisian women.[50]

The government's rather successful family planning program has maintained a population growth rate at just over 1 percent per year. Health-related social policies have included the legalization of the import and sale of contraception; the limitation of family allowances to the first three children to encourage smaller families; the legalization of regulated abortion in 1973; the creation of an agency for the protection of mother and child by the ministry of public health; and the creation of the National Office for the Family and Population. The fertility rate is 2.1 per woman, among the lowest in the developing world. While fertility rates are higher in rural areas, women's health has improved such that in the late 1990s, the maternal mortality rate was 70 per 100,000 women.[51] The proportion of women covered by family planning services is currently 66 percent.[52]

There is no documentation of gender-based harmful traditional practices such as female genital mutilation (FGM) in Tunisia. The average age at first marriage for Tunisian women is high—around 27.

Tunisian women are free to participate in and influence community life, policies, and social development at local levels. This is evident in women's roles as councilors at local decision-making levels (currently 20 percent of councilors are women); through the activities of local pro-establishment, nonpolitical NGOs, including women's NGOs; and through their research and advocacy work in pro-government national-level organizations.

The Tunis Institute of Press and Information Sciences, an academic institution providing basic training to Tunisian journalists, has increasingly admitted women to its student body. Women journalists comprise an estimated 34 percent of the total number of journalist cardholders in the country. Efforts to combat the negative stereotypes of women portrayed by the media have been organized by MAFFE, the Ministry of Women's, Family, and Children's Affairs, through awareness-raising campaigns for youth and for those who work in the media to help promote a positive image of women.[53]

Women in Tunisia are vulnerable to poverty due to the gender gaps and the existing disparities in populations, particularly among older age groups and in rural areas. However, overall poverty for men and women in Tunisia has declined significantly over the past few decades; the poverty rate in the 1960s was 40 percent; this fell to 7 percent by the mid-1990s and to 4.2 percent in 2000. Poverty-alleviation programs include the work of government-sponsored agencies; local NGOs like the Tunisian Mothers' Association (ATM), which operates mainly in rural areas; international NGOs, such as Enda-Arab, which provides targeted transfers to poor households; public works programs; microcredit/microfinance programs; and social development funds. Some of these programs are specifically geared to alleviate unemployment among women and to raise the economic status of rural women and girls—necessary steps for the enjoyment of the rights and freedoms afforded them by Tunisia's legal frameworks.[54]

Despite some progress, the needs of rural women are still pressing, and their integration in development continues to lag behind. The results of government-commissioned studies by CREDIF were incorporated into the country's Ninth Development Plan, which encompassed a national plan of action for rural women.[55] Nevertheless, overall studies on Tunisia demonstrate that there has been a noticeable reduction in poverty and discrimination against women, as well as a general increase in well-being.[56]

RECOMMENDATIONS

1. The government of Tunisia should allow women of all political affiliations to take part in the processes of local political bodies and to use government funds for the development of their local communities.
2. The government should prioritize the problems of rural women by expanding micro-credit programs to help reduce their poverty and isolation, and to enhance their economic and cultural participation.
3. The government and civil society organizations should initiate community development programs that include literacy programs for rural women.

AUTHOR: Valentine M. Moghadam is Chief of Section in the Gender Equality and Development Section of the Division of Human Rights and Fight against Discrimination at the United Nations Educational, Scientific and Cultural Organization (UNESCO). She is on leave from her position as Director of the Women's Studies Program and Professor of Sociology at Illinois State University. She received a Ph.D. in Sociology from the American University, Washington D.C. Her publications include Modernizing Women: Gender and Social Change in the Middle East, *and* Women, Work, and Economic Reform in the Middle East and North Africa.

Notes

[1] *Les Femmes en Tunisie 2000* (Tunis: Centre de Recherche, d' Etudes, de Documentation et d'Information sur la Femme [CREDIF], 2002), 212.

[2] Mounira Charrad, "Becoming a Citizen: Lineage Versus Individual in Tunisia and Morocco," in Suad Joseph, ed., *Gender and Citizenship in the Middle East* (Syracuse University Press), 74-76.

[3] *Les Femmes . . .* (CREDIF, 2002), 190–192.

[4] "Consideration of Reports Submitted by States Parties under Article 18 of the Convention on the Elimination of All Forms of Discrimination Against Women. Combined third and fourth periodic reports of States Parties. Tunisia." (New York: UN Committee on the Elimination of Discrimination Against Women [CEDAW], CEDAW/C/TUN/1-2, 2 August 2000), 14.

[5] Laurie Brand, *Women, the State, and Political Liberalization: Middle Eastern and North African Experiences* (New York: Columbia University Press, 1998), 213. See also "Tunisia" (CEDAW), 14.

[6] "Tunisia" (CEDAW), 13.

[7] Abdullahi An-Naim, ed., *Islamic Family Law in a Changing World: A Global Resource Book* (London: Zed Books, 2002), 184.

[8] Charrad, 79.

[9] *Country Reports on Human Rights Practices – 2003* (Washington, D.C.: U.S. Dept. of State, Bureau of Democracy, Human Rights, and Labor, 25 February 2004).

[10] Charrad, 83.

[11] *Tunisia News* 357, 15 January 2000.

[12] *Les Femmes* . . . (CREDIF, 2002).

[13] *Country Reports* (U.S. Dept. of State).

[14] See, for example, reports of the (Paris: Fédération Internationale des Ligues des Droits de l'Homme [FIDH], 2 June 1994); *Tunisia: Women Victims of Harassment, Torture, and Imprisonment* (London: Amnesty International, 3 June 1993); Fadia Faqir, "Engendering Democracy and Islam in the Arab World," *Third World Quarterly* 18, 1 (1997): 172.

[15] For details, see "Tunisia" (CEDAW), 58.

[16] Lilia Labidi, "Women, Politics and Islam: The Case of Tunisia" (Washington, D.C.: Woodrow Wilson International Center for Scholars, paper presented April 2002), 24.

[17] Table 26, "Gender inequality in education," in *Human Development Report 2004: Cultural Liberty in Today's Diverse World* (New York: United Nations Development Programme [UNDP], 2004), 226. http://hdr.undp.org/reports/global/2004/.

[18] *Les Femmes* . . . (CREDIF), 159.

[19] "Reply of Tunisia to the Questionnaire to Governments on the Implementation of the Beijing Platform for Action (1995) and the Outcome of the 23rd Special Session of the General Assembly (2000)" (Tunis: Ministry of Women, Family, and Children's Affairs [MAFFE], May 2004).

[20] Although this has often been projected as a source of women's disadvantage, particularly in terms of status and income, it is also arguably the reason why educated Middle Eastern and North African women are less averse to modernity and change than are MENA men.

[21] "Tunisia" (CEDAW), 118.

[22] Table 27, "Gender inequality in economic activity," in *Human Development Report 2004: Cultural Liberty in Today's Diverse World* (New York: United Nations Development Programme [UNDP], 2004), 229-232. http://hdr.undp.org/reports/global/2004/.

[23] "Reply of Tunisia to the Questionnaire to Governments on the Implementation of the Beijing Platform for Action (1995) and the Outcome of the 23rd Special Session of the General Assembly (2000)" (Tunis: Ministry of Women, Family, and Children's Affairs [MAFFE], May 2004).

[24] *Globalization and Gender: Economic Participation of Arab Women* (Tunis: Center of Arab Women for Training and Research [CAWTAR] and UNDP, 2001).

[25] *Les Femmes* . . . (CREDIF), 178-79.

[26] Pierre-Noel Deneuil, *Les Femmes Entrepreneurs en Tunisie: Paroles et Portraits* (Tunis: CREDIF, UNDP, and Tunisian State Secretariat for Technology and Scientific Research, 2001).

[27] *Les Femmes* . . . (CREDIF), 249–51.

[28] Ibid., 213–14.

[29] Many countries have a policy limiting child allowances as part of their family planning and population programs.

[30] "Tunisia" (CEDAW), 37.

[31] *Les Femmes* . . . (CREDIF), 214, author's translation.

[32] Others were representatives of the *Association des Femmes Tunisiennes pour la Recherche et le Developpement* (AFTURD), the Tunisian section of Amnesty International, *la Ligue Tunisienne des Droits de l'Homme* (LTDH), *l'Union Générale des Travailleurs Tunisiens* (UGTT), and *l'Union Syndicale des Travailleurs du Maghreb Arabe* (USTMA).

[33] See Valentine M. Moghdam, *Women, Work, and Economic Reform in the Middle East and North Africa* (Boulder, CO: Lynne Rienner Publishers, 1998), ch. 3; Mahmoud Ben Romdhane, "Social Policy and Development in Tunisia: A Political Analysis" (Geneva: UN Research Institute for Social Development [UNRISD] project on Social Policy in the Middle East, paper, 2004); Iyabode Fahm, "Institutional and Regulatory Issues in Pension System Reforms: Country Experiences and Policy Options," in Belkacem Laabas, ed., *Building and Sustaining the Capacity for Social Policy Reforms* (Aldershot, UK, and Burlington, VT: Ashgate, 2000).

[34] Fahm, "Institutional and Regulatory Issues."

[35] "Tunisia" (CEDAW), 67.

[36] *Les Femmes* . . . (CREDIF), 194–95.

[37] Ibid., 196.

[38] *Freedom in the World* (New York and Washington, D.C.: Freedom House, 2004) and Freedom House staff interviews with Tunisian women activists in Rabat, Morocco, 2004.

[39] *Country Reports* (U.S. Dept. of State).

[40] *Les Femmes* . . . (CREDIF), 184.

[41] "Tunisia" (CEDAW), 64.

[42] "Reply of Tunisia . . ." (MAFFE), 9.

[43] Ibid., 64.

[44] *Les Femmes* . . . (CREDIF), 185.

[45] *Freedom in the World* and Freedom House staff interviews with Tunisian women lawyers in Rabat, Morocco, 2004.

[46] "Reply of Tunisia . . ." (MAFFE).

[47] Freedom House staff interviews with Tunisian women lawyers in Rabat, Morocco, 2004.

[48] See, for example, the discussion in *Les Femmes* . . . (CREDIF), 202–203.

[49] "Pour les droits des femmes: Quelle Constitution?" (Tunis: Association Tunisienne des Femmes Democrates [ATFD], Commission pour le 8 mars, 8 March 2002). I am grateful to Pamela Pelletreau for bringing the document to my attention.

50 See Farzaneh Roudi-Fahimi and Valentine M. Moghadam, "Empowering Women, Developing Society: Female Education in the Middle East and North Africa" (Washington, D.C.: Population Reference Bureau, MENA Policy Brief, October 2003), Table 1, with data from UNESCO, UNDP, and UN Statistics Division.

51 *Human Development Report 2002* (New York: UNDP and Oxford University Press), Table 8.

52 "Reply of Tunisia . . ." (MAFFE).

53 Ibid.

54 "Tunisia" (CEDAW), 198.

55 Ibid., 199.

56 Moghadam, *Women, Work, and Economic Reform*; Mahmoud Ben Rhomdane, "Social Policy and Development in Tunisia," (UNRISD).

U.A.E.

by Shatha K. Al-Muttawa

Population: 3,900,000
GDP Per Capita (PPP): $22,420
Economy: Capitalist-statist
Ranking on UN HDI: 49 out of 177
Polity: Federation of traditional monarchies
Literacy: Male 75.6% / Female 80.7%
Percent Women Economically Active: 32%
Date of Women's Suffrage: No women's suffrage
Women's Fertility Rate: 3.0
Percent Urban/Rural: Urban 78% / Rural 22%

Country Ratings for United Arab Emirates
Nondiscrimination and Access to Justice: 1.7
Autonomy, Security, and Freedom of the Person: 2.1
Economic Rights and Equal Opportunity: 2.8
Political Rights and Civic Voice: 1.2
Social and Cultural Rights: 2.3

(Scale of 1 to 5: 1 represents the lowest and 5 the highest level of freedom women have to exercise their rights)

Introduction

The United Arab Emirates (UAE), previously known as the Trucial States, established its independence in 1971 after the British withdrew from the Persian Gulf.[1] The UAE is a federation of seven traditional monarchies: Abu Dhabi, the capital; Dubai, the cosmopolitan financial and commercial center; Sharjah; Fujairah; Umm al-Qaiwain; Ras al-Khaimah; and Ajman. Every five years, the rulers of the seven emirates, who constitute the Federal Supreme Council, the top legislative and executive body, choose one of their own to serve as federal president. However, the position of president was held successively by the ruler of Abu Dhabi, Sheikh Zayed bin Sultan al-Nahayan, from the country's independence until his death in November 2004. His son Sheikh Khalifa bin Zayed Al Nahyan was chosen to succeed his father as president.

The UAE has a closed political system in which elections have never been held. The president appoints the prime minister and cabinet, who manage

313

the country's daily affairs. Delegates of a 40-member council, the Federal National Council (FNC), are appointed every two years by the leaders of the seven emirates; however, the council serves only as an advisory body.

The UAE has the region's most diversified economy and a high per capita GDP of $22,420.[2] In addition to large oil reserves, the UAE possesses a leading free trade zone in Dubai, a large manufacturing center in Sharjah, a sophisticated financial-services and banking sector, and a built-up tourism sector. Of the 3,900,000 residents, less than 20 percent are citizens,[3] with foreign workers from South and Southeast Asia, the Middle East, and Europe comprising the remaining population. Non-nationals are predominantly men, and in 2002, only 34.2 percent of the total population of the UAE was women.[4] The vast majority of UAE's foreign workers and citizens practice Islam, the state religion, with the Sunni sect predominating; there are also small groups of practicing Hindus and Christians.

Political parties are prohibited in the UAE, and rights of assembly and association are limited. All nongovernmental organizations (NGOs) must register with the ministry of labor and social affairs and are subject to government closure. There are no trade unions, and foreign nationals are generally not offered labor protections. In 2002, the Dubai police created a human rights department to monitor prison conditions, rehabilitate prisoners, and conduct programs for crime victims. However, no independent human rights groups operate in the UAE.

Women's equality is not clearly established in the UAE constitution. In practice, women's social, economic, and legal rights are not consistently observed because of traditional biases against women and the incomplete and selective implementation of the law. Women's lives in the UAE and the laws that govern them differ dramatically depending on the conditions of their citizenship and employment status.

A woman's rights and legal status are often determined by her standing in UAE society as one of the following: a UAE citizen, a foreign professional woman temporarily residing on an employment contract, a foreign woman employed in the informal sector such as domestic work, or the wife of a temporary foreign worker. This situation creates a gap between women's experiences in the UAE, the implementation of their legal protections, and their abilities to exercise their rights. Furthermore, many women remain uninformed of the rights and legal protections available to them.

There are no known independent women's human rights organizations working on gender equality issues in the UAE. The officially recognized organization promoting women's issues is a semi-government body, the General Women's Union, which was founded in 1975 by the late president's wife, Sheikha Fatima bint Mubarak. It serves as an umbrella organization that monitors the work of all other women's groups, most of which work as charity groups or women's business clubs.

Discussion of women's issues in the UAE is difficult because the justifications for restrictions on women's rights are rooted in traditional interpretations of Islam, the criticism of which is a punishable offense. These circumstances contribute to a severe lack of data on women's rights issues in the UAE—the information available being contradictory or inaccurate—and government censorship of information and discussion exacerbates the problem.

Nondiscrimination and Access to Justice

The constitution of the UAE, adopted in 1971 and made permanent in 1996 by the leaders of the seven emirates, declares Shari'a as a principal source of law. Additional influences on the UAE legal system are the common law and Egyptian legal traditions, in addition to UAE customs and traditions.[5]

The UAE constitution declares all persons equal before the law. Article 25 states, "All persons shall be equal before the law. No discrimination shall be practiced between citizens of the Union by reason of race, nationality, religious belief or social position."[6] However, the constitution does not ensure women's equality, in that it fails to stipulate the prohibition of discrimination based on gender.

Article 15 of the constitution declares, "The family is the basis of society. It is founded on morality, religion, ethics and patriotism. The law shall guarantee its existence, safeguard and protect it from corruption."[7] In addition to the importance given to the family in the constitution, the ministry of Islamic affairs and Awqaf classifies women's roles in society as wives and mothers within its definitions of religion, ethics, and morality. These two factors often serve as the basis for legal discrimination against women in the UAE. As a result, laws and policies tend to promote traditional roles for women rather than uphold their independence and equality with men.

Implementation of both legislation and the country's protections against gender discrimination is often dependent upon a woman's status in UAE society. For example, laws that apply for professional foreign women, such as sexual harassment laws, do not apply for domestic workers, and laws that apply to female citizens, such as the ban on marriage to men of other nationalities, do not apply to foreign women. Furthermore, some UAE laws may be contradicted or limited by other laws. The law that makes education mandatory at the elementary level may be superseded by the law that allows a father to determine whether or not his daughter will be educated.[8]

An additional challenge to the legal protection of women's rights in the UAE is that laws that protect women's equality tend only to apply and be enforced in the public sphere—outside the home—a setting that in practice is off-limits to most UAE women. Women's rights therefore are not legally protected in the home; fathers and husbands have the legal authority to prevent their daughters and wives from participating in professional and social life.

Women are directly discriminated against as a result of their gender in some UAE legislation, particularly in laws governing citizenship. Foreign women who marry male UAE citizens are granted citizenship; however, female citizens are not permitted, under any circumstances, to transfer their nationality to their foreign-born husbands. A UAE woman national, in fact, is forbidden by law to marry a foreign man, and a 1996 law requires her to give up her citizenship if she marries a non-Gulf citizen. Exceptions may be made if a woman presents her case to the presidential council in Abu Dhabi and receives special permission, but she will still not be able to transfer her citizenship on to her foreign husband. The government established a marriage fund in 1992 to encourage male citizens to marry female citizens but has taken no steps to remove the ban on the right of women citizens to marry noncitizens.

Since 1983, male citizens have been able to sponsor their expatriate wives for work visas in accordance with Cabinet Order No. 149/2.[9] It was only recently that the government issued decree No. 3/455 of 2004, allowing 8,000 female citizens to sponsor their foreign husbands for three-year work visas.[10] This decree applies only to women who gained permission from the president to marry noncitizens. Up to this point, UAE national women married to expatriate men with presidential permission had to request social aid from the government because their husbands were not allowed to work.

Female non-nationals also face discrimination in the laws governing citizenship; in practice, the implementation of these laws is often dependent upon the women's class and income levels. Foreign women working in the UAE cannot sponsor their children to live in the country although expatriate men can sponsor their families. Exceptions are made for female doctors, teachers, and nurses who meet a certain salary requirement, although women working in these professions generally do not meet the minimum requirement. Recently, the Nationalities and Residence Department introduced measures that will allow widows and divorced women who were married to foreigners to pass their nationality on to their underage children.[11]

The UAE has a dual system of Shari'a courts that handle criminal and family matters in addition to secular courts for matters of civil law. Non-Muslims are tried for criminal offenses in Shari'a courts; however, non-Muslims most often receive civil penalties at the discretion of the judge instead of Shari'a penalties.[12]

A woman is considered an adult and a full person before the courts at the age of 18 and can seek legal counsel and representation. Article 41 of the constitution states that "every person shall have the right to submit complaints to the competent authorities, including the judicial authorities, concerning the abuse or infringement of the rights and freedoms stipulated in this chapter." In practice, however, women often have extremely limited access to justice due to traditional social norms that discourage women from entering police stations or courts of law—predominantly male spaces. The police often try to settle disputes involving women so that women do not have to go to court. In the cases of women accused of assault, police officers allow women to pay a penalty rather than go to jail.[13] It is considered a dishonor to the family in the UAE for a woman to go to prison.

The UAE signed on to the United Nations Convention on the Elimination of All Forms of Discrimination Against Women (CEDAW) in 2004, making reservations to Articles 2(f), 9, 15(2), 16 and 29(1), predominantly on the grounds that they conflict with the precepts of Shari'a regarding rights of inheritance, nationality, maintenance and divorce, legal capacity, testimony, and the right to conclude contracts.

RECOMMENDATIONS

1. The government should amend the constitution to prohibit gender discrimination, particularly discriminatory provisions in its nationality law.
2. The government should ensure that women have free and safe access to the police and the courts without fear of violence at the hands of family members.
3. The government should remove all reservations to CEDAW and take steps to implement it locally by bringing national laws into conformity with CEDAW.

Autonomy, Security, and Freedom of the Person

Article 32 of the UAE constitution declares, "the freedom to hold religious ceremonies in accordance with established custom shall be safeguarded, provided such ceremonies are consistent with public order and with public morals." Islam is the official religion, and virtually all UAE citizens are Muslim; approximately 85 percent are Sunni and 15 percent are Shi'a. While no official statistics are available, it is estimated that the foreign population residing in the UAE is 55 percent Muslim, 25 percent Hindu, 10 percent Christian, and 5 percent Buddhist, as well as small populations of other religions.[14] Non-Muslim groups are permitted to practice their religions and can establish houses of worship by requesting a land grant from the government and receiving permission from the local ruler to build a compound.[15] Religious groups that do not have their own buildings must share the facilities of other religious organizations or worship in private homes.

Some restrictions on the practice of religion do exist, however. The government controls and monitors the content of sermons in nearly all Sunni mosques. The ministry of Islamic affairs and Awqaf trains and supervises the imams, inspects the mosques, bans any materials that "defame" Islam or "raise doubts" about the religion, works to spread Islamic values and culture in UAE society, and gives opinions on legal cases.[16]

Women are free to teach the Quran to other women and form study groups to discuss religion. However, these groups tend predominantly to stress conservative and patriarchal Islamic views on women's roles and reinforce traditional ideas of women's subordinate position in society.

While the law provides for freedom of movement, by custom, a man may prevent his wife, minor children, and adult unmarried daughters from leaving the country by withholding their passports or by contacting the immigration authorities.[17] Employers of foreign domestic workers also commonly hold the passports of their employees, making it difficult for them to terminate their contracts, travel, or return to their countries if dissatisfied with the conditions of their work. This practice was banned by the ministry of interior in July of 2003; however, many companies and employers continue to withhold the passports of employees as leverage. Recent public discussions and media attention on this issue have encouraged the government to increase efforts to enforce the prohibition of this practice.

The personal status code, which is in accordance with the UAE's interpretation of Sunni Shari'a laws, governs the family matters of Muslims and is applied in local Shari'a courts. However, Shi'a Muslims in Dubai have the option of pursuing Shi'a family law cases through a special Shi'a council rather than the Shari'a courts.[18]

The personal status code of the UAE prohibits Muslim women from marrying non-Muslim men. Muslim men, on the other hand, are free to marry outside the religion.[19] A woman may go to a court of law as early as at age 15, the legal age for marriage, to defend her right to marry a Muslim citizen of her choice if her male guardian forbids her marriage. In practice, however, parents arrange most local marriages. Women are permitted to ask for specific rights to be stipulated in the marriage contract, such as the right to work and study after marriage. UAE family law continues to permit men to have more than one wife at a time; however, marriage law requires that the man obtain permission from his first wife to marry a second wife.

A Muslim man in the UAE is allowed to divorce his spouse verbally, but a woman cannot do the same. A woman may be granted a divorce in a court of law only if the judge agrees that her husband has either inflicted harm on her physically, emotionally, or otherwise; abandoned her for three or more months; or not provided for her or her children.[20] Local divorced women are not looked upon favorably in society, and women generally prefer not to get a divorce despite their legal right to one.

In cases of divorce, custody is usually given to the mother of female children until they reach the age of maturity or marry, and of male children until they reach the age of 13. However, should the mother remarry, she forfeits her rights to custody of the children from her previous marriage. In 2003, a number of UAE national women advocates and members of the UAE Women's Federation submitted a memorandum to the ministry of Islamic affairs and Awqaf expressing reservations over articles of the Personal Status Draft Law.[21] Articles criticized as eroding women's rights involved laws governing engagement, the marriage contract, dowry, divorce, trusteeship, pregnancy, and maintenance, among others.

Despite Article 33 of Federal Law No. 13, 1996, which forbids the trafficking of persons,[22] women are regularly trafficked into the UAE for the purpose of labor and sexual exploitation.[23] Women victims of trafficking primarily originate from South and East Asia and the former Soviet Union, with many being sold to illegal brothels in the UAE.[24] In response the government has taken some actions such as limiting the number of visas granted to single women and banning all visas to women under 30 from the former Soviet republics.[25] The police also organize patrols and raids in areas where they suspect illegal activities to be taking place. However, while the Dubai police created an anti–trafficking in persons department in 2003, many victims of trafficking are still not recognized as such and may be punished for immigration violations or prostitution, which carries a three-year prison sentence.[26]

Torture is illegal and prohibited in Article 26 of the constitution, yet UAE Shari'a courts impose flogging sentences for persons found guilty of drug use, adultery, and prostitution in all emirates except Dubai.[27] The UAE has not ratified the UN Convention on the Elimination of All Forms of Torture and Other Cruel and Inhuman or Degrading Treatment or Punishment.[28] In 2003, the federal court ordered the flogging and deportation of a 15-year-old Chinese girl who was sentenced to 90 lashes for adultery—a ruling upheld twice by the federal court despite the girl's young age, but later overturned by the Federal Supreme Court.[29] According to an Amnesty International report, 18 flogging sentences were passed in the year 2001, all allegedly for adultery.[30]

Rape, abuse, and harassment are considered criminal offenses under UAE law.[31] Nevertheless, many women are subject to domestic abuse, often at the hands of male family members. According to Shari'a law as interpreted in the UAE, a man may legally beat his wife—so long as he does not seriously injure her—in order to "discipline" her.[32] This type of abuse is common, but women are often reluctant to seek outside help. In 2003, for the first time, a comparison of yearly statistics on violence in divorce cases among UAE nationals was possible, as 2002 was the first year in which details were accurately recorded.[33] Figures released by the Dubai department of justice at the end of 2003 revealed that the number of divorces caused by domestic violence had leapt. Violence is now known to be a factor in more than one-fifth of divorces.[34] There are no shelters for victims of domestic violence in the UAE.[35] However, major hospitals have police officers on staff to register complaints from women who come for treatment.[36]

Men who harass women on the street or in public places such as shopping malls are subject to punishment by law. Pictures of men caught harassing women appear weekly in Dubai-based newspapers, a source of shame for the men's families. However, these legal and social punitive measures have not completely eradicated the problem of the harassment of women in public spaces.

Victims of rape in the UAE are often reluctant to admit or report the crime. As a result, the offending men go unpunished. It is believed that cases involving the rape of women by immediate family members are on the rise and are also not reported to the police.[37] Part of women's fear of reporting the crime of rape stems from the fact that women who report rape may be subject to punishment for adultery, which ranges from death by stoning in some emirates to imprisonment and deportation in others. A French businesswoman who reported to the police that she was gang raped in Dubai in 2002 was taken to court and faced a maximum sentence of 18 months in prison for having "adulterous sexual relations." She was bailed out of jail by the French consulate while the perpetrators were not punished at all.[38]

The UAE issues an estimated 300 visas per day for domestic workers—116,083 such visas were issued in 1999 alone—which has resulted in the number of domestic workers in the UAE being equal to the indigenous population.[39] As a result of the limitations placed on UAE national women by their male family members not to interact with unrelated men, families are increasingly hiring female drivers and cooks, as well as housekeepers. UAE households host an average of three domestic workers per home.[40] Most domestic workers come from South and Southeast Asian countries, with sizable numbers from India, Sri Lanka, the Philippines, and Indonesia, as well as increasing numbers from Ethiopia.[41] The salaries of domestic workers are dependent on the worker's national origin—women from the Philippines typically receive higher salaries than women from India for the same job.[42]

UAE labor laws do not apply to domestic workers, and these women have few rights protections. Employers sponsor their visas, and the workers are legally placed under the control of their employers. Domestic workers often have very limited freedom of movement and are isolated from society; many are not allowed to leave the house or use the phone. They may be monitored closely, and their dress and religious activities controlled.[43] Many domestic workers are subject to racism and ill-treatment from household members and may labor under slave-like conditions.[44] The average domestic employee works 15 hours a day, without any days off.[45]

About half of the female domestic workers interviewed for the International Labour Organization's Gender Promotion Programme reported being abused verbally, physically, and/or sexually.[46] The sources of abuse range from employers to family members of the employer to visitors. Many domestic workers are afraid to report abuse, and many simply live with it.[47] Housemaids who run away from their employers and are caught by the police or who approach the police in order to report abusive employers and end their contracts may be imprisoned by the immigration authorities.[48]

A victim care program was launched in March 2003 by the Dubai police's human rights department to provide psychological, emotional, and legal assistance to victims of sexual crimes and children who are victims of crimes.[49] Women who suffer from abuse can call the social services division of the human rights department at four different numbers or the social services section of police stations.[50] The women's Da'waa administration is said to have a telephone hotline for women and children with direct access to police stations in all emirates; however, there is no readily available information on this hotline, so women and children do not know about it and cannot access it.[51] The Al Maktoum charity organization also provides financial assistance for battered women who have no income or shelter.[52]

RECOMMENDATIONS

1. The government should amend its laws and procedures on rape to ensure that women victims of rape are not discriminated against and charged with adultery.
2. The government should provide services to female victims of violence and rape, including counseling and legal representation; initiate public education campaigns on all forms of violence against women; and provide gender-sensitive training to police and court officials so they can provide support and due process to female victims of violence.
3. The government should revise the marriage laws to ensure that women are protected from domestic violence and that all forms of domestic violence are considered criminal offenses.

Economic Rights and Equal Opportunity

A woman may independently own land and property when she turns 18, and many women exercise this right. A married woman is the sole owner of her property, and her husband has no right to it while they are married or if they divorce.[53] An unmarried woman's property, on the other hand, is not legally protected from her father or brother. Government policies do not provide equal housing benefits for men and women. Male UAE nationals are entitled to receive either pieces of land and 500,000 Dirhams (approximately $136,000) from the government or previously built houses.[54] Women nationals do not have this same privilege, as it is presumed that they will be provided housing by their husband.

For Muslims in the UAE, inheritance law is in accordance with the country's interpretation of Shari'a, which prescribes an unequal distribution of assets for men and women.[55] For followers of other faiths, inheritance is determined by the religion of the deceased.

Women who are citizens of the UAE do not face restrictions on licensing businesses in their names, and they are legally allowed to own businesses and serve as business heads. Official reports show that women are now running businesses in trade and maintenance, financial brokerage, real estate and rental, manufacturing industries, restaurants and hotels, and construction.[56] Nevertheless, as it is not considered respectable for women to interact with male non-relatives, many women are prevented by their fathers, brothers, or husbands from entering into such business-related contracts and activities.

Education is free for all citizens from primary schooling through the university level. Article 17 of the constitution makes schooling mandatory for girls and boys through the sixth grade, at which time students are usually 10 or 11 years old. Nevertheless, compulsory education is not enforced, and a woman whose father or brother does not allow her to go to school or to work has no legal protection. The enrollment of girls in primary education (86 percent) for the year 2000, however, was equal to that of boys (87 percent).[57]

The school system in the UAE is gender-segregated at all levels. Textbooks for all educational subjects and levels are issued by the government, and academic freedom is restricted. Islamic education is compulsory for all Muslims and instructs girls to obey their fathers and husbands and to accept their primary roles as mothers and wives. Schools that teach subjects that contravene Islam or question the government's ethics and beliefs or local culture are subject to closure.[58]

Women have made great gains in education, particularly at the university level. The literacy rate of women in the UAE was 80.7 percent in 2003, higher than the male literacy rate of 75.6 percent. Women currently make up 75 percent of the student body at the National University in Al-Ain.[59] This gender discrepancy, however, may be due in part to the limited fields of study offered for both men and women in local universities. Many local men choose to study abroad, while most UAE women are not allowed by their families to leave the country alone.

Article 34 of the constitution guarantees both men and women the right to choose a profession: "Every citizen shall be free to choose his occupation, trade or profession within the limits of the law, due consideration being given to any regulations prescribed for any such professions and trades." Nevertheless, in practice, a woman's right to choose her career is often limited.

Family restrictions are a major factor in women's unemployment, as the opinions of family members—especially males—are highly influential in a woman's educational and vocational decisions. Women nationals are generally not allowed by their families to work in firms or organizations that are not gender-segregated, which limits their options considerably. For example, many women are prevented from studying law because its practice involves appearing in court and working with men. A profession like teaching, on the other hand, is more acceptable because all schools are gender-segregated and prevent contact between the sexes. The public sector in general is gender-segregated. Some government ministries do not employ married women without their husband's written consent.[60]

Despite the challenges women may face in following the profession of their choice, many women have begun to work in diverse fields that were previously male dominated. In 2003, for the first time, the Abu Dhabi police trained 32 women to work with the special security forces.[61] In 2000, the Dubai Transport Corporation hired women taxi drivers to transport women and children, a first in the Gulf.[62] Women graduates in the UAE can now be found working in engineering, science, media, computer technology, law, commerce, and the oil industry.[63] In 2002, women nationals of the UAE reportedly filled 27.1 percent of senior decision-making administrative posts in the public sector, and in 2003 women held an estimated 40 percent of all public sector posts.[64]

Women nationals make up the largest unemployed group in the UAE; 1 out of 10 women nationals are unemployed, while only 1 out of 100 expatriate women cannot find work, according to a 1995 census.[65] The participation of women in the labor force was at 14.8 percent in 2000 and dropped to 14 percent in 2003.[66] To address this problem, the government has started to grant women licenses to start their own businesses.[67] The Dubai and Abu Dhabi chambers of commerce and industry established women's business councils in 2002 to encourage women nationals to participate in the UAE economy.[68] At the First Economic Business Women's Forum, sponsored by the General Women's Union, held in October of 2003 for Arab businesswomen, the participants discussed ways to enhance the role of Arab businesswomen.[69]

The UAE ratified the International Labour Organization Convention Number 100 concerning Equal Remuneration for Men and Women Workers for Work of Equal Value, but males continue to receive higher wages than females in some jobs, particularly in the informal sector.[70] Some women also face discrimination in job promotions.[71] Employers, both government and private, are legally allowed to specify in job announcements and advertisements the gender of the employee they are seeking to hire. Sexual harassment in the workplace, however, is prohibited in the personal status code, and women can report incidents at any police station.[72]

There is an unequal distribution of work-related benefits in the UAE, especially regarding housing. This is true for jobs in both the public and private sectors. For example, if both spouses are employed by the government, both housing allowances will be paid to the husband because he is obliged under law to provide for his wife's housing.[73] However, housing allowances are paid directly to single women and to married women who work for the government whose husbands are employed in the private sector.[74]

The ministry of labor issued a law that prohibits employers from firing or threatening to fire a female employee on the basis of pregnancy, delivery, or parenting.[75] Maternity leave in the public sector is two to six months. While on maternity leave, a woman is entitled during the first two months to full pay, the third and fourth months to half salary, and the last two months to no pay.[76] A woman may take one paid hour break from work per day for 18 months to nurse her baby.

According to Article 30 of the Labor Law, a foreign woman worker is entitled to 45 days of paid leave after completing a year of work with an employer, 45 days of half pay if she worked for less than a year, and 100 days of absence without pay in the case of illness related to child bearing.[77]

The UAE does not allow labor unions, and foreign workers, who comprise 98 percent of the work force in the private sector, are generally not offered any labor protections. Even though domestic workers are considered contract workers, the majority of domestic workers do not have contracts with recruiting agencies or employers to outline their rights and responsibilities. Instead, many have contracts from their embassies, which are not binding on the employer or any UAE official. As an employee's residence or visa is often reliant upon the conditions of employment and sponsorship, termination of employment can lead to deportation. This situation serves to complicate the efforts of employees wanting to file labor dispute complaints or protest poor working conditions. The United Arab Emirates has not ratified the International Convention on the Protection of the Rights of All Migrant Workers and Members of Their Families.[78]

RECOMMENDATIONS

1. The government should revise the labor laws to remove articles that result in gender-based discrimination and should enact policies to promote equal rights for women workers and protections for migrant women workers.
2. The government should allow all foreign women working in the UAE to sponsor their families to live in the UAE and provide services to all migrant women regardless of their national origin.

3. The government should enact complaint mechanisms for women who are prohibited from working by their family members and ensure that women have access to justice in these cases.

Political Rights and Civic Voice

UAE citizens have few political rights and cannot change their government democratically. The UAE has never held an election; neither men nor women have the right of suffrage. The 40 members of the Federal National Council (FNC) are appointed every two years by the rulers of the seven emirates; however, this body serves only as an advisory body. Political parties are not allowed in the UAE, and citizens have little influence on policies and decision-making. Citizens voice their concerns directly to their leaders through consultative mechanisms such as the open *majlis* (meetings).

The rights of citizens to organize gatherings or demonstrate for any cause are extremely limited. All public meetings require government permits. All nongovernmental organizations must register with the ministry of labor and social affairs. In 2003, approximately 100 domestic NGOs were registered with the government.[79]

Freedom of speech is guaranteed in the constitution; however, the government restricts this right in practice. The Law of Printing and Publishing No. 15 of 1980 applies to all media, prohibiting "defamatory material and negative material about presidents, friendly countries, religious issues and pornography."[80] Journalists practice self-censorship in order to avoid government punishment, which can include harassment and imprisonment.

Although women are not legally prohibited from holding senior-level positions in government, they are vastly underrepresented in public life and decision-making roles. Sheikha Fatima, wife of the former president, announced in 1998 that women observers would be appointed to the Federal National Council to train for eventual appointment to the body itself. However, no such appointments were announced by the end of 2003.[81] In 2002, in her capacity as the head of the National Council on Women, she announced: "The Women's Federation will nominate and submit to the President the names of two women to be appointed as members of the Federal National Council for the emirate of Abu Dhabi."[82] However, at the end of 2003, the 40 members of the FNC remained all male.

Women have made inroads, however, in some levels of the government in recent years. The ruler of Sharjah, Sheikh Sultan Bin Muhammad Al Qassemi, appointed five women to his consultative council in 2002.[83] In 2003, women served as undersecretary in the ministry of labor and social affairs and as assistant undersecretary for planning and evaluation in the ministry of education.[84] Women were accepted for the first time to the Judicial Academy in Abu Dhabi in 2004, and one was selected for an executive position in the ministry of justice.[85]

Women's representation in UAE media continues to be limited, and there are few women journalists. UAE television stations rarely address women's issues or gender-based violence problems such as rape or incest.[86] In 2002, the General Women's Union organized the "Arab Women and Media Forum," which drew delegations from various Arab countries.[87] Papers presented at the gathering demonstrated that the most prominent challenge for Arab women in the media is society, which still views working women negatively.[88] The forum called for the portrayal of stronger Arab and Islamic values in the media and issued a code of ethics.[89] Sheikha Fatima continues to encourage the media to portray women's issues from an Arabic and Islamic perspective.[90]

Women's freedom to gain access to and use information to empower themselves is often limited. Most women do not have access to information on developments in UAE society and around the world and are therefore unaware of their rights, especially in comparison to women in other countries. UAE women are also often uninformed about movements within the country to improve women's status, making sustaining such a movement a challenge. Independent legal aid groups and legal literacy NGOs are rare, and women lawyers are just beginning to form associations. Currently, there are no independent women's human rights NGOs working in the UAE. It is also extremely difficult for international human rights NGOs to freely operate in the country, particularly migrant women's rights groups.

Of the approximately 460,000 Internet users in the UAE,[91] only 6 percent are women.[92] As a result, women remain largely unaware of government web portals that detail services available to them. The UAE government censors some Internet sites, but Dubai Media City and Dubai Internet City, which are free trade zones for information and technology companies, are exempt, with the warning that this freedom should not be abused. Women, mostly migrant workers from East Asia, constitute 65 percent of Dubai Internet City workers.[93]

RECOMMENDATIONS

1. The government should ensure the right of assembly to all citizens and noncitizens and allow NGOs to advocate for the rights of all women.
2. The government should allow independent political parties to operate and should grant the right to vote to all men and women.
3. The government should create a legislative body that represents the people and is open to men and women.
4. The government should allow freedom of the press at all levels and encourage debate on women's rights issues in order to improve women's image in the media.

Social and Cultural Rights

Despite the cosmopolitan nature of the UAE, the country is segregated not only along gender lines but also by ethnicity. Schools, hospitals, and mosques are segregated by gender, while banks and post offices have separate lines for women. Likewise, immigrants to the UAE tend to self-segregate, forming separate communities characterized by the use of native languages and practice of foreign cultures, as well as separate institutions like schools and hospitals. Thus, the potential benefits of introducing into society new views and cultural norms regarding women remain largely unrealized.

The UAE has some of the best medical care facilities in the world,[94] but the extent to which women can make independent decisions on their health and reproductive rights is sometimes restricted. All public health clinics are free for citizens and have separate sections for women. However, free and reduced-cost health services are not extended to the 80 percent of the population who are foreign.

Efforts toward promoting women's maternal health have greatly decreased the infant mortality rate and helped to increase the life expectancy of women over the last decade. A UNICEF survey (1995–2003) of women aged 15 to 49, found that 97 percent of pregnant women received antenatal care, and 96 percent of births were attended by skilled health personnel.[95] Between 1980 and 1985, the total fertility rate was 5.23 children per childbearing woman.[96] This rate has now dropped to 3.0 children per mother.[97] However, the UNICEF survey revealed that only 28 percent of women aged 15 to 49 used contraception.[98]

According to the UN-funded Pan Arab Project for Family Health (PAP-FAM), the majority of women in the UAE who wish to use birth control pills obtain them through smugglers because they are not stocked in most pharmacies. The alternative is to special-order birth control pills at a pharmacy; however, no educational materials are available about this type of birth control.[99] In 2000, a 24-hour phone and e-mail hotline was launched by Johnson and Johnson Gynecare to answer women's medical questions in Arabic and in English.[100] This service is not advertised, but it continues to operate.[101]

Abortion is illegal under Article 64 of the penal code and Law No. 7 of 1975, unless it is required to save the life of the woman. It is not permitted on the grounds of rape or incest, fetal impairment, economic or social reasons, or preserving the physical or mental health of the woman.[102] No legal abortions were reported in 2002 or 2003.[103] However, in 2002, two female doctors were imprisoned for performing illegal abortions.[104]

A study in the UAE shows that 60 percent of women over the age of 50 may develop breast cancer.[105] The number of deaths caused by breast cancer has been rising dramatically, with doctors saying that diagnostic techniques have not improved much and that, in any case, many women are too shy or uneducated to seek medical care. This lack of awareness of the benefits of regular medical checkups results in many diagnoses being made 6 to 10 years after the onset of breast cancer.[106]

Female genital mutilation (FGM) is still discreetly practiced in the UAE, performed chiefly by female doctors on young girls in hospitals and dispensaries. One survey conducted in the country in the mid-1990s found that 30.8 percent of girls between the ages of 1 and 5 had been circumcised.[107]

Unmarried male and female nationals traditionally live with their families regardless of their age. Unmarried couples may not live together legally,[108] but this law is not generally enforced for foreigners. However, in all emirates except Dubai, foreign women who have children out of wedlock may be imprisoned and deported if they are found living with a man to whom they are not married. In Dubai, unmarried pregnant noncitizens are given the option of marrying the father or leaving the country before they are arrested for fornication.[109]

Women are not required by law to cover themselves, but women nationals often wear a *sheila*—a traditional black scarf that covers some, or all, of a woman's hair—and an *abaya*—an article of clothing that covers the entire body from the shoulders to the ankles. Those inclined to dress differently often do not for fear of verbal and physical abuse from male family members or restrictions that might be imposed on their freedom to leave the home. Domestic workers are often given clothes their employers find suitable and are usually ordered to wear them.

There are no restrictions on the dress of foreign women, who are free to wear their national or ethnic clothing. Noncitizen women in the UAE are free to take an active role in the cultural events of their communities. A large number of social and community groups run by noncitizen women in the UAE support programs, dance, music, and food native to their culture. Noncitizen women from wealthy families also manage and produce several magazines and media groups, particularly in Dubai.

RECOMMENDATIONS

1. The ministry of health should lead educational programs and awareness campaigns for all women, citizens and noncitizens, on women's health, reproductive health, and birth control.
2. The government should enact laws against female genital mutilation and initiate educational campaigns to inform doctors and the public about the dangers of this practice.
3. The government should initiate public education programs that address women's gender-specific health needs such as screenings for breast cancer.

AUTHOR: Shatha K. Al-Muttawa was born in Kuwait and is a local citizen of the United Arab Emirates. She received her B.A. from Mount Holyoke College in Massachusetts and is currently pursuing her graduate work at the University of Chicago. She is interested in the intellectual history of the Arab world and its interaction with other cultures and civilizations.

Notes

[1] "UAE Politics" (Abu Dhabi: United Arab Emirates Government Web site, 2005), http://www.uae.gov.ae/Government/politics.htm.

[2] Table 1, "Human Development Index," in *Human Development Report 2004: Cultural Liberty in Today's Diverse World* (New York: United Nations Development Programme [UNDP], 2004), 139, http://hdr.undp.org/reports/global/2004/.

[3] "UAE Politics" (United Arab Emirates Government Web site).

[4] "UAE" (Beirut: UN Economic and Social Commission for Western Asia [ESCWA], Country Profiles, 2003), www.escwa.org.lb/divisions/ecw/profile/uae/main.html.

[5] "Judiciary: United Arab Emirates" (Beirut: UNDP, Programme on Governance in the Arab Region [POGAR]), www.pogar.org/countries/judiciary.asp?cid=21.

[6] M. Cherif Bassiouni and Martha E. Dyba, "United Arab Emirates," in *Constitutions of the Countries of the World* (New York: Oceana Publications, 1982).

[7] Author's translation.

[8] Freedom House staff and author's conversations with women lawyers in UAE in the summer of 2004.

[9] "Expats can work under local wife's sponsorship," *UAE Interact:* The Official Website for the Ministry of Information and Culture in the UAE, 21 July 2004, http://www.uaeinteract.com/news/default.asp?ID=155.

[10] Nada S. Mussallam, "Local women can now sponsor expat husbands," *Khaleej Times,* 14 July 2004, http://www.khaleejtimes.com/DisplayArticle.asp?xfile=data/theuae/2004/July/theuae_July293.xml&section=theuae.

[11] "Developments in the Situation of Arab Women" (ESCWA, Centre for Women, accessed 30 July 2004), www.escwa.org.lb/divisions/ecw/more/developments.html.

[12] *United Arab Emirates International Religious Freedom Report 2003* (Washington, D.C.: U.S. Dept. of State, Bureau of Democracy, Human Rights and Labor, 2004), http://www.state.gov/g/drl/rls/irf/2003/24464.htm.

[13] Freedom House staff and author's conversations with women lawyers in UAE in the summer of 2004.

[14] *Religious Freedom Report* (U.S. Dept. of State), http://www.state.gov/g/drl/rls/irf/2003/24464.htm.

[15] Ibid.

[16] "Cabinet Decision No. 4, 1974, On Arrangement of Ministry of Justice, Islamic Affairs and Awqaf" (UAE Ministry of Islamic Affairs and Awqaf), http://www.uae.gov.ae/moia/English/e_rules.htm.

[17] *Country Reports* (U.S. Dept. of State), http://www.state.gov/g/drl/rls/hrrpt/2003/27940.htm.

[18] *Religious Freedom Report* (U.S. Dept. of State), http://www.state.gov/g/drl/rls/irf/2003/24464.htm.

[19] "United Arab Emirates: Women in Public Life" (POGAR), www.pogar.org/countries/uae/gender.html.

[20] *Country Reports* (U.S. Dept. of State).

[21] "Call to Amend Draft Personal Status Law," *Gulf News,* 16 February 2003, http://www.amanjordan.org/english/daily_news/wmprint.php?ArtID=973.

[22] Rima Sabban, *Migrant Women in the United Arab Emirates: The Case of Female Domestic Workers* (Geneva: International Labour Organization, Gender Promotion Programme, 2001), 37.

[23] "Trafficking in Persons Report" (U.S. Dept. of State, 14 June 2004), http://www.state.gov/g/tip/rls/tiprpt/2004/33195.htm.

[24] Alexander Zelichenko, "Kyrgyz Sex Trade Flourishes" (London: Institute for War and Peace Reporting) *IWPROnline,* 24 March 2000, http://www.iwpr.net/index.pl?archive/rca/rca_200003_00_09_eng.txt.

[25] Leila Saralaeva, "Gulf States to Curb Sex Trafficking," *IWPR Online,* 16 June 2004, http://www.iwpr.net/index.pl?archive/rca/rca_200406_293_2_eng.txt.

[26] Geoffrey York, "Ads for foreign jobs lure Russians into pimps' net," *Globe and Mail,* 17 May 2001, http://www.walnet.org/csis/news/world_2001/gandm-010517.html.

[27] *Country Reports* (U.S. Dept. of State).

[28] *Arab Human Development Report 2002* (New York: United Nations Development Programme, 2002), 114.

[29] Shireena Alnowais, "Teenage Girl To Get 90 Lashes, To Be Deported," *Gulf News,* 17 August 2003, http://www.gulfnews.com/Articles/news.asp?ArticleID=95354.

[30] "United Arab Emirates" (London and New York: Amnesty International, Report, 2002), http://web.amnesty.org/web/ar2002.nsf/mde/united+arab+emirates!Open.

[31] "Violence Against Women – Innocent Victims of Violence," *Gulf News,* 16 December 2000, http://www.gulf-news.com/Articles/print.asp?ArticleID=5016.

[32] "Husband Has Right to Beat Wife Rules Court of Cassation," *Gulf News,* 31 March 2002.

[33] Bassam Za'za', "Divorce Due to Domestic Violence Up," *Gulf News,* 7 January 2004, http://www.amanjordan.org/english/daily_news/wmview.php?ArtID=3629.

[34] Ibid.

[35] "Violence Against Women," *Gulf News,* 16 December 2000, http://www.gulf-news.com/Articles/print.asp?ArticleID=5016.

[36] *Country Reports* (U.S. Dept. of State).

[37] "Violence Against Women," *Gulf News,* 16 December 2000, http://www.gulf-news.com/Articles/print.asp?ArticleID=5016.

[38] "Rape victim faces jail for adultery in Dubai," *The Guardian,* 4 January 2003, http://www.guardian.co.uk/france/story/0,11882,868508,00.html; "Gang Rape Victim Faces Adultery Charges," *Telegraph,* 3 January 2003, http://www.telegraph.co.uk/news/main.jhtml?xml=/news/2003/01/03/wgang03.xml&sSheet=/news/2003/01/03/ixnewstop.html.

[39] Rima Sabban, *Migrant Women,* 9.

[40] Ibid.

[41] Ibid., 10.

[42] Ibid., 11, 24.

[43] Ibid., 19.

[44] Ibid., 20.

[45] Ibid., 22.

[46] Ibid., 27.

[47] Ibid.

[48] Ibid., 44.

[49] *Country Reports* (U.S. Dept. of State).

[50] Shalini John, "Wife Abuse: When Fighting Back Is Not An Option," *Gulf News*, 19 June 2004, http://www.gulfnews.com/Articles/specialreports.asp?ArticleID=124115.

[51] *Country Reports* (U.S. Dept. of State).

[52] Shalini John, "Wife Abuse," *Gulf News*, 19 June 2004, http://www.gulfnews.com/Articles/specialreports.asp?ArticleID=124115.

[53] *Country* Reports (U.S. Dept. of State).

[54] *UAE Interact*, http://www.uaeinteract.com/news/default.asp?cntDisplay=10&ID=35.

[55] *Country Reports* (U.S. Dept. of State).

[56] "Role of UAE Women in National Growth Hailed," *Khaleej Times Online*, 10 March 2003, http://www.amanjordan.org/english/daily_news/wmprint.php?ArtID=1152.

[57] "Gender" (POGAR), www.pogar.org/countries/gender.asp?cid=21.

[58] *Religious Freedom Report 2003* (U.S. Dept. of State).

[59] "United Arab Emirates: Women in Public Life" (POGAR), www.pogar.org/countries/uae/gender.html.

[60] *Country Reports* (U.S. Dept. of State).

[61] "Political Participation," in *Developments in the Situation of Arab Women (October – December 2003)* (ESCWA, 2004), http://www.escwa.org.lb/divisions/ecw/main.htm.

[62] "Women to Drive Taxis in Dubai," *Indian Express Newspapers*, 29 May 2000, http://www.expressindia.com/ie/daily/20000529/iin29013.html.

[63] "UAE" (ESCWA, Country Profiles, 2003), www.escwa.org.lb/divisions/ecw/profile/uae/main.html.

[64] "United Arab Emirates women occupy 40% of public sector posts, 70% of university students," *ArabicNews.com*, 6 May 2003, http://www.arabicnews.com/ansub/Daily/Day/030605/2003060503.html.

[65] "Jobless UAE women — Ranks of jobless UAE women are growing," Gulf News, 19 May 2001, http://www.mafhoum.com/press/50S2.htm.

[66] "Women and Men in the Arab Countries" (ESCWA, 2004), http://www.escwa.org.lb/divisions/ecw/main.htm; Mildred Fernandes, "Empowerment of women vital to achieve development goals," *Gulf News,* 22 September 2003, http://www.gulf-news.com/Articles/print.asp?ArticleID=98208.

[67] Nada S. Mussallam, "Commercial licenses for unemployed local women," *Khaleej Times Online*, 29 January 2004, http://www.amanjordan.org/english/daily_news/wmview.php?ArtID=3878.

[68] "Dubai Business Women," (Dubai Chamber of Commerce and Industry, 12 August 2004), http://www.dcci.gov.ae/PF_contents.asp?Page=Bus_Women&PF=YES&cook

ie%5Ftest=1; "UAE: Sharp rise in number of businesswomen in Dubai," *Arab Women Connect*, 23 May 2004, http://www.arabwomenconnect.org/hdocs/mainform. asp?p=news/readNews&id=240.

[69] *Country Reports* (U.S. Dept. of State).

[70] Rima Sabban, *Migrant Women*, 36.

[71] *Country Reports* (U.S. Dept. of State).

[72] "Legal Issues That You Need to Be Aware of," *Data Dubai*, http://www.datadubai.com/sexualh_legal.htm.

[73] *Country Reports* (U.S. Dept. of State).

[74] Ibid.

[75] "Rights and Legislation," in *Developments in the Situation of Arab Women (October – December 2003)* (ESCWA, 2004), http://www.escwa.org.lb/divisions/ecw/main.htm.

[76] *Country Reports* (U.S. Dept. of State).

[77] "Ask the Law," *Gulf News*, 21 February 2003, http://www.gulf-news.com/Articles/opinionlets.asp?ArticleID=78149.

[78] "United Nations Convention on Migrant Workers' Rights enters into Force," UNESCO.org, http://portal.unesco.org/en/ev.php-URL_ID=13200&URL_DO=DO_PRINTPAGE&URL_SECTION=201.html.

[79] *Country Reports* (U.S. Dept. of State).

[80] Bassam Za'za', "All laws applicable to Dubai Media City," *Gulf News*, 27 May 2003, http://www.gulf-news.com/Articles/news.asp?ArticleID=88752.

[81] "United Arab Emirates: Women in Public Life" (POGAR), http://www.pogar.org/countries/uae/gender.html.

[82] Nada S. Mussallam, "Project true image of Arab women, Fatima tells media," *Khaleej Times*, 24 August 2002, http://www.khaleejtimes.co.ae/ktarchive/240802/lead.htm.

[83] Lydia Georgia, "UAE First Lady Calls for Dialogue," *Middle East Times*, http://www.metimes.com/2K2/issue2002-14/women/uae_first_lady.htm.

[84] *Country Reports* (U.S. Dept. of State).

[85] Freedom House staff and author's conversations with women lawyers in UAE in the summer of 2004.

[86] "Kill Them with Your Brilliance," *Al-Ahram Weekly*, 25 November–1 December 1999, http://weekly.ahram.org.eg/1999/457/feat2.htm.

[87] "Arab Woman Fights on Several Fronts, Says Fatima," *Khaleej Times*, 19 August 2002, http://www.khaleejtimes.co.ae/ktarchive/190802/uae.htm.

[88] "Media Women Face Challenges," *Gulf News*, 4 February 2002, http://www.gulf-news.com/Articles/News.asp?ArticleID=40003.

[89] "Fatima urges Arab media to focus on women's concerns," *UAE Interact*, 10 February 2002, http://www.uaeinteract.com/news/default.asp?ID=200.

[90] Ibid.

[91] "Advertise with Us," Emirates Internet and Multimedia, 2003, http://www.emirates.net.ae/isp/channel/main/netads/why-eim-net@ds.html.

[92] "Overview of Women and Information Technology in the United Arab Emirates" (Phoenix, AZ: Cisco Learning Institute, Gender Initiative, 2004), http://gender.ciscolearning.org/Strategies/Strategies_by_Region/Middle_East/United_Arab_Emirates/Index.html.

[93] Lee Smith, "The Road to Tech Mecca," *Wired*, 12 July 2004, http://www.wired.com/wired/archive/12.07/dubai.html.

[94] "UAE" (ESCWA, Country Profile), www.escwa.org.lb/divisions/ecw/profile/uae/main.html.

[95] *At a glance: United Arab Emirates – Statistics* (New York: UNICEF), http://www.unicef.org/infobycountry/uae_statistics.html.

[96] "UAE" (ESCWA, Country Profile), www.escwa.org.lb/divisions/ecw/profile/uae/main.html.

[97] "2003 World Population Data Sheet" (Washington, D.C.: Population Reference Bureau), http://www.prb.org.

[98] *At a glance: United Arab Emirates – Statistics* (UNICEF), http://www.unicef.org/infobycountry/uae_statistics.html.

[99] Nicole Veash, "Rich Pickings for Drug Traffickers as Islamic Women Defy Their Husbands to Take the Pill," *Scotland on Sunday*, 6 January 2002, 23.

[100] The hotline phone number is (04) 3085298 and the e-mail address is womenshealth@jnjae.jnj.com.

[101] Anupa Prathap Mathew, "Health Hotline Helps Women Discuss Delicate Subjects," *Gulf News*, 12 October 2000.

[102] "United Arab Emirates Abortion Policy" (New York: United Nations Population Division, Department of Economic and Social Affairs, 2002), http://www.un.org/esa/population/publications/abortion/doc/uae.doc.

[103] Robert Johnston, "Historical abortion statistics, United Arab Emirates," http://www.johnstonsarchive.net/policy/abortion/ab-uae.html.

[104] Mona Al Khanjare, "Two Doctors Jailed for Abortions," *Gulf News*, 17 October 2002, http://www.gulf-news.com/Articles/news.asp?ArticleID=65884.

[105] Tahseen Shaghouri, "UAE seeks to slash breast cancer mortality rate," *Gulf News*, http://www.gulf-news.co.ae/24022000/EMIRATES/emirates13.htm.

[106] Mona Al Khanjare, "Breast Cancer Deaths Rising," *Gulf News*, 5 January 2003.

[107] Halima Embarek Warzazi, *The Implementation of the Human Rights of Women – Traditional Practices Affecting the Health of Women and the Girl Child* (New York: UN Economic and Social Council, Commission on Human Rights, 26 June 1998), http://www.hri.ca/fortherecord1998/documentation/commission/e-cn4-sub2-1998-11.htm.

[108] "Country Profiles: United Arab Emirates." (Manila: Commission on Filipinos Overseas); "Ask the Law," *Gulf News*, 17 October 2003, http://www.gulfnews.com/Articles/uae.asp?ArticleID=100450.

[109] *Country Reports* (U.S. Dept. of State).

Yemen

by Amal Basha

Population: 19,400,000
GDP Per Capita (PPP): $870
Economy: Capitalist-statist
Ranking on UN HDI: 149 out of 177
Polity: Dominant party (military-influenced) (traditional chiefs)
Literacy: Male 69.5% / Female 28.5%
Percent Women Economically Active: 30.8%
Date of Women's Suffrage: 1967
Women's Fertility Rate: 7.0
Percent Urban/Rural: Urban 26% / Rural 74%

Country Ratings for Yemen
Nondiscrimination and Access to Justice: 2.4
Autonomy, Security, and Freedom of the Person: 2.3
Economic Rights and Equal Opportunity: 2.3
Political Rights and Civic Voice: 2.6
Social and Cultural Rights: 2.1
(Scale of 1 to 5: 1 represents the lowest and 5 the highest level of freedom women have to exercise their rights)

Introduction

Yemen is one of the oldest centers of civilization in the Middle East, with a history dating back nearly 3,000 years. From the 16th to the 19th century, the Ottoman Empire ruled many of Yemen's cities. A succession of Zaydi *imams* governed areas of northern Yemen until military officers launched a coup and established the Yemen Arab Republic (YAR) in 1962. South Yemen was under British control from 1839 until it gained its independence in 1967 and soon afterward became the Marxist-dominated People's Democratic Republic of Yemen (PDRY). After the two parts of Yemen were united on May 22, 1990, in the Republic of Yemen, the country underwent unprecedented political reforms and took steps toward a democratic system of government.

In Yemen's first direct presidential elections, in September 1999, Ali Abdallah Salih, the former leader of the YAR, was elected to a second five-year term as president of the Republic of Yemen.[1] Constitutional amendments on

335

February 20, 2001, created a bicameral legislature consisting of a 111-seat *Majlis Al-Shura* (Consultative Council), to be appointed by the president, and a 301-member House of Representatives to be elected by popular vote. In the most recent parliamentary elections, held in April 2003, 19 political parties[2] participated, including the president's dominant General People's Congress (GPC). The GPC monopolizes Yemen's politics, holding 237 seats in the current parliament. Corruption is an endemic problem at all levels of Yemen's government and society.

The United Nations considers Yemen one of the least developed countries (LDC); it ranks 149 out of 177 countries in the UNDP 2004 Human Development Index.[3] Yemen is basically an agrarian society that depends heavily on a very limited quantity of oil exports to provide 80 percent of its public budget. Of Yemen's population of approximately 19.4 million, the youth population under the age of 15 makes up 46 percent. With an estimated poverty rate of 41 percent, Yemen has a birth growth rate of 3.5 percent, one of the highest in the world. An estimated 73 percent of Yemenis inhabit rural areas, most of which lack basic infrastructure and sufficient services. Most Yemenis are Sunni and Shi'a Muslims; those in the north and northwest of the country belong predominantly to the Zaidi sect of the Shi'a, while Yemenis in the south and southeast adhere for the most part to the *Shafa'i* school of Sunni Islam. Small numbers of Jews, Christians, and Hindus also live in Yemen.

Pre-Islamic and Islamic history demonstrate that women played significant roles and held high status in Yemeni culture. The Queen of Sheba is a source of pride for the Yemeni nation, as the *Quran* described her throne as great. Queen Arwa ruled Yemen in later Islamic history, which historians document as a time of prosperity and order due to the queen's attention to building water channels, schools, and agriculture. Nevertheless, Yemeni women today face many obstacles in their efforts to achieve gender equality and empowerment. Despite the constitutional and legal measures that guaranteed women's equality during the first four years of Yemen's unity (1990–1994), gradual legislative setbacks followed the country's 1994 civil war. Gender inequality in the law remains a major problem today, and legal implementation and protections for women are very poor. Women's equality continues to be impeded in a society in which social mores and norms are regulated by a largely agrarian, tribal, and patriarchal culture.

Yemeni women do not have access to most of their economic, social, and cultural rights and still face many challenges in exercising their full political and civil rights. Women are vastly underrepresented in the government and the labor field, and only 8.2 percent of women report paid employment.[4] The government of Yemen does not have effective mechanisms to enforce the compulsory education law, and many families deny their daughters the right to education for cultural or economic reasons. A large percentage of rural families also marry their daughters at an early age. Gender inequalities in education persisted in 2002, with female literacy at only 28.5 percent, in contrast to the 69.5 percent rate for male literacy.[5]

Nondiscrimination and Access to Justice

Article 41 of the 1990 unification constitution declared, "All citizens are equal before the law, and they are equal in public rights and duties, and there is no discrimination between them on the basis of sex, origin, language, profession, social position, or faith."[6] However, amendments to this article in 1994 eliminated the text specifying the unconstitutionality of discrimination, and Article 41 now simply states "All citizens are equal in public rights and duties."[7]

A further amendment to the unification constitution in 1994 involved the addition of Article 31, which declares, "Women are sisters of men and they have rights and duties as guaranteed by Shari'a and the law."[8] This article has served as the foundation of a number of Yemen's discriminatory laws, with Yemen's male clergy and legislators citing the Shari'a as justification. The wording of Article 31 implies that women are not equal citizens but rather are sisters of male citizens. This article has serious repercussions for women's equality and empowerment in a culture in which males are typically viewed and treated as superior to females within the family. Furthermore, Article 31 is in direct contradiction to Article 41, which emphasizes the principle of equality among citizens in public rights before the law. Such legal inconsistency leaves the many issues covered under these two articles open to judicial selectivity and multiple interpretations by individual judges, which in turn, contributes to practices of discrimination against women and impedes their access to justice.

Yemen's legal system is based on Islamic law, Turkish law, English common law, and local tribal customary law.[9] Due to women's limited access and minor participation in judicial institutions, the majority of lawmakers and law enforcement agents are men. While the 1994 constitution stipulates that all citizens are equal in rights and duties, a number of Yemeni laws, regulations, and policies are discriminatory against women, particularly those governing women's rights in the family that have been created by Yemeni legislators under the pretext of Islamic Shari'a. For example, women have fewer rights than men in Yemen's Personal Status Law, which governs matters of marriage, divorce, child custody, and inheritance.

Gender discrimination is present not only in Yemeni laws, but also in the implementation of laws, by-laws, and procedures, which may be subject to various interpretations and the personal whims of individual state agents and authorities. Discrimination is faced not only by women in Yemen, but also by ethnic minorities such as the community called *Akhdam* (servants),[10] refugees from the Horn of Africa, and the small Jewish minority who remain in Yemen. The government has not instituted a formal complaint mechanism whereby an individual or group can file a report if they become victims of discrimination.

A Yemeni woman citizen is required to have the approval of the Minister of Interior, along with a written letter of approval from her guardian, in order to marry a non-Yemeni. Furthermore, Article 6 of the Nationality Law of 1990 denies Yemeni women married to foreigners the right to pass citizenship on to their children, while the children of a Yemeni man married to a foreign woman are guaranteed immediate Yemeni citizenship. In 2003, Article 3 of the Nationality Law was amended to grant children of a Yemeni woman and a foreign husband citizenship at the age of 18 on one of three conditions: the divorce of the mother from her foreign husband, his insanity, or the death of the husband.

Women are legally eligible to work in the judiciary and appear in court. However, women in Yemen face tremendous obstacles in their struggle to gain access to justice within a legal system that is overwhelmingly male-dominated at all levels. While women who pursue legal charges in the courts may occasionally encounter compassion from court officials, the majority of police and court officials view women clients with suspicion, due to the social stigma associated with a woman's presence in the courts.

Along with gender discrimination, factors such as women's high rates of illiteracy and poverty, lack of awareness of their rights, and absence from public life and the workforce, may serve to restrict women's access to justice. Furthermore, a socially short-sighted view of women, combined with financial and administrative corruption at almost all levels of the state and judiciary, pose obstacles to women's justice. Access to justice is particularly difficult for poor and rural women without a male guardian and for members of marginalized communities. Moreover, the infrastructure of Yemen's judicial system, with its overcrowded courtrooms and overburdened court dockets, further deters women's pursuit of litigation. As a result, women more often resort to informal mechanisms that involve their families and communities in order to address their problems; however, this often increases women's susceptibility to family pressures and perpetuates their lack of protection from family abuse.

A woman in Yemen is not recognized as a full person before the court; the testimony of two women equals the testimony of one man. Article 45 (21) of the 1992 Evidence Law forbids the testimony of women in cases of adultery, libel, theft, or sodomy. In general, the testimony of a woman must be supported by the testimony of a man in order to be accepted in court; yet, a woman's testimony is partially accepted in cases involving financial rights issues. The only time in which the testimony of a single woman is fully accepted is in cases in which Yemeni men are not culturally permitted to be present, such as during the delivery of a baby.[11]

According to Article 12 of Yemen's 1994 Crime and Penalty Law, the value of the life of a woman or girl is equal to half that of a man or boy; therefore, financial compensation or blood money for a Yemeni female who is killed amounts to half that for a man who is killed. This disproportionate value system is also applied to victim compensation. For example, for the 27 crimes that involve attacks on the body, a surviving female victim is eligible to receive half the compensation that a male victim receives. Furthermore, Yemeni law provides greater leniency in punishments for men who commit so-called "honor killings" (violent assaults or murder of a female relative for her perceived immodest behavior, or when caught in the act of illicit fornication (*zina*)). Article 232 of law No. 12/1994 declares that a man who murders or injures his wife and/or her partner during the moment of their adultery (*in flagrante delicto*) should receive a maximum sentence of one year's imprisonment or a fine.[12]

Women are treated differently from men in cases of detention, arrest, or seizure. Yemeni police officials tend to exhibit a greater degree of interest in cases involving women, and proceedings may be lengthened, particularly if the charges against a woman are of a "moral" nature such as zina, involving illicit sexual activity like adultery or prostitution. In some cases, the police may allow a male relative to report to the police station and be held in detention on behalf of a woman suspect. The special attention given to cases involving women is mostly due to the social stigma associated with a woman who is arrested or imprisoned. Socially, a woman's incarceration is considered a great disgrace to her family, much more so than a man's imprisonment. Special treatment is not normally provided to women members of marginalized or powerless social communities, like the Akhdam or refugees, and is generally reserved for women of a high social and economic class.

By law, detainees must be arraigned within 24 hours of arrest or be released. Nevertheless, both men and women sometimes wait for long periods before being allowed access to legal proceedings or a lawyer. Women reportedly receive longer punishments than men for crimes such as zina or *khilwa*.[13] Khilwa is not specifically mentioned in Yemen's new penal code, but the former YAR penal code defines it as "the unjustified meeting between an adult male and an adult female who are not close relatives." There are also reports of women being detained for behavior considered improper but that may not fit within a clear legal definition. A woman arrested for crimes such as khilwa or improper acts outside legal definition may be considered guilty without an investigation and sent to prison by the police even before any legal procedures begin.

South Yemen first ratified the United Nations Convention on the Elimination of All Forms of Discrimination Against Women (CEDAW) in May

1984 before unification, with reservations to provision number 29 regarding the issue of arbitration. National laws in South Yemen were reasonably
compatible with the convention. While the country's ratification of CEDAW
still remained valid under the unified Yemen, unified national laws were not
amended to conform to the standards of CEDAW.

Although women's NGOs and civil society groups have created some social momentum and broadened an awareness of women's issues, they have
not yet achieved necessary reforms or the eradication of discriminatory laws.
Yemen's independent women's rights groups that advocate for legal rights,
greater public awareness, and women's equality issues are small and lack the
resources, funds, and equipment to launch national-level campaigns.

As a follow-up to the 1995 Beijing Platform of Action, gender affairs departments were created in most government ministries by 1999. Nevertheless,
these departments have not been very active, due to inadequate human and financial resources and limited decision-making authority. The Supreme Council
for Women's Affairs and its consultative, executive, and administrative body,
the Women's National Committee, are the main government entities that aim
to enhance women's status and integrate women's issues into governmental
affairs, acting as advocates for women's rights within the state system.

An increasingly powerful extremist religious movement contributes to the
restrictions on women's rights advocacy in Yemen. Growing support for the
extremist movement began soon after the Saudi Arabian government expelled
thousands of Yemeni workers during the second Gulf War of 1991, as a result
of Yemen's support of Iraq. Returning workers imported practices and beliefs
of Saudi Arabia's strict form of *Wahabbi* Islam, which have since gained momentum and become a powerful tool against women's efforts toward equality.
To compensate for a lack of freedom of expression, women's rights advocates
have carefully adopted an enlightened and progressive religious discourse in
which to promote women's human rights. Advocacy for equality and gender
empowerment is most often conducted in reference to Islam, rather than the
language of international human rights conventions, in order to avoid accusations of promoting western agendas.

RECOMMENDATIONS

1. The government should work with Yemeni women's rights organizations
   and legislators to amend all laws that discriminate against women.
2. The government should establish nationwide complaint mechanisms for
   women to access if they are discriminated against on the basis of their
   gender.
3. The government and women's rights NGOs should implement women's
   rights awareness programs to educate women on their rights and protections under Yemen's laws and constitution.

4. The government should remove all reservations to CEDAW and take steps to implement it locally by bringing national laws in conformity with CEDAW.

Autonomy, Security, and Freedom of the Person

Yemen's population is predominantly Muslim (Sunni and Shi'a), with a small Jewish, Christian, and Hindu minority who are free to practice their religions. Conversion from Islam to another religion is forbidden for all Muslims, and according to Yemen's laws, a person found doing so will be considered an apostate and killed. However, no such executions for religious conversion have been reported in Yemen.

Both family traditions and Yemeni laws may ser e to restrict a woman's freedom of movement. Women are not legally permitted a passport without the approval of their guardians (*wali*),[14] but women with passports are legally allowed to travel without their guardian's permission. Law enforcement officers, however, will often breach this law and restrict a woman's right to travel if her guardian disapproves and reports her to the authorities. In addition, while such actions are not legally permitted, a woman's guardian can prevent her from seeking an education or employment and may even restrict her ability to leave the home without permission.

South Yemen's progressive family code of 1974 provided women greater rights in matters of divorce, marriage, and custody than the family code of North Yemen. However, the government of the newly unified Yemen implemented a new Personal Status Law in 1992 that opted to integrate the more conservative and discriminatory laws that had previously applied under North Yemen's family codes, annulling women's equal rights under South Yemen's family code of 1974.

According to the unified Personal Status Law, a woman's guardian must conclude her marriage contract, and if a woman does not have a guardian, she may delegate a judge to sign the marriage contract on her behalf. A man, however, is entitled to conclude his own marriage contract. In theory, a woman can negotiate her marriage contract if her fiancé agrees to the conditions, such as allowing a woman to continue her education or employment after marrying; however, in reality, this does not frequently occur.

The Personal Status Law does not establish a minimum age of marriage for boys or girls, thus encouraging early and child marriage. Little research has been conducted on the percentage of girls married at an early age in Yemen; however, early marriage is a serious problem and a widespread phenomenon that can lead to serious health problems for girls. The law requires a non-virgin (usually a woman who has been previously married) to pronounce her consent to marriage verbally, while the law allows the silence of a girl or woman considered to be a virgin to signify her approval or consent to marriage. In practice, most judges do not verify the consent of a woman, and a majority of marriages take place at home, not in the courts. A man is allowed to be married to up to four women at one time in Yemen, and the law does not require him to obtain permission from his first wife or inform her of the other marriages.

Women do not have the same rights to divorce as men. A husband can divorce his wife at any time without needing to provide any justification, whereas a woman must litigate in court and present adequate justification in order to have the marriage contract nullified. Article 47 of the amended Personal Status Law provides women with the right to have their marriage contract nullified but only under the condition that the woman's husband has a defect or dangerous disease, which according to Yemeni laws includes such disorders as tuberculosis, leprosy, insanity, or castration. However, the court must agree to nullify the marriage contract; the wife may not do this on her own. Meanwhile, a man has the right to restore his relations with the wife who is divorcing him within the period of *edda* (a waiting period of three months before a divorce becomes legal) without her consent. This waiting period is mandatory and is intended to ensure that the wife is not pregnant by the husband she is divorcing. Yemeni law does not consider a woman's marriage to another man valid if it is performed before the conclusion of the period of edda.

Personal Status Law No. 20, amended in 1998, obligates wives to yield to the authority of their husbands. A wife is required to reside where her husband resides, no matter what the condition of the residence, and she is legally obligated to do the housework. In 2003, a legal statement of *Bait Al-Ta'a* (the House of Obedience) that had previously been passed by the parliament in 2001 was proposed for ratification. The legal implications of Bait Al-Ta'a would have been to authorize judges to use force to require married women to return to their conjugal homes against their will. After a nationwide campaign and extensive advocacy efforts by women's NGOs, Sisters Arab Forum for Human Rights (SAF), and select government officials, the legal statement was canceled.

While the trafficking of women in Yemen has not been a problem in the past, there are indications that it may become one. Little information on this crime is available, but cases have been reported of children trafficked within Yemen and to Saudi Arabia for child labor, as well as an increasing number of women trafficked to Yemen for prostitution, some of whom may have originated in Iraq. Yemeni law does not specifically prohibit trafficking in persons, and protections for victims have not yet been established, but several other Yemeni statutes are being used to prosecute traffickers.[15]

Generally speaking, the conditions of both men's and women's prisons are very poor, and health conditions are unsatisfactory. Prisoners are mistreated and suffer from extrajudicial torture, which is in violation of the constitution. By custom, children and babies born in prison usually remain with their mothers. Recently, the Prisons Law was slightly amended to stipulate that "pregnant women in prison must have access to medical care before and after delivery."[16] Accordingly, women who are pregnant and/or breast-feeding are exempted from punitive measures inside prisons.

Although there is no such law in Yemen, as a matter of cultural practice, Yemeni prison officials do not release women who have completed their sentences unless they can be released into the custody of a male family member. Partly due to the shame and social stigma associated with women in prison, many women who have served their time continue to wait for male family members to appear and authorize their release. Prison guards have been known to both impregnate women during their incarceration and marry off female inmates to men who bribe the guards. While the government began to take some measures a few years ago to remedy women's situations in prison, the state has mostly turned a blind eye to their plight. There are no state-sponsored services to help women reintegrate back into society once they have completed their sentences. In addition to Yemenis, a number of women inmates from neighboring African countries, particularly Ethiopia, languish in prisons past the expiration of their sentences.

There are no legal protections for women who suffer from domestic violence in Yemen. While a married woman may report acts of violence against her committed at the hands of her husband, a physical trace of the violence must be visible on her body. In the case of violence perpetrated by a husband, the court may rule for material compensation for the wife, according to the judge's discretion. An unmarried girl living in her father's home, however, has no legal recourse against abuse by a family member unless her legal guardian brings the charges.

Women may experience various forms of street violence in Yemen, particularly verbal harassment. Social norms in Yemen most often place the burden of proper social behavior on women instead of their male harassers. Verbal harassment serves to humiliate women and often leads families to prohibit daughters and women from leaving the home. Many women prefer to appear anonymous in public in order to avoid harassment and the resulting embarrassment felt by their families. Most Yemeni women fully cover their bodies in a black dress with their faces veiled except for the eyes. Very few women expose their faces, and those who uncover their hair are rare. While the veil is not legally imposed, some extremist religious groups exert pressure on women to veil as part of their duties as "good" Muslim women. Unveiled women face harassment and are strongly criticized.

While both women and their families may experience harassment on the streets, the government has failed to increase the availability of safe and affordable transportation for the many Yemenis limited by poverty. Another factor contributing to restrictions on women's freedom and safety in public space is the absence of protective laws and a lack of law enforcement officials on the street to deter violence directed at women. Despite the efforts of women's rights groups to demand improved access for women to safe transportation, the government continues to allow logistical and financial restrictions to perpetuate women's social obstacles.

RECOMMENDATIONS

1. The government should increase the minimum age of marriage to 18 years to help girls complete their high school education and protect them from early and forced marriages, and initiate campaigns to increase awareness of the harmful effects of early marriage.
2. The government should create adequate prison facilities for women and allow human rights organizations and individuals to monitor their conditions.
3. The government should introduce laws to criminalize domestic violence against women in Yemen and work with women's NGOs to establish shelters and counseling services for women victims of violence.

Economic Rights and Equal Opportunities

Yemen is one of the poorest countries in the region. Declines in oil prices served to stunt the economic growth of the 1990s. Yemen has embarked on an International Monetary Fund (IMF)-supported structural adjustment program designed to modernize and streamline the economy. However, high population growth, scarce resources, and political corruption challenge economic advances. An estimated 35 percent of the population is unemployed, and the illiteracy rate in Yemen remains as high as 47.2 percent.[17]

While no legal obstacles prevent women from having full use or ownership of their property, widespread illiteracy, patriarchal attitudes, and women's ignorance of their economic rights have produced a situation in which a majority of women hand over the administration of their possessions and property to their husbands or brothers. Most women, especially in rural areas, do not know about their property and inheritance rights, nor do they know how to gain access to them or use them. The government has not initiated programs for rural women to provide them with basic information on their economic or human rights.

Women legally have full and independent use of their incomes, but in practice, fathers and husbands may partially or completely control that income. Women, however, are not legally obligated to spend money on family needs, while a man is obligated to provide financially both for his family and for his wife's relatives if they are destitute.

Yemen's inheritance laws are in accordance with the country's interpretation of Islam, which suggests that a daughter and a wife should receive half the share inherited by a son and a husband. In Yemen's rural areas however, women are sometimes deprived of their full inheritance without their knowledge and without legal justification. Some wealthier families may forbid their daughters to marry anyone outside the family in order to protect their properties from being transferred to another family.

No legal provisions prevent women from participating in business, commercial, or economic activities at any level. However, social pressures work to ensure that women are monitored and criticized for "unconventional behaviors" that may fall outside the societal customs and traditions, including women's involvement in economic entrepreneurship. As a result, women's role in Yemen's commercial and economic activities is still relatively weak.

Article 54 of the 2001 Yemen constitution declares education compulsory, yet the government does not translate this provision into practice. Yemen has one of the highest gaps in the world between the net primary school attendance rates of boys and of girls. In rural areas, only 30 percent of girls, as compared to 73 percent of boys, are enrolled in primary school.[18] The main impediments to women's education are poverty and a social bias in which parents prefer to send sons to school and to avoid placing their daughters in a mixed-gender environment. Early marriage also plays a significant role in women's high dropout rate. Additionally, there are not enough schools to meet the needs of girls' education, especially in rural areas.

While there are no legal restrictions against women's education at any level, some technical institutes and schools do not admit women. The High Judicial Institute does not allow women, for example, which makes it practically impossible for women to be trained as judges. Women account for 25 percent of the total number of university students. An estimated 50 percent of women at the university level are in the field of education.[19]

The Labor Law of 1995 provides safeguards prohibiting discrimination against women in the workforce, but in practice such discrimination is common, and preference in hiring goes to men. Only a limited number of job skills centers and job opportunities are available for women in Yemen, and the government has undertaken no systematic efforts to provide job-training skills for women in the schools or to promote income-generating programs for rural women.

While only a few professions are legally off-limits to women's employment, a woman's family will most often determine the field in which she works. No legal or administrative remedies are available to women who are prohibited by their families from pursuing the profession of their choice. The state relegates its duties to protect the rights of Yemen's female citizens to the male members of families.

The government of Yemen does not allow women to join the army, although a few women recently graduated from the police academy and are eligible to fill positions in airports, prisons, and police stations to inspect women. Women have also started to work in shops and are able to work as engineers in offices. Social customs keep women from holding positions as taxi drivers or employees in construction or building projects. The socially preferred professions for women are teaching and medicine. Nevertheless, due to widespread corruption, employment opportunities for both men and women are often limited by nepotism and favoritism.

According to a report released by the National Women's Committee in 2004, Yemeni women represent 24.6 percent of the workforce. Nearly 86 percent of women in the workforce are in the agricultural sector, and most women work in the informal and unregulated sector. Many women are involved in non-wage work; the Women's National Committee reports that only 8 percent of women are employed in paid jobs.[20] Women make up 28 percent of the employees in the private sector, but only 9.3 percent in the civil service and public sector.

No laws protect women from sexual harassment in the workplace. Female employees who are subject to sexual harassment at work often choose to remain silent in fear of damage to their reputations or the loss of their jobs. If a woman reports harassment to her superior, the matter will be subject to that individual's judgment, due to the lack of applicable rules or regulations. Economic hardships and the high rate of unemployment eliminate this risk as an option for women workers.

Pregnant women are granted 60 days of maternity leave with full pay and 20 additional days in the case of a caesarian delivery or the birth of twins. Articles 43 and 45 of Yemen's labor laws reduce a woman's working hours from eight to five hours starting from the sixth month of pregnancy and continuing up until six months following the delivery. Yemen's labor laws also stipulate that any institution or company with more than 50 female employees must set up a children's nursery.

Organizations working to improve women's economic rights in Yemen have succeeded in raising awareness of the importance of women's education and women's participation in the workforce and have achieved some minor amendments to Yemen's laws. Yet despite this progress, women's organizations involved in women's economic rights are still relatively ineffective and have not made a significant impact due to their lack of technical skills and financial resources. Facilitating loans and expanding women's access to credit requires investments from the government and society—not, apparently, a state priority.

RECOMMENDATIONS

1. The government, in collaboration with women's organizations, schools, and donors should launch job development training programs for women and facilitate loans for small enterprises to help increase women's participation in the labor market.
2. The government should enact a law to protect women from sexual harassment in the workplace.
3. The government should work in cooperation with NGOs, media, educators, politicians, and religious groups to launch a national campaign to combat illiteracy among women, particularly rural women and girls.
4. The government should increase the number of schools for girls, and increase the availability of safe transportation for students and teachers.

Political Rights and Civic Voice

The constitution of unified Yemen, ratified in May 1991, confirmed the principles of the peaceful transfer of power, freedom of association, freedom to form political parties, and respect for freedom of speech and expression. Immediately after the 1990 unification, at least 48 political parties and many newspapers were established. Yemen is one of the few countries in the Arab world to organize regular elections at the national and local levels. On the surface, Yemen appears to have a relatively democratic system, yet in reality, the ruling party, the GPC, monopolizes Yemen's politics. While Yemeni legislation guarantees women equal political and civil rights, women remain greatly underrepresented in Yemen's political life. The government still cites Yemen's traditions and customs as justification for its failure to take affirmative steps to ensure women's political participation.

According to Article 58 of the constitution, Yemenis have the right to form associations, and respect for this right is evident in the presence of several thousand NGOs. However, Yemen's 2003 Law of Demonstrations and Strikes limits peaceful demonstrations by requiring groups to obtain advance permission from the Minister of Interior, declare the time and place of the demonstration, and pledge not to cause any material damages. These provisions were added in reaction to a series of violent demonstrations—some of which were political, while others protested economic conditions and governmental policies related to the IMF structural adjustment program. Women in Yemen, however, rarely participate in public demonstrations because societal norms and the country's conservative culture reserve this space for men.

While freedom of expression is guaranteed under Article 42 of the constitution, journalists practice self-censorship in order to adhere to Article 103 of the Press and Publications Law. Article 103 outlaws direct personal criticism of the head of state and the publication of material that might lead to dissent among the Yemeni people, contradict the principles of the Yemeni Revolution, or distort the image of the Yemeni, Arab, or Islamic heritage. Prosecutors have filed a number of lawsuits against journalists and newspapers over the years, targeting those affiliated with the political opposition. Sentences for libel range from suspension and fines to imprisonment. In 2003, when the Syndicate of Journalists demanded a halt to the harassment and sentencing of journalists, the president declared that imprisonment for journalists would be stopped in 2004. Women journalists have not specifically been targeted for harassment as a result of their gender; only one female journalist was interrogated in 1999 for reporting on a sensitive political issue. The proportion of female journalists registered with the syndicate is an estimated 10 percent of the total number of journalists.

The General Election and Referendum Law respects women's rights to participate in parliamentary elections as voters and candidates. The number of women registered to vote increased from 15 percent of the total electorate in 1993 to 42 percent in the 2003 parliamentary elections.[21] However, the number of female candidates saw a remarkable downturn, decreasing from 41 women candidates in 1993 to only 11 out of 1,400 candidates in the 2003 parliamentary elections. The number of women in parliament also declined from 11 (all members of the former parliament of South Yemen) in 1990 to 2 women in the parliaments of 1993 and 1997 to only 1 woman in the 301-member parliament in 2003. Moreover, only 2 women have been appointed to the 111-member Shura Council. In local councils, women comprise a low 0.6 percent of the total membership.

In 2001, SAF—a leading Yemeni NGO—and civil society leaders organized a national campaign for changes to the draft Election Law and demanded the adoption of a quota system of 30 percent minimum representation for women. Three years later, the Women's National Committee joined the movement and campaigned for the institution of a quota system for women.

Women are vastly underrepresented in the judiciary; estimates range from a low of 4 to a high of 32 total women judges as compared with 1,200 male judges.[22] Most women judges work in primary courts, and no criminal issues are referred to them. No new women judges have been appointed since the proclamation of unity in 1990.

Women's representation in governmental bodies remains nominal. While there is no shortage of highly educated women to fill senior-level appointments, the government seems to appoint only from among a select group of women. The same woman who was Yemen's first female ambassador now serves as the Minister of Human Rights, the only woman in Yemen's 35-member cabinet. Two women have been appointed as deputy ministers, and there are currently no women ambassadors.

The law guarantees men and women the right to form political parties and organizations. However, women's membership in political parties is very low, and the representation of women in upper leadership positions within parties does not exceed 2 percent.[23]

Women's participation in civic life is limited, and women's influence on policy development and decision making remains weak. Most meetings of official institutions, syndicates, and associations are held in all-male qat[24] sessions in the afternoons, where women are forbidden by social custom. Qat chewing is a national pastime for men in Yemen; it is an exclusively male function and privilege in public. Women's exclusion from qat sessions serves to impede their effective participation in the political arena. Women's rights groups are not demanding to chew qat in such sessions with men but are rather advocating for the establishment of improved professional and social standards and processes for the deliberation of key political issues in place of qat sessions.

The law does not infringe upon women's freedom to seek information; however, women's access is limited. Most women do not benefit from the print media because of their lack of literacy, and television does not reach the entire country. This is largely because electrical power reaches only 30.5 percent of Yemeni land, while rural access to electricity is only 13.2 percent.[25] The government occasionally censors media information by confiscating magazines and newspapers and suppressing sensitive political articles. Some Web sites are also suppressed for political and moral reasons. Women's exclusion from the social and official meetings held during qat sessions is a further factor serving to isolate them from equal networking opportunities, information sharing, and opinion exchange.

RECOMMENDATIONS

1. The government should ensure free, competitive, and democratic elections that are open to all political parties, which include the full and equal participation of women at all levels of the political process.
2. The government should work with women's organizations to adopt a quota system to enable women to participate in legislative and executive councils.
3. The government should prohibit qat chewing in all governmental meetings.
4. The government and international organizations should offer technical and financial support to Yemeni NGOs that are working in the field of women's political rights.

Social and Cultural Rights

The state of women's health in Yemen is among the poorest in the world. The Yemeni government spends a low 3.4 percent of its annual general budget on the health sector.[26] There are 4,185 people per doctor and 1,589 people per hospital bed.[27] Women from rural areas particularly suffer from limited access to reproductive health care; reproductive health services are limited primarily to the main cities, and the few health centers available are of poor quality. Most women give birth at home, contributing to Yemen's high rate of maternal mortality. The proportion of mothers who receive health care during pregnancy in the cities is 61 percent, while only 27 percent of women in the rural areas receive care.[28]

No legal provisions guarantee women's freedom to make decisions about their health or reproductive rights. A husband often controls a woman's choices regarding the number of children she will have, the length of time between births, and the use of contraceptives, as well as whether or not she may visit a hospital or undergo surgery. There are no sexual education programs, and Yemeni law prohibits sexual relations outside marriage. The share of married women using contraceptives was 23 percent in 2003.[29] Abortion is illegal, except in cases involving serious health risks for the mother.

Some harmful traditional practices still exist in Yemen, such as female genital mutilation (FGM), which is often performed during the first 40 days after a girl's birth. This widespread tradition is practiced predominantly in the coastal areas of Aden, Hadramout, Mahra, Hudiedah, and Taiz. While the Ministry of Public Health issued a decree banning FGM in official health centers, the state has remained silent on FGM practiced by traditional women in private places.

The Family Law in South Yemen before unity, stipulated that the conjugal house would be allocated to the wife if a couple divorced and she maintained custody of the children. However, this law was repealed after unity, and today a woman must already have ownership of the conjugal home in order to maintain possession of it for herself and her children after divorce.

Women remain underrepresented in the media, constituting only 18.6 percent of employees working in television and radio stations.[30] Most media institutions do not have any women in senior positions. The one woman who holds the post of Deputy Minister of Information is the same woman currently serving as the Minister of Human Rights. The government exclusively runs Yemen's broadcast media, including television and radio. Women in the media are generally stereotyped, with most images portraying women in limited and glorified roles as mothers and housewives.

The proportion of families in Yemen living under the Food Poverty Line is 17.5 percent, while 41.8 percent of the population lives under the Upper Poverty Line (education, health, and clothing poverty).[31] Poverty was exacerbated in 1994 by state-implemented restructuring and privatization programs. Few statistics on poverty are available disaggregated by gender, but women seem to be disproportionately affected by poverty as a result of higher rates of illiteracy and social discrimination and segregation. The Women's National Committee reported that of the families living below the poverty line, 13 percent are women-headed households, and the average income of a family headed by a woman is one-third less than that of families headed by men.

The ability of Yemen's women's groups to advocate for women's rights is often constrained by extremist religious leaders and some extremist religious parties who severely criticize and defame women's groups by citing the Islamic Shari'a as justification for their condemnation. At the same time, an enlightened movement has begun in Yemeni civil society to reinterpret women's rights within the Shari'a, finding the Shari'a to be in accord with full and equal rights for women and men. Their advocacy highlights the ways in which various interpretations of Quranic text, the influence of patriarchal cultural practices, and the authoritarian nature of the ruling political ideologies negatively affect Muslim women's abilities to exercise their human rights.

RECOMMENDATIONS

1. The government should work in cooperation with the media and NGOs to adopt policies aimed at changing the image of women in the media.
2. The government should facilitate practical coordination between governmental and non-governmental organizations concerned with women's issues in the area of housing and allocate resources for housing programs to meet the needs of all Yemeni women.
3. The government should increase budget allocations for the public health sector, with special attention and funding going to reproductive healthcare and women's health needs in rural areas.
4. The government should develop support services, including programs to build skills, obtain credit, and increase financial literacy, to help Yemeni women who are most exposed to social marginalization and poverty, including female heads of households, women with disabilities, and poor women who are divorced or widowed.

AUTHORS: Amal Basha is a human rights activist and a trainer in the fields of gender, development, and human rights. She serves as chairperson of the Sisters Arab Forum for Human Rights (SAF) in Yemen, and is a regional coordinator for the Middle East and North Africa Region for the International Coalition for the International Criminal Court (CICC). She holds an MA in international development and gender and has extensive working experience with UNDP, UNIFEM, the EU, and the ICRC.

Assistance on this report provided by researchers Rana Ghanem, Media and External Relations Officer of SAF, and Nabil Abdulhafid, Secretary General of Yemen Democratic and Social Forum.

Notes

[1] Constitutional amendments in 2000 extended the presidential term by two years. The next presidential elections will be held in 2006.

[2] "The April 27, 2003 Parliamentary Elections in the Republic of Yemen" (Washington, D.C.: National Democratic Institute for International Affairs [NDI], 2003), http://www.accessdemocracy.org/library/1701_yem_elect-rep.pdf.

[3] The UNDP Human Development Index considers such factors as life expectancy at birth, adult literacy rate, combined gross enrollment in schools, and GDP per capita.

[4] "National Report on Women's Status in Yemen (Beijing + 10)" (Sana'a: Women's National Committee [WNC], submitted to UN Economic and Social Council for Western Asia [ESCWA], May 2004).

[5] Table 24, "Gender-related development index," in *Human Development Report 2004: Cultural Liberty in Today's Diverse World* (New York: United Nations Development Programme [UNDP], 2004), 217-220. http://hdr.undp.org/reports/global/2004/.

[6] Yemeni constitution, Article 27 (1990).

[7] Yemeni constitution, Article 40 (1994).

[8] Yemeni constitution, Article 31 (1994).

[9] *The World Factbook—Yemen* (Springfield, VA: U.S. Central Intelligence Agency [CIA], 2003).

[10] Arabic word for servants. Akhdams are descendants of Abyssinian soldiers who stayed in Yemen after a failed invasion in the 6th century AD. They are limited to such jobs as disposing of human waste and collecting garbage and do not have access to most social services. There are few efforts by government to integrate them.

[11] Ahamed Al-Wadei, "Discrimination against women in the laws" (Sana'a: Sisters Arab Forum for Human Rights [SAF], study submitted 2003).

[12] Lynn Welchman, "Extracted Provisions from the Penal Codes of Arab States Relevant to 'Crimes of Honour'" (Centre of Islamic and Middle Eastern Laws/International Center for the Legal Protection of Human Rights: Project on Strategies to Address 'Crimes of Honour'; [CIMEL/INTERIGHTS] University of London, School of African and Oriental Studies), http://www.soas.ac.uk/honourcrimes/Mat_ArabLaws.htm.

[13] "Integration of the Human Rights of Women and the Gender Perspective: Violence Against Women" (New York: United Nations Economic and Social Council, Commission on Human Rights, 56th session, 27 January 2000).

[14] The *wali* is usually the woman's father, or in his absence, her brother, uncle, or other close male relative.

[15] "Trafficking in Persons Report" (Washington, D.C.: U.S. Dept. of State, Office to Monitor and Combat Trafficking in Persons, 14 June 2004).

[16] Prisons Law, Article 27, amendment, 2003.

[17] *Yemen in Figures* (Sana'a: Central Statistical Organization), 4.

[18] "Persistent Inequalities" (New York: UNDP, Yemen Country Profile, 2002), http://www.undp.org.ye/Inequalities.htm.

[19] "Yemen" (Beirut: ESCWA, Country Profiles, 2003), http://www.escwa.org.lb/divisions/ecw/profile/yemen/main.html.

[20] "Beijing +10" (WNC, 2004).

[21] "Yemen Strategic Report 2003" (Sana'a: Yemen Centre for Strategic Studies [YCSS]), 191.

[22] The Women's National Committee reports the presence of 32 female judges versus 1,200 male judges.

[23] "Yemen Strategic Report 2003" (YCSS), 178.

[24] The leaves of the shrub Catha edulis, which are chewed like tobacco or used to make tea; has the effect of a euphoric stimulant.

[25] Report of Women's National Committee (Sana'a: 2003), 79.

[26] *Yemen in Figures 2002* (Sana'a: Central Organization of Statistics), 5.

[27] Ibid., 10.

[28] "Beijing + 10" (WNC, 2004).

[29] Ibid.

[30] Report of Women's National Committee (Sana'a: 2003), 80.

[31] "Beijing + 10" (WNC, 2004).

Survey Methodology

Introduction:

The survey *Women's Rights in the Middle East and North Africa* provides a comparative evaluation of women's freedom to exercise their human rights. The survey's methodology is based largely on the Universal Declaration of Human Rights (UDHR), which has long guided Freedom House in its extensive work in the evaluation of the state of freedom, political rights, and civil liberties throughout the world. Each country report in the survey takes into account both the de jure and the de facto status of women's rights in all areas under study. In addition, the survey reports review the impact of both state actions and omissions, and the actions and influence of non-state actors that affect women's freedom in a country. Women's rights and freedoms in the Middle East and North Africa are examined by assessing the following key areas:

    I.   Nondiscrimination and Access to Justice
    II.   Autonomy, Security, and Freedom of the Person
    III. Economic Rights and Equal Opportunity
    IV. Political Rights and Civic Voice
    V.   Social and Cultural Rights

Overview:

The full promotion and protection of human rights remains an ideal in all parts of the world. In recent years, however, particular focus has been directed to the status of basic human rights protections in the countries of the Middle East and North Africa. There is an unprecedented need today to develop a comprehensive understanding of the challenges to full enjoyment of human rights by men and women in the region. Although the Middle East and North Africa region continues to lag behind global trends towards freedom, progress was seen recently in a number of countries with majority Muslim populations, defying some who argue that Islamic religious beliefs are somehow contrary to democratic development. Recent efforts toward expanding democracy, particularly in Bahrain, Morocco, Qatar, and Yemen, are small but important steps in the right direction.

Women make up half of the population of 325 million in the Middle East and North Africa (MENA). They are also the most affected by poverty, lack of equal opportunity, and the denial of democratic rights. Despite these obstacles—with the aid of governmental assistance and consistent advocacy by local women's groups, civil society actors, and educators—women in the region have made impressive progress in the area of education, with female literacy growing threefold since the 1970s. However, the overall condition of women's human rights remains challenging for most women in the region. For example, women in the Middle East have the world's lowest labor force participation rate (32%), and women's political participation within the MENA region is the world's lowest and even fully denied in some countries. It is in this context that Freedom House believes that an assessment of women's rights and freedom in the Middle East and North Africa is of critical importance. Throughout its existence, Freedom House has been guided by the conviction that women's rights are indivisible from all human rights. This first-of-its-kind, pilot study is also in keeping with a growing interest in the status of women in the Middle East region, as highlighted by recent reports such as the United Nations' *Arab Human Development Report* (2002) and the *Women in the Public Sphere* report of the World Bank (2003).

Region in Review:

During the last sixty years, Freedom House has conducted a number of global, regional, and thematic studies and special reports in order to highlight key issues at critical times. Issues explored by these special studies include religious freedom, press freedom, and economic conditions in regions such as Central and Eastern Europe, and in groups of countries selected for particular status, such as for the annual surveys *Nations in Transit* and *Countries at the Crossroads*. The overarching purpose and goal of the survey *Women's Rights in the Middle East and North Africa* is to facilitate national and international efforts to empower women in a region where women's rights protections remain most challenging.

The countries/territories selected for review in this project are: **Algeria, Bahrain, Egypt, Iraq, Jordan, Kuwait, Lebanon, Libya, Morocco, Oman, Palestine (Palestinian Authority and Israeli-Occupied Territories), Qatar, Saudi Arabia, Syria, Tunisia, United Arab Emirates, and Yemen.** These countries represent a narrow range of political systems: traditional or constitutional monarchies and dictatorships. In some, a modest degree of democratic reform has taken root. In others, reforms have failed to take root or have stalled. A further factor is the phenomenon of personal authoritarianism, in which a handful of individuals have maintained a monopoly over economic and political power. Each country report in *Women's Rights in the Middle East and North Africa* presents a brief analysis of the overall political, economic, social, and democratic rights status of the general population in that country, i.e. men and women from all ethnic, social, and economic groups. However, since the main focus of this survey is to highlight the presence of and obstacles to women's rights and freedoms, the majority of each country report is devoted to analyzing gender-specific issues that impact women's rights and freedom.

Survey Methodology and Process:

The survey offers a transparent and consistent guide to scoring and analyzing the countries under review. This process includes a rigorous and detailed methodology, the identification of key themes and questions for review, and the development of a system for monitoring, rating, and producing a written analysis of a country's progress on certain thematic issues. Because of the uniqueness of a survey that assesses the theme of women's rights, Freedom House has developed a new methodology that addresses questions that apply to all people, as well as issues that represent distinct obstacles to the full enjoyment of women's rights. In addition, each writer received instructional tools such as guidelines for interpreting complex questions, and suggestions for consulting relevant studies, reports, and human rights standards to help examine particular issues in depth. In general, however, this survey is largely based on the methodology that informs other freedom assessments published by Freedom House, including *Freedom in the World*. The methodology for these surveys has been developed and refined over a thirty-year period and validated by leading social scientists and democracy specialists. The methodology for *Women's Rights in the Middle East and North Africa* was drafted by Freedom House survey staff and experts, and reviewed and approved by a distinguished committee of senior academic specialists.

A. Analytical Country Reports:
The core of the survey consists of analytical reports for each of the 16 countries and one territory under study. The writers have been drawn from a vast pool of country and regional specialists, all possessing an expertise in women's rights, the history and politics of the Middle East, democracy issues, and international human rights standards. The reports are based on guidelines developed by the methodology committee and a checklist of questions that address the most critical issues of women's rights and freedoms in the region. The reports consist of narrative assessments of approximately 6,000 words, as

well as scores that rate the country's performance in the five key areas. Each report assesses the performance of state actions and omissions, the legal system and its impact on women's rights, the overall political environment of the country, and the actual implementation of laws and official policies. The role of non-state actors who have an impact on the strengthening or weakening of women's rights is also examined. In addition, the narratives highlight both the major obstacles to women's rights, and the consistent achievements and forward-looking strategies made possible either by the state or due to the efforts of non-state actors. Finally, the survey presents a human rights and democracy-oriented review of women's needs and priorities defined by women in the region, obstacles and challenges to their freedom, and recommendations for effective promotion and protection of women's rights.

B. Narrative and Ratings Review by Regional Experts:

After the completion of the country reports by the writers, the narrative reports and proposed ratings were reviewed and critiqued by a group of senior academic experts who specialize in women's rights, the history and politics of the Middle East, democracy issues, and international human rights standards. Each regional expert reviewed up to three reports and assessed the rating scores on both a country level and on a region-wide comparative basis. The system of evaluating each country's performance includes a score for each of the checklist questions addressed in the survey. Ratings are also provided for each of the five key areas that the survey has identified as crucial to women's freedom. By using identical benchmarks for both the narrative and the ratings, the two indicators are mutually reinforcing. The final result is a system of well-defined, comparative ratings, accompanied by a narrative that objectively reflects the legal and judicial, civil and political, economic, social and cultural conditions in a country, and the degree to which these conditions facilitate or obstruct a woman's freedom to exercise her basic rights.

C. Consultations in the Region:

In order to ensure that each country report includes the most up-to-date perspectives and opinions of the government, and a current analysis of the work of women's rights advocates in the region, Freedom House staff traveled to nine countries in the region for in-depth consultations during 2003-2004. Countries visited included: Bahrain, Egypt, Jordan, Lebanon, Morocco, Oman, Palestine (Palestinian Authority and Israeli-Occupied Territories), Syria, and United Arab Emirates. Survey staff also met with women leaders from Saudi Arabia and Yemen. The consultations were held with a large number of women's rights activists and advocates, civil society leaders, human rights groups, journalists, community leaders, politicians, labor leaders, and other important opinion makers in each country. The on-the-ground consultations focused on the particular issues assessed in the survey narratives, and the results of these consultations were used to inform country narratives and final report recommendations.

D. Focus Groups:

An additional dimension of the survey process was a series of focus groups conducted in Egypt, Kuwait, and Morocco. The focus group interviews and discussions were designed to elicit popular attitudes towards issues that affect the status of women, as well as the concrete and urgent concerns and recommendations of both men and women. Results of the focus group discussions are available on the Freedom House website and an essay summarizing the findings is included in this survey.

Results and Recommendations:

The country report writers were asked to draft concrete recommendations for the improvement of women's rights within the five key areas under review in each report. These recommendations focus on urgent issues and address national governments and international policy-making institutions. The survey *Women's Rights in the Middle East and North Africa* will be widely disseminated in both Arabic and English throughout the region and the world. Target audiences for the survey include women's rights advocates, civil society organizations, media in the Middle East and North Africa, and policy makers in the countries addressed in the survey. Freedom House will also make the survey easily accessible to international institutions, NGOs, educational institutions, and global media through its website. It is anticipated that the survey will be used as an advocacy instrument by those who are working for the expansion of women's rights and freedom in the region.

Checklist Questions

Interpretive Guidelines for Checklist Questions:

The writers were requested to consider the following conceptual factors while examining and addressing each survey question, both in the narrative and in the scoring process.

De jure and de facto status:
For each question, please try to examine both the de jure and de facto dimensions of the situation under study in order to assess the following:

A: Existence (or lack) of domestic or internationally-recognized laws, policies, and legal protection mechanisms available for women to use to advance and secure their rights, including legal institutions, funds, public services, special seats allocated to women, etc.

B: Actual practices within a society – consider acts and omissions of both state and/or non-state actors to negate or ensure women's de jure rights and freedoms in a country. This survey aims at measuring the *actual* freedom a woman has in a country to exercise her human rights during all stages of her life. Please try to assess the level of *implementation* of laws and policies supporting women's freedom and the obstacles to the practice and realization of these freedoms.

State and Non-State Actors:
Please examine each question by measuring the impact of state and non-state actors in facilitating or denying women's freedom. For example, consider the performance of state agents such as prison guards, police, or military who might prevent women from successfully accessing and/or exercising their rights. Also consider acts by non-state actors, such as religious groups who might issue statements to condemn women who take part in politics, or tribal or family members who stop a female family member from benefiting from legal rights accorded to her by domestic law or international human rights standards ratified by the state.

Status of All Groups of Women in a Country:
Your report should attempt to review the freedoms of *all* women within a society to exercise their human rights. In your analysis, please consider all ethnic groups, religious groups, cultural groups (including language identity), economic and social classes, urban and rural dwellers, and citizens and non-citizens (including female migrants).

Nondiscrimination and Rights of Women in Comparison with Men:
One of the core initiatives of this survey is to examine a woman's right to be free from gender-based discrimination in all situations and during all stages of her life. While the overall context of human rights in a country will be noted (e.g., no one has the right to vote in Saudi Arabia – men or women), the fact that women do not have the right to vote is still a denial of a universally accepted right. The status of women's freedom does not always need to be determined in comparison to men. In some cases, women have different and special needs, such as maternity leave or protection from gender-based violence, that need to be taken into account and assessed separately. Finally, the aim of our survey is to show the status of women's freedom in light of universally accepted human rights standards that may or may not be present for the men in a country under review, but nonetheless still remain important in their assurance of full and equal rights for women as human beings.

Checklist Questions for Five Key Areas:

Section I: Nondiscrimination and Access to Justice
1. To what extent does the national Constitution ensure equal rights for men and women as citizens?
2. To what extent do the country's laws and policies provide protection to all women from gender-based discrimination?
3. To what extent do women have the right to full and equal status as citizens (nationals)?
4. To what extent do women have nondiscriminatory access to justice in the country at all levels?
5. To what extent are women treated equally in the penal code and under the criminal laws?
6. To what extent are women protected from gender-based and discriminatory arbitrary arrest, detention, and exile?
7. To what extent is an adult woman recognized as a full person before the court?

8. Has the government ratified CEDAW, and if so, to what extent is the government compliant with implementing the stipulations of CEDAW?
9. To what extent are women's rights groups and/or civil society actors working freely and effectively to promote the status of women's freedoms addressed in this section?

Section II: Autonomy, Security, and Freedom of the Person

1. To what extent do women have the right to freely practice their religion or belief?
2. To what extent do women have the freedom of movement?
3. To what extent are women treated equally in the Personal Status Code (Family Law)?
4. To what extent can women negotiate their full and equal marriage rights?
5. To what extent are women protected from slavery or gender-based, slavery-like practices?
6. To what extent are women free from torture and cruel, inhuman, or degrading punishment?
7. To what extent do women have protection from domestic violence?
8. To what extent are women protected from gender-based violence outside the home?
9. To what extent are women's rights groups and/or civil society actors working freely and effectively to promote the status of women's freedoms addressed in this section?

Section III: Economic Rights and Equal Opportunity

1. To what extent do women have the right to own and have full and independent use of their land and property?
2. To what extent do women have the freedom to have full and independent use of their income and assets?
3. To what extent do women have the right to inheritance?
4. To what extent can women freely enter into business and economic-related contracts and activities at all levels?
5. To what extent are women free to access education at all levels and to be protected from gender-based discrimination within the education system?
6. To what extent do women have the freedom to choose their profession?
7. To what extent are women protected from gender-based discrimination in the area of employment?
8. To what extent do women have gender-specific protections in the workplace, including maternity leave, protections from sexual harassment, and child-care?
9. To what extent are women's rights groups and/or civil society actors work-

ing freely and effectively to promote the status of women's freedoms addressed in this section?

Section IV: Political Rights and Civic Voice

1. To what extent do women have the right to peaceful assembly?
2. To what extent do women have the right to freedom of expression?
3. To what extent are women guaranteed the right to participate in competitive and democratic elections with full and equal suffrage?
4. To what extent are women represented in the judiciary?
5. To what extent are women represented in national government (executive) structures?
6. To what extent do women have to the right to participate in local assemblies and the national parliament?
7. To what extent can women organize and participate in political parties and processes at all levels?
8. To what extent do women have the freedom to full and equal participation in civic life issues to influence policies and decision-making?
9. To what extent do women have the freedom to access and use information to empower themselves in all areas of their civic and political lives?

Section V: Social and Cultural Rights

1. To what extent do women have the freedom to make independent decisions about their health and reproductive rights?
2. To what extent do women have full and equal access to health services?
3. To what extent do women have the freedom to be protected from gender-based harmful traditional practices?
4. To what extent are women protected from gender-based discrimination in their right to own and use housing?
5. To what extent are women free to participate in and influence community life, policies, and social development at local levels?
6. To what extent are women able to participate in and influence media content, including the shaping of women's images in the media?
7. To what extent are women disproportionately affected by poverty due to their gender?
8. To what extent are women and/or women's rights activists free to advocate openly about the promotion and protection of women's human rights in the country?

Ratings and Scoring System

The survey is comprised of 17 narrative country reports and a set of corresponding ratings for each of the five key areas for the country/territory under study. The ratings should not be taken as absolute indicators of all women's freedom in a country, but as a general assessment of the degree of freedom women have within that country to exercise their human rights. While the opinions expressed in each report are those of the report writer, the ratings and scores reflect the consensus of Freedom House, the regional review experts, and the report writers. Each country or territory's key area ratings are presented in the statistics section that precedes the narrative report. These ratings are meant to help in assessing where, in a country, the most immediate attention should focus to improve women's rights.

Key Terminology: (for the purpose of this survey)

The term **Ratings** refers to a numerically expressed comparative rating of performance.

The term **Scoring** refers to an underlying system of numerical scoring along a spectrum of performance. The numerical scores are added or averaged to produce a rating.

The term **Survey** refers to the combined ratings and analytical efforts.

Steps in the Rating Process:

The writers have been assigned a checklist of questions for each of the five key areas examined in the survey. Each question from the checklist will be awarded a raw **Score** of one to five, of which the total raw scores from each key area's questions will be calculated and averaged. This averaged score will then reflect a total **Rating** of 1 to 5 for each of the five key areas, demonstrating the degree to which state and non-state actors affect women's freedom within each of the five key areas for that country/territory.

For all of the five key areas and their checklist questions:

A RATING OF 1 will represent a country where women's freedom to exercise their human rights is almost entirely restricted by the actions of state and/or non-state actors. Women have almost no adequate human rights protections and face systematic gender-based discrimination.

A RATING OF 2 is meant to characterize a country where women's freedom to exercise their human rights is mostly restricted by the actions of state and/or non-state actors. Women have very few adequate human rights protections and they often face gender-based discrimination.

A RATING OF 3 represents a country where women's freedom to exercise their human rights is sometimes restricted by the actions of state and/or non-state actors. Women have some adequate human rights protections, but they are poorly implemented. Women occasionally face gender-based discrimination.

A RATING OF 4 characterizes a country where women's freedom to exercise their human rights is rarely restricted by the actions of state and/or non-state actors. Women have adequate human rights protections that are mostly implemented. Women rarely face gender-based discrimination.

A RATING OF 5 represents a country where women's freedom to exercise their human rights is almost never restricted by the actions of state and/or non-state actors. Women have adequate human rights protections that are fully implemented. Women almost never face gender-based discrimination.

About Freedom House

Freedom House is an independent non-governmental organization that supports the expansion of freedom in the world. Freedom is possible only in political systems where free expression, association, and belief are guaranteed; the rule of law prevails; the rights of women and minorities are protected; and government is accountable to the people. Freedom ultimately depends on the actions of committed and courageous men and women. We support nonviolent civic initiatives in societies where freedom is denied or under threat, and we stand in opposition to ideas and forces that challenge the right of all people to be free. Freedom House functions as a catalyst for freedom through its analysis, advocacy, and action.

Freedom House Board Of Trustees